W9-BMS-877

This Book is on Loan to you & must
be returned in good condition

YEAR	STUDENT	COND.
90	Cari Dedman	
90/91	Mikaela Willett	
91	KIRSTY WILKIE	Good
	Jen Bawn	
92	Sunny Gyural	

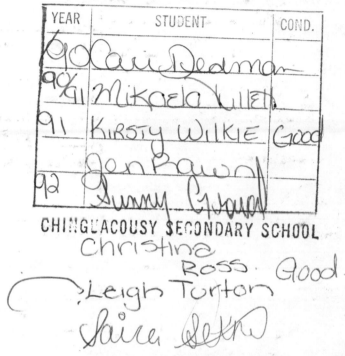

CHINGUACOUSY SECONDARY SCHOOL

Christina
Ross. Good.

Leigh Turton

Saira Seth

The Developing Child

Understanding Children and Parenting

The Developing Child

Understanding Children and Parenting

HOLLY E. BRISBANE

Fifth Edition

GLENCOE PUBLISHING COMPANY
Bennett & McKnight Division

Send all inquiries to:
Glencoe Publishing Company
15319 Chatsworth Street
P.O. Box 9509
Mission Hills, California 91345-9509

Printed in the United States of America

ISBN 0-02-668190-0 (Student Text)
ISBN 0-02-675910-1 (Teacher's Annotated Edition)

4 5 6 7 8 9   93 92 91 90 89

Design by: Design Associates; Paul Uhl & William Seabright
Design Photography by: Jim Ballard

Contributors

Susie Ball
Genetic Counselor
Yakima Valley Memorial Hospital
Yakima, Washington

Candice H. Bowers
Chairperson, Department of Child Development
Kilgore College
Kilgore, Texas

Becky Burgue
Gaither High School
Tampa, Florida

Evelyn Chikahisa
Banning High School
Wilmington, California

Jackie Harmon
Antioch High School
Antioch, Tennessee

Laurie A. Kanyer
Childbirth Education Assn.
Yakima, Washington

Catherine S. Krals
Temple High School
Temple, Texas

Judy Lee
Director, Campus Day Care Center
Yakima Valley Community College
Yakima, Washington

Dr. Mary Helen Mays
Editor, *Child Care Today*
San Antonio, Texas

Brenda Barrington Mendiola
Irion County Schools
Mertzon, Texas

Darlene Montz
Regional Preschool Coordinator and Parenting Consultant
Yakima, Washington

Mary Patrick
Coordinator of Home Economics and Family Life
Yakima Valley Community College
Yakima, Washington

Claudia Re
Merrick, New York

Mary Richmond
San Luis Obispo High School
San Luis Obispo, California

Judith-Anne Salts
Coordinator, Yakima Public Schools Backyard Center Programs
Yakima, Washington

Betty Schuler-Weingarten
Bryan Senior High School
Omaha, Nebraska

Contents

Children, Parenting, and You

Chapter 1: Children and Childhood
Chapter 2: Parents and Parenthood

 hildren—are they fascinating little people or endless sources of trouble? You probably have an opinion now. But after you finish this course, you will have a better idea of what children are *really* like.

What about parenting—how does it fit into your life? Did you know that parenting skills are needed by almost everyone who comes in contact with children, whether they are parents or not?

Chapter 1 begins with your present attitudes toward children. It will also give you some answers to the question, "Why study about children?" And it discusses the significance of the whole span of time called "childhood." Do you realize how different childhood was in the past? Can you think of ways in which your own childhood has influenced your present life?

Chapter 2 explores what "parenting" means. Have you ever been a babysitter, or helped care for a younger brother or sister? If so, you have already had an opportunity to practice parenting skills. Those who make a lifelong commitment to parenting find that the job brings both challenges and rewards.

The third part of the title of this unit is "you." In fact, you—the reader—are the most important ingredient of every chapter in this book. All of them were written for you. And throughout this course, you may find that you are learning as much about yourself as about children!

1 Children and Childhood

To help you to . . .

- Evaluate your attitude toward children.
- Identify benefits of studying children.
- Compare childhood in the past and in the present.
- Give examples of progress in understanding how and why children develop as they do.
- Describe five characteristics of development.
- Explain influences on development.

Terms to Learn

behavior	formula	sequence
child development	heredity	
environment	nutrition	

JoAnn sat in the guidance counselor's office with a class schedule on her lap. She chewed on the end of her pencil.

"Mr. Gerard," she said, "I'm having trouble deciding what courses to take next semester. I've been looking at this one, Child Development, but I don't know. I like kids, I guess. I like to babysit. But I don't know if I want to work with children or even if I'll ever have any of my own."

Mr. Gerard smiled. "I can't make the decision of what classes are best for you, JoAnn. But I can tell you that the child development course is a good way to find out about children. It can be valuable even if you don't become a parent or work with children as a career."

"I guess knowing more about kids could help me right now, couldn't it?"

"It certainly could," replied Mr. Gerard.

"I think I will take this class," said JoAnn, "and see what child development is all about."

Children in Your Life

How would you describe your relationships with the children in your life today? Do you like children? Can you talk with and enjoy children of all ages? Do you know what to do when caring for them? Just as important, do children like you?

Think about these questions seriously. Your honest answers tell a great deal about you—the person you are today, the child you once were, and the adult you will be. At the end of this course, you will have an even better understanding of these questions and the meaning of your answers.

Children may seem to naturally enjoy being with you. On the other hand, perhaps you feel uncomfortable around children and wish you understood them better. People vary a great deal in the way they feel and act toward children.

Your relationship with young children—brothers, sisters, friends, or babysitting charges—depends on your interest in children. It also depends on your knowledge of their changing stages and needs, and your skill in applying that knowledge.

Close-up

Jim, age 16, babysits three afternoons a week for his sister's kindergarten-age son Kevin and infant daughter Kelly. One day he was explaining to his friends Chris and Sue why he couldn't go with them after school.

"Babysitting? Boring!" Chris replied. "My kid brother's a pest. How can you stand two kids?" Sue had a different response. "That's a lot of responsibility. Aren't you nervous around a tiny baby?"

"It's not so bad," Jim answered. "My nephew reminds me of myself when I was a kid. We have a lot of fun playing with his toy cars. My sister leaves me plenty of instructions for Kelly. If I didn't help out, Joan wouldn't be able to keep her part-time job. And I get paid every week. Besides, I may decide to be a father someday — and maybe a teacher or doctor. This is a pretty good way to see if I'm cut out for working with kids."

Would you enjoy being in Jim's situation? Do you know someone your age who gets along especially well with children? ■

As a young child, do you remember how much fun it was when older children and teens spent time with you? Now you are on the other side of that relationship. The more you understand children, the more you will enjoy being with them.

Why Study Children?

Learning about children is important in more ways than you might realize.

- It can help you benefit from a better understanding of children.
- It can help you better understand yourself.
- It can help you think about your future in relation to parenthood and career choices.

Understanding Children

In your study of children, you will read about them, observe them, talk with them, play with them, and help them. In the process, your understanding of them will increase in many ways. The study of children can help you to:

- ***Better appreciate all characteristics of human development.*** **Child development** is the study of how children grow in many different ways—physically, mentally, emotionally, and socially. In discovering the variety and complexity of growth, you will begin to understand why children remain dependent on their parents for such a long time. You will learn why they need affection in order to grow emotionally. You will see why they need the guidance and support of older people.

- ***Sharpen your powers of observation.*** Everything you need to learn about children cannot come from books. Youngsters are all around you, perhaps even in your own home. With some background and interest, you can increase your knowledge of children every day.

Growth is a complex process. Just as a plant needs good soil, sun, and rain to grow, children need care and understanding.

The love of parents and others is one of a child's most important needs. Would you say that this baby is growing up in secure, happy surroundings?

■*Begin to see why children act, feel, and think as they do.* Have you ever misinterpreted or been puzzled by something a child said or did? That's normal. It is particularly difficult to understand children before they can talk and make their wants known. Yet there is predictable, appropriate **behavior**—a way of acting or responding—for every stage of life. An angry outburst from a two-year-old who cannot pull a tricycle up the steps is not unreasonable. But what about similar behavior in a ten-year-old? This is more complicated and takes deeper under-standing.

■*Apply learning to everyday life.* Merely studying child development is not enough. You need to apply your knowledge to real situations. For example, when your four-year-old sister plays with your softball glove, it's probably because she wants to be like you. Younger children naturally admire those who are older. They like to imitate. This may annoy those who do not recognize the compliment. When you understand the reasons behind children's actions, you will get along with them better.

■*Learn practical caring techniques.* Children respond favorably to those who care for them with confidence. Knowing how to bathe a baby, how to select and prepare a nutritious meal for a toddler, and how to encourage a nap from a reluctant three-year-old will give you that confidence. It will also bring you considerable satisfaction.

■*Discover that children are fun.* The more you are around children, the more you can appreciate how delightful they are. In their innocence, humor, and generous affection, you will find much that is fascinating and rewarding.

Understanding Yourself

Through understanding children, you will also come to know yourself better. You will learn more about what makes you the person you are. As psychologist Arthur Jersild wrote: "Our understanding of a child can go no deeper than our understanding of ourselves."

Your own childhood has influenced your life today. What do you remember about your childhood? What do others recall about you?

You may feel that you are a different person from the child you were only a few years ago. It's true that you have grown and changed in many ways. However, no one ever changes entirely. The young man or woman you are right now sums up the child you were and hints at the adult you will be. Experience, education, and life's situations help you mature. Still, the self you have developed through past years will always be a part of you.

Ask your parents what you were like as a child. Maybe you were "typical"—close to average development. Or maybe you were "quiet," "independent," or "constantly active." How much of your early personality is still evident? The amount might surprise you!

As you study child development, you will discover that all children are similar in some ways. You will also find that every child has characteristics that are unique. And you will see that development continues throughout life. All of these things can help you understand yourself.

Thinking About Your Future

Increased understanding of children will be valuable not only now, but throughout your entire lifetime. Today it may simply help you to better understand your family or the kids in your neighborhood. You may also put your knowledge and skills to work as a babysitter, a teacher's aide, or a playground supervisor. Tomorrow your understanding of children may help you become successful as a parent or as a professional in a career related to child care.

Studying children at this point in your life can help you make decisions about your future career. For example, a New Jersey high school student was planning to be a nurse at the beginning of a child study course, but now wants to go into teaching. The reason? "I like kids more than I used to. I want to work with a group of children."

For some people, such as this special education teacher, the study of child development leads to a rewarding career.

A classmate feels differently. "I thought I wanted to be a teacher, but now I don't know. I didn't have any idea how much responsibility was involved."

Learning about child development can also help you think about parenthood and prepare for its responsibilities. "It's made me more aware that having a child is really a lifetime commitment," one student commented. Another said, "I have the feeling I could handle anything now. I'm going to adopt about six children."

The instructor of the child study class in the previous examples stated, "Parenthood is the most important occupation most of us are ever engaged in. Whatever this course may or may not accomplish in helping these students make a choice of occupation, I know it will help them to be better parents."

Understanding the responsibilities of children and parenthood can affect other areas of life. Children are one possible outcome of sexual activity. Those who understand the responsibilities of children and parenthood are more apt to accept the responsibilities of human sexuality.

Check Your Understanding

1. How can knowledge of child development be applied to your everyday life? Give an example.

2. Explain this statement: "The self you have developed through past years will always be a part of you tomorrow."

3. How can studying about children help you think about your future?

Understanding children's needs and abilities at different ages is one way to become a more effective parent.

Childhood: A Time for Development

What does "childhood" mean to you? Do you picture a baby taking a few stumbling steps . . . a four-year-old playing on a swing . . . a classroom of fifth-graders? What makes children different from adults?

However you define it, you probably think of childhood as a period of life separate from adulthood. It is a time when development occurs very rapidly. Human beings begin childhood almost completely dependent on adults for every need. By the time childhood ends, most people have become mature and ready for independence.

You would probably also agree that children have special needs as they grow and learn. Imagine that you are going to spend a day with a five-year-old. You probably wouldn't plan the same activities or talk about the same things as you would if you were spending the day with someone your own age. You wouldn't expect the five-year-old to think, feel, or behave exactly as you do.

Not only do we look upon childhood as a distinct period of life, but many people have made a special study of it. They have devoted much time and effort to finding out more about how children develop and what their needs are. Later in this chapter, you will read about the ideas of some of those who have studied children. One of the most important ideas is that childhood has a great influence on later life.

on later life. Today's society emphasizes the importance of childhood to healthy development. Those who study children believe that each child has a right to a happy, healthy, loving childhood.

It may surprise you to learn that childhood has not always been viewed as a separate, important stage of life. In fact, childhood—as we know it—is a fairly recent "discovery."

What adjectives do you think of when you see the children in this picture? Is that how you would describe childhood?

Childhood: Past and Present

Prior to the 20th century, few people in Western civilization felt that there was anything unusual or important about the early years of life. During the Middle Ages and the centuries that followed, European adults were almost totally unaware of the special needs of children. They did not realize the importance of providing children with sunshine, wholesome food, protection, loving care, and a variety of learning experiences.

The art created in earlier centuries reflects society's attitude toward children. In paintings and statues, children appeared as miniature adults. They had the proportions, expressions, and clothes of grown-ups.

During colonial days in America, people still believed that children differed from adults only in size, experience, and abilities. They were dressed, fed, and doctored just as adults were.

These ideas persisted as recently as the 19th century. An example is Louisa May Alcott's famous book, *Little Women*. In it, Jo (the author herself) is constantly in trouble because she acts like the exuberant child she is rather than the little lady that girls of that time were expected to be. The title itself indicates this point of view.

Childhood in the past, therefore, was quite a different experience than it is today. Some of these differences have to do with changing attitudes toward children. Others are the result of advances in technology.

How old would you say these children are? Do you think 17th-century children really acted like "miniature adults," or did this scene come from the artist's imagination?

The Industrial Revolution of the 19th century created a need for cheap labor in shops and factories. Many young children worked long, hard hours under unsafe and unhealthy conditions.

Work

In the past, children were expected to work hard at an early age. In American pioneer families, children were needed for many of the farming and household tasks. During the Industrial Revolution, children often worked as laborers in factories.

Today, most children in our society are not thrown into the world of adulthood so abruptly. The "job" of young children is simply to grow, learn, and play. Children assume responsibility gradually by helping with household tasks or taking part-time jobs. Child labor laws protect them from physically demanding work and long hours.

Health

In past generations, no parents dared hope to raise every child born to them. Diseases such as diphtheria (dip-THEER-ee-uh), typhoid fever, and smallpox caused deaths of children in almost every family. Today in the United States and other developed countries, these and many other diseases have been controlled by medical advances, personal cleanliness, and strict public health regulations. Severe epidemics—uncontrolled outbreaks of disease—are almost unknown.

Nutrition

In the past, babies either thrived on breast-feeding or died. The first rubber feeding nipple and glass nursing bottle were not invented until the middle of the last century. It was not until much later that people realized the importance of disease-preventing cleanliness for these utensils. Older babies usually graduated from milk to "pap"—a bland mush. Some went from milk to the sausage, cheese, and rye bread their parents enjoyed.

Today, of course, breast-feeding still provides the infant with complete **nutrition**—a balance of all the food substances needed for health and growth. Parents also have the option of bottle-feeding their baby with a commercially prepared **formula**, which is a mixture of milk or milk substitutes and added nutrients. Infant formulas are safe and scientifically balanced for nutrition. Different formulas are available for infants with digestive problems or other special health needs. For older babies, strained, unseasoned foods—made commercially or at home—have replaced much of the table food of the past.

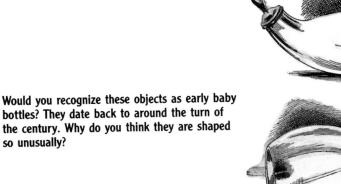

Would you recognize these objects as early baby bottles? They date back to around the turn of the century. Why do you think they are shaped so unusually?

Mother and Son
In the early 1900s, this was a typical outfit for a small boy or girl. What type of clothes would a boy like this wear today? Would a girl be dressed differently?

Dress

It was not until the 17th century that children stopped being clothed as small adults. Even early in this century, all children wore dresses for the first years of life. In an old family album, you may see pictures of your great-grandfather at age four or five in long curls, petticoats, and a pleated skirt. Preschool boys and girls were dressed alike until the early part of the 20th century. When your parents were babies, sex differences were reinforced in clothing styles and colors right from birth. Girls wore dresses and boys wore pants. Pink was for girls and blue for boys.

Today the circle seems to have been completed. Children most often wear clothing that is suitable in style for either boys or girls. You rarely find small children dressed daily in lace and ruffles today! Modern children wear practical, washable, lightweight garments designed to give freedom of movement and maximum comfort.

Parental Love

Although childhood in the past was different in many ways from what we know today, one thing has not changed. History is filled with examples of parents' love for their children. The Bible story of Moses is a good example. It tells how Moses' mother saved him when the Egyptian ruler decreed that all male Hebrew children be killed.

Despite such genuine affection, there was little awareness of the special needs of children. Parents did not know how to encourage the best physical, emotional, social, or intellectual development. Such knowledge is fairly recent.

The Growth of Child Study

The fact that you are studying and learning about children reveals the importance now attached to their understanding and guidance. Because of all the interest in studying children and their behavior in the past few generations, this is often called the "century of the child." For the first time, researchers and scholars have been able to study child growth and development scientifically.

A new awareness of children's physical development early in this century was followed closely by an appreciation of their intellectual and emotional growth.

- In France, Alfred Binet (buh-NAY) developed a series of tests to measure intellectual processes.
- Swiss psychologist, Jean Piaget (ZHAWN pee-ah-ZHAY), theorized that intelligence develops in stages that are related to age. According to him, the new mental abilities at each stage determine the limits of what the child can learn during that period. (You will learn more about Piaget's theories in Chapter 8.)
- In Austria, Sigmund Freud (FROID) developed the theory that the emotional experiences of childhood have a lasting effect on the personality of the adult.
- More recent theorists like Arnold Gesell (guh-ZELL) and Erik Erikson have continued to explore child development in terms of social and emotional growth.

Much remains to be learned about children—enough to keep researchers busy for years to come. But with the help of scientific research, the superstitions and misunderstandings of the past are being replaced by sound knowledge.

Today you have many resources available to help you in your study of children.

The results of scientific research are used by those who work for the rights of children. Teachers, day care workers, psychologists, social workers, and others concerned about children put new knowledge to practical use.

Information about children and their needs has become not only more complete, but more readily available. In the past, older family members were almost the only source of advice about child care and development. Today, those without this help nearby have other resources to turn to. Experts in many fields share their knowledge of child development and give advice. Everywhere you turn, you can find books, articles, and radio and television programs on the subject.

All of these resources can give you valuable knowledge about children. Still, the best way to truly understand human growth is to study and observe it for yourself.

Characteristics of Development

One of the many results that have come from the study of childhood is an understanding of some basic facts about human development. You should be able to see these characteristics in your own life and others' lives.

■*Development is similar for everyone.* Children all over the world go through the same stages of development in approximately the same order. For example, all babies lift their head before their body, and all stand before they walk. It does not matter where the baby is born—Indiana, Morocco, Russia, or New Guinea—or how the baby is raised.

■*Development builds on earlier learning.* The skills a child learns at age two build directly on those mastered at age one. After learning to walk, the child will soon be able to run. Before learning to speak in sentences, the child must learn to say simple words. Thus, development follows an orderly **sequence**, or step-by-step pattern.

■*Development proceeds at an individual rate.* Although each child follows a similar pattern of development, each is an individual. The style and rate of growth differ from one child to another.

Denise, Brett, and Karen are five-year-old playmates. Denise is taller and can run faster than the others. Brett is not as good at physical play. However, he seems especially well-behaved for his age and gets along well with the others in his kindergarten class. Karen likes numbers. This year she learned to tie her shoes—a task that Denise still finds frustrating. Each of these children is developing normally, but at his or her own rate.

All children follow a similar step-by-step pattern of development. Yet each child is unique in many ways. Can you see how physical, emotional, and social development influence one another?

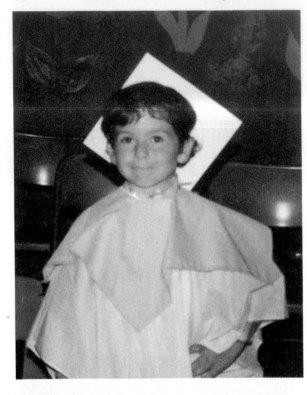

■*Development is interrelated.* When studying children, it is convenient to focus on one area of development at a time. That is how most of this book is organized. But you should remember that as a child grows, many changes are taking place at once. A child does not develop physically one week and emotionally the next week.

All areas of development continually interact. Think about the development that must occur before walking is possible. The baby's back and leg muscles must develop and strengthen. The mind and body must work together to coordinate movements and maintain balance. Social and emotional adjustments must allow the child to try new learning experiences. If the child has a setback in one area of development, all the others can be affected.

■*Development is continuous throughout life.* It does not stop at a certain age. Sometimes development is rapid, while at other times it is much slower. But we continue to develop in many ways throughout our lives.

As a young child, you were working toward becoming more independent. You learned to feed and dress yourself and to explore the neighborhood. Right now you are still increasing your independence— choosing your own friends, developing new abilities, thinking about a career. Soon you may be living on your own. Can you think of other ways in which development continues from childhood through adulthood?

Graduation is just as exciting to the kindergartner as it is to the eighteen-year-old. What does the occasion represent to each of them? What does this tell you about development?

Influences on Development

Have you ever thought of the many different forces that have made you what you are? Your widening circle of outside influences begins even before your birth and continues until death.

One important influence on development is **heredity**. This means that many of your characteristics are physically inherited from past generations. But **environment**—that is, the people, places, and things that surround you—also influences development. Scientists and philosophers have debated for centuries whether heredity or environment has more influence. Today, however, most agree that the two work together.

Think of how heredity and environment have helped shape your development. From your parents and past generations, you inherited your own particular physical characteristics out of millions of possibilities. When you were born, you became a member of a family whose relationships are unique. Directly or indirectly, your family passed on certain attitudes and ways of doing things. These reflect your family's personal and religious or moral values, and the customs of the society in which you live.

Eventually, everyone is claimed by or chooses to join many groups outside the family. These groups may include friends, classmates, coworkers, neighbors, social clubs, religious and political organizations, and many others. Each group exerts some influence on its members' thoughts and actions. You are also influenced by the type of community you live in, what you read, what you see on television, your personal experiences, and countless other forces.

Being encouraged to appreciate art is an example of an environmental influence. What else might account for this young woman's interest and skill in painting?

This is not to say that you copy the attitudes and actions of everyone you come in contact with. In fact, sometimes you may try to do just the opposite! Because you are an individual, you will always react to outside influences in your own unique way. Still, you are continually being shaped by people and experiences.

The same is true for every child. During infancy and early childhood, outside forces have an especially strong influence on development. That is why caring for children is such an important responsibility and opportunity.

Children and You

You are in an excellent position to study children—close to adulthood, yet not so removed from childhood that you cannot remember it clearly. Bring your resources—all of them—to enrich your study. Become involved personally and you will find the study of children enjoyable and rewarding.

As you learn, you will find some of your opinions challenged, others reinforced. You will discover answers to questions that have puzzled you. You will raise other questions to which there are yet no answers. Perhaps someday you will help find the answers to some of these questions.

Check Your Understanding

1. Why do you think people in the past treated children as "miniature adults"?

2. Explain this statement: "The 'job' of young children is simply to grow, learn, and play."

3. How might a setback in one area of development affect other areas? Give a specific example.

4. Describe three outside influences and how they might affect development.

Having fun with children is one of the best rewards of understanding their development.

Chapter Review

To Sum Up

- Your relationship with young children depends on your interest and knowledge.
- Study, observation, and practical experience help you understand children.
- Understanding children will help you better understand yourself.
- Your knowledge about children and your experiences with them can help you think about parenthood and career choices.
- Childhood is quite different today than in the past. Changes in attitude and advances in health care and nutrition are particularly significant.
- Study of child growth and development is a recent science.
- Development always follows an orderly sequence, but proceeds at individual rates.
- Development is interrelated and continuous.
- A variety of hereditary and environmental influences affect development.

To Review and Remember

1. Name the three main ways studying children can be beneficial.
2. Define child development.
3. What is behavior? Give an example.
4. Why didn't parents of past generations dare expect that all their children would live to adulthood?
5. What is nutrition?
6. Why is this era called "the century of the child"?
7. What theory did Jean Piaget contribute to child development studies?
8. Name five characteristics of development.
9. What is meant by saying "development is interrelated"?
10. What is the difference between heredity and environment?

To Discuss and Discover

1. In writing, tell why you enrolled in this course. What do you expect to learn from it? Describe the amount and types of experiences you have had with children.
2. Write about how some event in your childhood influenced your life. (It might be something as simple as why you now dislike meatloaf, or something more significant.) If the same thing happened to you today, would your reaction be the same? Why or why not?
3. In a class discussion, speculate about how childhood may be different in the future.

2 Parents and Parenthood

To help you to . . .

- Describe the main parenting skills needed to properly care for a child.
- Explain why parenting skills can be helpful to those who are not parents, as well as those who are.
- Explain how having a child affects all aspects of parents' lives.
- Discuss the rewards of parenthood.
- List factors that should be considered in evaluating readiness for parenthood.

Terms to Learn

adoption	foster parent	parenting
biological parent	guardian	potential
caregiver	nurturing	stepparent

Three-year-old Ricky climbed onto his father's lap and laid his head on his father's shoulder.

"I like being your little boy," Ricky said. "Do you like being my daddy?"

"Sure I do," replied Mr. Perez. He gave his son a hug.

"Why?" asked Ricky.

"Well, for one thing, I love you."

"Even when I'm naughty?"

"Yes, even when you're naughty," replied Mr. Perez. "I don't like the naughty things you do sometimes, but I always like you."

"Do you have a daddy?" asked Ricky.

"Yes, Ricky, your Grandpa Perez is my daddy. When you grow up and have children, you will be the daddy and I will be the grandpa."

"Then you won't be my daddy anymore?"

"Oh, I'll always be your daddy, Ricky. You can't get rid of me that easily."

Being a parent is a long-term responsibility. It requires a great deal of work, time, patience, and understanding. It also has many rewards.

What Is Parenting?

You may think of parenting as being a parent. That is true, but it is only part of the answer. **Parenting** is the process of caring for children and helping them grow and learn. It involves many different skills.

Meeting Children's Needs

Think of all the ways you have been cared for in your lifetime. As a baby, you were fed, bathed, clothed, and protected from harm. You were cuddled, talked to, and sung to. Someone encouraged you as you learned to stand and walk or to throw a ball.

As you grew older, you gradually learned to provide for more of your own needs. You learned to dress yourself, to make a sandwich, and to get to school on your own. But there were still people there to guide you. They made sure you didn't get hurt and saw that your physical needs were met. They helped you learn to get along with others and to feel good about yourself.

You could probably come up with hundreds of examples of parenting skills. But all of them fall into three main categories: physical care, nurturing, and guidance.

Physical Care

Children need food, clothing, exercise, rest, and a safe place to live. They need good health practices to keep them well and care when they are sick. Parenting means taking responsibility for all these physical needs.

Nurturing

Children need to feel loved and appreciated. **Nurturing** means providing love, support, attention, and encouragement. A warm, nurturing atmosphere gives children a feeling of confidence and self-worth. It helps them grow, learn, and develop social skills.

Guidance

Children do not know automatically what they should or shouldn't do. They need to have appropriate limits placed on their behavior for their own and others' welfare. As children grow older, guidance helps them learn self-control, positive values, and moral standards.

All of these aspects of parenting work together. Children whose physical needs are met and who are given loving support and guidance have a better chance of reaching their full **potential**. That is, they are better able to develop physically, intellectually, emotionally, and socially to the highest degree possible for them. Helping children reach their full potential is the primary goal of parenting.

Parenting begins with physical care, but it does not end there. Love, encouragement, and positive guidance are just as important.

Who Needs Parenting Skills?

There are several ways to become a parent—by the birth of a child, by marriage to someone with children, or by a legal process. In each case, parents need skills in providing physical care, nurturing, and guidance. But parents aren't the only ones who need these skills. So does anyone who helps care for a child, even for a short while.

Most often, those primarily responsible for parenting have a biological relationship to the child. **Biological parents** are the man and woman who conceive a child. (You will read about conception, pregnancy, and birth in Unit Two.) Every child has a biological mother and father.

In some cases, someone who is not one of the biological parents takes on or shares the responsibility for raising a child. For example, a person may become a **stepparent** by marrying someone who has children. Sometimes both spouses already have children. The relationship between stepparents and stepchildren can be as rewarding as that between any parent and child.

Some people become parents by **adoption**. Through a legal process, they take a child who is not biologically their own into their family. They raise the child as if they were the natural parents. The relationship is a permanent one.

Greeting a new son or daughter — few events in life are as exciting! The birth of a child is one of several ways that people can become parents.

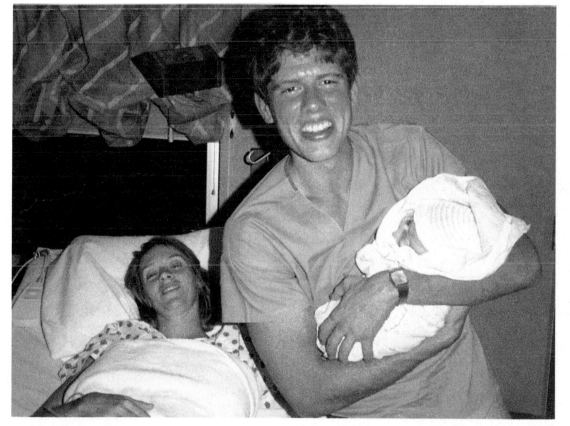

Although adoptive or foster parents and their children do not have a biological relationship, they do share a relationship of love and caring.

A **foster parent**, on the other hand, is someone who assumes temporary legal responsibility for a child. The child's own parents may be unable to care for the child for a while because of illness or some other problem. Or the child may be waiting for a permanent home through adoption. Foster parents need to provide loving care and guidance. But they must also be prepared to give the child up when the time comes.

Sometimes a member of a child's extended family—such as a grandparent, aunt, uncle, or other relative—must take on the responsibilities of parenting for a time. For example, the grandparents may become a child's legal guardians if the parents have died. (A **guardian** is someone appointed by a court of law to care for a child, usually until the child turns eighteen or twenty-one.)

No matter who is primarily responsible for caring for a child, many other people provide help. Often these are family members. Grand-parents may assist with the daily routines of child care or invite grandchildren to stay with them for the weekend. An older brother or sister may babysit when the parents are out. All family members can help provide nurturing and guidance when they play or talk with children. Other people, such as babysitters and child care workers, help care for children in many of the same ways as family members.

The term **caregiver** is sometimes used to refer to anyone who cares for a child, whether on a long-term or short-term basis. Therefore parents, foster parents, family members, babysitters, and child care workers can all be considered caregivers. All need the same skills in caring for children.

As you read about how to care for children in this book, you will find both the terms "parent" and "caregiver" being used. For now, however, the focus is on those who have primary responsibility for raising a child—in most cases, the parent or parents.

Changes in Parenting Roles

In the past, men and women in most societies had very distinct roles. This was especially true of roles related to parenthood. Each society worked out its own system of roles and responsibilities.

In earlier generations of our own society, most fathers took full responsibility for working to provide money for the family. Their main role in child care was to provide discipline. Most mothers stayed at home to provide full-time care for the children.

Many families still follow these roles. However, today many couples are more flexible in deciding who will do certain jobs. Tasks are not divided based on whether they are "man's work" or "woman's work." They may be done by the partner with the most interest, skill, or time. Child care responsibilities are often shared by both parents.

As a result, today's fathers tend to be more involved in the actual care of their children. Many fathers find that child care is not only rewarding and satisfying, but promotes a strong parent-child relationship that is important to the child's development.

Until recently, few fathers were actively involved in child care or household chores. Many of today's families find that these tasks require a teamwork approach.

Close-up

The family background of one young new father is typical of the gradual change toward greater involvement of fathers in day-to-day parenting. He described it this way: "I can't remember Dad or Grandpa doing any housework or taking care of us kids. Mom did all that, even after she got a job teaching school when my youngest brother started first grade.

"Now that I have a baby of my own, I can see that Dad missed a lot. I really enjoy taking care of Brad. I feed him, bathe him, dress him — everything. Linda and I talked it over before we got married. Since she works, too, we decided it was only fair that a baby should be a 50-50 job. The same with the housework.

"I especially like taking care of Brad. I enjoy that little guy so much. And I know Brad and I will be really close as he grows up. My own father and I love each other a lot. But growing up I felt closer to Mom because she was so involved with everything I did. I hope Brad feels that special closeness with both Linda and me."

Have you noticed differences in the ways fathers in your family or neighborhood interact with their children?

How might increased interaction with the father influence a child's development? ■

Parenting Styles and Abilities

Just as the roles of parents differ from one family to another, so do approaches to parenting. Of course, most parents want to do what is best for their children. They are concerned with providing for their children's needs and helping them develop in all areas. But there is no one right way to be a good parent. What works for one family may not for another.

For example, in one family the parents may set specific rules for their children. In another, the parents and children may work together to establish guidelines for behavior.

There are several factors that influence parenting styles. The experiences people have had, both as children and adults, affect how they will behave as parents. The community and society, or culture, in which they live influence parenting styles. Finally, the lifestyle of the parents affects how they carry out the parent roles.

Many different parenting styles can be successful. The important thing is that the child's physical, emotional, social, and intellectual needs are met. As long as the parents provide care, guidance, and a loving, supportive atmosphere, they probably need not worry about the particular methods they use.

Some parenting techniques, however, have been shown to be ineffective or even harmful. And some parents fall short in one or more of the aspects of parenting. They may fail to meet the child's physical or emotional needs, or they may not balance love and attention with firm guidance. In some cases, parents may even abuse their children physically or emotionally.

Fortunately, these problems can be avoided. One important way is through skills and knowledge relating to children. The more parents understand their children's needs, the better equipped they will be to meet them.

In the past, it was assumed that everyone naturally knew how to be a parent. Of course, that is not true. There is a vast difference between having children and being a good parent.

The importance of good parenting to individuals and society is now better recognized. One result is that there are now many classes to help adults and high school students learn about child development and parenting techniques. In this class you will learn how children grow and develop. You will acquire many of the skills needed to care for them. And you will learn about effective parenting techniques.

Right now, you may not know whether you would like to be a parent. No matter what decision a person makes about parenthood, the choice should be an informed one.

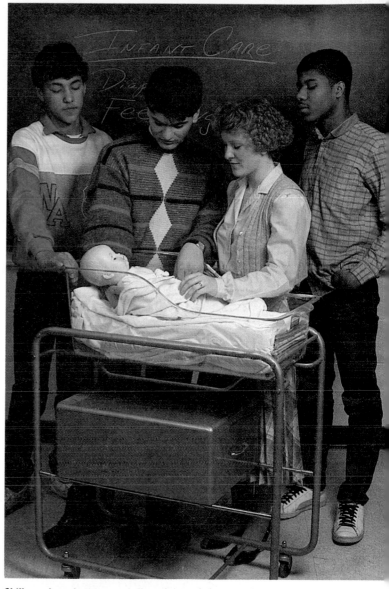

Skills such as bathing and diapering an infant aren't instinctive — they are learned through practice. One way to get that practice is through child care classes.

Check Your Understanding

1. Why isn't providing excellent physical care enough for a child's total development?

2. How can parents help their children reach their full potential?

3. Explain what is meant by the following statement: "There is a vast difference between having children and being a good parent."

Parenthood Brings Changes

Have you ever stopped to think about just how many ways having a child affects parents' lives? Few events have such dramatic and long-lasting effects. Some of these changes can bring great pleasure and satisfaction. Others can be difficult to deal with, especially when parents are unprepared for them. But they are all part of being a parent.

New Responsibilities

The arrival of a new family member brings with it many added responsibilities. For most people, it is the first time in their lives that another human being is completely dependent on them for every need.

Raising a child is more than just a day-to-day assignment. It is a lifelong commitment. The child's needs for physical care, financial support, love, and guidance continue until adulthood. Being a parent also means having a constant concern for the present and future welfare of another human being. Parents can no longer make choices and plan for the future based only on their own needs and wants.

For first-time parents, these new responsibilities can seem overwhelming. Good management is the key to meeting these responsibilities. Management involves planning and working out the best way to meet goals and responsibilities. In other words, parents use what they have to get what they want. New parents manage their time, money, energy, knowledge, and skills in meeting their responsibilities. They also may call on family, friends, and community resources for help and support.

A big part of being a parent is accepting responsibility for the child's welfare — not just for a few days or weeks, but for many years.

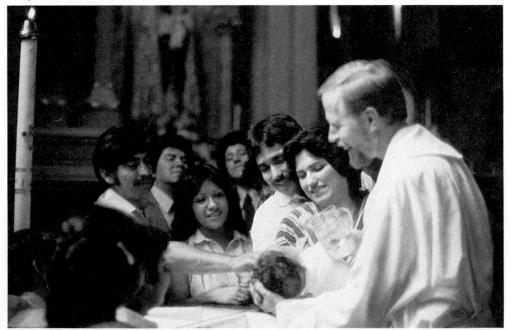

Changes in Lifestyle

One of the biggest initial adjustments new parents face is in their day-to-day living. Caring for a child—especially a newborn baby—takes a surprising amount of time and energy. A newborn must be fed every few hours around the clock, in addition to being diapered, bathed, played with, and comforted. When you add laundry and other household chores, it's not hard to see why new parents feel they have no time for themselves.

Not only is a lot of work involved, but it often seems that everything in the parent's life revolves around the baby's schedule of eating and sleeping. One new mother reported, "I couldn't be sure of anything—that I could nap after a feeding, clean house on a certain day, or fix meals without interruption. As for a good night's sleep—forget it!" Good management skills can help reduce the stress that comes from the demands on the parent's time and energy. However, caring for a baby is a demanding job.

With a child of any age, parents are faced with limits on their personal freedom. This is an especially difficult adjustment for new parents. Suddenly it's not so easy to go anywhere on the spur of the moment. Taking a baby on an outing is usually a major job. It requires advance planning and a bagful of supplies—diapers, feeding equipment, toys, extra clothes, and so on. Bringing a child along to a movie, a restaurant, the mall, or a friend's house is not always fun. The parent must be prepared to cope with a crying baby or a toddler who is tired and irritable. The alternative—leaving the child with a babysitter—must be arranged in advance and can be costly.

Taking a child along on an errand or visit requires a good deal of preparation. Even a short trip can seem to take all day! Parents must learn to expect some delays and handle them with a sense of humor.

Another common change in lifestyle occurs when a parent gives up an outside job to stay at home. A woman with a job outside the home must take at least some time off before and after the birth. Either a mother or a father may decide to stay at home full-time—permanently or temporarily—to care for a baby or young child. In any of these cases, staying home can require quite an adjustment. The parent must adapt to following an entirely different daily routine, to spending every day in the same surroundings, and to having limited contact with other adults.

Emotional Adjustments

Parenthood, with its changes in lifestyle and new responsibilities, requires a number of emotional adjustments. Going through so many changes at once is stressful in itself. It takes time for new parents to sort through their conflicting feelings and grow accustomed to their new role.

Most parents are happy, proud, and excited. But most also experience a variety of more difficult and confusing feelings. Common reactions include:

- Anxiety about the baby and how to care for him or her.
- Fear of not being a good parent.
- Frustration at losing personal freedom and adding responsibilities.
- Loneliness and isolation from being "cooped up" at home.
- Doubt about the decision to become a parent.
- Worry over financial matters.
- Jealousy of the baby and the attention he or she gets.
- Depression related to exhaustion or to the physical changes of pregnancy and birth.

The difficulty of these emotional adjustments depends on the particular situation and the attitudes of the parent. It helps for parents to be prepared for these reactions and to understand that they are normal. With the patience and support of family members, most parents eventually resolve their conflicting feelings. They are able to get over the rough spots and enjoy the positive side of parenthood.

Changes in Relationships

When a child is born or adopted, the parents have the unique experience of getting to know a new family member. In addition to this new relationship, there are likely to be changes in the way parents interact with each other, with other family members, and with friends. This is especially true for first-time parents.

It's natural for a new parent to feel a bit left out if the baby gets all the attention. What could this couple do to solve the problem?

The Couple's Relationship

There's no doubt that the birth of a baby can be a wonderful time for new parents. But it can also cause problems between them. As you have read, new parents are likely to be physically exhausted and under emotional stress. Suddenly they are faced with new roles, new worries, and a baby who demands a great deal of time and energy. All these can put a strain on their relationship.

Parents who are anxious or frustrated sometimes take out their feelings on their spouse. Without patience and understanding on both sides of the relationship, tempers may flare. A marriage may also suffer when one or both parents are so involved with child care that they neglect each other. Money problems are another source of conflict. Many new parents need more living space at a time when expenses for doctors, baby items, and child care are already adding up.

One thing a baby will not do is save a shaky marriage. Couples who argued before a baby's birth will continue to argue about the same things. Children just add one more area of disagreement.

The couples who sail most easily through the early, difficult time are those who plan carefully in advance. They read books and articles on parenting and child care. They talk to family members or friends who have been through the experience. Many take parenting or child care classes before or after the baby's arrival. You will find more suggestions for helping new parents avoid conflicts in their relationships on page below.

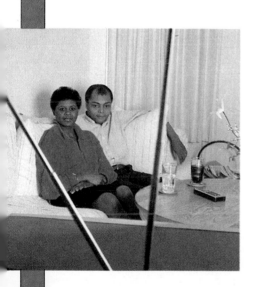

Parents and Partners

In addition to learning what to expect from parenthood, what can couples do to avoid problems in their relationship? Here are some suggestions:

- Talk things over ahead of time. If issues such as budgeting, sharing tasks, and philosophies of rearing children can be resolved before the baby arrives, they are unlikely to become problems later.
- Decide how parenting and household tasks will be shared. Exactly how responsibilities are divided doesn't matter, as long as both partners feel the division is fair. Couples who communicate well about such issues are less likely to become overwhelmed and divided by parenthood.
- Make time for each other. New parents need to occasionally take a break from their responsibilities and have some time to themselves. Supportive friends and family members can help out with the baby and other chores. It's also important for parents and baby to spend some time playing together and enjoying each other as a family.
- Relax and keep a sense of humor. New parents can reassure themselves that they are not the first ones ever to experience parenthood. No one feels completely confident as a parent, but most parents are successful ones. A sense of perspective can keep minor tensions from becoming major sources of conflict.

Grandparents can be a good source of assistance and experienced advice for the child's parents. Everyone benefits from good family relationships.

may resent what they see as interference in their decisions. Meanwhile, the grandparents may feel hurt that their offers of advice are rejected. Sometimes the situation is the opposite. The grandparents may feel overburdened if the parents expect them to provide more help than they can manage.

On the positive side, many new parents feel that having a child has brought them closer to their own parents. For the first time, they truly understand what being a parent is like. Grandparents and other relatives can share their experiences with the new parents and give help, advice, and support.

When there are already children in the family, the arrival of a new baby can bring on jealousy and misbehavior. Parents need to be understanding and provide special attention and love. (In later chapters, ways to handle this situation are discussed in more detail.)

The Rewards of Parenthood

In spite of all the adjustments and problems involved, parenthood can bring many joys. Nothing is quite like a baby's first smile or a hug from a three-year-old. Of course, you don't have to be a parent to experience the fun and delight of children. But parents discover special feelings of happiness, pride, and love that are different from anything they have felt before.

Relationships with Family and Friends

The family and friends of prospective parents are usually the first to share in the exciting news. They, too, will be affected by the event.

New parents will probably find that they have little time or freedom for the social life they once enjoyed. They may also feel they have less in common with some of their friends than before. New friendships may develop with other parents who can understand and share their experiences.

The new role of parenthood means that extended family members will have new roles too—grandparent, aunt, uncle, cousin, perhaps sister or brother. These roles may also take some adjustment. For example, a couple may feel that the well-meaning advice offered by the baby's grandparents is a criticism of their own ability to care for the child. They

One first-time father said, "Being a father to Carrie is the most important thing in my life. This is the happiest I've ever been." A new mother's view: "Vickie is more work than I ever imagined. But if we hadn't had her, we would have missed the most wonderful experience of our lives."

Raising children can give parents a great sense of accomplishment. They may also find that having children can enrich an already strong marriage. And by helping their children discover the world, they can see it with new eyes themselves.

How has parenthood changed Joan's views of the world and herself?

Do you think Joan and Terry were well prepared to become parents? ■

Those who genuinely love children, have a strong desire to be parents, and can accept the responsibilities of parenthood almost always find that their lives are enriched by it. Although there are ups and downs along the way, it is an experience they wouldn't trade for anything in the world.

Close-up

"I can hardly remember what our lives were like before Katie and Jeff came along," says Joan Chandler. "Being a parent is a lot of hard work, but I'm glad we decided to have children. Every day brings something new. It might be showing Katie how to feed the ducks at the park, or Jeff's new tooth. Watching them play makes me remember the fun I had as a kid. We love them so much — and Terry and I feel even closer than before."

"As we watch our children grow up, we can feel we've really made a difference in the world. The future seems more meaningful now. I used to think only about myself. Now I want to make sure the world will be a good place for my children and grandchildren to live. And I like to think that something of ourselves — our characteristics, our traditions, the things we believe in — will be carried on by our children. I feel good about that."

Check Your Understanding

1. What are some of the responsibilities new parents must face?

2. How can having a baby affect first-time parents' lifestyle?

3. Why won't having a baby save a shaky marriage?

4. How can parenthood enrich a person's life?

The Parenthood Decision

Deciding whether or not to become a parent is the biggest decision that most people will ever make. You have just seen how many ways parenthood can affect a person's life. Yet as important as the decision is to the would-be parent, it is even more important to the future child.

Children who aren't loved or cared for properly have a difficult time in life. Sometimes these early problems are overcome and the results are positive. In many cases, the children are not so fortunate.

In the past, parenthood was seldom viewed as a choice. Everyone was expected to marry and have children. Today, not everyone does. There is more realization of the importance of the decision to be a parent. Raising children is much too important a task to be left to chance.

Things to Consider

Those who are thinking about parenthood should get as clear a picture of it as possible before they make a decision. They should also take a realistic look at themselves. The decision of whether to have children—and when to have them—may well depend on these five important points: emotional maturity, desire for parenthood, health, management skills, and finances.

Emotional Maturity

Being an adult—and certainly being a parent—is not just a matter of physical maturity. It takes emotional maturity as well. That means being responsible enough to put someone else's needs before your own. It means being secure enough to devote your full attention to an infant without expecting to receive attention in return. And it means being able to hold your temper when you find that a toddler has dumped all the dirt out of the plants on the windowsill.

Parenthood is a major step. When a couple fully understands the responsibilities involved as well as their own feelings and motivations, they will be better able to make a wise decision.

Parents must be willing to do without some things they might enjoy in order to devote time, energy, and other resources to the child's needs.

Age is no guarantee of emotional maturity. However, most people do become better able to handle situations like these as they grow older. Prospective parents should take an honest look at their emotional maturity. Are their expectations of parenthood realistic? Are they equipped to handle the pressures and responsibilities involved? If they have any doubts, parenthood is best postponed.

Desire for Parenthood

"Do I really want to be a parent?" This question can be difficult to answer. Just as important, and often just as difficult, is for would-be parents to understand their reasons. Typical reactions might be, "I don't know why—I just want to have children, that's all!" or, "I think I want to (or don't want to), but sometimes I'm not sure."

Prospective parents should try to understand their own desires and doubts as clearly as possible. Only in this way can they be sure of their decision. Sometimes parents realize too late that their reasons for having children were not realistic. Look at some of the examples on page 52. Can you see why the reasons in the left column are not sound ones?

Health Considerations

The health of prospective parents is an important consideration, particularly before pregnancy. It is best for both prospective parents to go to the doctor for a checkup. If either has a medical problem, it could affect the health of the baby or their ability to care for the child.

The age of the woman should also be considered. If she is under seventeen or over thirty-five, pregnancy is riskier for both the mother and the baby.

In addition, couples should investigate the possibility of an inherited disorder. A child can inherit a physical problem even if both parents seem to be healthy. Special tests can determine whether this is likely to happen. They are sometimes recommended if other family members have inherited disorders. Chapter 3 tells more about how couples can get the information they need to make health-related decisions.

Shower gifts can help with some of the early expenses of parenthood. But they won't cover the continuing costs of raising a child through the teen years. Besides clothing, what examples of continuing expenses can you think of?

Management Skills

Because parenting is such a complex task, good management skills are needed. Parents must look at their family's needs and wants and decide what their goals are. Then they work to discover what resources they can use to reach these goals. Successful parents look at their options and make good decisions. Finally, they evaluate this process by looking at whether their decisions led to reaching their goals.

In using the management process, parents act as leaders of the family. They provide leadership in setting goals and standards for the family. They are planners and decision makers. If parents have good management and leadership skills, they will be better able to create a family setting where children can grow and develop in healthy ways.

Financial Considerations

Children can do quite well without expensive toys or closets full of new clothes. But even the basic necessities of adequate food, clothing, and shelter can cost a surprising amount. Before making a decision, parents-to-be should take a careful look at how much raising a child is likely to cost in the years ahead. They may need to make changes in their way of life and set aside some savings.

New parents need skill in money management. Expenses increase and, if one parent stays home with the baby, income drops. A personal checking account can help parents control and keep track of their expenses. If a loan is needed, parents must be able to shop for the loan, know how to apply for it, and plan for and manage its repayment. Understanding the various types of financial institutions can help parents manage their money better. In Chapter 4 you will read about how parents-to-be can estimate costs and plan to meet their expenses.

Teenagers as Parents

In spite of a national trend toward postponing marriage and motherhood, the number of teenage pregnancies has increased dramatically over the last decade. Today, one girl in ten is a mother before her eighteenth birthday. Most teen mothers are age fourteen to sixteen. The father is usually also a teen.

It is not impossible for teens to be good parents. But as you can see, teen parents are likely to start out with several major disadvantages. They may not be emotionally mature. Many teens have children without really thinking it through or understanding the lifetime responsibilities. Teenage pregnancy carries a higher risk of health problems. And most teen parents cannot afford to support themselves, let alone a baby. Many find the realities of parenthood quite different from their expectations.

Pregnancy and birth are risky when the mother is a teen. Once past that hurdle, teen parents face additional challenges as a lifetime of caring for the child begins. They may be able to get help through nutrition programs, infant care classes, counseling, and other services.

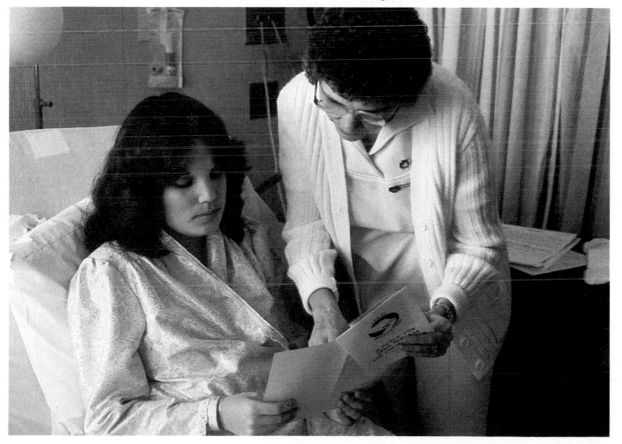

Close-up

Tracy and Gregg were married while still in high school. Gregg remained in school to graduate with his class, but Tracy dropped out to have the baby that caused their early marriage.

A small apartment in an older downtown building was all the young couple could afford. The dingy apartment depressed them, but after their rent was paid, there was only enough money left for necessities. They couldn't afford to go out and have a good time.

Gregg worked nights and weekends as a gas station attendant. Tracy got a job as a motel chambermaid. She was only able to work three months before her doctor told her she had to stop working.

When Jimmy was born, Gregg's mother came to stay with them for a week to help out. Then she went home to her own teenagers and part-time job. Gregg and Tracy were suddenly full-time parents. Though both had younger brothers and sisters and knew the basics of child care, they hadn't anticipated the work and time Jimmy needed.

The routine soon began to take a toll on their own relationship. Tracy, exhausted after nights of getting up with the baby, accused Gregg of not doing his share. Gregg said he was paying the bills and the baby was her job. Though he loved his new son, the baby's crying got on his nerves. Sometimes no amount of rocking or feeding made Jimmy stop crying.

When they quarreled, Gregg would leave the apartment. Hurt and angry, Tracy would bundle up the baby, drop him off with his grandparents, and join her friends. Often she would leave the baby overnight.

Tracy confided to a friend, "Sometimes I wish I could leave Jimmy there forever. It's not that I don't love him. But nothing's fun anymore. I'm so tied down! Sometimes I panic and think there will never be time for fun again. I wish I weren't married and I wish I weren't a mother. It's nothing like I imagined."

How might Gregg and Tracy's problems affect their son Jimmy?
What might be done to help their situation? ■

Parenthood requires a role of patience and giving that many teens are not prepared to assume. Some still need to be parented themselves.

The problems are compounded for the unmarried adolescent. Pregnancy is certainly a difficult time for both the parents, but especially for the girl. Unfortunately, the important decisions that must be made are often based on emotion rather than reason. Later, such decisions may be regretted. It is always important to think through alternatives carefully before making a major decision.

Many young women see a baby as a way to fill an empty spot in their lives. Yet the emotional and physical needs of a newborn are many times greater than their own. Many young men do not realize their legal responsibility for financially supporting their child, even if they do not marry the baby's mother.

Awareness and responsible decision-making can help teens avoid these difficult situations. Teens who do become parents need information, skills, and support if they are to be successful ones. You will read more about teen parenthood in Chapter 3 and Chapter 16.

Looking Ahead

As you can see, parenthood is not a decision to be taken lightly. Those who choose it should be prepared to meet the demands that will be placed on their time, energy, finances, and management skills. But when approached with good judgement, the experience can be a successful and enriching one.

Take time to learn about children—and about parenting skills. What you learn now may help you make decisions about human sexuality and becoming a parent. It will also make your experiences with children more enjoyable.

Many community agencies have programs designed to help teens and young adults become better prepared for parenthood. Find out what is available in your area.

Check Your Understanding

1. Explain the statement, "Deciding whether or not to become a parent is the biggest decision most people will ever make."

2. What can happen when a person who isn't emotionally mature enough becomes a parent?

3. Why do teen parents face so many more challenges than older parents?

Why Parenthood?

- "Our marriage is in trouble. Maybe this will solve our problems."
- "A baby is someone who will love me and belong to me."
- "I feel like I'm nobody. Being a parent will make me somebody."
- "I want someone who will take care of me when I'm old."
- "Our parents want grandchildren."

- "Having children will add depth to our already strong relationship."
- "I want to give a baby my care and love."
- "I feel good about myself. I believe that parenthood will be a meaningful and rewarding experience."
- "I want to experience the special bond between parent and child that lasts for a lifetime."
- "I love children, and I sincerely want to be a parent."

Chapter Review

To Sum Up

- Parenting skills fall into three areas: physical care, nurturing, and guidance.
- One can become a parent by birth, marriage, or legal process.
- Fathers today are more likely to take part in child care than in the past.
- Approaches to parenting differ. The important thing is meeting the child's needs.
- Parenthood brings on many added responsibilities and changes in lifestyle.
- A baby affects the new parents' relationship with each other, family, and friends.
- Parenthood can bring enrichment and many joys.
- Those considering parenthood should take a realistic look at themselves first.
- Teens are usually less well prepared for the responsibilities of parenthood.

To Review and Remember

1. Give examples of three main aspects of parenting.
2. Define nurturing. Why is it important?
3. What is the primary goal of parenting?
4. Give two examples of people who are not parents who need parenting skills.
5. What is the difference between an adoptive parent and a foster parent?
6. Define caregiver.
7. Name three possible ways in which a person's lifestyle could change because of parenthood.
8. Give two examples of how new parents can avoid conflict in their relationship.
9. Before making a decision about parenthood, what five points should be considered?
10. Name a poor reason for wanting to be a parent.

To Discuss and Discover

1. Discuss what might happen in a family in which the two parents have different styles and methods of parenting.
2. Ask a parent to explain whether his or her parenting style is similar to or different from the one his or her own parents used, and why. Write a report summarizing your interview.
3. Write a want ad describing the qualities a child might look for in a parent. In class, compare your ads. What qualities were mentioned most often? Would children of different ages list different qualities?

Pregnancy and Birth

The weeks preceding a baby's birth can seem like a very long time to anxiously waiting parents. But considering all that happens during pregnancy, the time is amazingly short. Whether they seem to pass quickly or slowly, these nine months can be summed up in one word—preparation.

The most important preparation takes place "behind the scenes," as a single tiny cell develops into a baby. Chapter 3 explains this miraculous process. It also discusses factors that can have harmful effects on the baby's development, and ways to predict or avoid problems.

More visible aspects of getting ready for a new baby are the subject of Chapter 4. From the mother's point of view, pregnancy is a time of growing—and a time to take good care of her health. Both parents have many plans and decisions to make. They must get ready for not only the birth itself, but the months and years that will follow.

It's a busy and exciting time. And it all leads up to a very special birthday—the newborn's first appearance. Chapter 5 explains how the baby is born. It also describes the events that follow a birth and takes you through the baby's first few weeks at home.

In studying this unit, you will learn how a baby comes to be and what newborns are like. Whether or not you ever care for a newborn, your understanding of young children starts with your understanding of the beginnings of life.

3 Prenatal Development

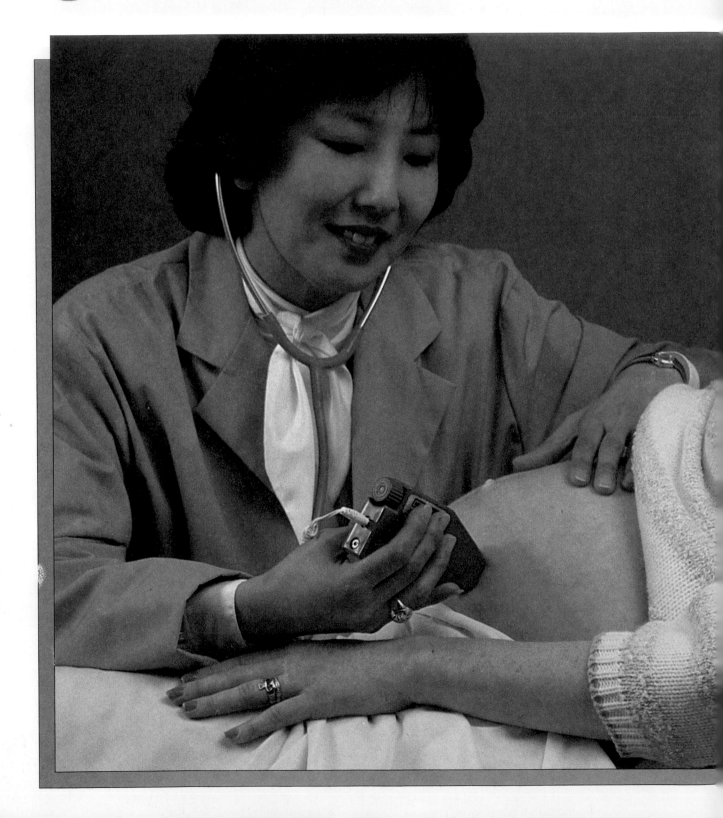

To help you to . . .

- Name the three stages of pregnancy and describe the prenatal development in each.
- Describe how personal characteristics are inherited.
- Explain how multiple births occur.
- Discuss possible solutions for infertility.
- Discuss the causes of birth defects and how they can be diagnosed and prevented.
- Explain why teen pregnancies are considered high risk.

Terms to Learn

amniocentesis	embryo	premature
amniotic fluid	fetus	prenatal
birth defects	genes	recessive
chorionic villi	infertility	sperm
sampling	miscarriage	ultrasound
chromosomes	ovum	umbilical cord
conception	placenta	uterus
dominant		

he term **prenatal** refers to the period before birth. It is a very special time. During this 40-week (or about nine-month) period, a single cell develops into a human being capable of independent existence. In this chapter you will learn how this miracle takes place. You will also gain an understanding of how problems that could interfere with prenatal development can be predicted or prevented.

The Forty-Week Miracle

Prenatal development begins at conception. It continues through three stages: the period of the ovum, the period of the embryo, and the period of the fetus. The chart on pages 59–60 shows how the unborn baby develops. It also shows corresponding physical changes in the mother.

Conception

Once each month, a female cell or egg—called an **ovum**—is released by the ovary of a woman. The egg moves through the Fallopian tube to the **uterus** (YOOT-uh-russ), or womb. This journey requires about two or three days. It is only in the Fallopian tube that fertilization can take place.

When the egg reaches the uterus, it usually disintegrates and is flushed away with the menstrual flow. However, if the egg meets and is fertilized in the Fallopian tube by a **sperm**, or male cell, **conception** takes place. This is the beginning of pregnancy.

Period of the Ovum

The first stage in the life of a human baby is called the period of the ovum. It lasts approximately two weeks.

When the fertilized egg reaches the uterus, it attaches itself to the thickened lining of the uterus and begins to grow. Since the lining is needed to nourish the fertilized egg, it cannot be shed in menstruation as usual. Therefore, menstruation does not take place. The woman's menstrual periods stop and will not begin again until after the baby is born.

The fertilized egg has found a soft, warm bed and food in the thickened lining of the uterus. It grows by a process called cell division. This single, complete cell divides and becomes two. Two become four, and so on until there is a mass of cells. Each cell is programmed to become a particular type. Some will help form skin or bones. Others will become brain or blood cells. In spite of the remarkable growth in this two-week period, the tiny ovum is still only the size of a pinhead.

Conception — the beginning of pregnancy — occurs when an ovum is fertilized by a sperm. In actuality, the sperm cells are many times smaller than the ovum. The ovum is about the size of the dot over a printed letter *i*.

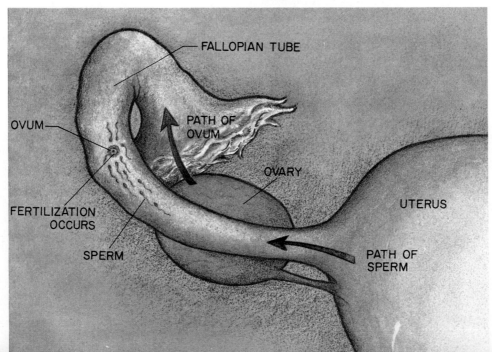

FALLOPIAN TUBE

OVUM

PATH OF OVUM

OVARY

UTERUS

FERTILIZATION OCCURS

SPERM

PATH OF SPERM

Prenatal Development Month by Month

Keep in mind that reactions and growth patterns are very individual. Not all babies develop at exactly the same rate. Nor does every pregnant woman experience all the things described here.

	Prenatal Development	Effects on Mother
During the First Month	■ Cell multiplication begins. ■ The fertilized egg attaches itself to the lining of the uterus. ■ Internal organs and the circulatory system begin to form. The heart begins to beat. ■ By the end of the month, small bumps show the beginning of arms and legs.	■ Missed menstrual period. ■ Other signs of pregnancy may not yet be noticeable.
During the Second Month	■ At five weeks, the embryo is only about ¼ in. (6 mm) long. ■ Face, eyes, ears, and limbs take shape. ■ Bones begin to form. ■ Internal organs begin to develop.	■ Breasts begin to swell. ■ Pressure on bladder from enlarging uterus results in need to urinate more frequently. ■ Possible nausea ("morning sickness"). ■ Fatigue is common.
During the Third Month	■ As this month begins, the fetus is about 1 in. (25 mm) long. ■ Nostrils, mouth, lips, teeth buds, and eyelids form. ■ Fingers and toes are almost complete. ■ All organs are present, although immature.	■ Breasts become firmer and fuller and may ache. ■ Nausea, fatigue, and frequent urination may continue. ■ Abdomen becomes slightly larger. Uterus has grown to about the size of an orange. ■ Weight gain totals 2-4 lb. (0.9–1.8 kg).
During the Fourth Month	■ Fetus is about 3 in. (76 mm) long and weighs about 1 oz. (28 g) at the beginning of this month. ■ Can suck its thumb, swallow, hiccup, and move around. ■ Facial features become clearer.	■ Size change continues slowly. ■ Most discomforts of early pregnancy are usually gone by now. ■ Appetite increases.
During the Fifth Month	■ As this month begins, the fetus is about 6½–7 in. (16–18 cm) long and weighs about 4–5 oz. (113–142 g). ■ Hair, eyelashes, and eyebrows appear. ■ Teeth continue to develop. ■ Organs are maturing. ■ The fetus becomes more active.	■ Enlarged abdomen becomes apparent. ■ Slight fetal movements are felt. ■ Fetal heartbeat may be heard through a stethoscope.

(Continued on next page)

Prenatal Development Month by Month (Cont'd.)

	Prenatal Development	Effects on Mother
During the Sixth Month	■ The fetus is now about 8–10 in. (21–25 cm) long and weighs about 8–12 oz. (227-340 g). ■ Fat is being deposited under the skin, but fetus still appears wrinkled. ■ Breathing movements begin.	■ Fetal movements have become strong kicks, thumps, and bumps. Some may be visible. ■ Weight gain may total about 10-12 lb. (4.5–5.4 kg) as this month begins.
During the Seventh Month	■ Fetus is about 10–12 in. (25–30 cm) long and weighs about 1½–2 lb. (680–907 g). ■ Periods of fetal activity are followed by periods of rest and quiet.	■ Increased size is beginning to affect posture.
During the Eighth Month	■ Weight gain continues rapidly. The fetus is about 14–16 in. (36–41 cm) long and weighs about 2½–3 lb. (1.0–1.4 kg). ■ Fetus may react to loud noises with a reflex jerking action. ■ Usually has moved into head-down position.	■ May have discomfort as size increases. Backache, leg cramps, shortness of breath, and tiredness are common. ■ Fetal kicks continue to be felt. Mother's rest may be disturbed. ■ Weight gain at the beginning of this month may total 18–20 lb. (8.2–9.1 kg).
During the Ninth Month	■ As the final month begins, the fetus is about 17–18 in. (43–46 cm) long and weighs around 5–6 lb. (2.3–2.7 kg). Weight gain continues until the week before birth. ■ Skin becomes smooth as fat deposits continue. ■ Fetal movements decrease as the baby has less room to move around. ■ Disease-fighting antibodies are acquired by the fetus from the mother's blood. ■ The fetus descends into the pelvis, ready for birth.	■ "Lightening" is felt as the fetus drops into the pelvis. Breathing is easier now. ■ Other discomforts of late pregnancy may continue. ■ Total weight gain of 24–30 lb. (10.9–13.6 kg). Uterus is the size of a small watermelon by the time of birth. ■ May have false labor pains.

Period of the Embryo

The increasing cluster of cells is called the **embryo** (EM-bree-oh). The second stage of development—the period of the embryo—lasts about six weeks.

The embryo is growing rapidly. It becomes firmly attached to the inner lining of the uterus. By the end of this stage, the connecting tissue between the embryo and the uterus has developed into the **placenta** (pluh-SENT-uh). Nourishment and oxygen from the mother's bloodstream are carried from the placenta to the developing baby through the **umbilical cord** (uhm-BILL-ih-kuhl).

Many mothers worry that during their pregnancy, the baby may become tangled up in the umbilical cord and strangle. This is very unlikely. The cord is filled with blood. It is as stiff and firm as a garden hose filled with water. It is not flexible enough to loop around the fetus. Only after the baby is born does the cord become limp and ropelike.

The growing embryo is soon surrounded by a bag of liquid called **amniotic fluid** (am-nee-OTT-ik). This acts as a cushion to protect it, even through minor bumps or falls of the mother. The baby remains within this sac of liquid until just before birth.

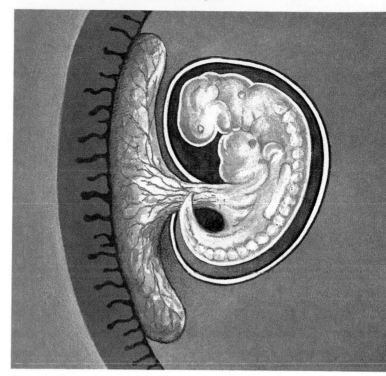

At three weeks after conception, the embryo is surrounded by a sac of amniotic fluid (shown in dark gray). Between the amniotic sac and the uterine lining is the membrane that will soon develop into the placenta. The heart is the largest organ so far and has already begun to beat.

The embryo has made its home by attaching itself to the inner lining of the uterus. The uterus is about 3 in. (75 mm) long at this stage. The embryo is still smaller than a grain of rice.

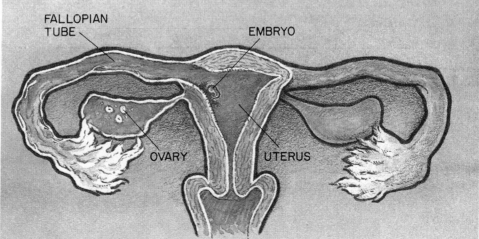

FALLOPIAN TUBE

EMBRYO

OVARY

UTERUS

Period of the Fetus

The third and last stage of pregnancy is called the fetal period. It begins about the seventh or eighth week of pregnancy and lasts until birth. The new life is now known as the **fetus** rather than the embryo.

The unborn baby is now more recognizable. Arms, legs, and even fingers and toes have developed. Facial features are also forming. All of the internal organs are present, but not all are ready to function yet. They continue to develop in the remaining months.

Somewhere between the fourth and fifth months, the fetus's movements and kicks touch the wall of the uterus. These fluttering movements will be faint and infrequent at first. Gradually, they become stronger and occur more often. This feeling life, sometimes called "quickening," tells the mother that she does, indeed, carry a live child within her. Actually, the baby has been very active long before this.

The doctor will want to know when the expectant mother first felt life. This helps the doctor estimate the baby's fetal age and establish a more accurate birth date. When life is felt, the fetus's heartbeat can also be heard.

As the growing fetus fills more and more of the space in the uterus, the surrounding fluid is lessened. Eventually, the amniotic fluid fills only the pockets around the baby's body. With less space to stretch out, the baby curls up. This is called the fetal position.

By the seventh month, the most rapid fetal development has already taken place. Now the fetus's main job is to get ready for birth. In these last months, the major organs become ready to sustain life outside the womb. The fetus also gains weight rapidly. Fat deposits are added under the skin. These will help the baby maintain body heat after birth. Gradually, the fetus, which had been thin, wrinkled, and old-looking takes on the smoother, rounder appearance of a baby. The fetus is also storing nutrients and building immunity to diseases and infections.

By the fourth month, the fetus looks more like a baby. The eyelids will remain shut until about the sixth month.

PLACENTA

UTERUS

UMBILICAL CORD

AMNIOTIC FLUID

FETUS

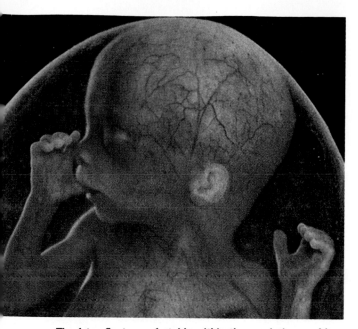

The fetus floats comfortably within the amniotic sac. After brief active periods, the fetus spends long hours resting. The same will be true of the baby after birth.

By now the baby is probably upside down with the head nestled in the pelvis. This is the most comfortable position for the baby. It is also the easiest and safest position for birth. The baby is less active now because it fills most of the available space.

The skin of the mother's abdomen appears stretched to capacity. So are the abdominal muscles. Nature has miraculously provided for this. The muscles of the uterus and abdomen are capable of being increased up to sixty times their original size during pregnancy. Yet they will return to nearly their original size within a month or so after the birth.

The nine months of pregnancy are over. The baby is ready to be born.

The unborn baby can do a surprising number of things for one so tiny. It can suck its thumb, cough, sneeze, yawn, and suffer hiccups. A baby can even cry before birth. Usually the crying is soundless. In one case, however, a doctor injected an air bubble into the uterus for medical purposes. The bubble happened to cover the baby's face. The moment the fetus had air to inhale and exhale, the sound of a protesting wail could clearly be heard.

One day during the ninth month the baby's weight seems to shift unexpectedly. Somehow the mother feels much more comfortable. "Lightening" has occurred. This means the baby has dropped into the lower pelvis. Birth is not far off. If this is not a first baby, lightening may not occur until just before labor begins. Sometimes lightening is accompanied by slight abdominal pains which first-time mothers may mistake for the beginning of labor.

At full term (after nine months of development), the baby has put on weight and settled into a snug, head-down position.

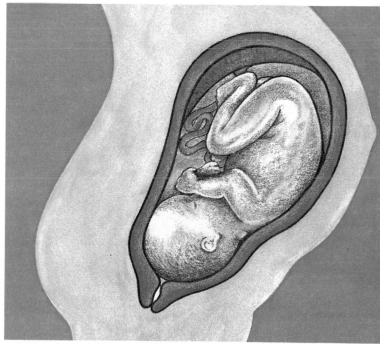

A Closer Look at Conception

You have seen how the unborn baby develops during these forty weeks. Now let us return to the moment of conception, when the sperm and egg meet to form a new life. In that instant, many of the baby's future characteristics are decided.

The Genetic Package

As you learned in Chapter 1, everyone inherits characteristics from previous generations. These include such traits as:

- Physical build.
- Skin color.
- Hair texture and color.
- Color and shape of the eyes.
- The shape and size of the ears, hands, and feet.
- Blood type.

Heredity—the passing on of these and other characteristics—has been observed since ancient times. However, only in the last century has science begun to understand how heredity works.

At the moment of conception, every human baby receives a total of 46 tiny, thread-like particles called **chromosomes**. Twenty-three of the chromosomes come from the sperm of the father and the other 23 from the egg of the mother. Each chromosome con-

Hair color is an example of a characteristic that is genetically determined. Each of these parents contributed one recessive gene for red hair to their son. As a result, the child's hair is redder than that of either parent.

tains thousands of **genes**. These genes determine all the characteristics—from appearance to physical size—that each of us inherits.

Each individual receives two genes for every inherited characteristic—one from the mother and one from the father. When both genes are the same—for example, both for blue eyes—the child is certain to have that characteristic. But an infant who inherits one blue-eye gene and one brown-eye gene will have the trait dictated by the **dominant**, or stronger, gene. (Weaker genes are called **recessive**.) In this example, the gene for brown eyes is dominant, so the child will have brown eyes.

Heredity explains why brothers and sisters often resemble each other. It also explains why they can look quite different. Out of the 46 chromosomes belonging to the father, only half go into the sperm cell—one from each of

his 23 pairs. Which chromosome from each pair is used? This is a matter of chance. The same is true of the mother's egg cell. Thus each sperm or egg cell contains a different combination of genes. The uniting of sperm and egg creates a unique individual.

At conception, the fertilized egg has instantly inherited all the physical traits its parents can ever give it. Though it is less than one-fourth the size of a pinhead, the fertilized egg has its own genetic blueprint. This may include its father's brown eyes, grandfather's tall, lean build, mother's dimples, and grandmother's talent for singing. The new life will have many other individual traits that this particular egg and sperm gave it.

A person with brown eyes may carry a recessive gene for blue eyes. If this is true of both parents, *each* of their children has one chance in four of having blue eyes. What would happen if only one parent carried the recessive gene?

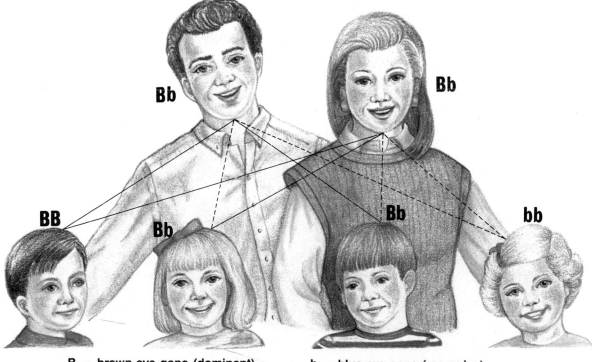

B = brown-eye gene (dominant)   b = blue-eye gene (recessive)

Identical twins share the same genetic pattern. That is why their appearance is so similar. Since a child's sex is determined by the genes, identical twins are always the same sex.

Sex Determination

The sex of a child is also determined at the moment of conception. It is determined by special chromosomes that come in two types, X and Y. The egg from the female contains an X chromosome. Male sperm contains either an X chromosome or a Y chromosome. If an X chromosome fertilizes the egg, an XX combination results and the child is a girl. If a Y chromosome fertilizes the egg, the XY combination produces a boy.

Multiple Births

As you have learned, the fertilized egg starts growing by dividing into two cells. These cells continue to divide until there are millions.

Sometimes the growing mass of cells splits apart soon after fertilization. Each clump of cells continues to divide and grow into a separate embryo. This produces identical twins. They are always the same sex and have very similar characteristics because the two babies have developed from one ovum. Why the ovum splits apart is still an unsolved mystery of nature.

If the split is not complete, Siamese twins result. The babies will be joined at some part of their bodies. Such births are very rare.

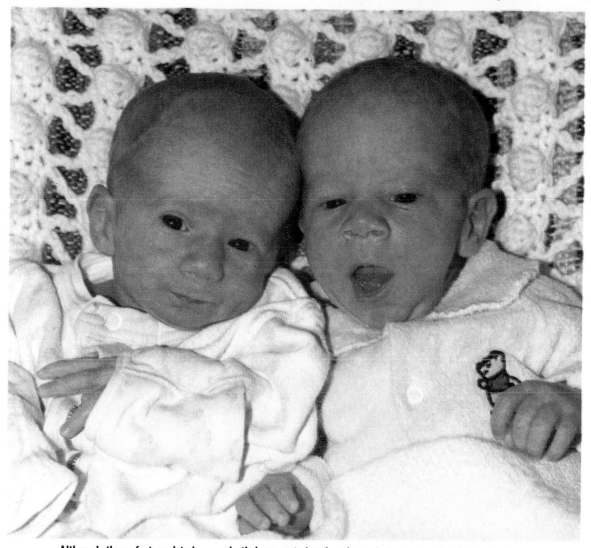

Although these fraternal twins are both boys, a twin of each sex is just as likely. Fraternal twins sometimes look very much alike. In other cases, they look quite different. Can you explain why?

Fraternal twins result when two eggs are released at the same time and each is fertilized by a different sperm. They grow side by side in the uterus. Fraternal twins can be the same sex or opposite sexes. They are not any more alike in appearance or personality than ordinary brothers and sisters.

In multiple births of more than two, the babies may either be identical, fraternal, or both. Triplets, for example, may be identical when the single fertilized ovum splits into three parts, each of which continues to develop independently. Or two eggs may be fertilized. If one of them splits apart, there will be two identical babies and the other egg will produce a single fraternal baby.

Multiple births are rare. The more babies born at one time, the rarer such an event is.

Infertility

What about couples who want to have children, yet fail to conceive? A couple's **infertility**, or inability to have children, may have many causes. If they seek medical help, the doctor will make a fertility analysis. This is a detailed study of the man and woman, both physically and psychologically. Medical histories are taken and thorough physical examinations are given.

In some cases, there seems to be no physical cause for infertility. Emotional factors may be affecting the ability to conceive. If so, help from psychiatrists and psychologists is usually most effective. Sometimes, however, it is discovered that the man, the woman, or both have a physical problem that is preventing pregnancy. Surgery or medication may solve the problem.

For example, the woman's ovaries may not be releasing an egg each month. In this case, the doctor may prescribe fertility drugs. These are powerful compounds that stimulate a woman's ovaries to release eggs. The drugs have several drawbacks. Some women who take them are troubled by serious side effects. Also, there is no accurate way to determine how much of a fertility drug a particular woman should be given. If too little is prescribed, there is no pregnancy. If too much is

Infertility can be a difficult problem for couples who want to have children. They may decide to undergo a fertility analysis. In many cases, the doctor is able to determine the cause of the infertility and suggest a course of treatment.

prescribed, there may be multiple births. Two, three, or even eight or more babies may be born at one time. Babies in such large births, however, have little chance of survival.

Despite problems such as these, it is estimated that half of all couples who would have been childless may be able to conceive after medical treatment.

Options for Infertile Couples

When a couple cannot be helped to conceive a child themselves, other options are available to them.

■*Adoption.* Couples who cannot become parents biologically may choose to adopt. Adoption is a way to provide loving homes for children who would not otherwise have them.

■*Artificial insemination.* This is the process of injecting sperm into a woman's uterus with a special surgical syringe. The doctor does this during the woman's fertile period. The sperm may be from the husband or from an unknown male called a donor.

■*Test-tube babies.* These are babies who are conceived in medical laboratories. When a woman's damaged Fallopian tubes prevent pregnancy, a surgical syringe is used to remove a mature egg from her ovary. It is placed in a small glass dish containing a special solution to which the husband's sperm is added. When fertilization takes place, the doctor inserts the fertilized egg into the mother's uterus. If the procedure is successful, a normal pregnancy proceeds.

■*Ovum transfer.* This is sometimes called "adoptive pregnancy." A fertilized egg obtained from a female donor is implanted in an infertile woman's womb. This method is sometimes used for women who lack working ovaries or who have a family history of inherited disorders.

■*Surrogate mothers.* These are women who carry and deliver a baby for another couple. In some cases, a "substitute mother" will carry a couple's fertilized egg which is removed from a biological mother who cannot carry a baby to term. Other surrogates are artificially inseminated with sperm from the husband of the infertile wife. Such options are usually managed through legal arrangements or according to various state laws.

As technology continues to advance, there may soon be other options available. However, the alternatives that science makes possible are not always considered acceptable by everyone. Procedures such as ovum transfer and surrogate motherhood are controversial. They raise many philosophical questions that society has not had to face before.

Check Your Understanding

1. Name and briefly describe the three stages of prenatal development.

2. Describe five characteristics you have that were determined by your genes. From whom do you think you inherited these characteristics?

3. Explain the differences between fraternal and identical twins.

Sometimes a baby is born with a serious health problem. Medical science is constantly working to find not only better ways of treating these problems, but ways to prevent them.

Prenatal development is a complex process. When something interferes with it, a birth defect may be the result. The development of these children's fingers was not completed the way it should have been.

Problems in Prenatal Development

The biggest concern of most parents-to-be is whether their baby will be all right. Fortunately, most babies are healthy. But sometimes, for a variety of reasons, prenatal development does not proceed normally.

Babies that are born before their development is complete are called **premature**. This usually means that the pregnancy was less than eight and a half months or that the baby weighs under 5½ lb. (2.5 kg). (At full term, a baby usually weighs about 7–8 lb. [3.2–3.6 kg].) Premature babies must be given specialized care. Their small size and incomplete development make them vulnerable to infection, lung ailments, and other problems. Some babies weigh less than 5½ lb. (2.5 kg) even though they have spent nine months in the uterus. These babies, too, may have health problems as a result.

Prematurity is an example of a **birth defect**—an abnormality that affects the structure or function of the body. Strictly speaking, almost everyone is born with some type of imperfection. Most, such as birthmarks, are relatively minor. However, some babies are born with more serious problems. These are referred to as **birth defects**.

Types of Birth Defects

There are hundreds of different kinds of birth defects. The one thing they have in common is that most are very rare.

Some birth defects affect the shape or size of the body or certain parts of it. For instance, a child may be born with a misshapen foot or missing fingers. Other birth defects involve a part or system of the body that does not function properly. Blindness, deafness, and mental retardation fall into this category.

Not all birth defects are apparent at birth. Sometimes the abnormality does not cause problems until months or even years later. Birth defects also differ in severity. Some are mild or can be corrected. Others result in severe handicaps or even death.

Actually, nature sees to it that the worst cases do not go beyond the embryo stage. Many pregnancies end before the mother even realizes she is pregnant. Any pregnancy that ends due to natural causes before the embryo or fetus could possibly survive is referred to as a **miscarriage**.

What Causes Birth Defects?

Just as the types of birth defects differ, so do the causes. Some are inherited from one or both parents. Others are caused by controllable factors in the environment. Researchers believe that most birth defects result from a combination of heredity and environment. However, the exact causes of many birth defects are not yet fully understood.

Environmental Causes

As you have learned, prenatal development occurs very rapidly. In just a few weeks, the baby develops all of the bodily systems needed for survival and a normal life. During this time the developing baby is completely dependent on the mother's body for nourishment and oxygen.

Many things that the mother does, or that happen to the mother, can be harmful to the development of her baby. Environmental factors include:

- Whether her diet is nutritionally balanced.
- Any diseases or infections that strike the mother during pregnancy.

- Harmful substances such as alcohol, tobacco smoke, and drugs (including some medicines that would ordinarily benefit the mother).
- Exposure to outside hazards such as radiation, especially early in pregnancy.

It used to be thought that the placenta was a barrier that protected the baby from many dangerous substances. But cases of defects resulting from drugs and other substances have proved this untrue.

Everything a pregnant woman takes into her body—pills, injections, food, tobacco smoke, even coffee—may affect her unborn child. True, the placenta does act as a partial barrier. Some substances have difficulty crossing over to the child. But it now appears that if the concentration of any substance in the mother's blood is high enough, some will leak across the placenta and reach the fetus. Later in this chapter you will learn more about how specific hazards can affect the baby's development.

Rh Incompatability

Rh incompatability is related to the Rh factor—an inherited substance present in most people. Someone whose blood contains this factor is called "Rh-positive." Someone lacking the ingredient is called "Rh-negative." The presence or absence of the Rh factor itself makes no difference in a person's health. It only causes problems if an Rh-positive male and Rh-negative female have more than one child.

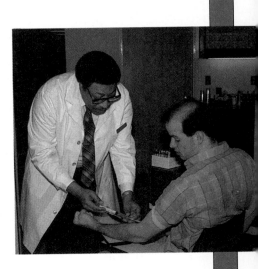

The first child of a positive-negative couple is usually not affected. But if the baby has Rh-positive blood, there is an increasing chance of trouble in later pregnancies.

The first child is almost always unaffected because very few blood cells pass from the baby to the mother during pregnancy. In effect, the mother does not notice the baby's foreign blood type. But during birth, some of the infant's blood may enter the mother's bloodstream. The mother's body reacts by producing antibodies to destroy the foreign blood cells. (Antibodies defend the body against germs and other foreign substances.) When the mother becomes pregnant with a second Rh-positive child, these antibodies cross the placenta to attack and destroy the baby's blood cells.

The production of antibodies increases as the pregnancy goes on. It also increases with each Rh-positive child. Therefore, some babies are more severely affected than others. Those that are mildly affected usually recover. Babies with more serious cases may suffer from mental retardation or physical defects. The most seriously afflicted infants die before or shortly after birth.

Fortunately, prevention is now possible. A vaccine can be given to the Rh-negative woman after her first pregnancy with an Rh-positive child. The vaccine prevents the Rh antibodies from forming in her bloodstream. She can then safely give birth to another Rh-positive child.

As you can see, how the mother takes care of herself during pregnancy is crucial. She should see a doctor as soon as pregnancy is suspected and follow the doctor's advice to stay healthy. (You will learn more about good prenatal care in Chapter 4.)

Hereditary Defects

Although everyone probably has a few imperfect genes among the thousands that make up his or her personal blueprint, these usually have no effect. However, sometimes a defective gene from one parent is matched with a similar defective gene from the other parent. Then there is a high risk of a birth defect. These defective genes are passed down to children, just as those that determine hair color and eye color.

Normal genes are usually dominant over defective ones, which are often recessive. A recessive gene will usually produce an effect only when transmitted by both parents. Very often it is not until an affected child is born that parents learn they carry recessive genes for a defect. If both parents have a recessive gene for the same disease, *each* of their children has one chance in four of developing the disease. Some defects that are passed on in this way include color blindness and sickle-cell anemia, a blood disease.

Not all hereditary defects work this way. For example, some inherited diseases affect only males. Hemophilia (HE-moe-FEEL-ee-uh), a condition which prevents the blood from clotting, is one such disease. The defective gene is inherited from the mother, although she does not suffer from the defect herself.

Heredity and Environment Interact

Many birth defects are believed to result from a combination of heredity and environment. For example, sometimes the structure of the heart is defective at birth. Such a defect is usually the result of two factors working to-gether. First, there was an inherited tendency for a heart defect. Second, the defect was triggered by something in the environment, such as a drug or virus. If only one of these conditions had been met, the heart probably would have been normal.

Another example is Rh incompatibility. This means that the baby inherits from the father a blood type that is not compatible with the mother's blood type. Under certain conditions, the health of the baby can be affected. Rh incompatibility is explained on page 73.

Errors in Chromosomes

A few types of birth defects are linked to a problem with the affected baby's chromosomes. For example, there may be too many chromosomes in each cell of the body or too few. Although this type of defect has to do with the genetic material, it is not the same as a hereditary defect. The child does not inherit the defect from the parents. Researchers are still working to understand why chromosomal errors occur.

The most common type of chromosomal error is called Down syndrome. One child in every 600 births has this condition. The risk increases if the mother is over age thirty-five. A child with Down syndrome has an extra chromosome 21, as shown in the photograph on page 74. Because each chromosome carries hundreds of genes, the defect can interfere with development in many ways.

Most Down syndrome children have recognizable physical features such as reduced height and characteristic facial features. They are almost always mentally retarded.

There is no cure for Down syndrome. In the past, many children were placed in institutions. Today, treatment has a more positive approach. Early therapy, parent counseling and training, and at-home care help such children to develop more normally than in the past.

A positive, encouraging approach can help children with Down syndrome make the most of their abilities.

Children with Down syndrome are usually happy and friendly. Their care is almost the same as that of normal babies, but their development is much slower. They walk and talk later, they get more respiratory infections, and they often suffer from heart defects.

The degree of mental impairment varies greatly. Most children are capable of learning and attending special education classes. However, they rarely achieve beyond grade school levels. As adults they often work in community sheltered workshops and live at home or in a supervised group residence.

Some genetic defects can be identified by making a photograph of chromosomes from the person's tissues. In the case of Down syndrome, there are three, rather than two, of chromosome 21 (bottom row).

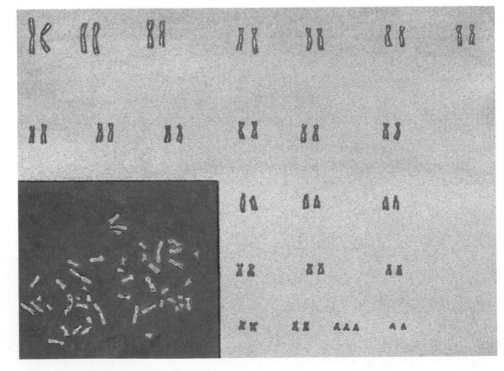

Prevention and Diagnosis of Birth Defects

In the past, little could be done to improve the chances of having a healthy baby. Today, organizations like the National Foundation–March of Dimes continually fund research into the cause, prevention, and treatment of all types of birth defects. As you have learned, some causes of birth defects, such as infections, drugs, and alcohol, can be controlled.

While many defects cannot yet be prevented, the probability that they will occur can often be determined. Advances in the detection of defects before birth allow treatment to be given as soon as possible.

It is difficult for a child born with a serious medical problem to lead a normal life. The rest of the family can also be hurt by the emotional and financial strain the defect causes. Responsible couples do everything they can to minimize the possibility of birth defects.

Raising a child who has a serious birth defect involves many challenges. Parents are faced with a drain on their finances, emotions, time, and energy. At the same time, family members should treat the child as normally as possible. They need to help the child gain confidence and overcome feelings of being "different."

Selected Birth Defects

Birth Defect	Description	Cause(s)	Detection	Treatment
CEREBRAL PALSY	General term for a variety of motor system disorders. Symptoms can include lack of coordination, stiffness, jerkiness, difficulty in speech, and paralysis. Other disorders may also be present.	Results from brain damage before, during, or shortly after birth. Causes vary.	Symptoms usually become recognizable sometime in the first year.	Brain damage is irreversible. However, physical and speech therapy, surgery, and medication can minimize handicaps in many cases.
CLEFT LIP and/or CLEFT PALATE	Gap in upper lip and/or palate, causing problems with eating, swallowing, speech, and appearance.	Hereditary and/or environmental; often unknown.	Apparent at birth.	Surgery to correct defect.
CONGENITAL HEART DEFECTS	Structural defect affecting the heart's ability to circulate blood. May be minor or severe. (Congenital means "present at birth.")	Hereditary and/or environmental; often unknown.	Examination at birth or later.	Surgery or medication.
CONGENITAL RUBELLA SYNDROME	Various defects such as blindness, deafness, cleft lip or palate, heart defects, brain damage. (Congenital means "present at birth.")	Infection of mother with rubella virus (German measles) during pregnancy.	Apparent at birth or later. Diagnosis confirmed through tests.	Depends on defects. May include surgery, hearing aids, physical therapy.
CYSTIC FIBROSIS	Functional defect involving respiratory and digestive systems. Many of those affected die before adulthood.	Hereditary. Carried on recessive gene.	Tests can identify carriers of the gene and diagnose an affected child or fetus.	Special diet, lung exercises, treatment of complications. No known cure.
DIABETES MELLITUS	Disorder affecting the body's ability to metabolize (process and use) carbohydrates. Symptoms include frequent urination, excessive thirst, tiredness, and weight loss.	Hereditary and/or environmental.	Symptoms appear in childhood or later. Blood and urine tests confirm the diagnosis.	Medication and/or special diet to control level of sugar in the blood. No known cure.

(Continued)

Birth Defect	Description	Cause(s)	Detection	Treatment
DOWN SYNDROME	A group of associated defects including mental retardation, delayed development, heart defects (in some cases), and other characteristics.	Chromosomal error. For reasons not yet understood, there is an extra chromosome 21.	Analysis of the chromosomes. Amniocentesis or chorionic villi sampling can detect the syndrome before birth.	Special therapy and schooling, corrective surgery.
HEMOPHILIA	Blood disease affecting clotting ability. In severe cases, even minor wounds can result in serious bleeding.	Hereditary. Hemophilia affects only males; females can pass the defective gene on to their children, but do not have the disease themselves.	A blood test confirms the diagnosis. Amniocentesis or chorionic villi sampling can detect the disorder in a fetus.	Medication, blood transfusions. No known cure.
LOW BIRTH WEIGHT and/or PREMATURITY	Baby weighs less than 5½ lb. (2.5 kg) at birth and/or is born before 8½ months of prenatal development. Creates a high risk of various physical problems.	May be caused by poor prenatal care (inadequate diet, smoking, etc.) or a medical condition in the mother.	Ultrasound; visual inspection at birth.	Intensive care of newborn until a healthy weight and level of development are reached.
MUSCULAR DYSTROPHY	Progressive weakness and shrinking of the muscles beginning between ages two and six. Death from infection before adulthood is common.	Hereditary. The most common form is transmitted by female carriers of the gene but affects only males.	Disease is apparent at onset. Genetic counseling can identify carriers.	Physical therapy to minimize handicaps. No known cure.
PKU (Phenylketonuria)	Inability of body to metabolize (process and use) a specific protein. Mental retardation can result.	Hereditary. Carried on recessive gene.	Newborn can be tested for condition (required by law in some states).	If diagnosed early, a special diet can reduce or prevent brain damage. No known cure.
Rh DISEASE	Antibodies in the mother's blood attack and destroy the fetus's red blood cells. Can cause anemia, brain damage, or death.	Results from incompatibility of mother's and baby's blood types. (The first such incompatibility usually causes no problem, but later pregnancies are endangered.)	Blood tests of prospective parents reveal whether there is a risk. Blood tests of fetus diagnose the problem.	A fetus already in danger can be treated by a massive transfusion before or just after birth. After each delivery, a vaccine is given to mothers at risk to help prevent problems in future pregnancies.

(Continued on next page)

Selected Birth Defects (Cont'd.)

Birth Defect	Description	Cause(s)	Detection	Treatment
SICKLE CELL ANEMIA	Malformed red blood cells interfere with the supply of oxygen to all parts of the body. Symptoms include tiredness, lack of appetite, pain. Can lead to early death.	Hereditary.	Blood tests. Amniocentesis or chorionic villi sampling can identify anemia in the fetus.	No known cure. Medication to treat symptoms.
SPINA BIFIDA and/or HYDROCEPH-ALUS	An incompletely formed spinal cord (spina bifida) resulting in partial paralysis. Often occurs together with an excess of fluid surrounding the brain (hydrocephalus), which can lead to brain damage.	Hereditary and environmental.	Apparent at birth. A combination of tests of the mother's blood, amniocentesis, and ultrasound can reveal suspected cases before birth.	Any paralysis or brain damage is permanent. Corrective surgery, physical therapy, and special schooling can minimize handicaps. Hydrocephalus can often be controlled by an operation shortly after birth.
TAY-SACHS DISEASE	Lack of a specific chemical in the blood, resulting in inability to metabolize (process and use) fats. Leads to severe brain damage and death by age two or three.	Hereditary. Carried on a recessive gene.	Blood test to identify carriers or to test for the disorder in a newborn. Amniocentesis or chorionic villi sampling to detect the disorder before birth.	No cure or treatment.
THALASSEMIA (Cooley's Anemia)	Inability of the body to make enough hemoglobin, the substance found in red blood cells that carries oxygen to the tissues.	Hereditary.	Blood test. Amniocentesis or chorionic villi sampling can test fetus for the disease.	Regular blood transfusions and medication are needed. No known cure.

Genetic Counseling

Many hereditary or chromosomal defects can be predicted and prevented by genetic counseling. This service combines a knowledge of heredity and birth defects with laboratory tests. It tells parents in advance the statistical odds that their children will have certain diseases or defects. Most people who seek genetic counseling do so because of a known need.

Genetic counseling may be provided by several different types of doctors, including family doctors. But the more specialized testing is done at one of the genetic counseling centers throughout the country.

The genetic counselor first obtains a complete family medical history from the patients. Each is asked for information relating to diseases and causes of death of all close relatives. They are also questioned about any marriages between relatives, previous pregnancies, and other relevant information.

Family members may be given a thorough physical examination. If necessary, special laboratory tests may be performed.

When all the tests are completed, the counselor may be able to tell the couple whether genetic problems are present. They may also be told their mathematical chances for having a defective child. The genetic counselor will explain the findings and describe alternative courses of action.

Prenatal Tests

If a woman is already pregnant and it is likely that a birth defect may appear, special prenatal tests can sometimes tell for certain. These prenatal tests may also alert the physician to a condition in the baby that must be treated before or immediately after birth. Although it is not yet possible to test for all defects, newer methods of prenatal diagnosis are constantly being developed. Three of the most useful procedures are **amniocentesis** (AM-nee-oh-sen-TEE-sihs), **ultrasound**, and **chorionic villi sampling** (CORE-ee-AHN-ik VIL-eye).

■*Amniocentesis.* In this process, a special needle is used to withdraw a small amount of the amniotic fluid surrounding the baby. Cast-off cells in the fluid are then examined for evidence of defects. The most common use of amniocentesis is to test for Down syndrome when the expectant mother is over age thirty-five. Because the procedure involves some risks, it is only performed when there is a valid medical reason.

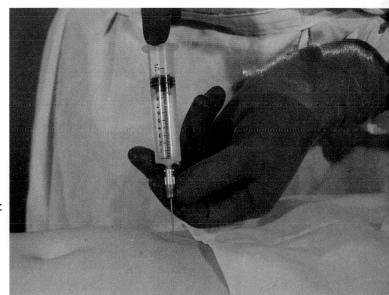

Amniocentesis can detect a number of rare genetic defects. It is performed in the fourth month of pregnancy or later, but only if there is reason to suspect a problem.

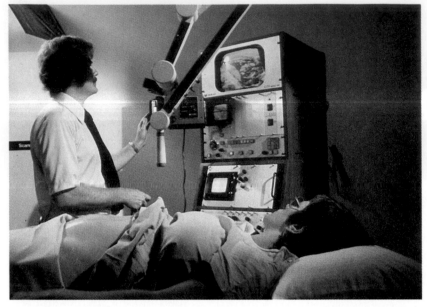

An ultrasound scan produces a picture of the fetus that can give the doctor information about its development.

■*Ultrasound.* This technique uses sound waves to make a video image of the unborn child. It can show whether the fetus is developing on schedule. Certain defects, especially those involving the skeleton and organs, can also be detected by the scan. When amniocentesis is performed, an ultrasound image is used to guide the needle.

Researchers are still studying possible risks of ultrasound. For this reason, most experts advise that ultrasound be used only as a part of necessary medical tests. When it is used, however, ultrasound can often provide additional information. It can help verify the due date. Often it reveals the sex of the developing baby or the presence of twins.

■*Chorionic villi sampling.* This newer test, available at major medical centers, detects the same disorders as amniocentesis but earlier in pregnancy. (The villi are fingers of tissue protruding from the chorion—the membrane encasing the fetus.) For this test, ultrasound is used to guide a catheter through the vagina into the uterus. Samples of the villi are snipped or suctioned off for analysis.

Over one hundred birth defects can now be diagnosed prenatally. Sometimes the problems can be treated before the baby is born. For example, the first child of a Boston mother died at three months of age from a hereditary disease. During her second pregnancy, the mother underwent amniocentesis. It indicated this child also had the disease. The biochemical defect would cause mental retardation. Vitamin therapy was administered to the mother and unborn baby to correct the problem. The baby was normal at birth.

Several other methods of prenatal diagnosis are now in the experimental stages. These may someday provide more accurate information at earlier stages of development. For example, it has become possible to view the fetus directly through a special instrument, obtain samples of fetal blood and tissue, and even perform surgery on the unborn child. Further breakthroughs may make these procedures safe enough for widespread use.

Environmental Hazards to Avoid

Genetic counseling and prenatal tests are useful when there is reason to suspect a particular hereditary or chromosomal defect. But in *all* pregnancies, the best thing the mother-to-be can do to increase the chances of a healthy baby is to take care of herself. An important part of good prenatal care is understanding the harmful effects of environmental hazards such as alcohol and other drugs, smoking, X rays, and infections.

Alcohol

Most people do not think of alcohol as a drug, but it is one. It is best avoided during pregnancy.

Ever since ancient times, writers have commented on the poor mental and physical health of children born to alcoholic women.

Modern medicine has confirmed this. Alcoholic mothers often do bear children with a variety of birth defects, some of which can be fatal.

The resulting condition of affected infants is called fetal alcohol syndrome. The degree of damage usually corresponds to the degree of alcoholism in the mother. Because the damage is done before birth, there is no help for affected children. By the time the symptoms are found, it is too late.

Researchers have found that alcohol interferes with tissue growth and development. The brain is most easily injured. Almost all babies born with fetal alcohol syndrome are mentally retarded. Most also have other problems, such as poor growth and coordination.

Alcohol abuse is dangerous at any time, but especially during pregnancy. Groups such as Alcoholics Anonymous can help people overcome their dependency.

Close-up

A twenty-four-year-old mother lives with the agonizing knowledge that she is the cause of her two daughters' handicaps. Susan is five and Emily four. Both girls have below-average intelligence, little strength, and at times no muscle control.

An observer watched as the children were playing. Emily ran to hide behind a tree. Her movements were slower than average. Instead of going directly to the tree, she stumbled past it. Though both girls were quite pretty, slight irregularities in their facial features indicated abnormalities.

Their mother married at age eighteen. Since her husband was serving in the army, the couple had to move from one military base to another. She found it difficult to make new friends, knowing that in a few months she would have to start over again somewhere else. She began drinking to relieve her loneliness and boredom. The habit continued through her two pregnancies.

Susan's ailments did not become apparent until after Emily was born. Several months later, the specialists gave the verdict. The children's defects resulted from the mother's alcoholism during both pregnancies.

In the heartsick mother's words, "If anyone had told me, I would have quit drinking!" She did, of course, but too late.

What could this mother have done to overcome her boredom and loneliness instead of drinking?

Where would you go for help if you had a drinking problem? ■

Doctors continue to study how alcohol leads to birth defects. It is not yet known how much alcohol is too much. Many health professionals recommend that all pregnant women play it safe by avoiding alcohol as much as possible.

The best advice is to give up alcohol during pregnancy. If the prospective mother finds this difficult, she should seek counseling.

Other Drugs

Many doctors believe that drugs taken during pregnancy are among the major causes of birth defects linked to environmental factors. The word "drugs" includes the following:

- Alcohol, as you have just read.
- Medicines that doctors prescribe.
- Over-the-counter remedies like aspirin, cold medicines, nose drops, and vitamins.
- Chemicals such as caffeine, found in some foods and beverages, and nicotine, found in tobacco.
- Abused drugs such as heroin, LSD, marijuana, and cocaine.

One recent nationwide study revealed that the average woman takes four drugs during pregnancy, not including home remedies and vitamin supplements. There is no such thing as a completely safe drug. Thalidomide, a so-called "safe sedative," was responsible for the birth of more than 2,000 severely deformed infants before its effects were discovered.

In the first four weeks of pregnancy, the effect of drugs on the unborn is usually an "all-or-nothing" reaction. The mother either suffers a miscarriage, or the baby is unaffected by the medicine.

During the second and third months, any medicines or infections that reach the fetus will have their greatest effect. Drugs reduce the flow of food-bearing blood from the mother to her baby. The chances of malformation occuring are greatest during this period because the body systems, organs, arms, and legs are being formed.

In the last six months of pregnancy, harmful substances that reach the fetus usually cause slow growth, infections, or abnormal bleeding at birth. Drugs taken just before birth will still be in the baby's body at birth and may cause serious problems.

An expectant mother should not take any medication unless it is prescribed or recommended by a doctor who knows of the pregnancy. Even vitamin supplements can pose a risk to the unborn baby unless taken under a doctor's advice.

Doctors are advising strict limits on the use of medication during pregnancy. Pregnant women should not take any medicines—even aspirin or vitamins—unless they are specifically prescribed by their physician.

Drugs that are necessary in managing serious conditions such as diabetes and high blood pressure can be taken under the doctor's direction. However, giving up medication for complaints like headaches and hay fever is a worthwhile contribution a pregnant woman can make to her baby's normal development. In fact, any woman who is likely to become pregnant would be wise to avoid taking unnecessary drugs. Usually a woman does not know she is pregnant until several weeks after conception has taken place.

■*Caffeine.* Of all the compounds that have been investigated as possible causes of birth defects, none has been so completely taken for granted as caffeine. This drug is widely used in beverages such as coffee, tea, cocoa, and many soft drinks. Caffeine is also used in many medications. Women who take in moderate amounts of caffeine probably need not worry about birth defects. It is known, however, that feeding large doses of caffeine to pregnant mice and rabbits causes birth defects in their young. Doctors advise heavy coffee, tea, and cola drinkers to cut down during pregnancy.

■*Tobacco.* Nicotine in cigarettes is also a drug. The more the mother smokes, the smaller her baby is likely to be. This is important because the weight of the newborn is a critical factor in the ability to survive. Heavy smoking is believed to cause premature birth. Doctors advise heavy smokers that if they cannot quit smoking, they should at least cut down during pregnancy.

■*Abused drugs.* The increase in the use of cocaine, marijuana, and other "street drugs" has presented physicians with new problems in preventing birth defects.

A mother who is addicted to drugs at the time of delivery usually passes her addiction on to her baby. Immediately after birth, these addicted infants must go through a period of withdrawal—painful illness resulting from the body's dependence on the drug. Severe withdrawal symptoms may lead to death. Even if the baby survives, experts are concerned that the long-range effects of addiction may be serious.

Little is known about exactly how such drugs as marijuana, cocaine, barbituates, and amphetamines affect the fetus. But considering that even over-the-counter medications are cause for concern, you can see the potential danger of these drugs. Preliminary studies in animals suggest cocaine may cause birth defects or the death of the fetus. Similar results have been suggested in studies on marijuana. While research continues, the best advice is not to take *any* drugs before or during pregnancy.

X Rays

X rays may also be dangerous to the unborn baby. Radiation from X rays or other sources can cause birth defects. A woman who is in an accident or sick should tell medical personnel if she is pregnant. They will take special precautions if X rays are needed. For the same reason, she should also tell her dentist or orthodontist if she is pregnant.

Rubella (German Measles)

The terrible effect of certain infections on unborn children was highlighted by the epidemic of rubella (German measles) that swept the country in 1964–65. Thousands of unborn babies were affected when their mothers came down with German measles during pregnancy. In most cases, the pregnant mothers had no symptoms. Others spent a few days in bed with a sore throat, runny nose, temperature, and a rash. However, the disease was not minor for their unborn children. Depending on when during pregnancy rubella strikes, it can cause deafness, blindness, heart defects, or mental retardation.

A rubella vaccine has been developed and millions of children have been vaccinated. The vaccine may be dangerous, however, for women who are pregnant or who become pregnant shortly after receiving it. Check your own health records. Have you had the disease or been vaccinated? A woman should take a rubella immunity test before she considers pregnancy.

Sexually Transmitted Diseases

Sexually transmitted diseases are also infections which can have dreadful effects on the unborn. Some of the diseases in this category include:

- Syphilis.
- Gonorrhea.
- Genital herpes.
- AIDS (acquired immune deficiency syndrome).

These and other sexually transmitted diseases can affect prenatal development or be passed on from an infected mother to the infant. The results can be serious illness, deformity, or even death.

It is possible for someone to be infected with a sexually transmitted disease without realizing it. Many states now require every pregnant woman to be tested for syphilis. Most states also require doctors to put a solution in the eyes of newborns to kill gonorrhea germs that could otherwise cause blindness.

Drugs and treatment can cure syphilis and gonorrhea and relieve the symptoms of herpes in adults. Untreated, the diseases can affect the heart, brain, reproductive system, and spinal cord, and eventually lead to death. No drug cures the damage to the newborn which results from a delay in diagnosis and treatment. Doctors should always be told of the presence of any sexually transmitted disease during pregnancy.

Other Infections

Not all infections in a pregnant woman are likely to cause damage to the unborn baby. However, she should tell her doctor about any illness, no matter how mild it may seem.

The availability of a rubella vaccine makes it unlikely that another epidemic will strike. However, every woman who might become pregnant should find out whether she is immune.

Teen Pregnancy: A Health Risk

The younger the mother is, the greater the physical hazards of pregnancy. During adolescence, a girl's body is not yet mature. It is much harder for her to support the physical demands of an unborn baby for nine months. Indeed, the death rate for the baby during or immediately after pregnancy is five times higher among mothers under sixteen than among those between twenty and twenty-four.

Young pregnant mothers are also more likely to suffer from complications during pregnancy. Their children are often underweight at birth. Underweight newborns are more likely to have brain damage or die at birth.

One out of every fourteen babies born in the United States has some sort of birth defect. Adolescent girls have an even greater chance of bearing a defective infant. Such babies may be born crippled, mentally retarded, deaf, blind, diabetic, or with any one of hundreds of other defects. You can imagine the emotional and financial impact on a young couple. Often these problems will continue throughout their lives.

In short, very young pregnant mothers are in the high-risk category. For that reason, pregnancy before the age of sixteen calls for extra prenatal care, good nutrition, and social and emotional assistance.

Check Your Understanding

1. Explain the differences between hereditary and environmental birth defects. Give three examples of each.

2. Why might a couple seek genetic counseling.

3. If you had a friend or relative who just found out she was pregnant, what would you advise her to do to help prevent environmental birth defects?

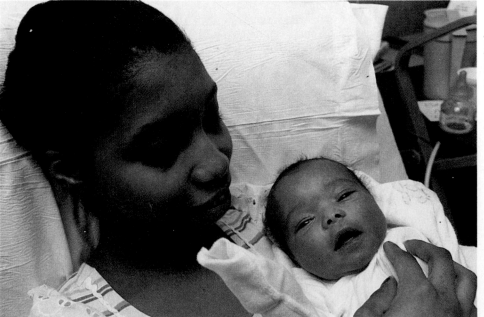

This sixteen-year-old was fortunate to give birth to a healthy baby. Many teen mothers are not so lucky.

Chapter Review

To Sum Up

- Prenatal development begins with conception. It includes three stages: the period of the ovum, the period of the embryo, the period of the fetus.
- Chromosomes contain the genes which determine all inherited characteristics.
- Infertility problems can sometimes be solved through treatment; if not, couples can try other options.
- Birth defects have a variety of causes.
- Genetic counseling and prenatal tests can help predict some birth defects.
- To minimize risks to her unborn baby, a pregnant woman should avoid environmental hazards such as alcohol, drugs, and smoking.
- Babies born to teen mothers are at much greater risk for health problems.

To Review and Remember

1. How do unborn babies receive their nourishment?
2. What is the fetus?
3. What is meant by "quickening"? When does this usually first occur?
4. Briefly explain the difference between a dominant and a recessive gene.
5. How is the sex of a baby determined?
6. Name three options available to people who have fertility problems that cannot be solved through treatment.
7. What is the defect that results in Down syndrome?
8. How is amniocentesis performed? Why is it used?
9. Describe the cause and effects of fetal alcohol syndrome?
10. Name three health risks of teen pregnancy.

To Discuss and Discover

1. Discuss the effects a multiple birth might have on a family's lifestyle, both positive and negative.
2. Choose one type of birth defect that you would like to learn more about. Find current information about its causes, symptoms, frequency of occurrence, and treatment. Share your information with the class in a paper or speech.
3. Create a poster, magazine advertisement, or radio or TV commercial aimed at prospective parents. Include facts about prenatal development and the hazards of alcohol, drugs, and smoking. Present the results to the class.

4 Preparing for Birth

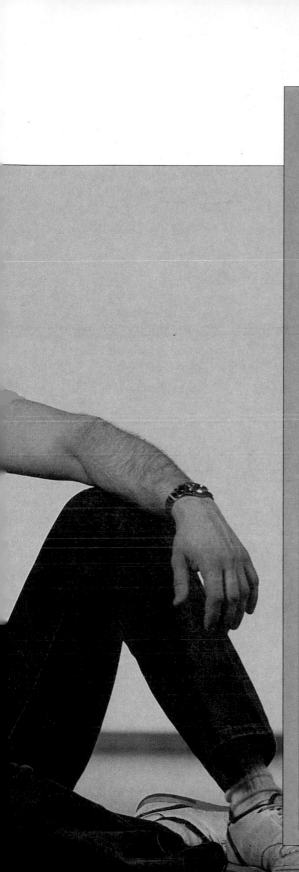

To help you to . . .

- List the early signs of pregnancy.
- Explain the importance of medical care and nutrition during pregnancy.
- Differentiate between discomforts and complications of pregnancy.
- Plan a well-balanced diet for a pregnant woman.
- Give recommendations for a pregnant woman's activities and personal care.
- Describe ways parents-to-be can plan for a baby's care.
- Give examples of how to reduce the costs of having a baby.
- Describe how parents can make decisions and preparations relating to childbirth.

Terms to Learn

alternative birth center	labor	postnatal
anemia	maternity leave	pregnancy test
budget	nurse-midwife	prepared childbirth
delivery	obstetrician	variable expenses
fixed expenses	paternity leave	

"Here, Jenny. Put your hand on my tummy." Mrs. Williamson placed six-year-old Jenny's hand on her abdomen.

"I feel something," Jenny said excitedly. "Your tummy is moving."

"That is your new little brother. The baby is stretching and turning over. That is what you feel."

"Does that tickle you?" asked Jenny.

"Not really, Jenny, but it does feel kind of funny. In fact, sometimes the baby makes me uncomfortable. He can get into a position that pokes me in the side. Then if I rub where his little foot or hand is poking me, he moves it to a different spot."

"Why is he inside you, Mommy?" asked Jenny.

"He needs to grow there for a while. When he is big enough and strong enough, then he will be born.

"Right now, though, he is depending upon me for food and a comfortable place to grow. That's why I have to take extra good care of myself now. I try to eat foods that are good for me and to get plenty of rest. I go to the doctor twice a month now."

"Well, I wish he would hurry up and get big enough to come out so I could see him," Jenny said.

"So do I, Jenny. It won't be long now."

We have explored the incredible development of the child from conception to the time of birth. The corresponding events in the lives of the parents are no less significant. The mother is going through many physical changes as the baby grows inside her. Both parents have important plans and decisions to make in preparation for the arrival of a new family member.

A Healthy Pregnancy

Staying in good health is the most important responsibility of a pregnant woman. Her child's life and health, as well as her own, depend on it. Consulting and following the advice of a good doctor is the first step. Using common sense about diet, activities, rest, and personal care will help avoid problems.

Early Signs of Pregnancy

A woman cannot tell immediately when conception has occurred. How, then, does she know when she is pregnant?
- Usually the first indication is a missed period, especially if her menstrual cycle is very regular.
- She may have an ache or feeling of fullness in her lower abdomen.
- Fatigue, drowsiness, or faintness may occur.

Unusual sleepiness, when combined with other signs, can be a clue that a woman might be pregnant. She should confirm the suspicion with a visit to the doctor for a pregnancy test.

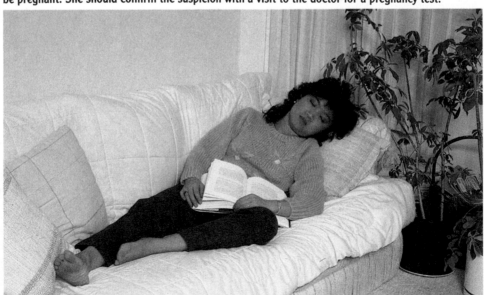

- She may find that she needs to urinate more frequently.
- She may have discomfort or tenderness in her breasts.
- Morning nausea is a first indication for some.

Actually, each of these physical signs can occur without pregnancy. Since the physical signs of pregnancy may not be accurate, a **pregnancy test** is needed to be sure. Various methods are used. For most, a laboratory test is performed on the blood or urine of the woman, and a visit to the doctor is required. Simplified versions of these tests are available for at-home use, but pregnancy should always be verified by a physician.

Medical Care During Pregnancy

A visit to the doctor is advisable as soon as a woman suspects she is pregnant. This can help prevent serious complications. Many women prefer to consult an **obstetrician** (OB-stuh-TRISH-un)—a doctor who specializes in pregnancy and birth.

Although the expectant mother probably feels as healthy as ever, her doctor will usually perform a thorough examination. An examination includes the following:

- Blood pressure, pulse, respiration, and initial weight are recorded.

Regular medical checkups are an important part of prenatal care. Checking the baby's heartbeat, examining the ankles for swelling, and recording weight gain are routine parts of each visit.

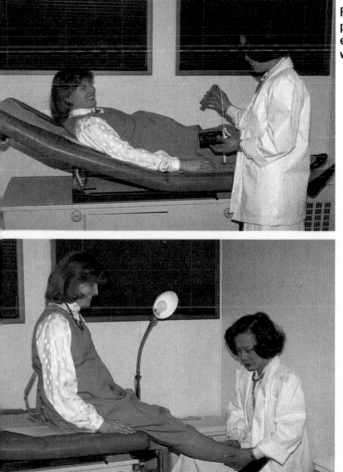

- Pelvic measurements are taken to determine whether the birth passageway is wide enough to allow a normal-size baby to be born without difficulty.
- An analysis of urine checks the condition of the kidneys, which carry a heavier burden during pregnancy.
- A blood test gives the doctor valuable information about the woman's health. For example, it tells if there is a tendency toward **anemia** Anemia is a condition caused by lack of iron that results in poor appetite, tiredness, and weakness. The blood test also determines the woman's blood type in case a transfusion is necessary.
- A history of past illnesses and operations will be recorded. These may reveal conditions which require special treatment or observation.

Under normal conditions, doctors usually see their patients about once a month until the sixth or seventh month of pregnancy. Then visits are increased to every other week. During the last month, the doctor will probably schedule office calls for once a week.

Examinations during these monthly visits seem fairly routine. They are, however, important to see that all continues to go well.

One of the first questions a prospective mother asks her doctor is, "When will my baby be born?" The calculations are simple. It takes about 280 days (40 weeks) for prenatal development to be complete. Nine months and one week after the beginning of the last menstrual period will be the approximate birth date. Most babies are born within two weeks before or after this date.

Discomforts of Pregnancy

Some women go through pregnancy without any problems. Others may be mildly annoyed by some of these common discomforts. Although they are probably no cause for concern, any discomforts should be discussed with the doctor to make sure they do not indicate a serious problem.

- Nausea is the most common complaint. It is commonly called "morning sickness." An easy way to combat this is to keep soda crackers by the bed to eat before lifting the head from the pillow in the morning. Many doctors recommend frequent, smaller meals so that the stomach is never completely empty. Fortunately, nausea rarely lasts beyond the fourth month. Severe and prolonged nausea should be reported to the doctor.
- Sleepiness is a fairly common condition during early pregnancy. Unusual fatigue is a result of not only chemical changes in the body, but also the carrying of extra weight. Fatigue can also be caused by a form of anemia and should be checked by the physician. By the third or fourth month, sleepiness usually decreases.
- Heartburn is a digestive disturbance not really associated with the heart. It is caused by increased pressure on the stomach from the enlarging uterus. The doctor can give advice to help relieve the problem.
- Shortness of breath is caused by the enlarging uterus pressing upward against the lungs.
- Varicose (swollen) veins develop from pressure on the blood vessels in the legs. Resting with the legs and feet elevated gives relief. The use of elasticized stockings and specific exercises can also help.
- Muscle cramps in the legs may be relieved by rest and gentle stretching. The doctor may also recommend a mineral supplement.
- Lower back pain caused by change in posture may be experienced during the last months of pregnancy. To avoid back strain, pregnant women should wear low-heeled shoes and be sure to bend the knees when lifting. Certain exercises can help relieve backache.

If no unusual problems develop, a woman can keep up her normal activities during pregnancy. Balancing work, rest, and recreation will help her feel her best.

Possible Complications

While the problems discussed thus far are usually minor, some women experience more serious complications. Any of the following symptoms should be reported to the doctor immediately.

- Vaginal bleeding.
- Unusual weight gain.
- Excessive thirst.
- Reduced or painful urination.
- Severe abdominal pain.
- Persistent headaches.
- Severe vomiting.
- Fever.
- Swelling of face and hands.
- Blurred vision or dizziness.

Nutrition During Pregnancy

Good nutrition is the single most important factor in prenatal care. The pregnant mother must eat a balanced diet if she wants to help her baby develop properly. It is also necessary if she wants to come through her pregnancy without damaging her own health.

Once it was thought that the developing baby would be fine, no matter how poorly the mother ate. The fetus was believed to take what was needed from the mother's system. We now know otherwise. The baby does take some things from the mother's system if they are not available in her diet. Calcium may be taken from her bones and teeth, for example. But her nutritional well-being before and during pregnancy determines much of the future health of her baby.

Most people are not aware that the baby's vital organs develop early in pregnancy. For example, improper nutrition has a direct, permanent effect on early brain growth. Often a

Protein is vital for the unborn baby's rapid growth. Fish is one good source of protein. What are some others?

woman is not even sure she is pregnant until after the second month of pregnancy. That is why every woman who might become pregnant should make sure she is in the best possible health at all times.

The Role of Nutrients

A good diet contains all the food nutrients—protein, vitamins, minerals, fats, and carbohydrates. A poor diet lacks the necessary amount of one or more of these nutrients. Every single nutrient performs very special functions.

■*Protein.* This nutrient is obtained from meat, fish, poultry, eggs, milk, cheese, and beans. It is vital for the growth of the baby. It also helps keep the mother's body in good repair. Because of the added needs of the growing fetus, protein intake must be increased during pregnancy. A diet lacking in protein is generally lacking in other nutrients, too.

■*Vitamins.* These promote general good health, help protect against infection and disease, and regulate body processes. More vitamins are also needed during pregnancy. If a mother's diet is lacking vitamins, her baby may be born with birth defects.

An increase in vitamin A is needed during pregnancy to assure proper development of the baby's eyes. Extra B vitamins are needed for good fetal development because they release the energy in foods. They build the nervous system, keep the digestive system working well, and promote healthy skin.

Vitamin C intake should also be increased during pregnancy. It helps build healthy gums and teeth, and helps make the material that holds body cells together. Vitamin D is important for the development of strong bones and teeth.

All of these vitamins are obtained through a proper diet. Vitamin-rich foods are usually those which are also rich in other nutrients. Fresh fruits and vegetables, whole-grain breads and cereal products, and fortified milk are especially rich sources. Vitamin supplements should not be taken unless recommended by the doctor.

Eating fresh fruits and vegetables is a good way to get the extra amounts of vitamins needed during pregnancy. These foods are also natural sources of energy.

An expectant mother should drink plenty of milk. The calcium and phosphorus in milk help keep teeth and bones strong, both for the mother and for her unborn baby.

■*Minerals.* These nutrients are needed for sturdy bones and teeth, healthy blood, and the regulation of daily elimination. Many foods are rich in minerals. If supplements are needed, the doctor will prescribe them.

Pregnant women need enough iron to prevent anemia. The developing fetus also needs iron to build a blood supply of its own. In addition, extra iron is stored in the baby's liver to last for several months after birth when the baby's diet lacks iron.

Meat is a good source of iron, especially organ meats such as liver and kidney. Other sources include beans, peas, spinach, raisins, and dates.

Calcium and phosphorus are other important minerals. They help build the baby's bones and teeth. The mother's body also has a greater need for calcium and phosphorus during pregnancy. Milk supplies much of the calcium and phosphorus needed, as well as protein.

■*Fats and carbohydrates.* These are necessary for heat and energy. Good sources are fruits, vegetables, whole-grain breads and cereal products, and vegetable oils. However, too much fat and sugar are not part of a healthy diet.

Daily Diet

It is not difficult to plan a daily diet that provides all these nutrients. Choosing foods from the Basic Food Groups is a simple way to have a well-balanced diet. The Basic Food Groups are recommended for anyone, young or old, pregnant or not—only the amounts vary.

■*Milk-Cheese Group.* A pregnant woman should drink four to five glasses of vitamin D fortified milk each day. Any kind will do—whole milk, skim milk, or buttermilk. Cheese, yogurt, cottage cheese, and ice cream can be substituted for some of the milk.

Foods from the bread-cereal group should be either whole-grain or enriched products. They supply important nutrients such as carbohydrates, B vitamins, and iron.

■*Meat-Poultry-Fish-Beans Group.* Three or more servings from this group should be eaten daily. Foods in this group include all types of meat, poultry, fish, eggs, nuts, dry beans and peas, and lentils. An expectant mother should have fish and liver at least once a week.

■*Fruit-Vegetable Group.* All fruits and vegetables are included in this group. A pregnant woman should eat at least four servings from the Fruit-Vegetable Group daily. One serving should be a deep yellow or leafy, dark green, fruit or vegetable. One food high in vitamin C, such as citrus fruit, berries, melon, tomatoes, or cabbage, should be eaten. Pregnant women should also have at least two more servings of any fruit or vegetable daily.

■*Bread-Cereal Group.* Four or more servings of grain products should be eaten each day. These may include whole-grain or enriched breads, cereals, and other grain products such as rice, macaroni, and noodles.

If a woman breast-feeds her baby, her need for extra nutrients continues after the birth. The chart on page 98 shows the Basic Food Groups. It also gives the recommended amounts for different age groups, pregnant women, and nursing mothers.

There are other important dietary recommendations for pregnant women. Six to eight glasses of water are needed daily. Rich and fried foods should be avoided. They are often hard to digest and usually provide few nutrients. And of course, alcohol is best avoided.

The Basic Food Groups

Food Group	Important Nutrients	Sample Foods and Serving Sizes	Recommended Number of Servings				
			Child	Teen	Adult	Pregnant Woman	Nursing Mother
MILK-CHEESE GROUP	Calcium Phosphorus Protein Vitamins B₂, A, and D	1 cup (250 mL) milk, butter-milk, skim milk, or yogurt 2 slices American or Swiss cheese 2 one-inch (2.5 cm) cubes cheddar cheese 1½ cups (375 mL) creamed cottage cheese	2–3	4	2	4	4
MEAT-POULTRY-FISH-BEANS GROUP	Protein Iron B vitamins	2 oz. (60 g) lean cooked meat, poultry, or fish 2 eggs 1 cup (240 mL) cooked dried beans or peas 4 Tbsp. (60 mL) peanut butter	2*	2	2	3	3
FRUIT-VEGETABLE GROUP	Vitamins A and C Calcium Phosphorus Iron B vitamins Fiber	½ cup (125 mL) juice ½ cup (125 mL) cooked vegetables 1 medium-size apple, banana, or orange 1 cup (250 mL) fresh berries or raw leafy vegetables	4*	4	4	4	4
BREAD-CEREAL GROUP	Carbohy-drates Iron B vitamins	1 slice bread 1 roll, biscuit, bagel, muffin, or pancake 1 cup (250 mL) ready-to-eat cereal ½ cup (125 mL) cooked cereal, pasta, rice, or grits 2 tortillas	4	4	4	4	4

*A child's serving size in these food groups is approximately 1 Tbsp. (15 mL) of food for each year of the child's age.

Teenage Diets

The kind of food that a girl eats in her teens affects the children she may have, even if she does not become pregnant until she is twenty or thirty. Good nutrition is vital during the teenage years. Even a crash nutrition program during pregnancy will not make up for poor nutrition earlier. This is especially true since the major organs are formed before most women are certain they are pregnant.

Poor nutrition during adolescence is not necessarily caused by lack of money. Popular foods such as potato chips, candy bars, and soft drinks provide little nutrition. Because some families do not always eat together, many teens choose their own meals. They often eat only their favorite foods or those which are easy to prepare, rather than balanced meals.

In most cases, just a few changes can make a great difference. Some people do not like milk, for example. In that case, using milk in creamed soups, desserts, and casseroles can help satisfy the milk requirement. Cheese can also be substituted for part of the milk. Other calcium sources include broccoli, yogurt, kale, sardines, and tofu (a soybean product often used in Oriental cooking). Women who are allergic to milk should consult their physician.

While meat is an excellent source of protein, it may be too expensive for families on low budgets. Poultry and eggs are less expensive, yet high in protein and other nutrients. Dried beans and peas are also inexpensive. They provide protein, although they are not as rich a source.

Improving Eating Habits

Every mother wants to have a healthy child. To do so, poor eating habits must be improved. It is not too much to ask when a child's health is at stake.

A well-balanced diet is important both before and during pregnancy. A variety of foods from each Basic Food Group should be eaten daily.

Close-up

Five months into her pregnancy, Elaine started having digestive problems that didn't seem like morning sickness to her. Instead of the usual nausea and vomiting, her symptoms included gas, bloating, slight abdominal pains, and diarrhea. Elaine thought the timing odd, since her problem didn't start until midway through her pregnancy. In addition, she always got sick a few hours after eating, not in the mornings when she first got up.

Concerned that something might be seriously wrong, Elaine consulted her doctor. Fortunately, in her case the problem was easily corrected. The doctor found that Elaine's body was unable to digest the sugar found in milk and milk products.

Elaine had not previously been aware of her problem since she seldom drank milk. But now that she was pregnant, she began following her doctor's instructions for a healthy diet. This included a quart of milk a day. The milk soon brought her hidden problem to the surface.

Elaine was pleased to find that she could still get the calcium she needed. Drinking milk in smaller amounts, and with meals, made it easier for her system to handle. She also found that yogurt was easier for her to digest than milk. And she learned to include other calcium-rich foods, like cabbage and broccoli, in her daily diet.

Was Elaine right to be concerned about her symptoms?

How would her unborn baby have been affected if she stopped drinking milk and did not substitute other sources of calcium? ■

Weight Gain During Pregnancy

For most women, pregnancy involves gaining about 24—30 lb. (11.0—13.6 kg). A 24 lb. (11 kg) weight gain does not mean the baby will weigh that amount. The chart on page 101 shows how added weight is usually distributed.

Fetal deaths increase when gains are below 20 lb. (9 kg). Mothers who gain less than 20 lb. (9 kg) are also twice as likely to give birth prematurely.

Many doctors recommend that pregnant women gain no more than 30 lb. (13.6 kg). However, it is never a good idea for the expectant mother to restrict her intake of nutritious foods. Pregnancy is not the time to go on a weight-loss diet. Moderate exercise and a diet that does not include sugary, fatty foods can help keep weight gain within the recommended levels. The doctor keeps track of the pregnant woman's weight gain at each prenatal visit and is the best source of advice.

Personal Care and Activities

In addition to practicing good nutrition, the expectant mother should take good care of herself in other ways. As you learned in Chapter 3, she should avoid alcohol, tobacco, and all drugs or medications except those prescribed by her doctor. Plenty of rest and moderate exercise are also important.

- **Rest.** The expectant mother needs at least eight hours of sleep at night and rest periods several times a day. She should avoid becoming overtired. If a nap is not possible, relaxing for 15 minutes with feet elevated can be just as refreshing.

- **Exercise.** Moderate exercise can help keep the expectant mother in good physical condition. It can also control weight gain and make pregnancy more comfortable.

Distribution of Weight Gain During Pregnancy

	Customary	Metric
Weight of average baby at birth	7–8 lb.	3.2–3.6 kg
Placenta	1–2 lb.	0.45–0.9 kg
Amniotic fluid	1½–2 lb.	0.7–0.9 kg
Increased size of uterus and supporting muscles	2 lb.	0.9 kg
Increase in breast tissue	1 lb.	0.45 kg
Increase in blood volume	1½–3 lb.	0.7–1.4 kg
Increase in fat stores	5 lb.	2.3 kg
Increase in body fluids	5–7 lb.	2.3–3.2 kg
Total	24–30 lb.	11.0–13.6 kg

Many doctors recommend exercise such as walking, swimming, or biking during pregnancy. Special programs of prenatal aerobics are offered in some communities. Hobbies such as tennis and golf can also be continued. However, pregnancy is not a time to begin any strenuous new activities. The expectant mother should take care not to strain herself or become overtired. Sports that might cause injury should be avoided.

Special exercises can also help the body prepare for giving birth. These are often taught in childbirth classes.

Regular exercise can help a pregnant woman stay fit and feeling well. As long as she is careful not to tire herself out, she can continue most of the physical activities she enjoys.

■ *Hygiene.* Daily baths or showers are especially important during this period. The skin helps to maintain correct body temperature and eliminate waste, so it should be kept clean. Just before bed is an excellent time to bathe or shower because the warm water encourages relaxation and sleep.

■ *Other activities.* Work routines of the mother-to-be will remain much as they were before her pregnancy. If she works outside the home, she can continue to do so as long as she desires unless her physician advises differently. Daily household chores can also be continued. However, a pregnant woman should be especially careful when bending, reaching, and lifting to avoid injuring her back.

Travel should be discussed with the doctor. Most doctors advise no long-distance travel during the last two months of pregnancy. This is mainly to avoid giving birth unexpectedly away from home.

The most important point for a woman to remember is that her lifestyle should not change radically during pregnancy. Moderation may be necessary in some circumstances, but on the whole she should continue her life as before.

Emotional Health During Pregnancy

As you read in Chapter 2, new parents must make a number of emotional adjustments during pregnancy. It is normal for both the

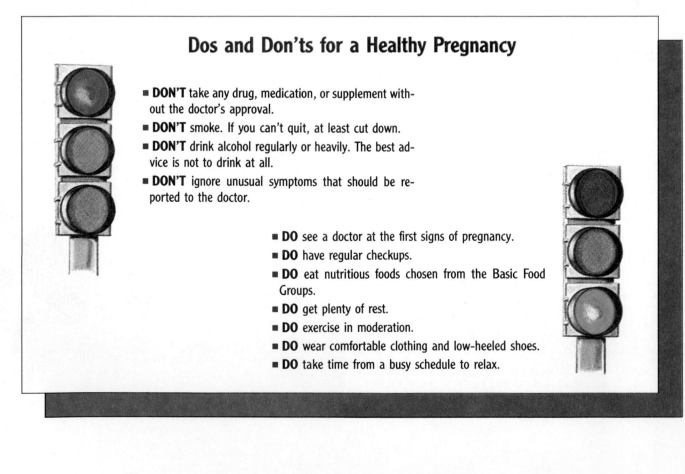

Dos and Don'ts for a Healthy Pregnancy

- **DON'T** take any drug, medication, or supplement without the doctor's approval.
- **DON'T** smoke. If you can't quit, at least cut down.
- **DON'T** drink alcohol regularly or heavily. The best advice is not to drink at all.
- **DON'T** ignore unusual symptoms that should be reported to the doctor.

- **DO** see a doctor at the first signs of pregnancy.
- **DO** have regular checkups.
- **DO** eat nutritious foods chosen from the Basic Food Groups.
- **DO** get plenty of rest.
- **DO** exercise in moderation.
- **DO** wear comfortable clothing and low-heeled shoes.
- **DO** take time from a busy schedule to relax.

mother and father to have some worries and fears about the baby's arrival. Talking over their concerns with family members and each other can be reassuring.

On the mother's part, emotional changes can also be brought about by physical ones. Hormonal changes caused by pregnancy sometimes produce swings between happiness and depression. Even the most even-tempered woman may be upset at times. As the body adjusts to pregnancy, these moods usually disappear.

Too much stress or too many emotional upsets are not healthy for anyone. Any unusually upsetting problems or situations should be talked over with a family member or counselor. Lasting feelings of anxiety, depression, or stress should be discussed with the doctor. In general, however, a pregnant woman who takes good physical care of herself—especially by exercising moderately and relaxing often—is helping to assure her mental and emotional health as well.

Check Your Understanding

1. Why should a woman see a doctor regularly during pregnancy, even if she feels good?

2. Describe a good daily diet for a pregnant woman. Give a sample menu for one day.

3. Why is it dangerous for a pregnant woman to go on a weight-loss diet? What would you recommend instead?

4. What changes, if any, would you recommend a pregnant woman make in her daily schedule? Why?

Some extra concerns and changing moods are to be expected during pregnancy. A calm, relaxed attitude can help minimize stress.

Working parents often arrange to take time off for the birth of their child and to settle into their new roles.

Planning Ahead for Changes

Have you noticed how much better a special event goes if someone has thought out the problems and made careful plans? A school dance where no one remembers to arrange for a band or have tickets printed is not much of a success. If you are going to college, you will not decide where to go by just drawing a name out of a hat. You will see which school can best help you reach all your goals.

Having a baby also requires planning. Responsible parents-to-be will have already thought carefully about what they must do to meet their baby's needs. Now, during their nine months of waiting, they have many decisions and preparations to make in order to be ready for the new family member.

Roles, Responsibilities, and Decisions

During pregnancy, every couple must decide how they will meet the responsibilities of child care. Many things should be taken into consideration—each partner's goals, skills, schedule, and personal characteristics, as well as the financial needs of the family.

If all parents could stay home to give full-time care to their children, decisions about child care would be much simpler. In most families, at least one parent—and often both—must work to provide income. Decisions about the employment of parents have a major effect on the baby's life and development. Therefore they should be made only after careful consideration.

Many new mothers who work outside the home take a **maternity leave**. This lets the woman take time off to give birth and recuperate. She may then spend several weeks or months caring for the baby full-time before returning to work. Some employers grant a similar leave to fathers, called **paternity leave**. These arrangements allow parents to spend more time with their baby during the important early stages of development.

If finances permit it, a couple may decide that one parent will stay home to care for the child on a long-term basis. In most of these situations, the mother is the one who becomes the primary caregiver. But some couples have reversed the traditional roles either temporarily or permanently. The father stays home to care for the house and children, and the mother becomes the chief wage earner.

There is nothing either masculine or feminine about caring for a baby. The infant feels comforted whether the father or the mother is holding it. The father gets the same feeling of protective tenderness and pride that the mother feels in giving the baby comfort. Regardless of who is primarily responsible for daily care tasks, every parent should know the basics of child care.

Sometimes neither parent stays home to care for the baby after the first few weeks. This may be by necessity or by choice. Parents look to a variety of arrangements for providing their children with care during the hours they work. Sometimes the child stays with a relative or other caregiver in the baby's own home, or perhaps another home. For toddlers and older children, various kinds of day care centers provide opportunities for group play and learning. (You will learn more about different types of child care arrangements in Chapter 16.) Whatever decision parents make, it should be carefully considered.

Some parents must find someone to care for the baby while they return to work. Day care centers are one option. It is best to consider this decision early so that any necessary arrangements can be made in advance.

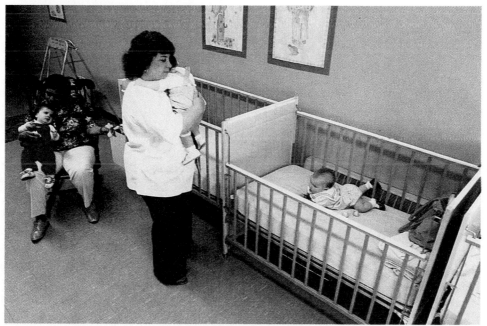

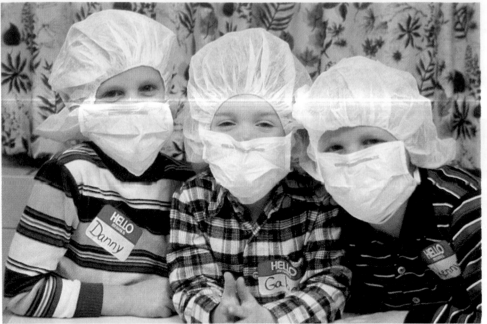

Many hospitals offer special programs for young children who will soon be welcoming home a new baby brother or sister. This helps the youngsters understand and feel a part of what is happening.

Preparing to Be a Good Parent

Most parents-to-be wonder whether they will be able to take good care of their child. Considering all the different ideas about children and parenting they have probably heard, it is no wonder. Even the most confident mothers and fathers worry about doing the right thing.

A couple should discuss their ideas about parenting methods with each other before the baby is born. Of course, they cannot plan what they will do in every possible situation. And as they become experienced at parenting, some of their early ideas may change. But by agreeing ahead of time on general philosophies of raising children, they can avoid conflict later on.

Preparing for parenthood also involves adjustments in the other roles parents fill. Parents may be spouses, family members, workers, volunteers, and citizens. Good management practices help parents balance their roles. Management of time, money, and energy are especially vital for good parents.

Other Children in the Family

Much has been written about the problems a new baby can cause in a family with other children. However, much depends on the kind of family—their attitudes and relationships. Children who feel loved and accepted are less likely to react negatively to a new baby. But it is normal for any young child to react with at least some feelings of jealousy or confusion. These will either fade or grow according to the parents' handling of the situation.

During pregnancy, parents should prepare their other children for the arrival of a new baby. Encouraging the attitude that the coming baby belongs to the child, as well as to the parents, lessens the feeling of being replaced. Giving a child a chance to help with the preparation for the baby's coming makes the child feel needed. Chapter 10 gives other suggestions for minimizing problems of jealousy.

Getting Ready for the New Arrival

Part of the excitement of expecting a new member of the family is gathering the "baby things." New parents are sometimes surprised at how much is required. The newborn will need food, clothing, and a place to sleep. Taking care of the infant also requires some special equipment and supplies. With careful planning, the parents can have everything ready when the baby arrives and still keep expenses to a minimum.

Decisions about Feeding

Whether to breast-feed or bottle-feed the baby is a decision usually made during pregnancy. Actually, it is impossible to tell any difference between a six-year-old who was fed formula and one who was nursed by his or her mother. However, medical experts recommend breast-feeding whenever possible, at least for the first few weeks after birth.

Breast-feeding has many advantages. It is ideally suited to the needs of a baby. It provides temporary immunity against some diseases. Experts also feel that the physical closeness of breast-feeding helps create a special bond between mother and child. Bottle-fed babies sometimes miss this closeness. Parents who bottle-feed must be sure to hold the baby during feedings and communicate their love.

Bottle-feeding with formula is a convenient alternative for mothers who are unable to breast-feed or do not choose to do so. Formula—a mixture of milk or milk substitute, water, and nutrients—provides nearly the same nutrition as breast milk. It may be made at home or purchased in a variety of convenient forms. Powdered, concentrated, and ready-to-use formulas are available.

The decision to breast-feed or bottle-feed is a personal one. It will depend on the mother's attitudes and perhaps her schedule. Some mothers breast-feed for some feedings and supplement with bottles. It is not so much the method of feeding chosen as the feeling behind it. The chart on page 108 shows some of the pros and cons of both methods.

One advantage of using formula is that family members can enjoy helping to feed the baby, too.

Comparing Breast-Feeding and Bottle-Feeding

Breast-Feeding

Advantages

- Creates a bond through physical closeness with the mother.
- Provides some natural immunity against diseases.
- Speeds the return of the mother's uterus to normal size.
- Causes fewer digestive upsets.
- Is conveniently available at all times.
- Babies have fewer allergies.

Disadvantages

- Father is unable to participate in feeding.
- Mother's breasts become enlarged and heavy.
- Medication the mother is taking may harm the infant.
- Some mothers find nursing painful.
- May be difficult due to work schedule.
- Anxiety or illness can interfere with ability to produce milk.

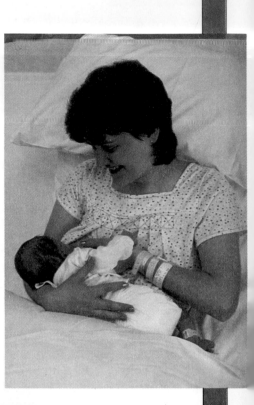

Bottle-Feeding

Advantages

- Father can participate in feeding.
- Makes return to work easier.
- Baby can be fed by anyone, anywhere.

Disadvantages

- Formula can be expensive.
- Greater chance of allergies.
- Baby may not be given close physical contact during feeding.

By shopping carefully, an expectant mother can put together a basic wardrobe of mix and match items that will see her through many different occasions.

Clothing and Equipment Needs

Basic supplies for a baby include clothing, bedding, feeding equipment, and bathing supplies. Wise parents begin with only a minimum number of the basic items needed at birth. Gifts and loaned articles may supply some of these, as well as later necessities.

Many baby gifts are unnecessary "extras." Practical items are often more appreciated. Most parents would gladly trade a fancy baby garment stored in the bottom of a drawer for an extra bottle or a dozen diapers.

The chart on pages 101–111 shows basic needs for a typical baby. This list merely suggests possibilities. The doctor may give specific suggestions for the individual baby. Advice is also given at the hospital and at classes for new parents.

Maternity Clothes

By about the fourth or fifth month, the mother-to-be will need special clothing. Attractive maternity clothes need not be expensive, but they are important for good morale. Maternity clothing must be comfortable. It should be loose enough for freedom of movement and allow for good circulation. Tight clothing of any kind should never be worn.

Simple garments are the best choice. The expectant mother should consider how they will fit in the last month of pregnancy. Knit fabrics stretch to allow room for the growing baby. Skirts and pants may include a stretch panel for comfort. Some manufacturers use large stitches that are easy to remove on wide side seams. The garment can be let out as needed.

Comfortable, low-heeled shoes with good support are recommended throughout pregnancy. High heels should be avoided. They not only throw the body out of balance, but increase the risk of falling.

Basic Baby Supplies

Clothing

- Disposable diapers. (Quantity depends on whether they will be for regular or occasional use.)
- 3–4 dozen cloth diapers, if preferred.
- 4–6 waterproof pants (for cloth diapers).
- 6–8 undershirts.
- 4–6 one-piece footed sleepers.
- 4–6 gowns.
- 3–4 cotton receiving blankets.
- 1 warm outer wrapping blanket.
- 1 sweater and cap set.
- 1–2 sun hats or bonnets.
- 1 dress-up outfit, if desired.

Feeding Equipment

- 6–8 large bottles (8 oz. or 237 mL) if the baby is bottle-fed.
- 2–3 large bottles (8 oz. or 237 mL) if the baby is breast-fed.
- 2–4 small bottles (4 oz. or 118 mL) for water and juice.
- Nipples (the same number as the bottles, plus a few extra).
- Bottle caps (the same number as the bottles).
- Sterilizer or saucepan. (This is not needed if bottles with disposable liners are used or the doctor says sterilization is unnecessary.)
- Bottle and nipple brush.
- Nipple jar and cover.
- Pan for hot water to warm bottle, if desired.

Bedding

- 4 fitted crib sheets.
- Waterproof mattress cover.
- 2–4 absorbent pads.
- 2 lightweight blankets or spreads.
- 1 heavier crib blanket.
- Bumper pad (fits around inside of crib just above mattress; keeps baby's arms and legs in, drafts out).

Bathing and Other Supplies

- Baby bathtub or other container.
- Mild, pure soap.
- Baby shampoo.
- Several soft washcloths.
- 2 soft bath towels.
- Cotton balls.
- Petroleum jelly.
- Baby powder or lotion, if desired.
- Safety pins (for cloth diapers).
- Blunt-tipped nail scissors.
- Baby comb and brush set.
- Rectal thermometer.
- Baby syringe.

Travel Equipment

- Car seat (safety-approved).
- Tote bag for carrying supplies.
- Stroller, carriage, or infant carrier, if desired.

How to Evaluate a Crib for Safety

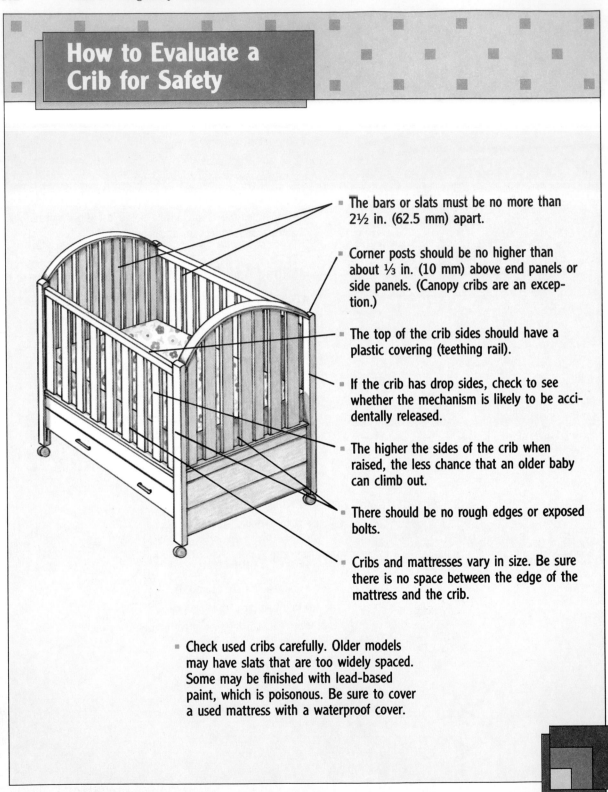

- The bars or slats must be no more than 2½ in. (62.5 mm) apart.

- Corner posts should be no higher than about ⅓ in. (10 mm) above end panels or side panels. (Canopy cribs are an exception.)

- The top of the crib sides should have a plastic covering (teething rail).

- If the crib has drop sides, check to see whether the mechanism is likely to be accidentally released.

- The higher the sides of the crib when raised, the less chance that an older baby can climb out.

- There should be no rough edges or exposed bolts.

- Cribs and mattresses vary in size. Be sure there is no space between the edge of the mattress and the crib.

- Check used cribs carefully. Older models may have slats that are too widely spaced. Some may be finished with lead-based paint, which is poisonous. Be sure to cover a used mattress with a waterproof cover.

Baby's Room

Every baby needs a place to sleep. If possible, the newborn should have a room alone. During the first six months, most babies sleep 15 to 18 hours a day. A separate room will allow better rest and help develop proper sleep habits. Later it will give the baby a feeling of security and belonging.

Love and pleasant conditions can make up for limited living space. If a room alone is not possible, the next best arrangement is a quiet corner of a room. A room divider can be used for more privacy.

The baby's first bed need not be a crib, or even a bassinet. A clothes basket, long enough to allow the baby to stretch out, will do nicely. With slight padding to protect against rough sides, and extra padding on the bottom to serve as a firm "mattress," it makes a good inexpensive portable bed.

If a crib is used, it should be large enough to last several years. Adjustable sides and mattress eliminate unnecessary bending. When a child is old enough to get in and out of bed alone, the sides on some cribs can be dropped or removed. This is a good feature to look for when shopping. Safety is also an important consideration. The chart on page 112 shows safety features to look for when choosing a crib.

A firm spring and mattress are important for development and a straight spine. Doctors advise against a pillow. It is bad for the posture and creates a risk of suffocation. Other bedding needs are listed on page 111.

A place for changing and dressing the baby will be needed. Special dressing tables are available. However, any surface of convenient height that is padded with blankets will do. The top of a chest of drawers can serve as a fine dressing table if it is the correct height and size. A crib with adjustable mattress height also works well.

The baby's room should also have storage space for clothes and equipment. Items should be stored near where they will be used. A wastebasket, covered diaper pail, and clothes hamper should be kept in the baby's room or the bathroom. A chair to use while feeding and holding the baby completes the needed furnishings. All furnishings, including curtains and rugs, should be easily cleaned.

Adequate and convenient storage in the baby's room makes daily routines easier. Clothing and supplies can be kept in many types of storage areas — closets, drawers, stacking cubes, or shelves, for example.

Managing to Meet Expenses

The financial aspects of having a baby are a concern for most parents. The costs do not end with the hospital bill for birth, or the first few years. They continue until the child can live independently. A couple that understands all of the costs involved can plan early to meet them.

Was this a wise choice as a way to save money?
What could some of the consequences have been? ■

Estimating Expenses

The expenses begin with the first doctor's appointment. Many doctors charge a lump sum which covers prenatal care, delivery, and care during the **postnatal** period (after the baby's birth).

Close-up

Julie and Steve Kalton wanted to save money on the doctor bill during Julie's first pregnancy. They decided to eliminate the cost of the monthly visits by consulting a doctor only toward the end of her pregnancy. After all, Julie had come from a large family and had often heard her mother say she had little medical attention during pregnancy. All her brothers and sisters had been delivered by a local doctor, consulted only during the last two months.

Julie and Steve were in for a real surprise. When Julie finally made an appointment, she learned that all the doctors in their community charged a lump sum for pregnancy care. The fee was the same whether it covered nine months or nine days.

The hospitalization fee is another major expense of the birth. Costs for a hospital stay vary, but usually depend on the kind of room and whether it is shared. Extra charges are often made for the labor room, delivery room, laboratory tests, medicine, and supplies. Expectant parents can check with local hospitals for current rates and policies.

Because costs change so rapidly and are not the same in all parts of the country, it is difficult to give the exact cost of having a baby. In addition to doctor and hospital fees, parents should consider these costs:
- Maternity clothes.
- The clothing, equipment, and supplies listed on pages 110–111, and any others desired.
- Formula and baby foods.
- Medical care for the baby.
- Furnishings for the baby's room.
- Child care services, if needed.

In addition, having more family members often creates a need for larger living quarters. The cost of raising the child must also be considered. Food, clothing, medical care, and education will all be major expenses over the years the child must be supported. Parents should have a clear idea of the total expenses involved and how they will manage them.

Reducing Expenses

Some of these necessary expenses can be reduced or eliminated. Ways to do this include:
- Good health and hospitalization insurance.
- Secondhand (but safe) equipment and supplies.
- Careful shopping.

Health Insurance Coverage

Health insurance can enable parents to meet the major expenses of birth. Newly married couples should immediately see that they are covered by a good health insurance plan. If they already have one, they need to review the hospital and medical coverage to see what it includes. This should be done before the pregnancy. It is also a good idea to find out whether the insurance company will pay the hospital directly, or reimburse the parents.

Almost all states now require family health insurance policies to include coverage of newborn infants. Check to see if you have such a law in your state. (In the past, some companies required waiting periods of anywhere from three weeks to three months after birth to make sure the baby was healthy.)

Some large hospitals have free or special rate clinics to help those without insurance who are unable to pay the full fees. Social workers may help with budgeting problems and financial arrangements.

The medical costs of pregnancy and birth are high. Expectant parents should make sure they have adequate health insurance and find out exactly what is covered.

Secondhand Equipment

Baby supplies and equipment need not be new, even for a first baby. Borrowing or buying used items can reduce costs considerably. Relatives and friends often share needed supplies and equipment among themselves. Other sources of bargains include neighborhood yard sales, rummage sales organized by community groups, and secondhand clothing stores. Everything from maternity clothes to cribs, bedding, and garments are available secondhand for only a fraction of the cost when new. These items may show little wear because babies outgrow things rapidly.

Secondhand purchases should be washed thoroughly, even though they may appear clean. Caution should be taken with equipment. Secondhand or borrowed cribs, playpens, car seats, and other items should meet current safety requirements.

Careful Shopping

With nine months' advance notice, expectant parents have time to watch for sales on needed items. Every few months, stores and mail-order catalogs have special sales. It also pays to comparison shop. The same item may be three different prices in three different stores.

Cost comparisons are also useful when choosing between alternatives. For example, the costs of diapering an infant vary depending on whether the family uses disposable diapers, a diaper service, or cloth diapers washed at home. Each method has advantages and disadvantages which must be weighed against the differences in cost.

Making a Budget

Do you keep a personal budget today? If not, it would be a good experience to do so. A **budget** is a spending plan. Its purpose is to help people set financial goals and work toward those goals in steps. Everyone can benefit from a spending plan. Expectant parents find a budget especially useful as they plan for added expenses.

The first step is for the parents-to-be to take a look at where their money currently goes. **Fixed expenses** are items that cannot be changed. They include rent or mortgage payments, taxes, insurance payments, and loans that must be paid. **Variable expenses** are areas in which spending can be cut back if need be. Usually this category includes food, household maintenance, recreation, clothing, and other expenses.

Next, expectant parents should get an idea of the added expenses they will soon face. How much of their medical expenses will be covered by insurance? What items will they need to buy instead of borrow? Another important consideration is whether there will be any income lost if the mother (or father) will be taking time off from a paying job.

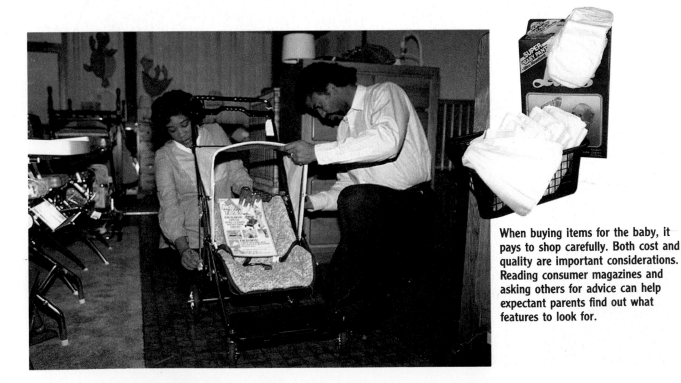

When buying items for the baby, it pays to shop carefully. Both cost and quality are important considerations. Reading consumer magazines and asking others for advice can help expectant parents find out what features to look for.

Once they have an idea of their new expenses, the parents can plan how to meet them. Having a baby must be budgeted like any other expense. Money spent for a new baby must be subtracted somewhere else. Variable expenses may have to be cut back.

If the parents have set aside some savings, it will be easier for them to meet the early, large expenses. It is often difficult to set aside money for the future. However, a budget can make it easier. It is a good idea for the parents to include a regular savings plan in their new budget as soon as they can afford it. Even a few dollars set aside each month can help pay for the baby's future needs.

Many couples decide to prepare for childbirth by taking a class together. They can choose from among several different methods designed to reduce the discomfort of giving birth.

Childbirth Choices

Even a few years ago, birth practices in all hospitals were very similar. Today, there are more options from which to choose. There is also more emphasis on helping the expectant mother prepare for childbirth physically and mentally. Fathers, too, are becoming more involved in the birth of their babies.

During pregnancy, arrangements must be made for someone to deliver the baby. The expectant parents should also decide on a place for the birth and the methods or procedures they prefer. These decisions are interrelated. The choice of a particular method may limit the choices of who will deliver the baby or where, and vice versa.

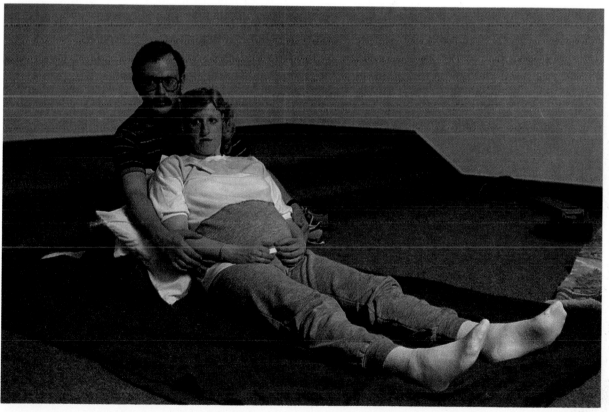

In Lamaze classes, the expectant mother learns special breathing techniques to use during labor. The coach's role will include keeping track of how labor is progressing and guiding the mother's breathing.

What Is Prepared Childbirth?

Prepared childbirth, sometimes called "natural childbirth," is becoming increasingly common. It means that the pain of childbirth is reduced through the elimination of fear, special conditioning exercises, and rhythmic breathing. This decreases or eliminates the need for pain-relieving drugs. The mother remains conscious and able to actively participate in the delivery. The baby suffers few, if any, complications caused by medication that might otherwise have been administered to the mother.

A mother who chooses prepared childbirth usually registers for a course during pregnancy. There are many types of childbirth preparation courses. Common ones include Lamaze classes and Bradley classes. All emphasize the same important points: understanding childbirth, relaxation, and control over the natural body functions of birth.

Class members learn about what will happen during **labor**—the process by which the baby gradually moves out of the uterus to be born—and **delivery**—the birth itself. They see films of childbirth and receive reading material. A tour of a hospital maternity department is usually included.

Most of the class time is spent learning and perfecting exercises to control muscles and breathing. The father, or anyone else the mother chooses to serve as a childbirth coach, learns along with the mother. She depends on her coach for moral support and guidance in practicing her exercises. The father or childbirth coach is also an active participant throughout the labor and birth.

Childbirth is recognized as a stress, but one that can be coped with. Class members are instructed in the risks and benefits of drugs and various medical procedures. The couple can then work with their doctor to make decisions about their use during childbirth.

Who Will Deliver the Baby?

Most babies today are delivered either by an obstetrician or by a family doctor. Another option for women who expect a normal, uncomplicated delivery is a nurse-midwife.

Obstetricians. These doctors specialize in prenatal and postnatal care of the mother and baby. They are qualified to handle any emergencies or special situations that may arise.

Family doctors. Some general-practice doctors also deliver babies and offer prenatal and postnatal care. If complications arise during pregnancy or delivery, the doctor may need to call in an obstetrician.

Nurse-midwives. In the past, a midwife was a woman who was skilled in helping other women give birth. Today, a midwife is a highly trained and capable man or woman called a **nurse-midwife**. Nurse-midwives are registered nurses with advanced training. Some states require licensing of nurse-midwives. They work as a team with an obstetrician and supervise routine pregnancies and births. Some experts feel that in the future there will not be enough obstetricians to go around. As in other countries, obstetricians may only take care of complications and train and supervise other health personnel.

How is the birth attendant chosen? Expectant parents can get recommendations from their family doctor, the county medical society, or a local hospital. They should visit and talk with each doctor or nurse-midwife that they are considering. They will want to be sure the person they choose is not only well qualified, but makes them feel comfortable and can answer their questions clearly.

The parents should find out how emergency calls will be handled at night and on weekends. Another consideration is whether the doctor or nurse-midwife is affiliated with a particular hospital or other medical facility, as most are. The parents should find out what programs and facilities the hospital has. They will also want to know whether the birth attendant's preferences toward delivery procedures agree with their own. If the parents want the father to be present during delivery, for example, they should ask whether this is allowed and encouraged.

A nurse-midwife is qualified to give prenatal care and to supervise routine, normal births. If complications arise during pregnancy or delivery, an obstetrician will be called in.

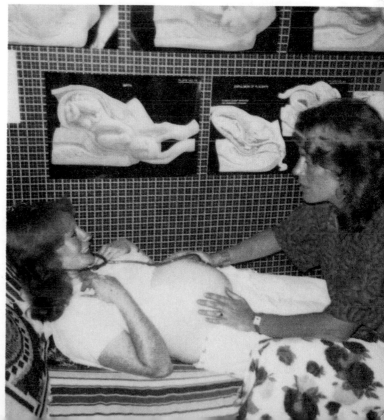

Although the mother-to-be should get medical care as soon as she is pregnant, she may not feel ready to make a decision about the delivery at that time. There is no reason why she cannot switch to a different doctor or nurse-midwife during pregnancy if she wishes. The sooner a final decision is made, however, the better prepared both the parents and the birth attendant will be.

Where Will the Baby Be Born?

Until this century, almost all babies were born at home. Today about 98 percent of all American births occur in hospitals. There, clean conditions, trained personnel, and special equipment help make the birth process as safe as possible.

Traditionally, a hospital birth has offered few choices for those involved. Recent trends are changing this. Increasingly, hospitals are providing services designed to better meet the needs and preferences of the expectant mother and her family. These are often referred to as "family-centered maternity care." For example:

- Childbirth and parenting classes may be offered to help the parents get ready for the big event.
- Some hospitals also offer special programs to help young children prepare for their new baby brother or sister.
- Fathers and other family members are often allowed to help the mother through labor and to be present during birth.
- "Birthing rooms" are becoming more common. They provide a home-like atmosphere for labor and birth. The need to move from the labor room to a separate delivery room is eliminated. Medical equipment is kept out of sight, but ready for use at a moment's notice.

- Different positions for birth may be offered. Instead of lying flat, the woman may be able to be propped up, lie on her side, or sit in a special chair. Many women find that these positions are more comfortable and make delivery easier.
- Special procedures may be allowed. For example, the lights in the delivery room may be dimmed so that the newborn can open his or her eyes without discomfort.
- The baby and mother may be able to be together for all or most of the hospital stay, instead of being kept in separate rooms.

Expectant parents should find out about services offered by local hospitals. Many offer tours of their maternity department.

Close-up

Ashley and Philip Riley were surprised when they visited the new birthing rooms at a local hospital. They liked the setting — a place that looked and felt like home but could handle any emergency. The early labor room was a large lounge with comfortable furniture, lamps, TV, and a stereo.

It was more than atmosphere, however, that drew the Rileys to this kind of birth experience. As Ashley explained, "We wanted to have the baby right there with us. We didn't want to be separated." The nursing staff helped Ashley and Philip learn to take care of their daughter, Megan. They felt very confident when they went home as first-time parents.

Why do you think staying with the baby after the birth helps new parents feel more confident?

What might be some other effects of this kind of birth experience? ■

Many hospitals offer birthing rooms that combine a comfortable, home-like setting with full medical facilities. Both labor and delivery take place in the same room, and mother and baby can stay there together until they go home.

A hospital tour helps the expectant mother become familiar with the procedures that will be used. In some hospitals, a birthing chair like this is used for delivery.

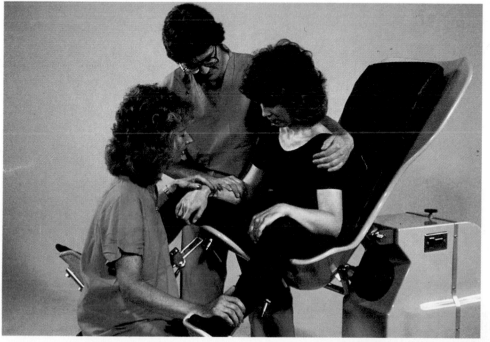

Another relatively new development is called an **alternative birth center**. This is a separate, home-like facility rather than part of a hospital. Alternative birth centers emphasize prepared childbirth and offer many of the nontraditional approaches already described. The delivery is usually performed by a nurse-midwife. Most alternative birth centers allow only low-risk mothers to give birth there. However, a hospital is usually nearby, and mother and baby can be transferred there if need be.

The costs of family-centered hospital maternity care or alternative birthing centers are usually less than those of traditional hospital maternity care. The time involved is also much less. If there are no complications, parents leave the hospital or birth center within 24 hours, compared to the two- to four-day stay for traditional births.

Check Your Understanding

1. What might happen if an expectant couple did not talk over their ideas about parenting methods ahead of time?

2. When making a budget, why is it important to differentiate between fixed expenses and variable expenses?

3. Compare the advantages and disadvantages of a traditional hospital birth to those of using an alternative birth center.

National Association of Childbearing Ctrs., Allentown, PA

Alternative birth centers are often located in large converted homes. Family participation and a relaxed atmosphere are emphasized.

National Association of Childbearing Ctrs., Delaware

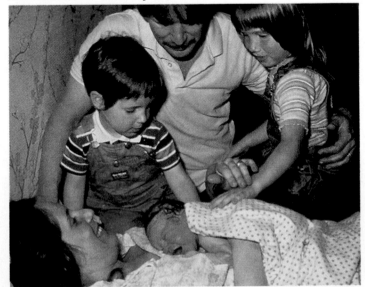

Chapter Review

To Sum Up

- A woman should visit a doctor as soon as she suspects she might be pregnant and should have periodic checkups during pregnancy.
- Good nutrition is very important for both the developing baby and the mother.
- A pregnant woman needs plenty of rest and moderate exercise.
- Preparations to be made include discussing child care and parenting, deciding on a feeding method, and assembling the items needed for the baby.
- Parents-to-be should estimate the expenses of having a baby, look for ways to reduce those expenses, and make a budget to meet their financial needs.
- Prepared childbirth classes help the expectant mother become physically and mentally ready for labor and birth.
- Expectant parents must choose who will deliver the baby and in what setting.

To Review and Remember

1. Name at least four early signs of pregnancy.
2. What are three signs of possible complications of pregnancy?
3. Why is good nutrition so important in prenatal care?
4. Name the Basic Food Groups and tell how many servings of each a pregnant woman needs each day.
5. When planning for daily child care responsibilities, what five things should parents-to-be consider?
6. What are two advantages of breast-feeding? Of bottle-feeding?
7. Describe four safety features to look for in a crib.
8. Name three ways expectant parents can reduce expenses.
9. What is a budget and what is its purpose?
10. What is prepared childbirth?

To Discuss and Discover

1. Write a thank-you note from the point of view of a newborn. Describe all the things the new mother did while pregnant to assure the birth of a healthy baby.
2. Check the want ads in newspapers or on bulletin boards for the prices of baby items. Compare with the cost of new items by checking in stores or catalogs.
3. Interview a mother who had a baby at least ten years ago. What did she do to prepare for childbirth? What does she remember about the birth itself?

5 The Baby's Arrival

To help you to . . .

- Recognize the ways in which labor may begin.
- Outline the three stages of labor.
- Describe a newborn's physical changes and appearance at birth.
- Describe common hospital procedures following a birth.
- Give recommendations for the postnatal care of the mother.
- Explain the special needs of a premature baby.
- Describe babies' basic needs and how they are best met.

Terms to Learn

Apgar scale	dilate	pediatrician
bonding	episiotomy	reflexes
cervix	fontanels	rooming-in
cesarean birth	forceps	rooting reflex
colostrum	grasp reflex	startle reflex
contractions	incubator	

aria is expecting her first baby in two weeks. She is very excited—and a little nervous, too. As she packs a small suitcase for the hospital, she thinks about her pregnancy. She has seen her doctor regularly and eaten a well-balanced diet. She and Mark have taken prenatal classes. They have purchased baby equipment and clothing.

"I think I'm ready to go to the hospital now," Maria says to herself, "whenever my baby is ready." Many thoughts race through her mind. "Will the baby be a boy or girl? How will I know when to go to the hospital? Will I remember what I'm supposed to do?"

Maria sets the suitcase in the corner. The next step is up to her baby.

The Birth Process

A normal birth always follows the same pattern. As the unborn baby becomes developed enough to exist independently, the muscles of the mother's uterus push to expel the fetus from her body. This process is known as labor. It is still not known what signals the uterus to begin the birth process.

Although the distance the fetus must travel is short—only 4 in. (10 cm)—it is a difficult journey. The baby must be pushed through the bony pelvic passage and the narrow vaginal canal. Fortunately, nature has arranged to make this easier. The unborn baby's skull is soft and flexible so it can become longer and narrower. It consists of five soft, pliable bones which overlap each other to fit through the pelvis. This "molding" helps the baby's skull pass through the mother's pelvis more easily.

The Beginning of Labor

Labor may start in one of three ways:
- The expectant mother may notice slight cramps and a backache. This may not concern her at first because she has probably felt this way occasionally for the last few weeks. Gradually she will realize that these cramps are different. They are not getting weaker as they did before; they are getting stronger and longer. As she has been told, she will watch the clock to see if these cramps come at regular intervals. At first they may appear every half hour or so, then every 25 minutes. As each cramp comes, the muscles of the abdomen tighten. As the cramp passes, the muscles relax.

When these cramps—or **contractions**—become very regular and continue to become stronger, active labor has probably started. It is time to notify the doctor or nurse-midwife. He or she will want to know two things—how often the mother is having contractions and how long each one lasts. The doctor will advise the mother from there.

- For another expectant mother, labor may begin differently. She may feel fine and be following her usual routine. Suddenly, she feels a warm trickle or gush of liquid from her vagina. She has been told of this possibility and knows what it is. The membrane holding the amniotic fluid which surrounds the baby has broken and the fluid is draining away.

When this happens, the mother should note the time, the amount of fluid, and the color and odor of the fluid. She should then inform her doctor or nurse-midwife. He or she will probably want to deliver the baby within 24 to 48 hours after the membrane has broken to avoid possible infection to the baby.

- Other mothers may become aware that labor is near when "show" appears. This may be a few drops of blood or a slight pinkish vaginal staining. This often means that the plug of mucus that sealed the **cervix**—the lower part of the uterus—has become loose.

Show does not always mean that labor has begun. It is possible to have show several days before labor begins. It does mean that things are ready to start. The mother should notify the doctor or nurse-midwife if this happens.

Stages of Labor

When actual labor begins, it progresses through three stages:
- First stage: Contractions open the cervix.
- Second stage: The baby is born.
- Third stage: The placenta is expelled.

The First Stage

The first stage of labor is the longest. It may last as long as 12 hours. In the beginning, the contractions are mild and brief. They probably occur about 15 to 30 minutes apart. These contractions cause the cervix to **dilate** (widen) and become thinner.

Ordinarily, the opening of the cervix is about the size of the end of a pencil. For birth, it must widen to about 4 in. (10 cm) in diameter. The cervix, normally about ¾ in. (19 mm) thick, becomes as thin as a piece of paper.

As the hours pass, the contractions become progressively stronger, more frequent, and longer lasting. The doctor or nurse-midwife will tell the expectant mother when to go to the hospital or birthing center.

As the cervix is opening, the baby will probably move down into the lower pelvis and into position for birth. The baby is usually head down, but occasionally babies are born in other positions.

In this stage of labor, the mother can help most by relaxing as much as possible between and during contractions. Fear and tension cause muscles to tighten. This slows up labor and makes it more difficult. If the mother has taken a prepared childbirth education class, she will do breathing exercises with her coach to relax and help the labor progress. She should also change her position every 30 minutes.

This drawing shows the baby at the end of nine months of pregnancy, before labor begins. The cervix (between the baby's head and the birth canal) is its normal size and shape. On the following pages you will see how the cervix becomes wider and thinner as labor progresses.

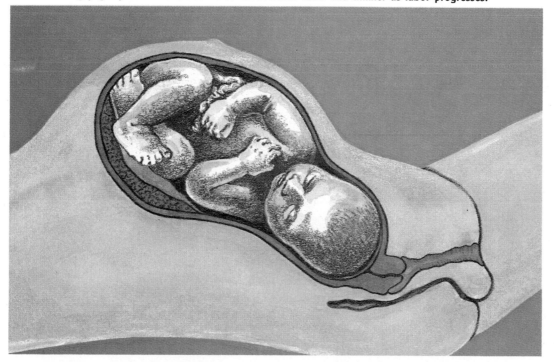

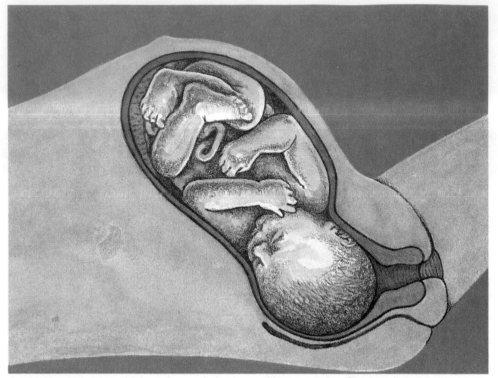

During the first stage of labor, the cervix begins to dilate, or widen. The baby's head moves lower in the pelvis.

The first stage of labor ends with the cervix fully dilated. The opening of the uterus is now 4 in. (10 cm) wide.

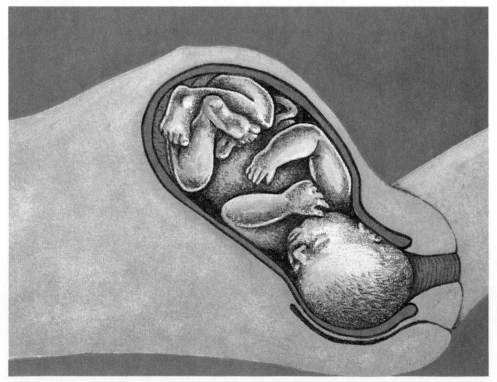

If necessary, the mother may be given medication to reduce the discomfort of labor. Depending on what type is used, the effects range from numbing the area around the cervix to putting the mother to sleep. Many of these drugs can affect the newborn, making the baby sluggish instead of alert. Some also interfere with the mother's ability to push during labor. Most doctors and childbirth educators encourage expectant mothers to give birth without drugs, if possible. However, medication will be given if the mother requests it or if complications call for its use.

As the first stage of labor ends, the contractions are very strong and frequent. With each contraction, the cervix stretches and opens more. When the cervix is fully dilated, the first stage is over.

The Second Stage

As soon as the cervix is completely dilated and the contractions are about two to four minutes apart, the second stage of labor will begin. This stage lasts from a few minutes up to three hours. It includes the actual birth. During the second stage, the movement of the uterus changes. The cervix is no longer opening. Instead, the contractions push the baby out through the pelvis and vagina.

In some hospitals, the mother having a normal delivery may remain in the birthing room, a home-like room designed especially for a comfortable labor and safe delivery. In other hospitals, the mother may be moved from the labor room to a separate delivery room.

During the second stage of labor, strong contractions push the baby out of the uterus and down the vagina, or birth canal. Notice that the baby begins to rotate to a face-down position.

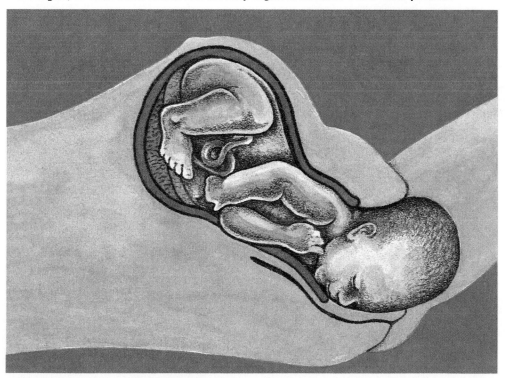

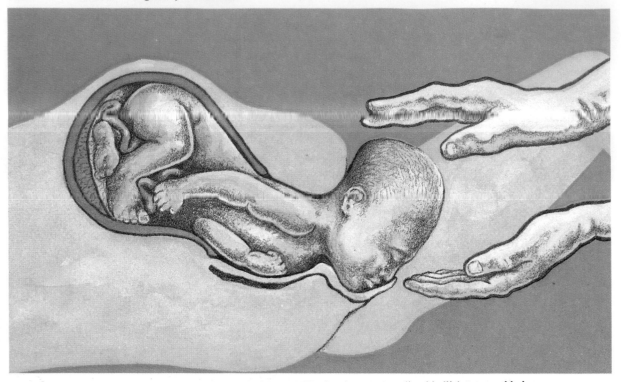

As the head emerges, the baby stretches out. The head may seem "molded" into an odd shape after traveling through such a narrow passageway. This is normal and temporary.

Almost there . . . Getting the head and shoulders out is the "tricky" part of delivery. After that, the rest of the body slips out easily.

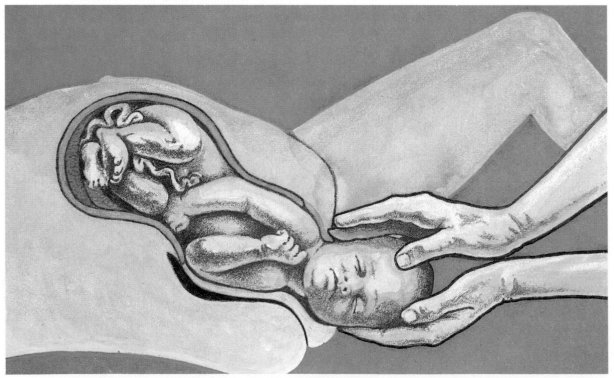

The mother can usually help during this stage. She will be told how and when to help her muscles bear down to make the baby come along. The mother will feel a constant and uncontrollable urge to bear down. However, she will be instructed to push only during a contraction.

If necessary, the doctor will perform a surgical procedure called an **episiotomy** (ih-PIHZ-ee-OTT-uh-mee). For this, the physician makes an incision (cut) to enlarge the external opening of the vagina. (The normal opening is about 1 in. [2.5 cm] smaller than the baby's head.) Enlarging the opening this way is occasionally done to protect a larger baby's head from excessive pressure from the muscles. It also prevents the mother's tissues from being torn by the baby. The clean incision heals better than a ragged tear.

The mother is now ready for delivery. The most common procedure is for the mother to lie in a semi-sitting position with her knees flexed. Her legs are supported at the sides of the delivery table in stirrups. Sometimes an ordinary hospital bed or a special birthing chair is used instead.

The baby's head usually emerges first. This is followed gently by one shoulder, then the other. Then the rest of the slippery little body slides through. The baby is born!

Sometimes, **forceps** must be used by the doctor to help guide the baby's head during delivery. Forceps are specialized tongs made from bands of surgical steel that are molded to fit the shape of a baby's head. With this instrument, the doctor can better control the movement of the head, helping the baby emerge more quickly or slowly as needed.

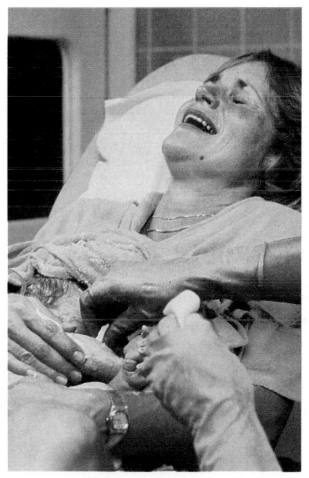

Success! Though she may have felt tired and discouraged earlier in labor, the mother experiences a great surge of energy just before delivery. She is ecstatic and eager to hold her baby.

The Third Stage

In the third stage of labor, the uterus continues to contract to expel the placenta—sometimes referred to as the "afterbirth." This stage lasts anywhere from two minutes to half an hour. It involves little or no discomfort.

The uterus contracts as the baby leaves, much as a balloon shrivels when the air is let out. As this happens, the placenta begins to separate from the uterus. It is soft and comes away easily. The doctor will ask the mother to push again to expel the placenta. The birth process is now completed.

The Newborn at Birth

The newborn is no longer completely dependent on the mother's body for life support. During birth, many changes take place in the infant's circulatory system so that it can survive on its own.

As the birth process begins, the baby's lungs are filled with fluid. The pressure of being squeezed down the birth canal forces much of the fluid out. When the baby emerges, the pressure is released and the lungs automatically expand. The baby's first breath is taken.

Usually the breathing reflex continues on its own. If necessary, the doctor or nurse-midwife may gently rub the baby's back to get the process started. Any fluid that remains in the lungs or mouth is gently suctioned out.

The placenta — no longer needed to nourish the baby — is expelled from the body in the third stage of labor.

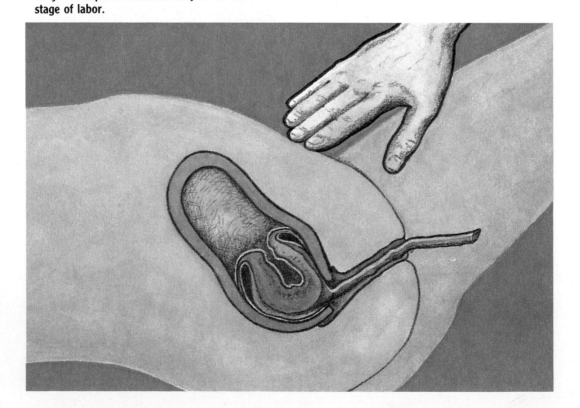

Once the lungs have begun taking in oxygen, the baby's circulatory system changes. A valve in the heart closes and over the next few days becomes permanently sealed. Blood now circulates to and from the lungs, instead of bypassing them as before. The umbilical cord, through which the baby has received oxygen and nourishment, is no longer needed. Within a few minutes it stops pulsing and begins to shrink. The cord is clamped, tied, and cut off.

How Does the Newborn Look?

The newborn's head is wobbly and large—one-fourth the size of the body. It may appear strangely lopsided or pointed from the passage through the birth canal. The bones of a baby's skull are not tightly knitted together as they are in adults. They can be molded together during birth without harm. Any such lopsidedness is temporary.

Babies have two **fontanels**—or open spaces—in the bones of the head. The largest of these "soft spots" is just above the baby's forehead. Most babies also have a fontanel toward the back of the head. These spaces allow the bones of the baby's skull to move together during birth. As the baby grows older, usually between the ages of six and eighteen months, the bone structure comes together to cover the space completely. Meanwhile, the soft spots are protected by skin that is as tough as heavy canvas.

The newborn typically has fat cheeks, a short, flat nose, and a receding chin. These features are useful for sucking purposes because the nose and chin are out of the way.

At birth, a baby's eyes are nearly adult size. They are usually dark grayish-blue at birth. Permanent eye color becomes apparent within several months.

The skin of the newborn is blotchy. The baby's circulation is not yet regulated, so the fingers and toes may feel cold and appear bluish. The hands and feet may peel if any of the cheesy material that covered the baby's skin before birth remains.

The newborn may have a full head of hair or no hair at all. Red marks on the skin are common. Can you see how the newborn's facial features make sucking easier?

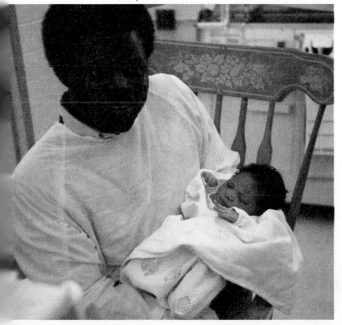
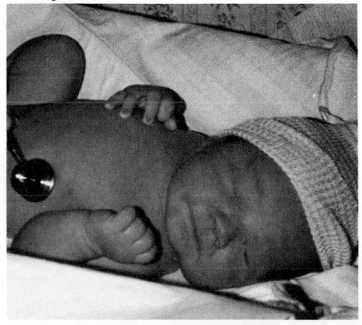

Cesarean Birth

Not all births follow the pattern just described. A **cesarean birth** is chosen when complications arise in a normal delivery. The baby is delivered through a surgical incision in the mother's abdomen. Depending on what type of medication is given, the mother may remain awake during cesarean surgery. The father or coach may also be present with the doctor's permission. When a cesarean birth is a possibility, a special cesarean childbirth education class may be recommended to help parents prepare for the event. After the surgery, the mother and baby usually leave the hospital in about four days.

Check Your Understanding

1. After reading about the birth process, how do you think childbirth classes might make this process easier?

2. Why is a healthy newborn's first breath usually taken automatically?

3. Some babies are born with misshapen heads, which greatly alarms their parents. Should this be a major concern? Why or why not?

The Postnatal Period

The moment of birth signals the end of nine months of development and anticipation. But, of course, it is also a beginning. In a short time the newborn, also called a neonate, and parents will go home to begin their new life together. First, however, the staff at the hospital or birthing center must make sure the new family gets off to a good start.

Examining the Newborn

Shortly after delivery, the neonate's physical condition is evaluated using a rating system called the **Apgar scale**. The infant is given a rating from 0 to 2 on each of five items: pulse, breathing, muscle tone, responsiveness, and skin color. A total score of 7 to 10 is considered normal. A lower score is a sign that the baby needs special medical attention. Usually the Apgar evaluation is given one minute after birth and repeated at five minutes after birth. The baby is also given a brief examination to check for any conditions that would require special care.

Within 60 minutes of delivery, drops of silver nitrate or an antiseptic ointment are put in the baby's eyes to guard against infection. The baby is weighed, measured, and perhaps washed. A permanent copy of the baby's footprints are made for public record. Two bands giving the baby's family name are clamped to the wrists or ankles. The mother wears a bracelet which contains the same information. Identification is done before the baby leaves the delivery room or birthing room to avoid any mix-up in identity.

The Apgar Scale

	Score		
	0	**1**	**2**
HEART RATE	Absent	Under 100	Over 100
BREATHING	Absent	Slow, irregular	Good, crying
MUSCLE TONE	Limp	Some movement of extremities	Active motion
RESPONSIVENESS (Baby's reaction when nose is irritated)	No response	Grimace	Cough or sneeze
COLOR	Blue or pale	Body pink, limbs blue	Completely pink

Bonding

In recent years, research has increasingly focused on the emotional needs of the newborn. Many experts feel that it is natural for lifelong emotional ties to be formed between parents and the newborn soon after birth. This process is called **bonding**. It is becoming more common for procedures such as cutting the umbilical cord, cleaning the infant, and giving eyedrops to be delayed for a time so that bonding can take place more naturally.

Immediately after birth, a healthy baby may be placed in the mother's arms or on her stomach. The baby can feel the mother's skin and hear her heartbeat and voice. The newborn instinctively focuses on the mother's face. In turn, the mother—and father, if present—enjoy stroking and talking to the baby.

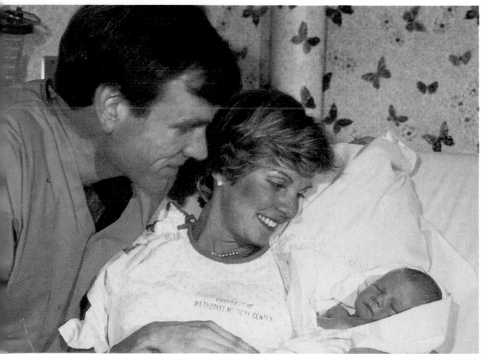

Bonding takes place as the parents and baby interact through sight, sound, and touch. This process is important for the baby's development. It also brings out the parents' natural desire to love and care for their baby.

If the baby will be breast-fed, the mother may nurse the baby within minutes after birth. The baby knows instinctively what to do. Although the mother's breasts do not supply milk yet, they secrete a fluid called **colostrum**. The colostrum is easy for the newborn to digest and is rich in antibodies to protect against disease. Nursing the baby also helps the mother's uterus shrink back to its normal size.

Bonding is not limited to the moments after birth, although many experts believe it occurs more quickly then. As the parents hold, cuddle, and talk to their baby during the first days and weeks, the bond between them gradually strengthens.

The Hospital Stay

The process of birth is a momentous undertaking for both mother and baby. The newborn must adjust to a whole new world. The mother, too, needs time to adjust. In a matter of hours her body has gone through many physical changes, from pregnancy to labor and birth and back to the nonpregnant state. Although she is probably thrilled and excited, she also needs to rest and recuperate.

In many hospitals, the mother will spend an hour or two in the recovery room for close observation following the birth. Her blood pressure, pulse, and other vital signs are monitored closely until all body functions have re-

The Leboyer Method of Birth

The room is warm and dimly lit. Carpeting absorbs the sound of footsteps on the floor. Doctors and nurses give instructions in whispers against a background of soft music.

What's going on here? Something very special — the birth of a baby. What sets this birth apart from most is the use of methods advocated by Dr. Frederick Leboyer, a French obstetrician.

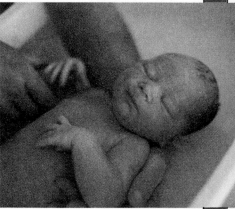

California Birthplace, Angora Hills

In the late 1960s, Dr. Leboyer became concerned with the way babies commonly entered the world. He felt that the newborn's first experiences outside the womb should be gentle and soothing, not harsh and unpleasant. In his 1975 book, *Birth Without Violence*, he questioned the typical medical procedures of childbirth. A newborn should not, he wrote, be subjected to bright lights or loud noises, be held upside down and spanked, or be taken from the mother and placed on a hard, cold metal scale. Instead, Dr. Leboyer recommended that the infant be placed on the mother's abdomen and given a gentle massage, followed by a warm bath.

Today, an increasing number of obstetricians follow Dr. Leboyer's methods, although they are still in the minority. Many more doctors have adopted at least some of his ideas. In fact, some standard procedures for childbirth have changed since the 1960s, in part because of Dr. Leboyer's influence. Newborns are almost never held upside down and spanked anymore! As Dr. Leboyer hoped, there is now more awareness of a previously neglected aspect of birth — the experiences and emotional needs of the newborn.

turned to normal. Other hospitals and most birthing centers allow the mother, father, and newborn to spend several hours together right away.

Hospitals also differ in how long the mother and baby are usually expected to wait before going home. At minimum, the mother needs a chance to eat, bathe, and rest. She and her infant must also be medically checked to make sure everything is going well. In some hospitals and birthing centers, a mother and baby who are both healthy may then go home if that is where the mother feels she can recuperate best. This may be as soon as 12 hours after the birth. However, a two- to four-day stay is average.

Rooming-In

As mentioned in the previous chapter, many hospitals allow newborns to stay with their mothers after birth rather than in a central nursery with other babies. This type of plan is called **rooming-in**.

In some cases, the newborn stays at the mother's bedside both day and night. In other programs, the baby stays with the mother during the day and in a central nursery at night.

The main disadvantage of traditional hospital birth is that mothers and babies are separated at a time when bonding should be taking place. Rooming-in brings them back together. It is a natural beginning to family unity and warm parent-child relationships. Fathers are allowed to visit whenever they wish.

Getting to know your new baby brother is easier when you can visit Mom in the hospital and even hold the baby yourself.

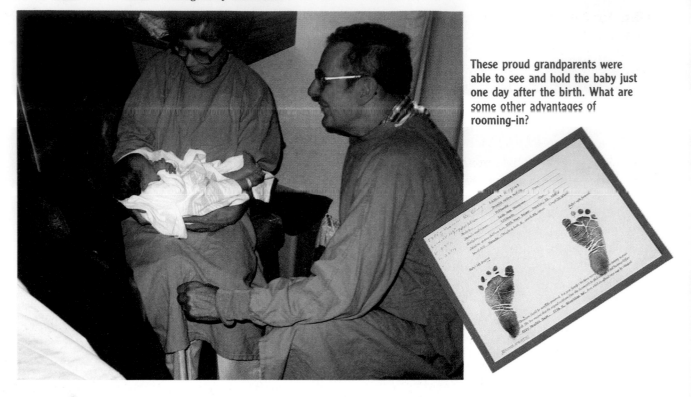

These proud grandparents were able to see and hold the baby just one day after the birth. What are some other advantages of rooming-in?

In some hospitals, grandparents and older brothers and sisters also can visit and hold the new baby. Couples can get to know their baby and learn proper care. The baby can be fed when hungry, rather than being brought from the nursery on a set schedule. Under a good rooming-in program, parents worry less and babies seem more content.

Birth Certificate

All new parents should check to see that their baby has a birth certificate. Usually the birth certificate is issued free of charge soon after the baby is born.

Getting a birth certificate when a baby is born is very simple. Proving a birth years later may be a real problem. It is time-consuming and may be expensive. In our society, a birth certificate is considered the most important piece of personal identification anyone has.

Postnatal Care of the Mother

After the baby is brought home, it is natural for most of the attention to be focused on the new family member. But care of the mother is just as important as the baby's care. A new mother has special physical and emotional needs that will continue for several weeks or months after the birth. A doctor or nurse will explain these needs before the mother and baby go home.

The Mother's Physical Needs

Physically, the mother needs to recover from pregnancy and childbirth and regain fitness. She must also take good care of herself so that she is able to care for her child. The best way to accomplish these goals is through rest, exercise, nutrition, and a medical checkup.

■ **Rest.** For the first few days and weeks, the new mother is likely to be tired. She should try to sleep whenever the baby does. This will help her get the rest she needs, even with late-night feedings. It is best if a relative or friend can help both parents with the baby and household chores for a time.

■ **Exercise.** As soon as the mother feels able, and her doctor approves, she should begin mild exercise. At first this may be just a few simple stretches while lying down. Gradually other exercises can be added. Even getting up and walking around is beneficial. Postnatal exercise helps the woman return to her normal figure and correct posture.

■ **Nutrition.** Eating right is just as important after pregnancy as during it. A mother who breast-feeds her baby should be sure to eat the number of servings from the Basic Food Groups shown in the chart on page 98. She should also drink plenty of liquids. Just as before the birth, the food she eats is supplying nutrients for the baby as well for her own needs. Even if the mother is not breast-feeding, good nutrition helps her feel well and regain her energy. If she needs to lose a few extra pounds, her doctor can recommend a well-balanced diet plan to control her weight.

■ **Medical checkup.** About four to six weeks after the birth, the new mother should have a postnatal checkup. The doctor will make sure that her uterus is returning to normal and that there are no unusual problems. The mother can discuss any questions she may have about caring for the infant or adjusting to parenthood.

The "baby blues" usually clear up in a few days. In the meantime, friends and relatives can help take some of the pressure off the new parents.

The Mother's Emotional Needs

Having a baby is a joyous event, but also a stressful one. Many new mothers go through a few days of mild depression sometime after the birth. They may have feelings of disappointment, loneliness, or resentment. No one knows for certain why the "baby blues" occur, but they are very common. Actually, new fathers often have these feelings as well.

New parents should expect to go through some unhappy moods after the birth. It helps to talk over their feelings with each other and with sympathetic relatives or friends. If possible, they should arrange to take some time away from the baby for short periods—even just a few minutes a day. Taking good physical care of themselves will also help minimize the blues.

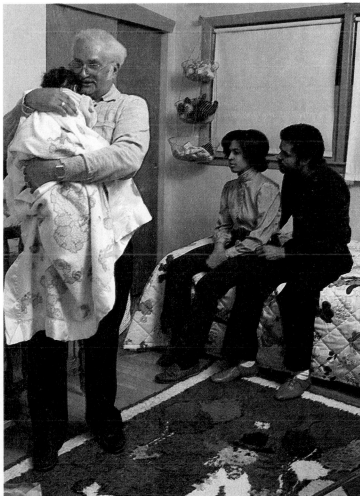

Caring for Premature Babies

As you learned in Chapter 3, some babies are premature—born before prenatal development is complete—or are much smaller than normal at birth. This can happen for a variety of reasons, not all of which are understood. Any newborn who weighs less than 5½ lb. (2.5 kg) or who was born before eight and half months needs special medical care. The more the baby weighs and the closer the pregnancy comes to full term, the better the baby's chances of survival.

Although premature babies look complete, they are not really ready to live outside the mother's body. Their systems for heat regulation, breathing, and digestion are not yet mature. To make up for these problems, a premature baby is usually placed in an **incubator**. This is a special enclosed crib in which the oxygen supply, temperature, and humidity can be closely controlled. Sometimes a special type of incubator is used that has arm-holes through which a nurse can work with the baby.

In the incubator, the baby's heart and lungs are electronically monitored. Special medical procedures may be needed to combat infections, breathing difficulties, and other problems. Advances in medical technology allow many premature infants—even some weighing close to 1 lb. (454 g)—to survive and become healthy.

Modern medicine is also concerned about the emotional needs of premature babies. Sometimes the infants are gently stroked. In one experiment, a tiny, heated waterbed was designed to simulate the warmth and free-

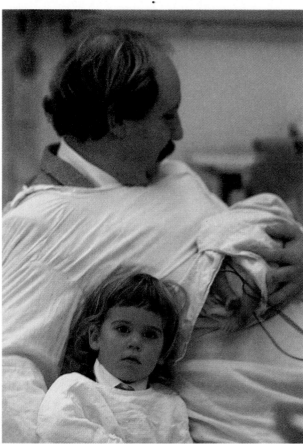

The first incubators were designed for the sole purpose of keeping the premature baby warm. Today, advanced medical technology is combined with a recognition of the premature infant's emotional needs, including close contact with the parents when possible.

floating sensations the baby experiences before birth. In addition, the sounds of the mother's heartbeat, her voice, and music were played to the infant. These devices soothed the infants, saving precious energy for growth.

When they become healthy enough to leave the incubator, premature babies are usually kept in the hospital to grow and gain weight. However, a new approach allows them to go home sooner.

Close-up

Erica Edwards was born six weeks before expected. She weighed 3½ lb. (1.6 kg). However, she had no other health problems except for her low birth weight.

Erica was part of a special study involving 79 infants that weighed from 2-4 lb. (0.9–1.8 kg). Like Erica, they were otherwise healthy. Half of these babies were kept in the hospital for standard treatment. The others were sent home 11 days earlier and given intensive nursing services.

Erica was one of the babies sent home early. With loving care from both parents and frequent checkups by the medical team, Erica gained weight steadily and developed no health problems. During the first weeks, however, she did sleep more and ate oftener — and in smaller amounts — than full-term newborns ordinarily do.

The medical study was completed when Erica was almost a year old. According to the report, average costs for babies discharged early, including home nurses' fees, were almost $20,000 less per infant. These babies experienced no more medical complications than ones kept in the hospital.

Erica is now a preschooler. As a toddler she had been smaller than average for her age, but each year closed the gap in her development. Erica showed a typical premature growth pattern. Lateness in physical, emotional, and intellectual growth usually levels off by school age. By that time, most premature children have caught up with their peers. Today, there is no longer any evidence of Erica's premature start in life.

How might being cared for at home affect a premature baby's emotional development?

If you were the parent of a premature baby like Erica, would you rather have her come home early or stay in the hospital? Why? ■

Medical science continues to work at increasing the survival rate of premature and underweight babies. Efforts are also being made to reduce the percentages of such births. One way is through educating the public in the importance of good nutrition, good health practices, and medical care during pregnancy. Awareness of the dangers of teen pregnancy is also important. Researchers have found other factors that increase the risk of prematurity and low birth weight. They are still learning more.

If premature labor is caught soon enough, medication can be given in an attempt to stop the contractions before they progress to delivery. Recently, a small device that monitors uterine contractions has been successfully tested. The device is worn for short periods, beginning in the fifth month of pregnancy, by women considered at high risk for premature delivery. If premature labor begins, the doctor can be quickly alerted.

Check Your Understanding

1. If a newborn needed medical care immediately after birth, and therefore, could not be given to the mother right away, would bonding ever take place? Explain.

2. Describe a rooming-in arrangement. What are some of its advantages?

3. Why is good nutrition so important for the mother after birth?

A New Family Member

For the first month of life, every baby is considered "new." It takes from two to four weeks for the normal body systems to coordinate and work together smoothly. The baby is also "new" in terms of the relationships among family members. Welcoming this tiny person home and getting to know him or her are exciting aspects of the days ahead.

The Amazing Newborn

In one respect, a newborn baby cannot do anything. Infants are unable to take care of themselves. A baby who was abandoned would surely die without someone to provide food and protection.

Viewed another way, however, this helpless baby has remarkable capabilities. In the past, it was thought that newborns could not focus their eyes, hear, or even taste. Recent studies have changed these ideas.

A researcher at Harvard University discovered that babies less than a day old could follow a pattern printed on paper and rolled before their eyes. Other studies show that newborns seem to select certain outlines for attention, such as edges and angles. They also prefer human faces. Although their hearing is not yet fully developed, newborns can hear many sounds and distinguish between different pitches. Taste, smell, and touch are also at work right from birth.

The newborn can breathe, and cries to signal a variety of needs. In this way, the baby can get food, attention, or a dry diaper.

What Are Reflexes?

Nature has helped newborns to handle their needs involuntarily until they learn to do things voluntarily. Babies are born with **reflexes**—instinctive, automatic responses, such as sneezing and yawning. These coordinated patterns of behavior help the baby's body to function. For example, a sneeze helps to clear the baby's nose of lint. Swallowing lets the baby eat without choking.

Some reflex actions, including sneezing and swallowing, continue throughout life. Others are temporary. They last only until voluntary control develops and takes over. Three of a newborn's temporary reflexes are the rooting reflex, the grasp reflex, and the startle reflex. They are shown on page 143.

How to Observe a Newborn's Reflexes

Newborns have a number of reflexes, or automatic responses. They can easily be observed if you know what to look for.

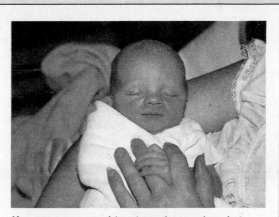

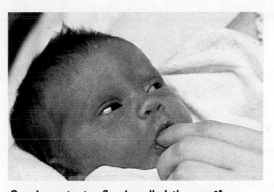

One important reflex is called the **rooting reflex.** If something touches the baby's cheeks or lips, the baby turns toward the touch and begins to suck. This response is completely automatic and helps the baby find food. When babies become aware of their surroundings and use their eyes to search for the bottle or mother's breast, the rooting reflex stops.

If you press something into the newborn's palms, the tiny fingers will curl and hold tight. This is known as the **grasp reflex.** The grip is often so strong that the newborn can be lifted off the bed. However, the baby will let go without warning. When a three-month-old baby begins to reach for objects, the grasp reflex disappears.

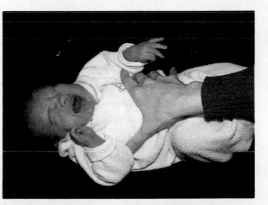

Newborns also have a **startle reflex.** This can happen if there is a loud noise or if the baby's stomach is touched. Babies respond by throwing the arms apart, spreading the fingers, extending the legs, and throwing back the head.

Learning to Care for the Newborn

At first, new parents may feel awkward caring for their baby. But they soon gain confidence and become attuned to the baby's way of communicating. They learn how to recognize the baby's needs and how to adapt their responses to the baby's individual style.

What Do Babies Need?

Being a good parent starts with understanding the baby's needs. You will learn more about caring for a baby in later chapters of this book. For now, here are some basics.

■*Babies need food.* Hungry newborns are hungry with their whole body. They squirm about, their mouth eagerly searching for mother's breast or a bottle nipple. Crying is the most effective way newborns show they are hungry.

Newborns want food immediately when they are hungry, and it is important to give it to them—right away. This is how they learn to trust their world.

■*Babies need sleep.* Newborns sleep and wake throughout the day and night. They usually average half an hour of alertness for each two or three hours of drowsiness or sleep. Long rest periods are needed to make up for all the energy they use eating and crying.

■*Babies need exercise.* In their brief, wakeful periods, newborns will wave their arms and legs. This helps their muscles and nervous system develop. Before a feeding, they become very active, moving all parts of their body. They can kick freely while being diapered, as long as someone watches them closely. Splashing and wiggling during a bath is another way small babies get exercise.

■*Babies need to be kept safe, clean, and warm.* Bathing and diapering soon become a familiar part of the new parent's routine. They must also protect the baby from anything that might be harmful. A baby, when awake, should always be under the watchful eye of a responsible person. Anything the baby might come in contact with—a toy, a crib, a garment—should be checked for safety, and any harmful objects should be kept away.

When parents set aside "play time" with their baby, they are helping to fulfill the baby's needs for exercise, stimulation, and close contact.

Crib Death: Mysterious Tragedy

Sudden infant death syndrome (SIDS), or "crib death," refers to the mysterious death of an apparently healthy baby. Most of these deaths occur from the second week through the sixth month of life. The victim dies while sleeping. There is no warning or cry.

Researchers are looking at several theories, but so far the cause or causes of SIDS are not understood. It is known, however, that the baby's parents or other caregivers are not at fault. There is nothing they could have done to prevent the tragedy.

Counseling can help parents who have lost a baby to SIDS learn to deal with their grief. They can also get help from support groups such as the National Sudden Infant Death Syndrome Foundation. Local chapters, made up of parents who have gone through this heartbreaking experience, are found in many cities across the country. For information about SIDS or the Foundation's chapters, call 1-800-221-SIDS.

■*Babies need medical care.* Throughout the first year, periodic checkups are given to make sure the baby is healthy and developing normally. A baby may be cared for by a family doctor or by a **pediatrician** (PEE-dee-uh-TRISH-un)—a doctor who specializes in the care of babies and young children. The process of choosing a pediatrician is similar to that of choosing someone to deliver the baby (see page 119). Ideally, the parents should visit a prospective pediatrician before the birth and discuss any questions they have about baby care.

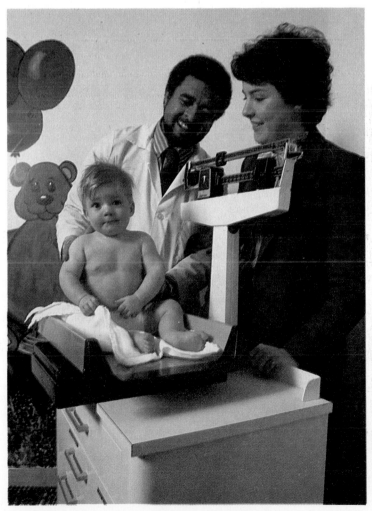

"Weighing in" to check the baby's physical growth is a routine part of each visit to the doctor.

■*Babies need things to look at, touch, listen to, and play with.* Interesting, stimulating surroundings help them learn. However, expensive toys are not necessary. In fact, an infant's favorite thing to look at is a human face. A gentle voice is the baby's favorite music.

■*Babies need love.* How do you feel about the people you love? You probably want to be near them. Newborns want nearness too. They need close contact with warm, affectionate adults. Love is as important as food and sleep to babies.

There is no one way to love a baby. Just as every newborn is different, so is every parent. It is more important that real love is shown than how it is shown. Love is one of the strongest forces affecting every person's life. When a healthy baby feels love, the infant is at ease and feels secure.

Adjusting to New Routines

All of these care tasks will keep the new parents quite busy for a while. Both they and the baby must get used to a new pattern of life.

In the 1930s, many doctors believed that babies should have strict schedules. It was important to train them from birth to eat and sleep with clocklike regularity. To busy doctors and efficient parents, this sounded like a splendid idea. However, babies did not agree.

Newborns need a few weeks of trial-and-error to get used to a new way of life. At first, a new baby does not follow any predictable pattern of eating and sleeping. Parents must adjust their schedule to the baby's. That means feeding the baby whenever hunger strikes, day or night.

You cannot spoil newborns by giving them what they need when they need it. Later, when they are more mature, babies can begin to learn self-control.

What Do Parents of Newborns Need?

- Knowledge of how to care for an infant.
- Resources to turn to for answers to their questions.
- Information about normal happenings and feelings they experience with their newborn.
- Time to fill their many roles — parent, spouse, family member, worker, and citizen.
- Emotional support from a network of family and friends.
- Financial planning.
- Reassurance and confidence that both parents are capable and needed.
- Agreement about parenting and household responsibilities.
- Personal health, rest, and nutrition.
- Privacy and time alone.

Newborns set their own pace at first, and parents must respond to it. This is how infants learn that their world is safe and dependable. As the baby grows a little older, daily routines will fall into a comfortable pattern.

Of course, every newborn benefits from order in life. Soon a certain rhythm emerges to hunger, sleepiness, and wakefulness. It takes about a month, for example, to establish a fairly predictable feeding schedule. Meanwhile, the key is flexibility.

Understanding the Baby's Language

Babies have one way to communicate with the world—by crying. While newborns never cry for fun, their reasons may be far less serious than the worried new parents imagine. Hunger is usually the reason. Sometimes babies cry because they are too hot or too cold. Other times they may be lying in an uncomfortable position and need to be moved. Parents soon learn to recognize their baby's different cries—one for hunger, another for discomfort, and so on.

Newborn babies will often stop crying when you pick them up and hold them close to your chest. This may be because the up-right position relieves gas or because they can hear the familiar sound of your heartbeat.

Going to small babies when they cry will help them feel secure. Babies soon learn that someone will come to make them feel better. This attention will not spoil them. They have not yet learned to cry just for attention.

Early Temperament

Babies differ markedly in their inborn temperament, or style of reacting to the world and relating to others. For example, one baby changes from sleep to wakefulness with a startled jump and cry. Another awakens gradually and begins quietly looking around. Some babies may be so easily upset that extra-gentle handling and a smooth routine are needed to maintain happiness. Others can be handled more playfully without objection. Just as no two babies look exactly alike— even identical twins—no two react in just the same way.

Those who care for a baby need to be sensitive to the baby's own style. But the baby, too, learns to adapt to the style of the parents. Studies have shown that babies as young as two weeks of age adjust their reactions depending on how parents handle and talk to them. If parents are very gentle and soothing, the baby tends to respond with soft cooing and gentle motions. If parents relate to the baby more playfully, the baby tends to react with excited grunts and active motion. These natural adjustments help parents and babies feel at ease with each other.

The next unit gives more detailed information about babies' characteristics and needs. Now that you have learned about what babies are like at birth, you are ready to learn how they grow physically, emotionally, socially, and intellectually.

Check Your Understanding

1. Why do babies need reflexes?

2. If the parents only handled a newborn when feeding or bathing, would the baby's needs be adequately met? Explain.

3. Why is it important to respond to an infant's crying?

Every baby has a unique temperament. Parents and other caregivers soon become attuned to these individual differences.

Chapter Review

To Sum Up

- Labor is the process by which the baby is expelled from the mother's body. A normal birth includes three stages of labor.
- Physical adjustments in the newborn's body make life outside the uterus possible.
- A cesarean birth is performed when medically necessary.
- Bonding is the formation of emotional ties between parent and child.
- To recover from childbirth, a woman needs rest, exercise, proper nutrition, medical checkups, and attention to her emotional needs.
- Premature babies need special care.
- Reflexes help a newborn's body function until voluntary actions take over.
- Babies need food, sleep, exercise, medical care, safe and interesting surroundings, and love.

To Review and Remember

1. Name three possible indications that labor is beginning.
2. What purpose do contractions serve in the first stage of labor? In the second stage of labor?
3. What happens in the third stage of labor?
4. What causes a newborn to begin breathing?
5. What are fontanels? What purpose do they serve?
6. What is a cesarean birth?
7. What five items are observed using the Apgar scale?
8. When should a new mother have a postnatal checkup?
9. What is an incubator and why is it used?
10. What are reflexes? Name and describe three of a newborn's temporary reflexes.

To Discuss and Discover

1. Life outside the mother's body is very different from life inside. Pretending you are a newborn, write a paper on what your first day of life is like. (Keep in mind the development of the senses at birth.)
2. Find out more about the Leboyer or Lamaze methods of childbirth. Share your information with the class.
3. Investigate the special facilities for premature babies closest to you. What equipment, personnel, and counseling services are available? What special care do premature infants receive there?
4. Discuss the ways you feel a parent can best show a baby that he or she is loved.

Chapter 6: Physical Development
Chapter 7: Emotional & Social Development
Chapter 8: Intellectual Development

What is the most important year of a person's life? In terms of development, it is the first year. An infant might appear to be doing nothing special—just eating, sleeping, looking around, and squirming. You may be surprised to learn what that baby is up to!

Physical growth predominates during the first year. There is an obvious size difference between a newborn and a one-year-old. Physical abilities improve through constant practice. Chapter 6 discusses these changes and will also teach you the skills needed to care for infants.

During their first year, babies' individual personalities—hinted at from birth—become more evident. They learn to get along with others in order to fulfill their needs. Early experiences with people influence lifelong attitudes toward self and others. Chapter 7 explains important emotional and social influences in this period.

Intellectual development is the subject of Chapter 8. Children are born with a certain intellectual potential, but their home and environment influence whether that potential is reached. One of the most important ways that babies learn is through play.

Growing, changing, learning—a baby's life is really quite a busy one after all!

6 Physical Development During the First Year

To help you to . . .

- Explain patterns of physical development.
- Describe physical growth and proportion during the first year.
- Discuss the development of the senses.
- Describe the development of motor skills during the first year.
- Discuss nutritional concerns during infancy.
- Demonstrate how to hold, feed, diaper, bathe, and dress a baby.
- Tell how to encourage good sleep habits.

Terms to Learn

- cradle cap
- depth perception
- diaper rash
- eye-hand coordination
- malnutrition
- motor skills
- primary teeth
- proportion
- strained foods
- weaning

Would you recognize a baby you had seen first as a week-old infant and next on the child's first birthday? If you have ever watched the development of a baby, you know that many changes occur from week to week and month to month. In the first twelve months, most babies change so much that they would be difficult to match up with pictures taken in the first weeks of life.

Development and growth during the first year are the most rapid of any time in life. In twelve months, the helpless newborn triples his or her birth weight, learns to stand alone, and may even be able to walk.

Patterns of Physical Development

As you learned in Chapter 1, all development follows an orderly sequence. It proceeds step-by-step in about the same order for every baby. Physical development is no exception. You will find it easier to observe physical development if you understand the three basic patterns it follows. Physical development proceeds from:

■*Head to foot.* Long before birth, the baby's head takes the lead in development. Two months after conception, the head is about half the size of the entire fetus. The arms and legs do not catch up until later. A newborn's head is still large in proportion to the body. The same head-to-toe pattern continues after birth. First, babies learn to lift their head to see a bright red block. Later they will be able to pick it up. Still later, they can walk to it.

There is quite a difference in appearance between this newborn (left) and the same child soon after her first birthday (right). What signs of development do you see?

■**Near to far.** Development starts at the trunk of the body and moves outward. First, babies are able to scoot their entire body toward the object they want. Then they wave their arms at it. Later they are able to grab at the object with the palm of the hand. Finally they learn to pick up objects with their thumb and fingers.

■**Simple to complex.** At first, babies' main activities are sleeping and eating. Gradually they learn more complicated tasks. From being fed, they progress to eating with their fingers. Eventually, they are able to use a spoon and fork for eating.

Growth During the First Year

You also learned in Chapter 1 that children grow and develop at individual rates. Charts are available that show average weight, height, and abilities at certain ages. These help give a general understanding of child growth and development. Remember, however, that these charts are based on averages. Very few babies are precisely average. Unless a child is significantly above or below average, there is no need for concern. All babies simply do things at their own rate.

Weight

In babies, weight gain is one of the best indications of good health. Most babies experience a slight weight loss just after birth. From then on, they gain weight rapidly. For the first six months, a healthy baby gains 1–2 lb. (0.45–0.9 kg) per month. During the last half of the first year, the average is 1 lb. (0.45 kg) per month.

The weight of year-old babies varies widely. The average weight is about 20–22 lb. (9–10 kg). Heredity has some effect on a baby's weight pattern.

Height

Growth in height is steady during the first year. You know that the average newborn is 20 in. (51 cm) long. By one year of age, the average infant is about 30 in. (76 cm) long.

Heredity influences height more than weight. If both your parents are tall, you are more likely to be tall than the child of short parents. This does not mean that tall parents will always have tall children. Human beings carry a mixture of genes. The results of a child's particular mixture cannot be predicted.

Proportion

Proportion is a size relationship. In child development it refers to the size relationship between different parts of the body. Compared to adult proportions, a baby's head and abdomen are large. The legs and arms are short and small.

The head grows rapidly during the first year to provide room for the swiftly developing brain. Over half of the total growth of the head throughout life occurs at this time. The fontanels provide for this growth of the head. (As you learned in Chapter 5, fontanels are open spaces in the bones of the skull, sometimes known as "soft spots.") The fontanels close by about eighteen months.

156

Signs of a Healthy Baby

Both appearance and behavior give clues to a baby's health:

- A healthy baby is plump, but not fat.
- Increases in height and weight are steady.
- Eyes are bright and clear, alert and interested.
- Hair is glossy.
- Skin is velvety and smooth.
- A healthy baby is generally happy, active, and curious.
- The baby does not tire easily.
- Muscular control is appropriate for age.
- Movements are quick and positive, never listless.

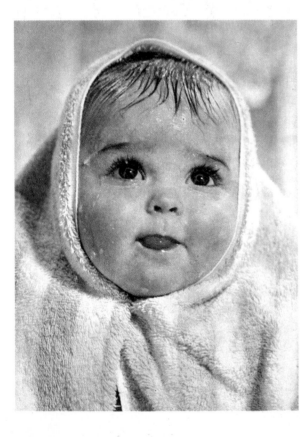

Development

Although the terms "growth" and "development" are often used to mean the same thing, there is a difference. Growth refers to measurable change in size. Development refers to an increase in physical, emotional, social, or intellectual skills. Growth and development are both rapid during the first year.

If you observed a group of teens, you could probably tell the older teens from the younger ones, but it would be difficult to identify the exact age of each individual. A fifteen-year-old and a sixteen-year-old look and act much alike. In contrast, it is easy to tell a newborn from a one-year-old. A healthy baby not only grows bigger, but develops many observable skills during the first year of life.

Sight

Development of sight in the unborn baby is limited by lack of bright light. The fetus's eyes, however, do open and shut before birth.

A newborn's eyes are closed most of the time. When they are open, the baby's stare seems blank and uncomprehending. Uncoordinated muscles cause the eyes to blink separately or look in different directions. Crying produces no tears at first.

Eyesight improves rapidly. Within a week or so, the newborn is increasingly aware of the surroundings. The eyes begin to work together. By about three and one-half months, a baby's vision is almost as good as a young adult's.

Depth perception (recognizing that an object is three-dimensional, not flat) is not noticeable until the second month. By the third month, babies prefer to look at three-dimensional or real objects rather than flat pictures of objects.

A newborn baby does not spend much time looking around at first.

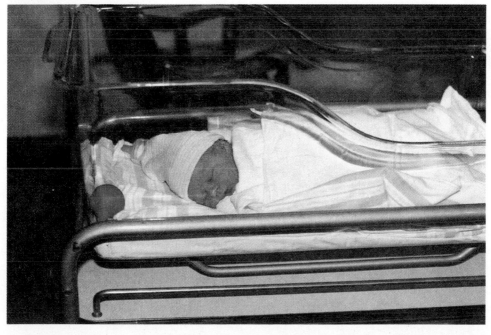

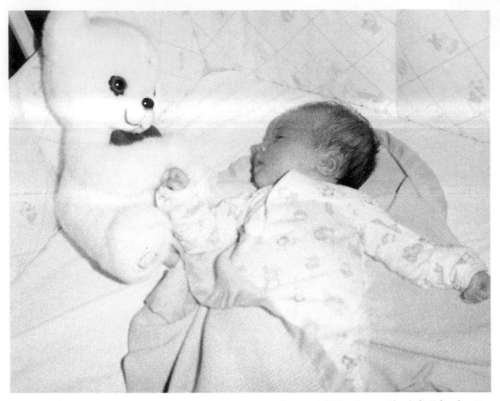

As eyesight improves, the infant begins to pay more attention to nearby objects. Next the baby tries to reach for them as well.

Eye-Hand Coordination

Gradually, a baby learns to coordinate sight with hand movement and control. The infant not only sees an object, but reaches for it. This is called **eye-hand coordination** and is an important milestone. Its development continues throughout childhood and is necessary for many skills such as eating, catching a ball, and coloring.

Hearing

The sense of hearing develops even before birth. In fact, babies still in the uterus react to sounds in a variety of ways. At birth, a baby can already tell the general direction a sound comes from.

Newborns respond to the tone of a voice rather than the words themselves. A soothing, loving voice calms them. A loud or angry voice alarms them. Remember this when caring for any child, but especially a newborn.

Hearing is essential for normal language development. Many physicians recommend that babies have a hearing test by about six months of age. This is especially important if they have had frequent ear infections which can cause hearing problems.

How can a parent tell if a child may have a hearing problem? Some signs are:

- If a newborn is not startled by a sharp clap.
- If a three-month-old never turns toward the source of sounds.

- If a child is not awakened by loud noises, does not respond when called, and pays no attention to ordinary sounds.

    If one of these signs is present, a complete hearing test is in order.

Smell

Since a baby's nose is underwater until birth, the sense of smell does not have much chance to develop. Studies at Brown University have shown, however, that even newborns respond to disagreeable odors. During the first few days of life, infants become sensitive to less strong smells and adjust quickly to familiar odors. Within ten days they can distinguish by smell their own mother from another person.

Taste

The sense of taste develops rapidly. Through their sucking behavior, two-week-old babies have shown they can taste the differences in water, sour liquids, sugar solutions, salt solutions, and milk.

When babies begin eating solid foods, they may not be picky at first. But as the baby's sense of smell improves, likes and dislikes develop. This is because the sense of taste depends to a great extent on the sense of smell. You may know this from having a head cold. When you cannot smell, everything tastes about the same.

Voice

The newborn's cry becomes less shrill as the lungs mature and the voice is used. This change in the baby's voice also results from the physical growth of the throat muscles, tongue, lips, teeth, and vocal cords. The tongue and interior of the mouth change in shape and proportion during the first months of life. The tongue is exceedingly large at birth.

These physical changes affect feeding. At first, the infant is able only to suck liquids. Later in the year when the baby is better able to swallow foods easily, solid foods may be added to the diet.

Growth of the mouth and related areas also affects speech development. Distinct speech depends upon it. Teeth are necessary to produce some sounds, such as "f," "s," and "th."

Infants are soon able to recognize their mother by smell. Why do you suppose this is true?

Many babies are physically ready for speech by the end of the first year. However, some normal children do not speak until much later. Albert Einstein, for example, did not speak as a young child. Even at age nine, his speech was not smooth. His parents thought that this might indicate mental retardation.

Teeth

The development of a baby's teeth actually begins about the sixth week of pregnancy. The first **primary teeth** (or "baby teeth") usually do not appear, however, until six or seven months of age.

Occasionally, one or more teeth are present at birth or appear in the first month of life. These teeth are often loose and immature. If so, a physician or dentist should be consulted.

The first sign of teething may be when a normally contented infant suddenly becomes cranky, restless, and wakeful. Some babies refuse food and drool a lot. Soon a small, pearl-white lump appears at the center of the lower gum.

The two lower front teeth are the first to come in, at six or seven months. By age two or three, most children have a full set of 20 primary teeth.

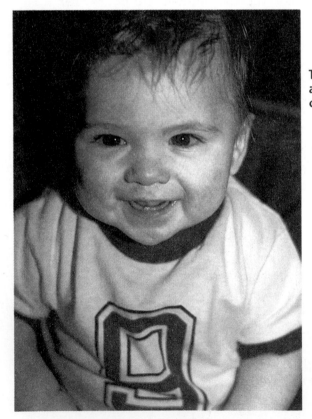

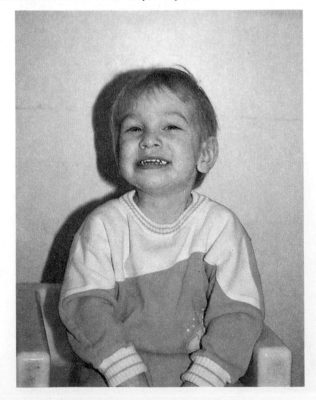

Teething is an entirely normal process but often a painful one for the infant. The teeth must force their way up through the baby's gums. As they do, they stretch and tear the tender gum tissues. This often causes pain and swelling. In addition to the symptoms mentioned above, teething can cause an increased desire for liquid, coughing, diarrhea, constipation, vomiting, fever, or even convulsions. Discomfort usually lasts from two to ten days for each tooth. The chart on page 162 gives suggestions for easing teething pain.

The teething process continues periodically for about two years until all 20 primary teeth have come in. The order in which primary teeth appear is fairly predictable. The timing, however, varies widely.

Motor Skills

Much of a baby's development during the first year is in the area of motor skills. **Motor skills** are abilities that depend upon the use and control of muscles. Although motor skills seem to be signs of physical development, mastering them requires intellectual, social, and emotional development as well. This is because development in each area affects all other areas.

One of the first motor skills infants must acquire is control of the head. At birth, the head is large and heavy; the neck muscles are weak. By age one month, babies placed on their stomach can lift their head slightly. By two to three months of age, they can also lift their chest. And when propped in a sitting position, they can keep their head steady. The chart on pages 162-163 shows other motor skill accomplishments during the first year.

As the baby grows older, the ability to support and control the head improves.

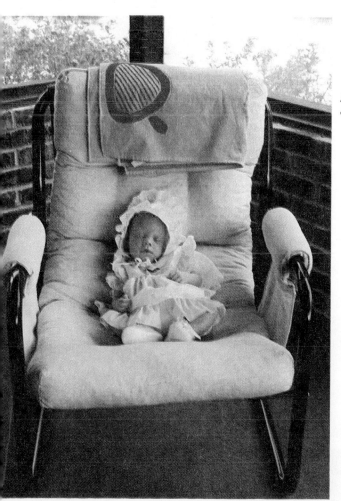

Tips for Teething Problems

- Teething babies like to bite down hard to relieve the pressure on their gums. Offer hard crusts of bread or teething rings.
- Since cold is a good painkiller, try chilling a liquid-filled teething ring in the refrigerator.
- Rubbing an ice cube on the baby's gums may ease the pain temporarily.
- Commercial medications specifically for teething pain are available. These liquids are rubbed onto the swollen gums to reduce pain. Read and follow all directions.
- If teething pain persists or other serious symptoms develop, consult a doctor.

Average Motor Skills Development
Birth to Twelve Months

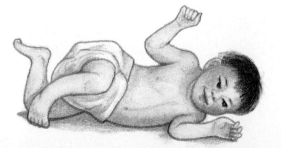

One Month

- Lifts chin when placed on stomach.

Two Months

- Lifts chest well above surface when placed on stomach.

Three to Four Months

- Reaches for objects, but unsteadily.
- Holds up head steadily.
- Rolls from side to back or back to side.
- Has complete head control when sitting on lap.
- Holds head erect when carried.

Average Motor Skills Development
Birth to Twelve Months

Five to Six Months

- Sits alone briefly.
- Reaches and grasps successfully, but awkwardly.
- Turns completely over when laid on back or stomach.
- Prefers to sit up with support.
- Uses hands to reach, grasp, crumble, bang, and splash.

Seven to Eight Months

- Reaches for spoon.
- Pulls self up in playpen.
- Sits up steadily.
- Propels self by arms, knees, or squirming motion — cannot creep or crawl.
- Eats with fingers.
- Picks up large objects.

Nine to Ten Months

- Walks when led.
- Reaches for and manipulates objects with good control.
- Picks up medium-size objects as well as larger ones.
- Stands holding on to furniture or other supports.
- More skillful with spoon.
- Creeps on hands and knees.

Eleven to Twelve Months

- Stands alone.
- May be walking alone.
- Shows preference for one hand over the other.
- Holds and drinks from a cup.
- Fits blocks or boxes inside each other.
- Picks up small objects using thumb and forefinger.

Close-up

"My husband and I are foster parents," Karen Li explained. "We've taken care of children of varying ages for up to two years at a time. It's been a good experience for us and for our own two kids, as well."

"At one time we had a set of infant twins until they were ten months old. That was a fascinating, but hectic, time! It really gave me an opportunity to see the similarities and differences among children the same age."

"Erin, the girl, was an extremely active baby. She squirmed and waved her arms around from the first day she came. Her brother Seth was much more easy-going, but he took in absolutely everything that went on around him.

"In the first few months, both babies progressed at about the same rate. But after that, each seemed to be on his or her own schedule. Erin sat up early and walked alone by ten months. That's unusual. Seth's large motor skills progressed more 'by the book.' He accomplished most skills at an average age. But he was better than Erin at picking up and handling toys and things. He also was talking a bit by the time they left us, but Erin wasn't."

"It's always hard to have kids leave after you have grown to love them. But the twins were able to go to a good adoptive home. Some of the other children have returned to their own homes after staying awhile with us. Each of them has helped us learn more about children and has brought our own family closer together."

If the twins had been identical, rather than fraternal, would their development have been more similar? Would it have been identical?

What are some ways a baby's home life may influence physical development? ■

Check Your Understanding

1. Explain the difference between growth and development. Give two examples of each.

2. Which of a baby's senses are most well developed at birth? Which are least developed? Use what you know about prenatal development to account for these differences.

3. Explain how the three patterns of physical development relate to motor skills. Use examples from the chart on pages 162–163.

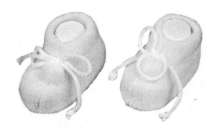

Providing Care: Handling and Feeding

The newborn is completely dependent upon others for care. Parents, and others who provide that care, must understand the baby's needs and develop skills to meet them. Among the first skills needed are those of holding, carrying, and feeding a baby.

Handling a Baby

How to handle a baby depends on the infant's age. But all babies need gentle, careful handling.

Picking up, carrying, and holding newborns requires the greatest care. Remember that a newborn's neck muscles cannot yet support the head.

To lift a newborn, slide one hand under the baby's buttocks, the other under the shoulders and head. When holding an infant upright, cradle the baby in the curve of your arm against your body. The baby will be face up. You can also hold the baby against your shoulder, facing backward. Always support the infant's head. The pictures below show the correct procedures.

Supporting the infant in the curve of your arm lets you stay face-to-face.

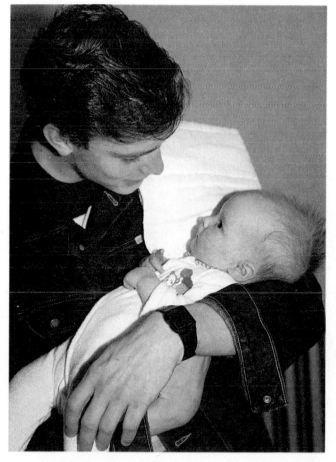

Another method is to hold the baby against your shoulder. Be sure to gently support the neck and head with one hand.

When you lay a newborn down, do so slowly and gently. Otherwise, the startle reflex is triggered and the baby will cry.

The sight of a baby gives some well-meaning adults an irresistible urge to pick up and jiggle the infant. Some babies are even tossed in the air. When parents are angry, they often shake small children vigorously. All these common practices can be dangerous. Shaking a baby younger than two years old creates a high risk of severe bleeding in the brain. Such bleeding may cause membranes to form around the brain and prevent it from growing properly. Brain damage, or even death, may result.

In one famous example, a baby nurse in Connecticut confessed to shaking two infants to death. They died of bleeding in the brain. Dozens of other babies cared for by the same woman became mentally retarded. She admitted having shaken them, too.

Always be gentle when playing with or caring for young children. Never physically punish a child when you are angry. Instead, call a friend or go into another room and calm down. Chapter 17 has additional suggestions for preventing physical harm by parents or caregivers.

Feeding a Baby

The newborn's early mealtime experiences give more than physical nourishment. Only during feeding is the infant fully awake with all the senses stimulated. Mealtime is also the baby's closest contact with other people. The cuddling, body contact, and soft words that go with feeding are as important as the food.

During a feeding, it is important that the baby feel loved and cared for.

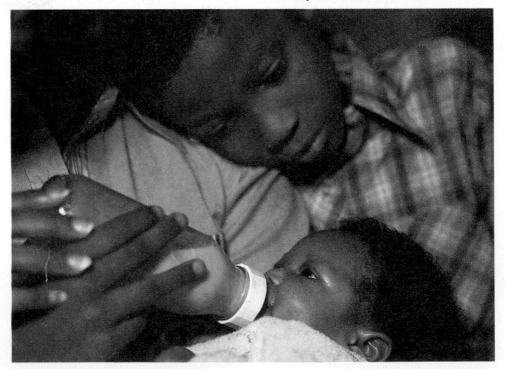

The baby's bottle can be warmed slightly, if desired. The formula should feel lukewarm, not hot, when tested on your inner arm or wrist.

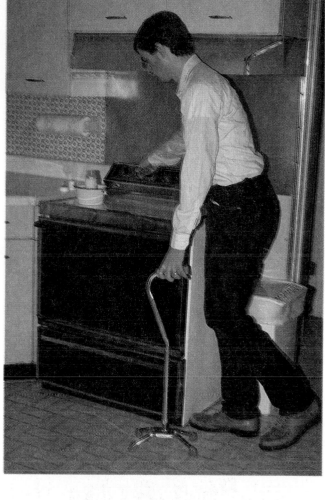

Feeding Schedules

As you read in Chapter 5, a newborn's schedule of eating and sleeping is unpredictable at first. Newborns need to eat about as much as they want and as often as they want. In the first few weeks of life, a baby feeds six to eight times or more in 24 hours. The stomach can only hold a small amount at a time.

By the second or third month, a regular pattern emerges. The baby may wake for a feeding every three or four hours around the clock. Eventually the late-night feeding is no longer needed. The schedule continues to change. By the end of the first year, a baby eats three meals a day plus snacks.

Mealtime Methods

The mother who breast-feeds her baby will receive instruction while still in the hospital. Information is also available from the La Leche League (la LAY-chay), an organization that promotes breast-feeding. The La Leche League has chapters across the country.

For bottle-feeding, hold the baby closely in a semi-upright position. Check the condition of the nipple frequently. The nipple should be kept full of milk to avoid excessive air swallowing. Continue the feeding until the infant seems satisfied. Healthy babies usually eat the amount they need.

Many parents prefer to give their baby a warm bottle, although this is not really necessary. If a warm feeding is desired, the bottle can be heated to lukewarm in a pan of water. A special warmer can also be used. Shake a drop of formula onto your wrist or inner arm to check the temperature.

Never "prop" a bottle for the baby to drink from. A New Zealand physician, Dr. Bruce Duncan, discovered that propping up the bottle while the baby is lying down causes the milk to gush in. This frequently leads to digestive problems and ear infections. In addition, the baby loses the physical contact with the parent or caregiver during feeding.

Other research on feeding has found that letting children go to bed with a bottle of milk or juice can cause tooth decay. When a baby drifts off to sleep sucking a bottle, the teeth are exposed to decay-producing carbohydrates for a long period. The teeth are more likely to decay.

How to Burp a Baby

All babies, whether breast- or bottle-fed, must be burped during and after feedings. This expels air swallowed during feeding which can cause discomfort. Here are two methods of burping a baby:

Lay the baby, stomach down, across your knees. (Protect your clothes with a clean diaper or cloth.) Pat the baby's back until you hear the air expelled.

Don't worry if no burp comes. There may not be one every time. It depends on the amount of air swallowed during feeding.

Hold the baby upright, head erect and supported. Pat the baby gently on the back until you hear the air expelled.

Introducing New Foods

Strained foods are usually added to a baby's diet between the fourth and sixth months. (Strained foods are solids processed to make them smooth and somewhat runny.) The baby's pediatrician will recommend when these "solids" should be added. Maturity, or "readiness," is as important in feeding as in learning to sit or stand. A baby cannot swallow and digest food well for several months after birth.

Choose a time when the baby is well, content, and happy to begin new foods. Don't begin solids, for example, if the infant has been sick or the family is moving. There is no real hurry to begin. Breast milk or formula provides adequate nutrition.

The attitude of the person feeding the baby can influence the baby's acceptance of new foods. First attempts at feeding solids are usually unsuccessful. The taste and texture of the foods are very different from milk. The baby's natural reaction is to spit the new food back out. If the person feeding becomes upset, the baby senses it and may take longer to adjust. Patience and a sense of humor help!

A baby's first solid food is usually cereal. Strained fruits, vegetables, and meats are gradually added later. Such foods can be made at home or purchased. It is important to feed only strained foods because the baby cannot yet chew.

After the baby accepts the first solid food, other types can be added. Be sure to add only one new food at a time. If a certain food causes a rash or digestive trouble, it will be easier to tell what is causing the problem.

Gradually, the baby will learn to eat a wider variety of foods. Many foods from family meals can be used if they are not highly seasoned and are strained or chopped fine. As more teeth appear, the foods can be coarser.

Tips for Feeding Solid Foods

- For the first feedings, hold the baby comfortably in a fairly upright position.
- If the baby is used to warm milk, solid foods should also be warmed to lukewarm. Check the temperature of warmed foods by placing a drop on your wrist.
- Early feedings will be messy. A bib for the baby will help somewhat. Wear old clothes yourself and plan on a shower afterwards.
- A baby often spits out an unfamiliar food. This does not necessarily mean dislike. It may be several weeks before the baby accepts the food eagerly.
- Babies often like cereal very runny (diluted with milk or formula, because the feel of the food is closer to milk.
- If baby food from a jar is used, take out a small portion and place it in a bowl. Return the rest to the refrigerator immediately. Do not feed directly from the jar. Bacteria from the spoon will multiply rapidly in the food and cause any leftovers to spoil.

Weaning

Weaning means changing a baby from drinking from the bottle or breast to drinking from a cup. It is a sign of the increasing independence of the baby.

There is no precise age at which babies should be weaned. Nine months is common, but the age varies greatly. The baby will usually show some signs of readiness such as playing or looking around while sucking, pushing the nipple away, or preferring to eat from a spoon. An unwilling child should not be forcibly weaned. This will only cause other feeding and behavior problems.

Self-Feeding

At about eight or ten months, babies start to eat with their fingers and reach for the spoon. They open their mouth when they see a spoon coming. Next they want to hold the spoon themselves. These are signs that the infant is ready to begin feeding himself or herself.

Begin self-feeding with "finger foods" like toast or crackers. Choose nutritious foods that are easy to grasp. For safety, however, avoid raw vegetables, nuts, candies, and similar foods that may cause choking.

A baby's first efforts with a spoon will not get much food into the mouth. Use a separate spoon and place a bite of food in the baby's mouth now and then yourself.

It takes patience to encourage self-feeding. You could feed the baby yourself in a fraction of the time. This would also eliminate scrubbing the baby, high chair, floor, and sometimes even the walls!

Nutritional Concerns

Feeding a baby involves more than mastering the needed techniques. Those responsible for the care of an infant must make sure that the baby's nutritional needs are being met. Fortunately, this is usually not difficult if the feeding recommendations already given are followed. However, problems can result if the baby is given too much, too little, or the wrong kinds of food.

Overfeeding

There has long been a debate over the proper weight for babies and whether overfeeding in infancy contributes to weight problems in

It's important to know the basics of good nutrition. These young women are taking part in a community program that helps them learn how they and their babies can eat healthfully.

adulthood. There are still no final answers. However, it is known that eating habits are established very early in life. A baby who is encouraged to overeat is more likely to have a weight problem later. A baby who is frequently given sweet snacks instead of nutritious foods is more likely to develop poor eating habits. Infancy is the time to begin a lifetime of healthy eating.

Bottle-fed babies have a greater chance of overfeeding than breast-fed babies. Parents and caregivers are often tempted to urge the baby to take any formula left in the bottle. Nursing mothers, on the other hand, are inclined to take their baby's word for it when the baby stops sucking.

Malnutrition

Some babies suffer from **malnutrition**—a lack of enough food or the proper type of food. Infants have very specific nutritional needs. They need:

- Enough calories to provide for rapid growth.
- Food that contains needed nutrients.
- Food that is easy to digest.
- Adequate amounts of liquid.

Throughout most of the first year, a baby's main source of nutrition is breast milk or formula. Cow's milk alone does not provide the same nutrition. A baby may begin drinking some whole milk after solids have been added to the diet.

Infant malnutrition isn't just a problem in developing nations in other parts of the world. It occurs in this country as well. Some parents do not provide their babies with enough food because of lack of money. Others simply do not know about babies' special food needs.

Some parents, for example, put their infants on diets very low in fat and cholesterol during the first year. They use low-fat or skim milk to prepare formula and later for drinking. While cholesterol has been linked to adult heart disease, low-fat and skim milk do not

provide enough calories for normal infant growth and they strain a baby's kidneys. There is also no real evidence that limiting cholesterol in early childhood prevents adult health problems. Breast milk, considered the ideal food, is high in cholesterol.

Malnutrition in infancy can cause lasting physical problems. Severe malnutrition is also linked to poor brain development and learning problems.

Many government and community programs try to eliminate infant and childhood malnutrition. Some provide food, while others teach parents about the nutritional needs of children. The federal government's Women, Infants, and Children Program (WIC for short) helps meet the special food needs of new mothers and young children. Find out what other programs are available in your area.

Check Your Understanding

1. Give four examples of different types of foods that might be a part of a baby's diet during the first year. List them in the order that they should be introduced to the baby. Explain why the order is important.

2. Nine-month-old Joey's parents don't want to let him try to feed himself because the process is so messy. How will this affect Joey's ability to learn?

3. Why is infancy the best time to begin learning good eating habits?

Other Care Skills

As you read in Chapter 5, a baby has many needs. Besides feeding, other tasks involved in infant care include bathing, dressing, and diapering. Proper sleep habits are also important for the baby's health.

Bathing a Baby

A bath helps keep a baby clean and healthy. As with other care skills, confidence comes from knowing what to do and from a bit of practice. Anytime is fine for a bath except right after feeding. Then the baby needs to sleep and digest the meal.

A newborn is given sponge baths until the navel heals. This takes about two weeks. After that a tub bath—first in a basin of water and later in the bathtub—may be given. Both require the caregiver's careful attention to insure safety.

Sponge Baths

Many of the same basic supplies are needed for both sponge baths and tub baths. These include:

- Two soft bath towels.
- A soft washcloth.
- Diaper.
- Mild soap.
- Baby shampoo.
- Cotton balls.

Assemble these articles and the baby's clean clothes in a warm place with no drafts. The temperature of the room should be 70°–80°F (20°–26°C). Choose a room with a good work surface—usually the bathroom, kitchen, or baby's room. Place a soft bath towel over the work area for the baby's comfort and safety.

For sponge baths, it is often most convenient to put the bathwater in a basin on the work surface. Test the water with your elbow. (The skin there is more sensitive than that on your hands or wrists.) The water should feel lukewarm, or about 98°F (37°C).

Remove the baby's clothes and place the infant on the towel. Wash the baby's face with clear water and a soft washcloth. Then pat it dry. A young baby's skin is very tender, so never rub it with a towel.

Wash the rest of the body with mild soap and water, one area at a time. Rinse thoroughly. Pay particular attention to skin creases. They should be gently separated, washed, and thoroughly dried.

During the bath, keep the baby covered except for the area being washed. It is a good idea to keep a diaper folded under and over the infant. A small baby usually wets while being bathed.

It is not necessary to clean the inside of the mouth, ears, eyes, or nose. Nature takes care of this. Never use cotton swab sticks. Babies move very suddenly and can easily be injured by them. Just wipe the outer ears and use a pinch of cotton to remove any visible mucus from the nose.

Wash the baby's scalp with mild soap or baby shampoo once or twice a week. On other days, just wipe the scalp with clear water and pat dry.

Sometimes babies develop a condition called **cradle cap**. These patches of yellowish, crusty scales on the scalp are common in young babies. To treat cradle cap, apply baby oil to the scalp at night. In the morning, gently loosen the scales with a washcloth or a soft hairbrush (not a stiff one!) and shampoo the hair.

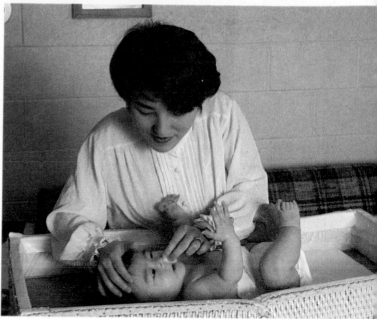

The baby's nose can be gently cleaned with a cotton ball.

Baby powder or lotion may be applied to a baby after a bath, but neither is really necessary. Powder should be used with caution. If it accumulates in skin creases, it can cause irritation. If the powder is inhaled, the baby can develop breathing problems or even suffocate. Never let a baby play with the container of powder. Apply powder by first shaking it into your own hand and then rubbing it onto the baby's skin.

Tub Baths

With proper handling, even a two-week-old baby can be bathed in a tub if the navel has healed. At first the "tub" can be a large dishpan or special baby bathtub. At age six or seven months when the baby can sit alone steadily, the regular tub can be used.

Place a rubber mat or towel in the bottom of the tub for comfort and to prevent falls. Add lukewarm water to a depth of about 2–3 in. (5–8 cm). Assemble the other equipment and the baby's clothes before starting the bath.

Begin by washing the baby's face with clear water and patting it dry. Then lift the baby into the tub with a secure grip—like the one illustrated on page 174. Slide your left wrist under the baby's head and grasp the baby's left arm under the armpit. Slide your right hand under the thighs, gripping the baby's left leg above the knee. (Reverse these directions if you are left-handed.)

While the baby is in the tub, the left hand stays in much the same position. This way you can support the baby's back and head while washing and rinsing with your right hand. Lift the baby from the water with the same secure grip. Place the infant on a clean towel and wrap quickly to prevent chilling. Then pat the baby dry.

Most older babies enjoy baths, especially when they are able to sit by themselves in the tub. They love to splash and play in the water. A few floating toys add to the fun. But safety is the primary concern when bathing a baby of any age. See page 174 for bathtime safety tips.

Bathtime Safety Tips

The bathtub can be a dangerous place for babies, so safety precautions must be taken:

- A baby should never be left alone while bathing, even for a few moments. Drownings can happen very quickly and even in shallow water.
- The baby should remain seated while in the tub. Standing or climbing can lead to falls.
- Always check the water temperature before the baby is placed in the water.
- Faucets present a double hazard. They are hard, sometimes sharp, surfaces. They may also be hot. Keep babies away from them.
- To prevent the baby from trying to drink bathwater or suck on the washcloth, offer a drink of water.

Dressing a Baby

Choose a baby's indoor clothing according to the temperature in the home, rather than the season of the year. A good rule of thumb is to check your own clothing needs. An infant does not need to be warmer than you do. Since a newborn's hands and feet usually feel cool to the touch, check the baby's body temperature by feeling the arms, legs, or neck instead. Babies who are too cold usually begin to fuss. Babies who are too warm perspire and become cranky.

The Newborn

A newborn's clothing needs are minimal. Many babies wear a "sleeper" (a one-piece stretch garment with feet) for both sleeping and waking. Or the baby may be dressed in a cotton undershirt and a gown. In warm or hot weather (if there is no air conditioning), the baby may wear only a diaper and perhaps a short-sleeved undershirt. For going outdoors in cool weather, warm outer garments or blankets can be added.

Babies are happiest when dressed with the least amount of handling possible. Choose shirts that open down the front. If a pullover garment is necessary, dressing and undressing will be easier using the techniques illustrated on pages 176-177.

Whenever you dress or undress a baby, work as smoothly and quickly as possible without being rough. Quick, jerking movements often frighten babies.

In spite of the fact that a baby's feet may feel cold, socks and booties are not necessary for everyday wear. They may bind and usually get wet or kicked off. The newborn's feet usually stay covered by a sleeper or blanket.

Older Babies

When babies begin to creep and crawl, their clothing needs change. Overalls and long or short pants with elastic waistbands are popular. Pants with padded or reinforced knees are a good choice. Soft, cotton knit shirts are usually worn with the pants. For bed, a sleeper keeps the baby covered even if blankets are kicked off.

Shoes are not really necessary unless the baby is outdoors or the floors are very cold. Many physicians feel the best way to learn to walk is barefooted. This leaves the toes free to grip the floor and gives the ankles flexibility. When used, either sneakers or leather shoes are satisfactory.

As babies get older, they are better able to help with dressing. However, they may also be uncooperative. Be firm, but gentle. Distracting the baby or making dressing a game often helps overcome stubbornness.

Choosing Clothes

In choosing baby clothes, both comfort and ease in dressing are important. Since clothing is expensive, it is wise to look for clothes with generous hems and extra buttons on shoulder straps and waistbands to allow for rapid growth.

The clothing available today is much better suited to babies' needs than in the past. Clothes are simple and comfortable. Many are made of knit fabrics which provide ease of movement for the baby and ease of care for the parents.

The size of infantwear is indicated by both weight and age of baby. Weight is a more reliable guide. It is best not to buy anything smaller than a six-month size for most newborns. At first, the infant will probably "swim" in the shirts and gowns. But babies grow quickly. Even the tiniest sizes are soon too small. Simply fold up the garments for the first few weeks until the baby catches up with the clothes.

Which of these garments would be most practical for everyday wear?

How to Dress a Baby

Babies are happiest when dressed with the least amount of handling possible. They especially dislike having garments of any kind pulled over their face. Here are some tips to make dressing easier for both you and the baby.

Pullover Garments

These garments have a small, but stretchable, neck opening.

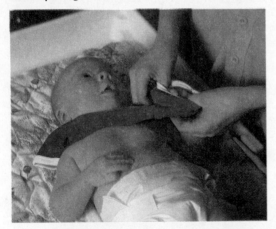

1. Gather the garment into a loop and slip it over the back of the baby's head.
2. Stretch the garment forward as you bring it down past the forehead and nose. (This keeps the face and nose free so the baby does not feel smothered.)
3. Put the baby's fist into the armhole and pull it through with your other hand. Repeat with the other arm.

Slipover Gown or Shirt

If the garment has a larger neck opening than a pullover, use this method.

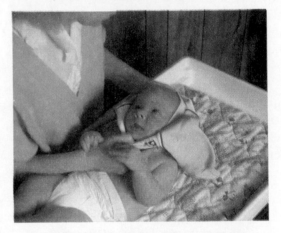

1. Gather the garment into a loop and place it around the baby's face like an oval frame.
2. Slip the garment down the back of the head.
3. Put the baby's fist into the armhole and pull it through with your other hand. Repeat with the other arm.

Open-Front Shirt

The "secret" of this method is first laying the baby face down. This helps the baby feel secure.

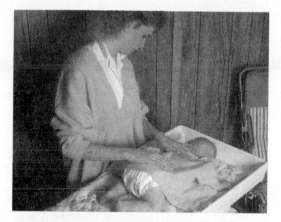

1. Place the baby on his or her stomach.
2. Lay the shirt on the infant's back.

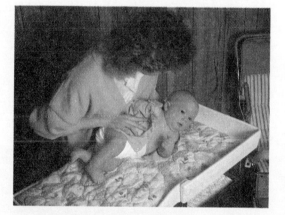

3. Gently turn the baby face up so that the shirt is underneath.
4. Put the baby's arms through the sleeves.

 ## One-Piece Garment with Feet

Putting on this type of garment is easier when the zipper or snaps go from neck to toes.

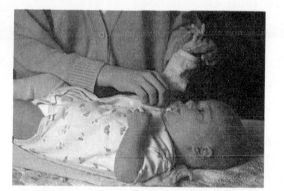

1. Put the bottom part of the garment on first.
2. Gently pull the sleeves over the baby's arms.

 ## Undressing the Baby

To take off a garment, reverse the steps given above. For example, to remove a pull-over top, first take the baby's arms out of the sleeves. Gather the garment into a loop as it lies around the neck. Stretch the garment up and over the baby's face and slip it off toward the back of the head.

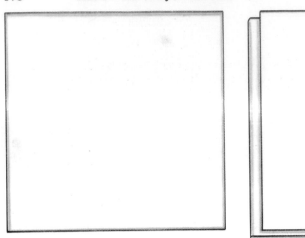

Fold a square diaper in thirds lengthwise so that it is a little wider than the baby's hips. Then turn up one end of the diaper partway.

Diapering a Baby

Diapers are the most essential part of a baby's wardrobe. Parents have a number of options. Cloth diapers, the traditional favorite, may be the least expensive if home laundry facilities are available. Although they are more expensive, some parents prefer disposable diapers for their throw away convenience. (They do add to the country's environmental problems.) Commercial diaper delivery services are available in some areas. They deliver clean cloth diapers and pick up used ones. They are convenient and may not be much more expensive than other options, in some circumstances.

Very young babies need eight to ten diaper changes daily. The newborn wets several times an hour, but in small amounts that do not require changing with each wetting. In fact, most babies are not bothered by being somewhat wet, if they are warm. It is not necessary to wake a baby to change diapers unless the doctor tells you to do so.

With a baby around, changing diapers soon becomes routine. Begin by assembling the supplies you will need by a sturdy, padded surface (such as the crib). Cloth diapers must be folded to the correct size. (The illustration above shows a good method.) Disposable diapers come in several sizes, with thicker diapers available for nighttime wear. A wet washcloth and cotton and baby oil (or special disposable baby washcloths) are also needed.

Follow these steps to change a diaper:

1. *Remove the diaper.* If the diaper was merely wet, clean the baby with cotton and baby oil. After a bowel movement, use soft tissue or toilet paper to remove the soil from the baby. Then wash with a washcloth and apply baby oil.

2. *Put on a fresh diaper.* Hold the baby's ankles and lift the body enough to slide the diaper under. If cloth diapers are used, place the extra thickness in the back for girls, in the front for boys. Bring the diaper up between the legs. Disposable diapers fasten with special adhesive tabs. Safety pins are needed for cloth diapers. To protect the baby, place the pins crosswise, keeping your finger between the diaper and the baby's skin as you pin. Waterproof pants may be added, if desired.

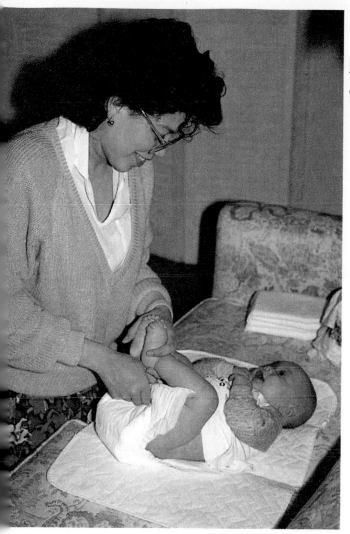

Babies sometimes fuss while being diapered. Talking or singing to them helps keep them contented.

Washing Cloth Diapers

Washing a baby's cloth diapers requires more care than you might think. Washing machines do not always wash out bacteria which can cause skin problems. Special laundry sanitizers can be added to the wash to destroy bacteria. Also use *hot* water and a mild soap. (Cold or warm water leaves too many bacteria in the fabric.) Always wash diapers separately, never with other clothing. Thorough rinsing is essential. Soap left in diapers can irritate a baby's skin. Diapers may be dried in a dryer. However, drying them outdoors in the sunshine destroys even more bacteria.

Diaper Rash

Control of bacteria in diapers is important because babies often develop **diaper rash**. Patches of red, rough, irritated skin appear in the diaper area. Sometimes, there are painful raw spots. Bacteria from wet or dirty diapers or improperly washed diapers are the usual cause. A sensitivity to disposable diapers can cause similar symptoms.

Mild diaper rash can be treated at home. Change diapers more frequently. Clean the baby thoroughly after soiling. Products containing zinc oxide and cod liver oil help protect against diaper rash and help it heal more quickly. Expose the diaper area to the air as much as possible and avoid waterproof pants. Consult a doctor if the rash continues or gets worse.

3. ***Dispose of used supplies.*** Cleanliness is important in diapering. Promptly dispose of used tissues, cotton, and other soiled supplies. Place disposable diapers in a covered trash container. (Never flush them down a toilet. They will clog the plumbing.) Place wet cloth diapers in a covered container filled with a mixture of water and borax or vinegar. Rinse soiled diapers before placing them in the container. A good method is to hold the diaper firmly in a clean, flushing toilet.

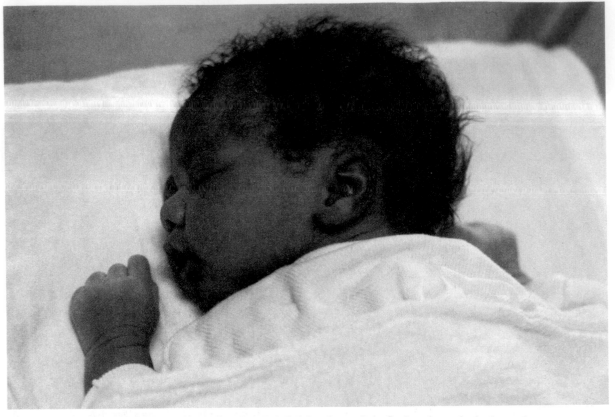

Sleep lets infants regain energy after their brief active periods. During sleep, the body repairs itself and builds new cells for growth.

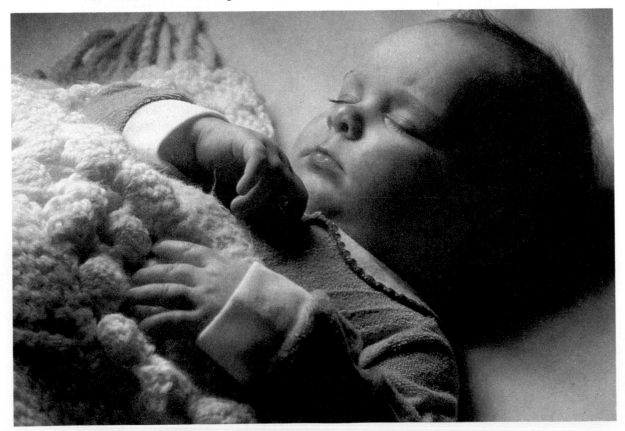

Sleep

Sleep is necessary for a baby's proper growth. However, the amount of time the infant spends sleeping decreases considerably during the first year. A newborn may sleep from 12 hours a day to almost continuously. But by one year, a baby often has as few as two or three sleep periods, including naps.

The amount of sleep needed also depends on the individual baby. An active baby needs more than an inactive one, just as active babies need more food. Babies also require more sleep on some days than on others.

Home environment and teaching influence sleeping habits. Parents must provide both a good place to sleep and proper attitudes toward sleep.

It is not always possible for a baby to have a room alone. If an infant must share a room, the parents' room is the best choice for the first weeks. When the baby sleeps through the night, the bed can be moved to a room with another child.

Preparations for Sleep

Before putting a baby to bed, wash off any obvious dirt and change the baby's diaper and clothes. Specific sleeping garments remind the older baby it is time to go to bed.

Rocking or a soothing lullaby is relaxing and reassuring to a baby at bedtime. Keep your manner calm and unhurried, even if you don't feel that way. Otherwise the baby will pick up your feelings and probably not sleep as well as usual.

Place the baby in bed with adequate covering. (Never let a baby sleep in a draft, even in very hot weather.) Young babies usually sleep best on their stomachs.

For a normal baby, sleep should never be brought about by the use of drugs or sleep medicines of any kind. Consult the baby's pediatrician if sleep problems continue.

Bedtime Problems

Active babies sometimes sleep restlessly. Occasionally during the night they may be half-awake and suck their fingers, cry out, or rock the crib. It is best not to respond to these activities. If you do, your presence may become a necessary part of the baby's pattern for getting back to sleep. Infants need to learn to use their own resources for returning to sleep. Of course, this does not mean you should ignore a baby who needs feeding or a diaper change. Prolonged crying should also be checked.

Although all babies need sleep, some simply need more than others!

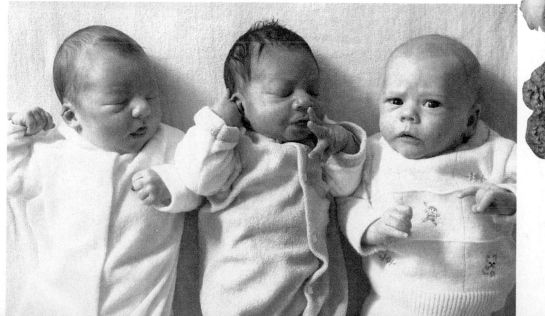

Close-up

By the time Rachel was a year old, her bedtime routine was well established. She was put down for the night around 7:30 p.m. Then the fussing and crying would begin. If no one responded, the cries would turn to screams until one or the other parent could take it no more. One would go into Rachel's room, pick her up, and soothe her.

When Rachel's crying stopped, she was put back in the crib. Instantly, the screams would begin again. It always ended the same way. Rachel was eventually brought to the family room where the parents relaxed before going to bed. Rachel would fall asleep in her parent's arms. When she was sleeping soundly she was put back to bed for the night.

Rachel's parents mentioned the problem to her pediatrician. The doctor asked a few questions, then responded, "Rachel's got you trained, not the other way around. You've given in to her crying so long that the habit will only get worse. Bedtime problems usually develop when parents aren't firm enough. Even small babies need to be taught conformance and control."

"It won't hurt Rachel to cry herself to sleep. If you don't pick her up, she'll soon learn that screams won't help her get her way. It'll be tough for a while — for all of you — but she'll soon learn that when she's put down for the night, she'll stay there. Babies don't long continue behavior that doesn't work."

The doctor was right. It was difficult to listen to Rachel's screams, but her parents held firm. Surprisingly, within a week, Rachel's crying gradually lessened in intensity and duration. It wasn't long before bedtime was no longer a problem.

How could the lesson Rachel's parents learned be carried over to other situations?

How could her parents be certain Rachel's crying didn't indicate a real physical problem?

Should the same technique be used with a two-week-old baby? ■

Check Your Understanding

1. What are the advantages and disadvantages of both cloth diapers and disposable diapers?

2. What kinds of clothes would be good choices for an active eight-month-old?

3. Why is it usually best not to interfere if a baby is half-awake or restless during the night?

Chapter Review

To Sum Up

- Development and growth are most rapid during the first year of life.
- Physical development proceeds from head to foot, near to far, and simple to complex.
- As babies' senses develop, they learn more about their world.
- Development of motor skills depends on physical, intellectual, social, and emotional development.
- Daily care routines include feeding, bathing, dressing, and diapering.
- During the first year, eating habits change from breast- or bottle-feeding to self-feeding a variety of foods.
- Clothing should be easy to put on and take off, suit the activity of the baby, and "grow" with the baby.
- Bedtime should be handled with a soothing, familiar routine.

To Review and Remember

1. What is meant by saying that physical development proceeds from near to far?
2. How do a baby's proportions compare to an adult's?
3. What are three signs of a baby's hearing problem?
4. What are motor skills?
5. Why shouldn't babies and young children be bounced up and down or shaken?
6. Why is it important to hold a baby during feeding?
7. What is weaning? Name two signs of readiness for it.
8. Give two reasons why caregivers should avoid feeding skim milk to infants.
9. What is cradle cap and how is it treated?
10. Describe how cloth diapers should be laundered.

To Discuss and Discover

1. Take a survey of students in the class. How does their height compare with that of their parents? Give some possible reasons for differences.
2. Using pictures from magazines and catalogs, find examples of positive and negative features of babies' clothing. Cut out and mount your pictures on paper or posterboard, indicating why they are good or poor choices.
3. Discuss how talking—which might be described as a physical ability—requires a combination of physical, emotional, social, and intellectual growth and development.

7 Emotional & Social Development During the First Year

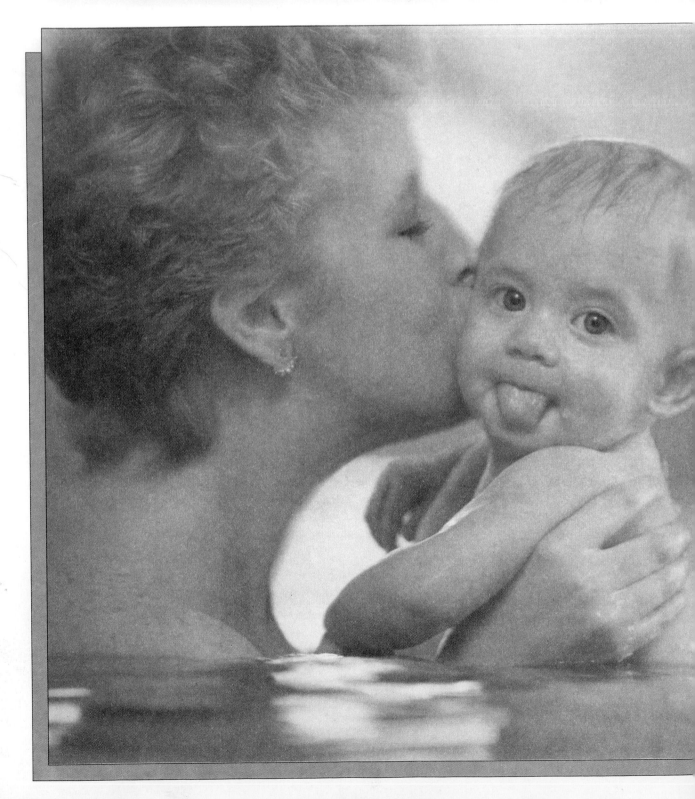

To help you to . . .

- Recognize signs of emotional and social development in babies.

- Explain how a baby's care affects emotional development.

- Describe how emotions change during infancy.

- Explain the importance of attachment to emotional and social development.

- Describe how behavior is learned.

- Define personality and describe how it develops.

- Recognize different personality types in babies.

Terms to Learn

aggressive	marasmus	self-concept
attachment	pacifier	sensitive
consistency	personality	social development
emotional development	placid	stranger anxiety

"It's amazing what a difference ten months can make," remarked John Spurgeon. "For the first few months after Lisa was born, she was this cute, but demanding, *baby*. All we thought about was keeping her fed and dry—and quiet! We would ask each other, 'How did the baby sleep?' or 'Does the baby need changing?'"

"Suddenly, she's turned into Lisa. She's not just a baby, but a real *person*. Her eyes light up and she gets excited when she sees her mom or me. She laughs and she gets mad. And you should see the faces she makes when we feed her something she doesn't like. It's pure disgust! I guess this is what they mean by the joys of parenthood."

Understanding Emotional and Social Development

In the preceding chapter you learned about physical development during the first year of life. In the chapter following this one, you will learn about intellectual development. Both of these dimensions of development can be easily observed. Physically, you can see a child's weight gain and ability to hold up the head. You can also observe the child's increasing ability to think and understand.

Emotional and social development cannot be observed or measured so simply. **Emotional development** deals with children's changing feelings about themselves, others, and the world. **Social development** is the progress a person makes from a baby's complete self-centeredness to an adult's ability to live and work with others. Good social development results in an adult whose behavior conforms to the expectations of society.

Often those who do try to observe a child's feelings and relationships with others misunderstand what they see. This usually happens because they fail to recognize the child's age level and maturity. They try to judge a child by adult standards. Behavior of small children may be perfectly normal for their age, but irritating to grown-ups who expect them to act like "small adults."

Everyone likes a happy baby. But babies need love and attention just as much — or even more — when they are crying or fussy. Their health and well-being depend on it.

Close-up

After retrieving Sammy's toy duck from the floor for the third time, Sammy's father dropped his newspaper in exasperation and said, "If he's old enough to deliberately throw it down, he's old enough to learn not to."

He placed the toy on eight-month-old Sammy's high chair tray. "No, no," he said sternly. "Don't throw it." He was rewarded by a bright smile as the duck promptly clattered to the floor. "No, no!" Sammy's father banged it on the surface. "Don't throw it! No — " He replaced the toy again, this time slapping Sammy's chubby hand. Sammy's big eyes surveyed his father uncertainly, and he tried again. This was a favorite game. Then, at the third slap, Sammy gave up and wailed. As he cried, he twisted away from his father, looking around for comfort from anyone who might be near.

Was Sammy's father's response appropriate? Why or why not?
What might Sammy learn from this experience? ■

This chapter will help you learn the "signs" of emotional and social development during a baby's first year. It is important to remember that emotional and social development cannot really be separated. How children act toward others depends upon their feelings.

At this age, children can't tell you what they are thinking or feeling. It takes understanding to interpret their moods and behavior.

Emotional Development

Emotional development begins at birth and continues throughout life. Like physical development, it follows predictable patterns. However, each baby's timing differs.

Every baby also copes with life in a very personal way. This is because each brings his or her own individuality to a situation. For example, all babies react to a sudden shaking of the surface on which they are lying. However, one baby will respond by screaming, while another will simply squirm a bit and quickly calm down again.

Emotional responses depend on other factors besides the child's individuality. The type of care the baby receives and the atmosphere of the home are major influences on emotional development.

A baby who experiences a world of caring people and interesting things has a good start in life. These influences are important for building trust.

Building Trust Through Care

The world is a strange place for newborns. The attitudes they develop about that world depend on how well their needs are met. If the newborn is kept warm and dry and is fed when hungry, soothed when fussy, and talked to when awake, the infant comes to feel that this is a comfortable place. The baby develops a sense of trust. On the other hand, if the newborn is made to conform to a rigid schedule of feeding, and crying brings no comfort, the baby learns that the world is not such a nice place. This also happens when parents are inconsistent in their care or responses. If schedules are changed often or parents are sometimes loving and other times sharp and impatient, the baby has difficulty building trust.

Building trust in infancy is important because it helps the child meet the inevitable frustrations of later life. Look on pages 230 to 231 for more information on building a sense of trust.

Establishing a happy, loving home environment is one of the best and most important ways in which parents can provide for their children.

Emotional Climate of the Home

Affection and harmony between parents are the foundation of successful family life. If the parents also love and understand each child as an individual, the conditions are ideal for emotional and social development.

Undoubtedly, you have days when you are grumpy. Have you ever noticed how contagious such feelings are? If you snap at someone, the chances are that person will snap back at you. Babies react the same way. Long before they know the meaning of words, babies catch the "tone" of their parents' feelings. Nervous, worried parents are likely to be tense or awkward in handling their baby. They may cuddle the infant less soothingly or rush through a feeding. The baby senses the parents' mood. In turn, the baby becomes irritable and fussy.

Every family has its normal ups and downs and a baby adapts to these. However, it is important that a baby feel that warm affection is the basis of the family, rather than bitterness or mistrust. A baby senses these emotions as easily as an adult.

Crying and Comforting

One obvious sign of infants' emotions is crying. Newborns vary greatly in the amount and intensity of their crying. Some cry infrequently, with little intensity, and are easily comforted. These are what parents call "easy" or "good" babies! Others cry often, loudly, and are difficult to comfort.

A young baby who is crying needs attention and care. The first step is to check for any physical problem. Is the baby hungry or in need of a diaper change? Is the infant too cold or too hot? Perhaps there's a burp left over from the last feeding. If none of these are the cause of the crying and the baby doesn't seem ill, it's time to try other comforting measures:

- Grandma's rocking chair really does work. The combination of being held and the rocking motion often soothes a crying baby. You can also cuddle the baby and walk around.

- Sometimes changing the baby's position brings relief.
- Talking softly or singing to the baby may bring comfort. (You don't need to be a great singer!)
- Try distracting the baby with a toy.

Babies also have ways of comforting themselves. The most common is by sucking on a thumb, fist, or **pacifier**. (A pacifier is a nipple attached to a plastic ring.)

Many children develop an attachment to a soft object such as a certain blanket or stuffed toy. They use this for comfort when they are sleepy or anxious. Others may twist their hair or rock themselves back and forth in their crib.

Children almost always outgrow their need for self-comforting techniques. They eventually give them up on their own without a problem.

Some rocking and soothing, along with a visit from a favorite stuffed toy, have chased away the tears. What self-comforting technique do you see here?

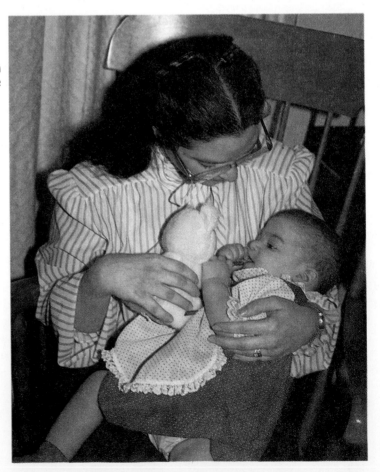

Emotions in Infancy

Think about all the different emotions you experience. You may be happy, angry, anxious, fearful, or excited. Babies, however, only gradually develop such specific emotions. A study by K. M. B. Bridges showed how dramatically emotions change during infancy. The chart below illustrates her findings.

At birth, the only emotion is excitement. Even mild discomfort may cause screams. By the second month, however, babies produce different cries to express different things—hunger, pain, or discomfort. These more specific responses continue to develop as babies connect their feelings with inner sensations and outer experiences. Pages 192-193 show how a baby's emotions develop.

Check Your Understanding

1. Describe how to build trust in an infant.

2. Describe what you would do if a baby is crying.

3. Name three common ways infants comfort themselves. How should caregivers respond to such practices?

4. What are some possible reasons babies' emotions become more specific?

Emotions in Infancy

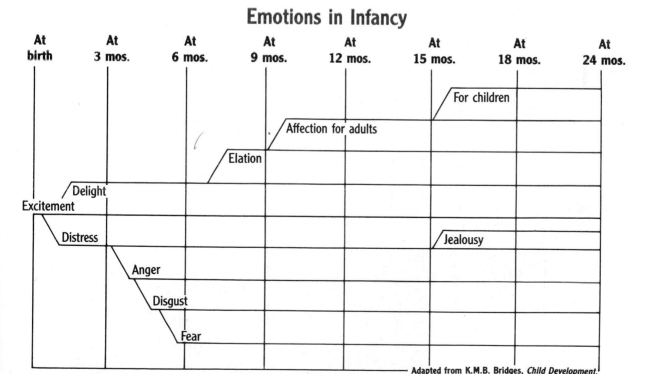

Adapted from K.M.B. Bridges, *Child Development.*

How Emotions Develop

Positive Emotions

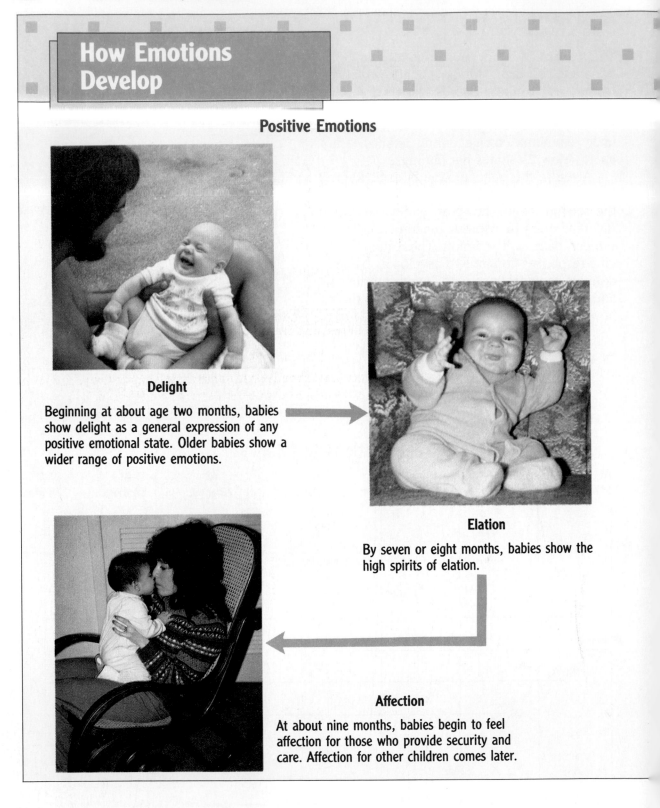

Delight

Beginning at about age two months, babies show delight as a general expression of any positive emotional state. Older babies show a wider range of positive emotions.

Elation

By seven or eight months, babies show the high spirits of elation.

Affection

At about nine months, babies begin to feel affection for those who provide security and care. Affection for other children comes later.

Negative Emotions

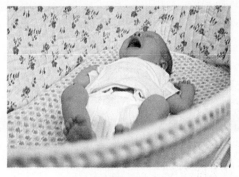

Distress

In very young babies, any discomfort or un-happiness is expressed in the same way.

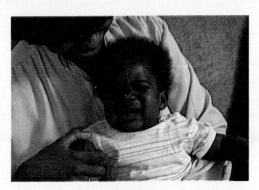

Anger

By about four or five months, babies show anger when they don't get their way. Older babies show anger at objects as well as at people.

Disgust

Disgust can also be observed at four or five months of age. Babies show their dislike very clearly.

Fear

Until about age six months, babies do not show fear because they can't recognize threatening situations. Fear of strangers be-gins at about eight months of age.

Social Development

Physical helplessness is what prompts a baby's social development. Newborns learn ways to respond to others in order to satisfy their physical and emotional needs. Therefore, long before they learn to talk, babies know a great deal about how they are expected to behave.

■*The first days of life.* Babies respond to human voices from birth. A calm, soothing voice will quiet them. A harsh or loud voice will upset them.

■*One month.* Most babies stop crying when lifted or touched. Their face brightens when they see a familiar person—usually a parent.

Social development is a natural part of being with parents and other family members. How does the older boy's level of social development compare with his baby brother's?

■*Two months.* Babies begin to smile at people. Since their eyes can follow moving objects, they especially enjoy watching people move about the room.

■*Three months.* Babies turn their head in response to a voice. They now want companionship as well as physical care.

■*Four months.* Babies laugh aloud. They look to others for entertainment.

■*Five months.* Babies' interest in family members other than parents increases. They may cry when left alone in a room. At this age, babies babble to their toys or themselves.

■*Six months.* Babies love company and attention. They delightedly play games like "peek-a-boo" and "pat-a-cake."

■*Seven months.* Babies prefer parents over other family members or strangers.

■*Eight months.* Babies are beginning to creep. They prefer to be in a room with others. Parents should provide a safe environment and encourage their baby to explore.

■*Nine and ten months.* Babies are quite socially advanced. They creep after their parents and are often underfoot. At this age, babies love attention. They enjoy being chased and like to throw toys and have them picked up so they can throw them again.

■*One year.* Babies are most often friendly and happy. They are also sensitive to the emotions of others. They know how to influence and adjust to others' emotions. At one year, babies like to be the center of attention. They like to play games with the family and are usually tolerant of strangers.

Attachment

At about six months of age, a baby comes to understand that he or she is a separate person. The baby then works to develop a special, strong **attachment** to parents or other major caregivers. This relationship is a strong emotional bond, but also represents the baby's first real social relationship.

Researchers have discovered that physical contact is an important factor in this attachment. In a famous experiment, Harry Harlow offered baby monkeys a choice of two substitute "mothers." The first was merely a body made of chicken wire. The second was similar, but was covered with soft cloth. A feeding bottle could be attached to either one.

In the experiment, some of the babies were "fed" only by the wire "mother." But all the monkeys clung to the cloth-covered form between feedings. Clearly, the monkeys needed the feeling of physical closeness, not just food. But none of the baby monkeys raised by substitute "mothers" developed normal social relationships. They did not know how to relate well to others. Harlow believed this was due to lack of interaction between the babies and "mothers."

Human babies, of course, are quite different from monkeys. But such research does give some possible clues to social development. Interaction with adults seems critical to human development as well.

All babies need lots of love. Even very young babies experience loneliness. If a baby is left alone most of the time except for physical care, the infant begins to fail to respond to people or objects.

This problem happens frequently in some institutions for children. These children are given physical care, but no emotional support or social practice. They may start out as normal, demanding babies. However, if they get little attention or encouragement from caregivers, their cries weaken, their smiles fade, and they turn inward.

This also happens in some babies with families. Impersonal, infrequent care results in withdrawn and unresponsive attitudes. Children are emotionally crippled when they have no one to love and nobody to love them. As they grow up, they lack the ability to form normal social relationships with others.

Social relationships are important for many animals as well as for humans. A famous example is Koko the gorilla's attachment to her favorite kitten.

In extreme cases, babies can die from a lack of love. This mysterious condition of young infants is known as **marasmus** (muh-RAZ-muhs)—the Greek word for "wasting." It usually strikes babies between the ages of six and twelve months. For no apparent reason, such a baby completely stops eating. Weight loss is rapid. The infant will die unless treated promptly.

In the past, most cases of marasmus occurred only in institutions in which children were routinely neglected. However, it is becoming increasingly common in modern homes where parents think they are taking good care of their baby. The parents are often intelligent, efficient, and very neat. They give their baby everything except what is most important—love and attention. Once the parents understand that spending time with the baby is much more important than keeping the house immaculately clean, or anything else, the problem is soon solved.

Stranger Anxiety

One obvious signal of attachment and social development occurs at about age eight months. A baby who used to sit cheerfully on anyone's lap suddenly screams when an unfamiliar person approaches. This is called **stranger anxiety**.

Stranger anxiety occurs because a baby's memory has improved. The child is better able to remember parents' faces. They are the ones who give comfort and security. Most other faces suddenly seem strange and cause fear.

Babies who often go places with parents or have regular contact with other people seem to have less stranger anxiety. But all normal babies go through this stage to some degree. It's a sign of social development.

Improved memory allows older babies to realize whether they are in familiar place with familiar people. Stranger anxiety may be less of a problem if the child is given opportunities to grow used to being around others.

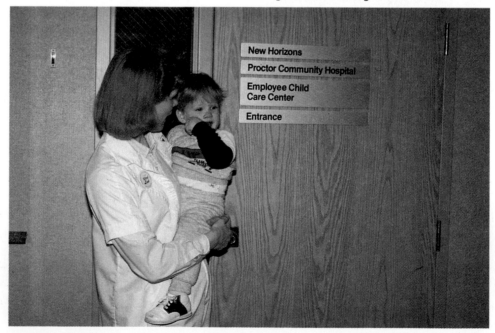

New Horizons
Proctor Community Hospital
Employee Child Care Center
Entrance

To a very young child, everything is meant to be explored and played with. Only gradually does the child learn that not all behavior results in praise or approval.

How Behavior Is Learned

An infant learns to behave in certain ways through relationships with others. The behavior learned depends mainly on the expectations and attitudes of those who provide care.

Babies learn some behavior through their daily routine. Running water may signal bath time or the rattle of keys may mean a ride in the car. A baby begins to respond to these clues with predictable behavior.

As babies mature, they learn that certain kinds of behavior are rewarded by such things as smiles or praise. Because love is very important to them, they begin to repeat behavior that brings approval. Babies also learn that negative behavior provokes punishment. This may be a frown, a scolding, or perhaps physical punishment.

Babies are sensitive to attitudes before they learn the words to describe them. For example, if a mother says "No" as her ten-month-old blows food all over, yet laughs at the same time, the baby thinks she approves.

Consistency—acting in the same way repeatedly—is necessary for a child to identify the behavior expected by parents. If a baby gets approval sometimes and punishment other times for the same behavior, this inconsistency confuses the child. Children react best to definite expectations. Parents who are always changing their mind or switching moods make learning good behavior more difficult.

What is Personality?

Personality is the total of all the specific traits (such as shyness or cheerfulness) that are consistent in an individual's behavior. To be consistent, the characteristic must be present over a period of time and in a variety of activities. We may say, for example, that babies who always pick themselves up after a tumble and try again are determined or persistent.

There are many personality traits. Each trait can have many degrees. For example, a person might be described as somewhat shy or very shy. With all the possible traits and all the degrees of each, you can see why no two people are exactly alike!

Influences on Personality

Some personality traits seem to be inborn. If you observed a group of newborns for a few weeks, you would see striking differences. Linda is very active when she is awake. She waves her arms and legs and squirms constantly. Jeremy is quite different. He cries at the slightest change in his surroundings. Arturo rarely cries except when he is hungry.

Every baby seems to have a unique way of reacting to the world. Inborn differences may be part of the reason, but environment has a great deal of influence.

Of course, family and environment also play a role in shaping a child's personality. Children tend to identify with or pattern themselves after parents. They adopt some of the parents' likes and dislikes, their interests, and their ideas. Children may imitate their parents' mannerisms and share many of their attitudes.

A wide range of personality is possible within the same family. Why? Part of the reason is that each child has a unique heredity pattern and responds in different ways to the same environment. But in addition, the environment is slightly different for each child. Each will be influenced by the various ways relatives and friends feel about, speak to, and treat him or her. Maybe the youngster is the oldest or youngest in the family. It is not the same, is it? Parents' attitudes change as they grow older and become more skilled at parenting. Therefore each child has different experiences.

How children feel about themselves—their **self-concept**—also influences personality. Janie's parents constantly compare her to her older sister, Cynthia. Janie feels she isn't as pretty, as smart, or as loved as Cynthia. Janie's shyness is related to her poor self-concept.

This does not mean, however, that a child's personality is completely determined by others. A child who finds his or her noisy home irritating may consciously strive as an adult to create a quiet home. Harsh, domineering parents may have children who purposely guide their own children with more understanding and affection. Generally, however, home, experiences, and self-concept greatly influence a child's personality.

Common Personality Patterns

No two personality traits necessarily go together. We may think that timid people are always unhappy, but this is not necessarily true. Not all shy people are unhappy, nor are all outgoing people happy.

However, it is true that certain characteristics do appear together frequently. This is why we tend to classify people by certain general personality patterns. Activity and behavior during the first months of life do not necessarily predict adult personality. However, understanding common personality patterns can help you care for children more effectively.

The Sensitive Child

Children who might be classified as **sensitive** are more aware of their surroundings and changes in them than other children. A sensitive child is often fussy and irritable as a baby. Babies who cry a great deal need more than the average amount of love and tenderness. Unfortunately, they often produce the opposite response in parents.

The baby who is easily startled and frightened is likely to become fearful of new experiences. Parents should encourage this type of baby to explore and try new things, but should minimize failure. Understanding parents will choose first toys that are easy to hold. A good choice would be a ring of plastic keys that is easily grasped. A bright ball that slips from small hands and rolls out of sight would not be as good. When the baby tries to stand and walk while holding onto furniture, a row of chairs is less likely to tip over than a single chair.

Parents need to be patient and understanding. Establishing self-confidence early in life will help the child through later frustrations.

The Placid Child

The **placid** child is the easiest personality type to live with. Placid babies are easygoing. They are less easily upset by changes in schedule and the demands of family life than any other personality type.

When older, a placid child is usually cheerful and patient or simply quiet and willing. Placid children adjust easily to new people and situations. They make friends readily and seem to handle life with a minimum of fuss and upset.

The sensitive child needs more reassurance when introduced to new situations.

Sandra seems content to examine a toy while she waits for her snack. How would you describe her personality?

Aggressive children are more willing to explore and try new things, but they are also more determined to have their own way.

The Aggressive Child

From birth, an **aggressive** baby seems strong-willed and determined. When awake, such babies are constantly active. Their responses are extreme. They eat more heartily, cry more loudly, and kick more strenuously than placid or sensitive babies.

Aggressive babies love activity. They try new things and are less likely to be concerned about failure. They simply pick themselves up and try again.

Aggressive children do, however, often get angry when they do not get their own way. It is best to ignore such outbursts.

Such children need love and praise. They also need to be made aware of the feelings and interests of others.

Do Boys and Girls Have Inborn Emotional Differences?

If someone handed you a diapered newborn, could you tell whether it was a boy or a girl? It's unlikely. But people tend to "see" in a baby what they expect to see. According to research, most parents perceive boy and girl babies differently. They continue to handle them differently, punish them differently, and make different demands as the children grow.

In an experiment at Tufts University, psychologists asked thirty mothers and fathers to describe their newborn babies soon after birth. The parents of girls described them as tiny, soft, and delicate. Boys were described as strong, alert, and well-coordinated.

Many mothers report distinct emotional differences in their babies. Boys are more often described as active and energetic, girls as passive and feminine. However, at least in some cases, cultural expectations subtly condition mothers to expect their babies to have these characteristics.

Many researchers believe that sex roles are learned rather than inborn. From infancy, boys and girls are subject to influences that help them develop characteristics viewed as appropriate to their sex. Parents, whether consciously or not, reinforce these differences. Girl babies are fussed with, hovered over, and their clothes are arranged more. They are likely to be handled more gently or protectively. Boy babies are allowed more freedom and activity.

Often the tone of voice people use implies femininity or masculinity. Softer, cooing tones are used with baby girls. For boys, the tone is often matter-of-fact or authoritative. Have you noticed how often people say, "What a nice, big boy!" whether the baby is big or not?

It is most important to remember the emotional characteristics of the individual rather than a stereotyped idea of what a male or female should be like. Dr. John Money, a researcher at Johns Hopkins Hospital, stated, "We're used to talking about the differences between sexes, but we must also learn to talk about the differences within the sexes." There are as many differences among girls and among boys as between girls and boys.

At this point, it is not known to what extent emotional differences are inborn and to what extent they are learned. Check your library for the latest research findings.

Check Your Understanding

1. How does a baby's physical development affect his or her social development?

2. How does consistency on the part of parents or caregivers affect how an infant learns behavior? Give an example.

3. Compare the types of toys and activities a sensitive child might enjoy to the types an aggressive child would enjoy.

Chapter Review

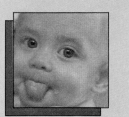

To Sum Up

- Emotional development deals with feelings. Social development deals with relationships.
- The type of care a baby receives and the atmosphere of the home are major influences on emotional development.
- Babies' emotions gradually become more specific and recognizable.
- Babies develop socially to satisfy their physical and emotional needs.
- Physical closeness, interaction, and a strong attachment to caregivers are necessary for normal development.
- Behavior is learned through relationships with others. Consistency on the part of caregivers aids this process.
- Each baby has an individual personality although general personality patterns can be identified.

To Review and Remember

1. Define both emotional and social development.
2. Why can't emotional and social development be separated?
3. Why is it important to build trust in infancy?
4. Give an example of how emotions change during infancy.
5. What initially prompts a baby's social development?
6. What is marasmus? How does it relate to attachment?
7. Why does a nine-month-old baby act differently toward strangers than a two-month-old does?
8. Define personality and name three influences on it.
9. Define self-concept.
10. Describe the characteristics of a placid child.

To Discuss and Discover

1. Discuss how a physical problem such as deafness or blindness could affect a baby's emotional and social development.
2. Collect pictures of infants that show various emotions. Analyze them in terms of the pictures on pages 192-193. Mount and label the pictures with the emotions and explain why you think each child is expressing that particular emotion.
3. List as many adjectives as you can to describe a person of each of the three general personality types discussed in this chapter.

8 Intellectual Development During the First Year

To help you to . . .

- Give examples of signs of intellectual growth in infants.
- Describe how a baby learns.
- Identify and give examples of Piaget's stages of learning.
- Discuss ways parents and caregivers can help babies' intellectual growth.
- Identify toys appropriate for a baby's age.
- Explain how babies develop communication skills.

Terms to Learn

attention span	cortex	perception
cause and effect	egocentric	preoperational
central nervous	formal operations	period
system	period	sensorimotor period
concrete operations	object permanence	symbolic thinking
period		

ewborn babies appear to be helpless. They depend on parents and other caregivers for food, shelter, and clothing. They even need someone to turn them over.

However, you already know that newborns do have a number of capabilities. They can hear, taste, smell, feel, and see. Right from birth, infants use these abilities as the building blocks of learning.

Newborns follow pleasant sights and sounds with their eyes. They move their bodies in rhythm to people's voices. They will even imitate an adult's facial expression! If the mother sticks out her tongue at her baby, the baby soon does the same. You might say that infants are focused on learning.

Understanding Intellectual Development

Researchers still do not fully understand the complex process of learning. They have, however, discovered much about how quickly and efficiently infants learn. Understanding the basics of the learning process will help you care for babies more effectively.

Think again about the differences between a newborn and a one-year-old. The newborn knows virtually nothing. The one-year-old, however, has an impressive store of knowledge. At age one the child can:

- Move to a desired location by creeping or walking.
- Understand some words and perhaps speak a few.
- Make his or her wants known, primarily by gestures.
- Play simple games such as peek-a-boo.
- Handle objects skillfully and do things with them, such as put one inside another.

Each of these actions is a sign of significant intellectual development. How does it happen?

Learning takes place very rapidly as infants develop new skills and explore their world.

The Mind-Body Connection

Newborns learn about the world primarily through their senses—sight, hearing, smell, taste, and touch. The blanket is soft and fuzzy. A fist or finger tastes different than milk. Mother's heartbeat sounds familiar.

Information moves from the senses through the nerves and spinal cord to the brain. This pathway is called the **central nervous system**.

The brain is the key to intellectual development. It receives and interprets the messages from the body. Gradually, it also sends messages to the body to tell it what to do. (The responses of newborns are mainly reflexes, not signs of real intelligence.)

The brain is divided into distinct sections, each controlling specific functions. By the second or third month, the baby's **cortex**—the outer layer of the brain which permits more complex learning—is better developed. **Perception**—learning from the senses—improves, too.

Memory is also beginning. The information from the senses can be crudely interpreted in light of past experiences. Babies may stop crying when someone enters the room because they know they are likely to be picked up and comforted. This simple act also indicates association. The baby associates parents and comfort.

Each area of the brain has specific functions to perform.

CEREBRUM: Receives information from the senses and directs motor activities. Controls such functions as speech, memory, and problem solving. Most of these activities occur in the outer layer of the cerebrum called the **cortex**.

THALAMUS: Connects the spinal cord and cerebrum. Controls expression of emotions.

CEREBELLUM: Controls muscular coordination and balance.

PITUITARY GLAND: Secretes hormones that regulate growth, metabolism, and sexual development.

SPINAL CORD: Transmits information and messages to and from the brain.

BRAIN STEM: Controls involuntary activities such as breathing, heart rate, and blood pressure.

Understanding **cause and effect** is another basic aspect of learning. When babies close their eyes, it gets dark. When they open them, it gets light. A baby can reach out a hand and feel a soft, warm surface. Sucking causes milk to flow. But if the baby stops sucking, the milk stops. In short, when the infant does something, something else happens and it happens consistently. Gradually, the baby develops some awareness of such control.

As babies' motor skills develop, cause and effect learning changes. By seven or eight months, they find they can deliberately throw things. Pulling the string on a toy will make it move. At this age babies better understand that they have the power to make some things happen. What are some other common infant behaviors that depend on this understanding?

Babies' **attention span**—how long they do something before they get bored—gives valuable information. A lessening of response when the same objects are presented over and over again indicates how quickly the baby loses interest. It is as if the infant were saying, "That's old stuff. I've seen it before." The sooner the child gets bored, the brighter the child usually is. It also indicates how rapidly the baby learns. (Note: Beyond infancy, bright children have a longer attention span than other children.)

Average Intellectual Development
Birth to Twelve Months

One to Two Months

- Follows moving objects with eyes.
- Gains information through senses.
- Prefers faces to objects.
- Cries to indicate needs.
- Can distinguish between familiar voices.

Three to Four Months

- Recognizes caregivers' faces.
- May show fear of strangers.
- Grasps objects that touch hand.
- Tries to swipe at objects.
- Interested in own hands and feet.
- Practices making sounds.
- Responds when caregiver talks.
- Smiles and laughs.

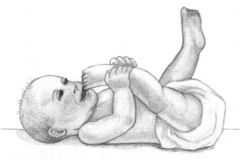

Five to Six Months

- Is alert for periods up to two hours.
- Reaches and grabs objects.
- Studies objects carefully.
- Looks for objects that are dropped.
- Plays peek-a-boo.
- Recognizes own name.
- Distinguishes between friendly and angry voices.
- Indicates pleasure and displeasure with sounds.

Seven to Eight Months

- Imitates the actions of others.
- Understands cause and effect.
- Remembers things that have happened.
- Smiles at self in mirror.
- Sorts objects by size.
- Solves simple problems.
- Recognizes some words.
- Babbling imitates inflections of speech.

Nine to Ten Months

- Searches for hidden objects.
- Handles medium-size objects skillfully.
- Takes objects out of containers and puts them in.
- Plays pat-a-cake.
- Responds to some words.
- May say a few words.
- Obeys simple commands or directions.

Eleven to Twelve Months

- Handles objects skillfully.
- Like to look at picture books.
- Fits blocks or boxes inside one another.
- Knows parts of body.
- Can pick up small objects.
- Recognizes many words.
- Speaks some words regularly.

Piaget's Theories

Jean Piaget, a Swiss psychologist, greatly influenced what we know about how children learn. His theories of learning and the research they inspired have helped us better understand and appreciate infants and children.

While investigating the development of intelligence, Piaget found that children's responses fell into patterns according to their age. This timetable seemed to control the development of intellectual skills. Piaget believed it suggested that the capacity for logical thought is not learned, but is determined—along with eye color and sex—in the genes. These capacities do not mature, however, unless they are used.

Children cannot be forced by parents or teachers to develop understanding any faster than their abilities mature. This is why it is a waste of effort to try to teach most two-year-olds to read. On the other hand, children who do not get the chance to apply their developing abilities and test their limitations may never reach their full intellectual ability.

According to Piaget, learning stages appear in the same order in all children. What differs is the age at which the stages develop, although average ages can be given. He identified four major periods of development from infancy through adolescence.

The Sensorimotor Period

The first learning stage is what Piaget called the **sensorimotor period**. This usually lasts from birth until about two years of age. Babies learn through their senses and actions during this stage. They are completely **egocentric**—they think only about themselves.

When a toy is held out of sight, this infant simply finds a new interest. Later the baby will learn to look for objects when they "disappear."

It is during the sensorimotor period (at about ten months) that a baby learns the important concept of **object permanence**. This means the child understands that an object continues to exist, even if it is removed from sight. At four months, Maria drops her rubber ring toy and it rolls behind her. She shows no concern. She just looks for something else to play with. But at eleven months, Maria's memory has improved a great deal. When her ball rolls out of sight, she actively looks for it. She looks for her favorite stuffed animal when she feels lonely. It is clear that she has learned the concept of object permanence.

The sensorimotor period can actually be broken down into shorter stages. At each stage, a baby has specific intellectual abilities. The chart on page 212 explains the stages within the sensorimotor period. It will help you better understand how early learning occurs.

The Preoperational Period

Usually, the **preoperational period** lasts from about the age of two to seven. Children think about everything in terms of their own activities and what they see and hear at the moment. They may believe that the moon follows them around, or that dreams fly in through the window at night. A child this age may think that water becomes "more to drink" when it is poured from a short, wide glass into a tall, thin one. To the child, it looks like the water is higher in the second glass, so there must be more of it.

Children in the preoperational period love to act out situations like playing house. However, they have trouble thinking about things that they aren't experiencing at the moment.

The Sensorimotor Period

Birth to Age Two

Stage	Approximate Ages	Characteristics
STAGE 1	Birth to one month	■ Applies reflexes. ■ Does not understand self as separate person.
STAGE 2	One to four months	■ Combines reflexes. ■ Develops hand-mouth coordination.
STAGE 3	Four to eight months	■ Acts intentionally to produce results. ■ Improves eye-hand coordination.
STAGE 4	Eight to twelve months	■ Begins to solve problems. ■ Finds partially hidden objects. ■ Imitates others.
STAGE 5	Twelve to eighteen months	■ Finds hidden objects. ■ Explores and experiments. ■ Understands that objects exist independently.
STAGE 6	Eighteen to twenty-four months	■ Solves problems by thinking. ■ Can think symbolically. ■ Begins imaginative thinking.

Pretending and imitating are the tools that young children use to understand their world.

In the preoperational period, children begin to understand abstract terms like "love" and "beauty." Concentration, though, is limited to one thing at a time. The child cannot think about both pain and the softness of a kitten at the same time, for example. Most problems are solved by pretending or imitating rather than thinking them through. You can observe many examples of this "pretending" behavior in children this age. Many times the child is not even aware of what is real and what is make-believe.

The Concrete Operations Period

The learning stage from about seven to eleven years is called the **concrete operations period**. Thinking processes are noticeably improved, although the child still learns best through direct experience. Problem-solving still relies on actually being able to see or experience the problem. However, logical thinking is possible. Children understand that pouring water from one container to another does not change the amount. They can also comprehend that the operations can be reversed. For example, subtraction will "undo" addition and division is the opposite of multiplication. It is also during this stage that children learn to classify objects into categories.

The Formal Operations Period

During the **formal operations period**, which begins at about age eleven and continues throughout adulthood, children become capable of abstract thinking. In other words, they can think about what might happen or what might have been the cause without really experiencing it. This allows problem-solving just by thinking. Abstract thinking also allows adolescents to make more realistic future plans and goals. They do not automatically accept everything that is said or read, but think things through critically first. Adolescents can also form ideals and understand double meanings.

The abstract concept of "three" has no meaning for a young child unless it is associated with something concrete—like three balls or three fingers.

Applying Piaget's Ideas

While Piaget's theories have been criticized by some for setting boundaries of learning stages too rigidly, his work revolutionized our understanding of child development. He focused attention on intellectual development of the infant, an area of study previously ignored. He drew attention to the importance of developmental steps that researchers continue to study today.

To summarize, Piaget has shown that adult intelligence has its origins in infancy. But his work also shows that attempts to impose adult ideas or understanding on children are bound to fail. Why? Older children and adults can learn through **symbolic thinking**—using words and numbers to represent ideas. However, "I have three red balls" means nothing to a small child. The child has to see the balls. That is also why a three-year-old will hold up three fingers when asked how old he or she is, even though the child may say the words, too. The preschool child needs lessons presented with objects or activities, not just symbols. Verbal instruction from a teacher or parent has only a minor role in the early years.

Heredity vs. Environment

In Chapter 1 you read that not everyone agrees whether heredity or environment has more influence on development. Much of this debate focuses on intelligence. In the past, intellectual ability was thought to be mainly determined by a child's inheritance—bright parents had bright children. But findings now indicate that a child's environment can actually increase or decrease intelligence.

It is true, however, that limits for intelligence are present at birth. A child may have the best environment and the finest education, but even this cannot turn a person of low or average mental ability into a genius. Most people, though, never develop or use their full potential (the highest level of learning possible for them). You have probably felt at times that with more effort you could make better use of your talents.

Check Your Understanding

1. Explain why two crying babies— one a week old and the other three months old—would respond differently to a parent entering the room.

2. Explain how motor skill development contributes to cause and effect learning.

3. Babies are described as being egocentric. What does this mean? Give an example.

4. Why are heredity and environment both important to a child's intellectual development?

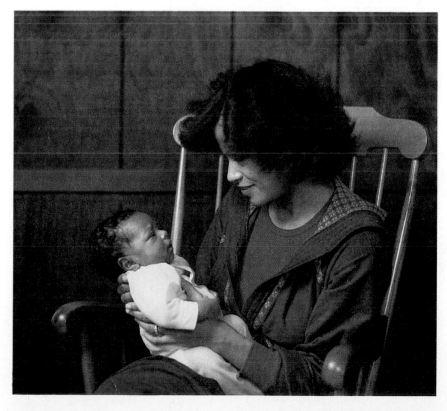

Both heredity and environment influence intelligence. The influence of heredity is determined before birth. Environmental influences begin before birth, but continue to affect development throughout life.

Babies who receive loving care and attention are more likely to approach their full potential, in learning as well as in other areas of development.

Children learn a great deal just by interacting with parents and caregivers.

Helping Babies Learn

The intellectual development of an infant is closely linked to the responsiveness of others. That is, babies learn more and learn faster when caregivers comfort them, smile at them, talk to them, and play with them. A baby treated this way is likely to be brighter than a similar child who does not receive loving, attentive care. Parents are babies' first and most important teachers.

Providing Care

If a newborn is hungry, the baby expresses that feeling by crying. Most parents respond by picking up, talking to, and feeding the baby. The uncomfortable hunger goes away. If parents do this whenever the baby feels hungry and cries, the infant soon learns that these things are related. There is a consistent pattern—discomfort, crying, parent, feeding, and comfort.

However, some infants never learn this way. Perhaps their crying is usually ignored. Or they may be fed on a strict schedule decided by someone else and not related to the baby's own sensations. There is no predictable pattern for the baby to learn.

When babies learn that their behavior has consequences, that they can affect and change their environment, they are motivated to learn.

Encouraging Learning

Those who care for children have a real influence on their intellectual development. Encouraging children to learn does not require money or special toys. It depends on the knowledge and time of parents and other caregivers. Here are some specific suggestions for encouraging learning:

- **Learn about child development.** When you understand how an average child develops, it is easier to provide learning experiences that are appropriate for a child. A young baby, for example, needs information for the senses.

- **Give your time and attention.** No baby needs attention every waking hour. But when an adult talks to and plays with a baby, learning takes place more quickly. Pages 232–233 suggest simple games you can play with babies.

- **Provide positive feedback.** When a baby accomplishes a skill or even tries something new, respond with praise. This encourages the child to try again.

- **Express your love.** Babies who feel loved are more self-confident. They are more likely to try new things.

See page 220 for additional ways to promote intellectual development.

Providing an Environment for Learning

It's not difficult to provide an environment that encourages learning. It just takes a bit of know-how.

Think again about the child's stage of development. Bright colors, objects that are easy to grasp, and music are just a few basic tools for stimulating a baby's senses. Pages 228–229 give specific ideas for creating a stimulating environment for babies of different ages.

In the home, allow the child as much freedom of movement as possible. In the first few months, this may mean moving the baby from room to room to be with the family. A baby kept in a crib most of the time rarely sees anything new. Older babies who can crawl or walk should not be restricted to playpens for long periods of time. It is better to make as much of the home as possible "childproof" and monitor the child's activities. Learning occurs best when children can explore and try new things. The chart on page 221 gives tips for checking a home for infant safety.

Remember that a baby's environment should go beyond the home. Trips to the store, a walk to the park, or a ride in the car all provide stimulation and learning.

Close-up

Jim and Heather Grant's first baby, Jeremy, was eight months old. The Grants were a bit nervous about parenthood. The shelf in their bedroom was filled with books on child development and parenting. It was easy to tell from the books' well-worn pages that they were consulted frequently.

When Heather and Jim took Jeremy to Dr. Lopez for a checkup, their concern about his development was obvious. Jim said, "Jeremy seems happy enough and is now walking, but we're worried that he is slow for his age intellectually. The development charts in all the books say he should be recognizing words and imitating what we do. But he's still at the stage of putting toys in his mouth — not really *doing* anything with them."

Heather added, "We've signed up with a company that sends an educational toy each month. They're geared to the baby's abilities at that age. Jeremy's development should be above average, not below."

Dr. Lopez had met many anxious parents in her years as a pediatrician. She assured the Grants that Jeremy was developing well. "You need to look at Jeremy's development as a whole, not at intellectual development all by itself. At this age, there's a very strong interrelationship among all the areas of development."

"You mentioned that Jeremy is walking. He is months ahead of 'average' babies in that regard. Sometimes babies put all their energy for a time into learning one skill. Other skills seem to lag behind for a while, but the baby soon catches up. Remember, too, in infancy physical abilities are often a good indication of intelligence."

"Educational toys," continued Dr. Lopez, "are no guarantee of a boost in intelligence. In fact, some aren't even appropriate for the age level indicated on the package. For the most part, a baby learns just as much from simple household items, like clothespins and empty plastic containers. But the best way for you to help Jeremy's intellectual development is to spend time with him. Talk to him. Play with him. Take him places with you. And relax. If you stop worrying about his development, you'll enjoy him more. I check for normal development every time I see him and I will let you know if there are any problems."

What factors seemed to contribute to the Grants' concern about Jeremy's development?

How could the Grants learn to feel more secure about their parenting skills? ■

Take a look at everything that is going on in this scene. What sights, sounds, smells, and other sensations did the child experience that day? How does taking a child to new places enrich learning?

Tips for Promoting Intellectual Development

Dos

- **DO** provide access to as much of the home as possible so the child can exercise curiosity and explore the surroundings. Check areas for safety first.
- **DO** provide a wide range of materials for the child to explore. Plastic jars with covers, large containers filled with interesting objects, a kitchen cabinet with pots, pans, and canned goods are all fine for a child 7–18 months of age.
- **DO** be sure the child has a caring adult to interact with at least half of the child's waking hours.
- **DO** respond as promptly as possible to a child's needs.
- **DO** respond favorably as often as possible.
- **DO** make an effort to understand what the child is trying to do.
- **DO** set limits.
- **DO** provide encouragement and enthusiasm.
- **DO** use words as often as possible. Choose words the child understands or ones that will help the child learn.
- **DO** encourage make-believe or "pretend" activities.
- **DO** provide things to do if the child seems bored.
- **DO** give assistance when needed.

Don'ts

- **DON'T** rely on prolonged use of such things as playpens and jumpseats. Research shows that regular confinement is associated with poor development.
- **DON'T** worry that the child will not love you if you say "no" from time to time. Accepting limits is an important part of learning.
- **DON'T** stifle a baby's curiosity to keep the home neat.
- **DON'T** be overprotective. Babies are more cautious than people think.
- **DON'T** overpower the child. Babies should be allowed to do what they want as often as possible.
- **DON'T** worry about when the child should learn to read, count, say the alphabet, or even talk. As long as the baby seems to understand more and more language, development is normal.
- **DON'T** try to force learning with "lessons" or many special educational toys. Learning will occur naturally with good care.

Checklist for Home Safety

Infants

√ Cribs and safety gates meet new requirements for narrower space between bars.

√ Plastic bags are never used on cribs or anywhere accessible to the baby.

√ Unused electrical outlets have safety covers. Electrical cords are secured or kept out of the baby's reach.

√ Stairs are kept off limits with safety gates or closed doors.

√ All toys are inspected for small or loose parts which could be swallowed. All small objects are kept out of reach.

√ When an infant seat or high chair is used, the baby is strapped in securely.

√ The baby is never left alone in a bath or on a bed or other high surface.

√ Once the baby begins to walk, loose rugs and tippable furniture are removed.

√ Cleaning supplies, medications, and other poisons are kept well out of reach.

√ Windows have locks and safety latches.

√ The baby is not allowed to move freely in the kitchen when meals are being prepared.

√ Items with sharp or pointed edges are not used as toys.

Toys — The Tools of Learning

Ten-month-old Beth sits on the kitchen floor thumping a spoon against the bottom of a saucepan. She has discovered her own "educational toy." With it she learns that a certain action will produce a particular sound. If she repeats that sound often enough and loudly enough, she may also learn that adults do not always enjoy the same sounds that delight children!

For children, play is work as well as pleasure. Researchers have found that playtime is not aimless or wasted. It is essential to intellectual development. Toys are the tools with which a child learns. Toys do not have to be expensive, but they should have a purpose.

Play is also a physical necessity through which growth and development take place. When you see a baby shake a rattle, stack blocks, throw a ball, or chew on a magazine, the activity is not just for amusement. These are serious, absorbing tasks through which babies strengthen muscles, refine motor skills, and learn about the world.

Different Toys for Different Ages

Because babies mature rapidly during their first year, their toy needs change, too. Here is a list of some appropriate toys for different stages:

- *Birth to three months.* A baby can do little except look and listen. Bright colors and interesting sounds stimulate development

Infants are just as happy to be playing with simple household objects like these as with expensive toys. Be sure, however, that all playthings are safe and suitable for the baby's age.

Books are fun to look at, even if you don't know how to read yet!

of the senses. A mobile hung above the crib is interesting to watch. Random arm and leg movements set the objects in motion and produce sounds. Brightly colored crib liners, wallpaper, and pictures also provide interest.

■*Four to six months.* The sense of touch is more important during this period. Babies need things to touch, handle, bang, shake, suck, and chew. Choose toys that are small enough to handle easily, but too large to swallow. All items and pieces should be at least 1½ in. (3.8 cm) in size. Teething rings, cups, rattles, and plastic toys are good choices. Stuffed toys are fun to touch. "Squeaker" toys give results for the baby's actions. At this age, babies like simple picture books. Choose washable ones with colorful pictures of familiar objects.

■*Seven to nine months.* Babies need things to handle, throw, pound, bang, and shake. Anything that makes a noise fascinates them. They enjoy blocks, balls, large plastic beads that pop apart, and roly-poly toys. Safe household items are just as interesting as real toys. Jar lids, pan covers, clothes-pins, and containers make great playthings. So do stacking toys.

■*Ten to twelve months.* Babies need things to creep after. Those who are walking like toys to push or pull. Children this age especially enjoy toys to manipulate. Provide baskets, boxes, or other containers. Babies like to put things in them and dump them out again. Simple books are good for looking at alone or brief storytimes before bed.

When choosing toys for a young child, look for ones that encourage participation and use. Younger children need simple toys. As abilities increase, toys can be more complex.

Close-up

Seven-month-old Tina sat in a stroller beside a park bench. Her mother was nearby, helping Tina's three-year-old sister and five-year-old brother play on the swings and slides.

Tina watched them from time to time, but she gave most of her attention to a red, plastic cup. Tina's mother had brought orange juice for a snack and gave Tina the cup to amuse herself while the older children were playing.

Tina turned the cup over and over, staring at it intently. She chewed on the bottom, the rim, and the handle. She would stop long enough to bang the cup on the stroller, then bring it back to her mouth. Tiring of that, Tina threw the cup on the ground. Immediately, she reached for it, straining, but the cup was out of reach. After several tries, Tina settled for a leaf from a bush nearby. The leaf promptly went into her mouth, but she immediately spit it out again.

Her eye caught the red cup again — and again she reached for it. Failing at that, she picked up a dry twig beside the stroller. She handled it, turned it, bit on it, and pounded it on the stroller, listening to the noise. The stick left dusty streaks on her cheeks and chubby fingers.

At that point, Tina decided she had been neglected long enough. Twisting in her stroller seat, she reached an arm toward her mother, protesting loudly. Her mother soon came to comfort her.

To an observer, all of this might have just seemed like another excursion to the park. But there was a remarkable amount of learning taking place. By the older children?

They were learning, too, of course, but probably not as much as seven-month-old Tina.

Make a list of Tina's learning experiences. Which stage of the sensorimotor period do they correspond to?
What toys did Tina use? ■

Toys are expensive, especially many "educational" toys. These special toys are not always good choices. You can often provide a baby with as much fun and learning with items from around the home.

When you do buy toys, consider ones which will remain interesting and appropriate for a number of years. A set of blocks is a good example:

- At six months Richard grasps and inspects his blocks.
- By his first birthday, he can stack several into a tower.
- At age three, they are used to make roads for his cars.
- At six, Richard creates elaborate houses and castles using every available block.

Richard's parents purchased his first blocks. Later they made more by cutting wood into shapes and sanding them smooth. Their efforts paid off in hours of fun and imaginative play.

Developing Communication Skills

One of the major tasks for infants is to learn to communicate effectively with others. This skill depends on development in all areas—physical, emotional, social, and intellectual. There are wide differences in the rate of development from baby to baby. However, a normal baby should show steady improvement in communication skills.

Communicating Without Words

Babies communicate long before they are able to talk. By the end of the first year, even without words, they can effectively make most of their needs and wants known.

Crying is a baby's first means of communication. Discomfort automatically causes crying. Someone usually responds to the baby's cries and attempts to relieve the discomfort. Within a month or so, the baby's crying takes on a pattern. A cry is followed by a pause to listen for reactions. If none is obvious, the baby resumes crying.

The baby soon develops different cries for different problems. A cry indicating hunger is interrupted by sucking movements. A cry of pain includes groans and whimpers. Those providing care can identify the problem by the type of cry.

A baby also communicates by sounds. Some noises just provide practice in use of the voice. The nonsense syllables of babbling, for example, help the baby learn to make sounds needed for speech. Others like giggles, grunts, and shrieks carry obvious messages.

Babies also communicate effectively with gestures. It's clear a wiggling baby just does not want to get dressed. An eleven-month-old who pushes the bowl of peaches to the floor is full. And a baby attached to a parent's leg is a sure sign of fear or shyness. The use of gestures continues into adulthood, but they are used more to reinforce words than as a substitute for them.

Learning to Speak

Before babies can learn to talk, they must learn to associate meanings with words. This is a gradual process. It depends on caregivers talking to a baby, even when the baby doesn't respond. When taking a baby for a walk, talk about what you see. Use simple words, but not baby talk. Tell the baby the names of everyday objects. Although the infant won't understand much of what you say, it is important to get into the habit. Listening to others talk—especially to them—is essential for infants' language development.

When you talk to an infant, you are laying a good foundation for the child's speech development.

As you learned in Chapter 6, a newborn is physically unable to speak. Over the first year the shape of the tongue and mouth change. Other speech organs also mature. These changes allow the baby to make the sounds necessary for speech.

Babbling—repeating syllables and sounds—helps babies get ready for real speech. You have probably heard babies endlessly repeating sounds like "mamamama" or "gogogo." Responding to babbling encourages the baby to continue.

A child's first real words are usually understandable sometime between eight and fifteen months. Because the infant has been babbling and coming close to real word sounds for some time, it isn't easy to know exactly when a specific word is purposely spoken. First words are usually common, simple ones like "mama," "dada," and "bye-bye." Most children don't have a large vocabulary or combine words into simple sentences until after their first birthday.

Check Your Understanding

1. How could a child of rich parents have a poor learning environment?

2. Describe the toys and activities that would appeal to a baby at each of the following ages: one month, six months, eight months, twelve months.

3. How can household items like pan lids, clothespins, and empty plastic containers be considered good educational toys for babies?

4. Describe the ways a baby communicates during the first year of life.

Baby's first words are among the events that parents look forward to the most.

Chapter Review

To Sum Up

- Babies first learn through their senses, but they gradually develop memory, learn cause and effect relationships, and develop a longer attention span.
- Jean Piaget, a Swiss psychologist, identified four periods of intellectual development.
- Both heredity and environment influence learning.
- An infant's intellectual development is linked to the responsiveness of others.
- Babies need a safe, stimulating environment for learning. Toys are tools for learning.
- Learning in the first year is a combination of intellectual ability and motor skill development.
- Communication skills depend on development in all areas—physical, emotional, social, and intellectual.

To Review and Remember

1. How do newborns learn about their world?
2. What is cause and effect learning? Give an example.
3. Name Piaget's stages of intellectual development and give the approximate ages at which each occurs.
4. What is object permanence? During which of Piaget's learning stages is this concept learned?
5. Why does a preschool child need lessons presented with objects or activities?
6. How does heredity influence intellectual development?
7. How does promptly caring for a baby's needs promote learning?
8. Why isn't it a good idea to keep a baby in a crib or playpen most of the time?
9. Why is play important for a baby?
10. Why should caregivers talk to babies?

To Discuss and Discover

1. Discuss why a newborn and a year-old baby learn differently. What factors influence what is learned and how it is learned at these ages?
2. List five commercial toys and five everyday objects that might be used as toys for babies. Evaluate each for safety and usefulness in development.
3. Read the section on the first year in Burton L. White's book *The First Three Years of Life.* What toys does Dr. White recommend for different stages during the first year? Why? What toys are popular, but not recommended? How can caregivers encourage learning?

Creating a Stimulating Environment

Babies begin learning from the moment they are born. Almost everything is new to them. An environment that offers a variety of experiences helps them use their natural learning abilities to the fullest. Here are some ideas for helping infants develop their senses and abilities.

A good learning environment can start from the first day. It is a natural part of providing loving care. Holding, cuddling, gentle stroking, and soft singing are ways to stimulate the senses. They also give the infant a message of love.

Give the baby new things to look at every now and then, but just one or two at a time. Babies like simple shapes and bright or contrasting colors. You can decorate the baby's room using colorful decals, posters, pictures, sheets, or wallpaper.

A mobile over the crib provides both color and movement. You can also hold a toy close to the baby's face and move it slowly, letting the baby's eyes follow it.

Infants like human faces even better than colorful objects or toys. Let the baby look into your eyes as you hold and play with him or her.

The caregiver's voice is the first sound a baby learns to recognize. Rattles and squeak toys introduce other types of sounds.

Babies especially enjoy music, whether it comes from a wind-up toy, a record, or a caregiver's singing. The rhythm of the music is soothing. So is the rhythm of being carried in someone's arms or being rocked in a rocking chair.

As babies begin to experiment with their voice, they soon learn that their sounds bring a response from an attentive caregiver. When you care for a baby, talk to him or her. Imitating each other's sounds can be fun for both of you. Reading to infants also helps them to become familiar with the sound of words.

Surrounding the baby with interesting things to touch also stimulates learning. Variety is more important than the number of toys. Stuffed toys can have different textures, ranging from furry teddy bears to simple beanbags. Different shapes encourage baby to touch, too. Empty spools, small plastic squeeze bottles, and empty plastic containers with lids are both educational and inexpensive.

A stimulating environment can help babies learn about their own movements. As the baby learns to reach and grasp, reinforce these skills by encouraging the baby to reach for a special toy. Objects, such as shiny spoons and colorful blocks, motivate the baby to examine things with the fingers. As large motor skills develop, caregivers can gently pull the baby up to sitting and standing positions, or hold a tiny hand while the baby takes those first hesitant steps.

Developing a Sense of Trust

In the first year, babies are almost entirely dependent on others. The kind of care they receive determines how they begin to view themselves and the world around them. The foundation of a strong, healthy self-concept is trust.

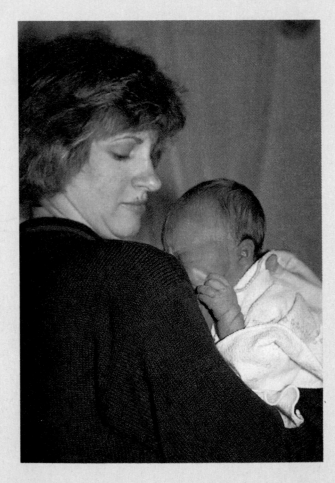

Responsive Care

A sense of trust begins to develop in newborns when they feel that their needs are being met. One of the most obvious ways to promote trust is to feed a baby who is hungry. Understanding and responding to the baby's emotional needs is just as important.

An infant who is upset or fussy needs to be soothed. But that doesn't mean you should ignore a baby who seems content. Here are some ways to let a baby know that you are responsive to his or her needs and wants:

- Hold and cuddle the baby often. Carry the baby with you as you walk around.
- When the baby is able to crawl, don't rely on a playpen. Give the baby the freedom to explore independently in a safe, accessible environment.
- Answer the baby's babbles and "funny noises" by talking back.
- Let the baby sense your caring and love in your facial expression, voice, and touch.
- Learn to read the baby's signals. Smiling and cooing can mean, "Let's play." Turning or looking away is the baby's way of saying, "That's enough — time to rest."
- Calm an unhappy baby with close contact, rhythmic movement, and soothing sounds.

Your responsive care will help the baby feel secure. It lets the baby know that the world can be a satisfying place.

Familiar Routines

Following a consistent schedule is another way to encourage the baby's sense of trust. Babies seem to need a predictable daily routine in order to thrive. Start with the baby's unique pattern of eating, sleeping, and waking. Then you can work out a routine that makes sense for you and the baby. For example, if you always change the baby after a feeding, the baby begins to learn what to expect. He or she will accept and look forward to that pattern of dependable care.

New Faces, New Places

Although it is important for babies to have a consistent routine, they must also learn to accept new situations. A trusted caregiver can soothe away fears and help the baby feel secure in unfamiliar surroundings.

Most babies go through a stage of fearing strangers. Don't force an infant to sit on an unfamiliar lap. Instead, give the baby some time to get used to the new person's presence. Stay close by and show that you trust this person.

You can help babies get used to strangers by taking them to stores and places where small children play. Talk to the baby about what to expect and what is happening. Speak in a calm, reassuring voice.

Babies who have been helped to develop a sense of trust are happy, loving, and secure. They have the confidence to explore and learn with enthusiasm.

Games to Play with Babies

Playing games can delight a baby and also stimulate all areas of development. Even very young babies can benefit from short play sessions. Choose times when the baby is happy and comfortable, not hungry or tired. Play should be fun for both of you. Here are some suggestions for games appropriate for different ages.

Looking Games

- **Funny faces.** Shake your head, stick out your tongue, make funny faces. Even babies a few days old often imitate facial expressions. (Birth-6 months)
- **Light games.** Shine a flashlight on the walls and ceiling of a darkened room. Make different designs by placing your fingers in front of the beam. (3 months and up)
- **Mirrors.** Sit with the baby in front of a mirror. Point to the infant's eyes, nose, mouth, and other features, naming each. Do the same with your own features. Eventually, the baby will also point and name them. (6-8 months)

Listening Games

- **Musical games.** Play music and nursery rhymes. Encourage the baby to respond by swaying or humming. (3 months and up)
- **Sound effects.** Give the baby paper to crackle, pie tins to clatter, blocks to bang together. Let the baby listen to your watch tick. (5-10 months)
- **What's that?** Record everyday sounds like running water, the washing machine, the doorbell. Play back and identify each sound for the baby. (5 months and up)
- **Mimic.** Make car noises, motorcycle noises, and other noises. See if the baby will mimic you. (11 months and up)

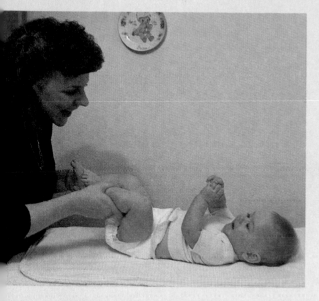

Baby Exercises

- **Bicycle.** Lay the baby face up, gently holding his or her ankles. Revolve the baby's legs as if riding a bike. (2 months and up)
- **Tug of war.** Give the baby large rings to grasp. Gently play tug of war. (3 months and up)
- **Airplane.** Playing airplane helps strengthen the back and neck muscles. Hold the baby just above the waist and lift up above your face. The baby's back will bend and arms and legs will stretch out. (4-5 months)

Old Favorites

- **Peek-a-boo.** Establish eye contact with the baby. Quickly turn your head, then turn back again saying "Peek-a-boo" (3-5 months). For older babies, cover your eyes, then uncover them and shout "Peek-a-boo!" Or cover the baby's eyes with a blanket briefly.
- **Hide and seek.** Make a toy disappear behind your back. Let the baby crawl to find it. Help the baby find toys you have hidden elsewhere. Or hide from the baby yourself, then reappear. (8 months and up)
- **Catch me.** Chase the baby. Then let the baby have a turn chasing you. (8 months and up)

The Child from One to Three

Chapter 9: Physical Development
Chapter 10: Emotional & Social Development
Chapter 11: Intellectual Development

A child one, two, or three years old can be described as struggling between the need to be babied and the need to be "grown up." This stage of development is the bridge between infancy and childhood. It is perhaps the most interesting stage of all.

Physically, growth in size is much slower than during the first year. Still, by the fourth birthday the child has undergone a remarkable change in appearance. And you will learn in Chapter 9 about the amazing number of physical skills that are mastered.

Children's feelings about themselves and others also change during this time, as do their ways of coping with these feelings. Chapter 10 discusses the recognizable stages of emotional and social development that most children go through. Have you ever heard of the "terrible twos," for example? Understanding the forces at work in this normal stage can help you handle the difficult behavior that often results.

By their first birthday, some children can say a few words. But by their fourth birthday—the end of this stage—children can think, remember, and speak quite well. Chapter 11 explores this fascinating progression. You will find out how learning takes place and how caregivers can encourage it.

Children this age are sometimes charming, sometimes frustrating, sometimes funny. But the more you know about them, the more you will agree that they are always interesting.

9 Physical Development from One to Three

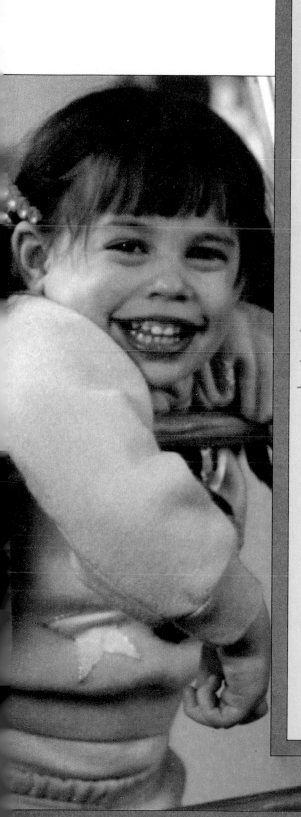

To help you to . . .

- Describe the changes in an average child's height, weight, posture, and proportion from ages one to three.

- Identify habits that influence tooth development and care.

- Distinguish between small and large motor skills and give examples of each.

- Plan meals appropriate for small children.

- Identify desirable characteristics in children's clothing.

- Describe common bedtime problems and how they can be minimized.

- Discuss the process of toilet training a child.

Terms to Learn

- circumference
- large motor skills
- manipulation
- natural fibers
- plaque
- small motor skills
- sphincter muscles
- synthetic fibers
- toddlers
- training pants

"**Y**ou weigh 30 pounds," Miss Mary said to Ellen as she lifted her off the scale. Ellen beamed.

"There, children. I wrote the height and weight for each of you on your charts. Now let's all sit down in our chairs," said Miss Mary.

The ten two-year-olds gathered around the little table at the day care center. They were very excited. Each of them was making a booklet to take home. First, they drew pictures of themselves. The teacher helped them learn the color of their hair and eyes. She wrote down their favorite colors and their favorite foods and she helped them staple the pages together.

"My daddy will like this 'Me Book,'" Ellen said. "I'm his favorite little girl!"

Physical Growth and Development

The time between the first and fourth birthdays is one of many physical changes. It is during this period that the transition from babyhood to childhood is made.

Actual physical growth slows considerably after the first year. However, the child's physical skills show dramatic improvement. Most children begin to walk a few unsteady steps about the time of their first birthday. (From this time until about age three, they are often called **toddlers**.) But by the time they turn four, they not only walk steadily, but can also hop, jump, and run. Similar advances are made in most other areas of physical development.

Height and Weight

Slower growth is apparent in both height and weight. Toddlers gain only about ½ lb. (0.2 kg) per month. That is less than half the average weight gain during the first year. Growth in height also slows by about half. The chart on page 239 shows average heights and weights of children one through three.

Hereditary and environmental influences on height and weight are more noticeable at this age. Children show more variation in size than before. Some are much larger than average, others much smaller. Height differences are particularly significant. A tall two-year-old will probably be a tall adult. An unusually short toddler will probably be shorter than average as an adult.

Proportion and Posture

Because of changes in proportion, posture also improves. Until age two, a child's head, chest, and abdomen all have about the same **circumference** (measurement around). Each grows at the same rapid rate. Between ages two and three, however, the chest becomes larger than the head and abdomen. There is rapid growth of the arms, legs, and lower body. These changes in proportion help improve balance and motor skills.

By two years of age, the child stands straighter. The abdomen still protrudes and the head is somewhat forward. Knees and elbows are still slightly bent.

By the third birthday, the toddler's posture is more upright. The spine has strengthened, so the back is straighter. The child has lost some baby fat.

Walking is related to growth and changes in posture.

Average Heights and Weights
Ages One to Three

Age	Height		Weight	
	Customary	Metric	Customary	Metric
1	29.8 in.	75.7 cm	22.5 lb.	10.2 kg
2	34.0 in.	86.4 cm	27.7 lb.	12.6 kg
3	37.7 in.	95.6 cm	32.4 lb.	14.7 kg

Changing proportions through out life are evident in this drawing. A newborn's head is relatively large compared to the body. As the child grows, the arms, legs, and trunk begin to catch up until the body takes on adult proportions.

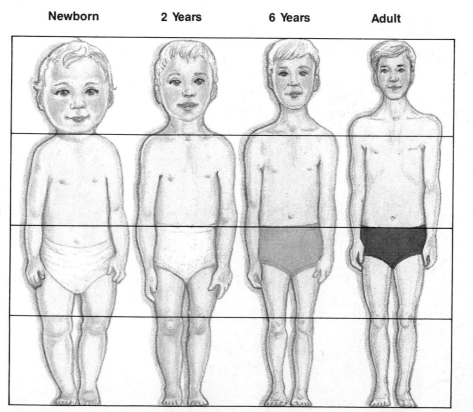

Newborn   **2 Years**   **6 Years**   **Adult**

Drinking plenty of milk helps build strong teeth that are more resistant to decay. What else influences the health of the teeth?

Teeth

One-year-olds have an average of eight primary teeth. Many children, however, have more or fewer. There is a great deal of variation. During the second year, eight more teeth come in. For most children, the last four back teeth emerge early in the third year. That makes a complete set of twenty primary teeth.

The quality of the teeth is greatly influenced by diet. The diet of the mother during pregnancy and of the infant during the first two years lay the foundation for a lifetime of good or poor teeth. Dairy products, which are rich in calcium and phosphorus, are especially beneficial. The vitamin D in milk also contributes to sound tooth and bone development. The American Dental Association has also endorsed the use of the mineral fluoride to minimize tooth decay. Fluoride helps harden the outer layer of teeth, called the enamel, and makes it more resistant to decay.

Heredity also appears to play a role in tooth quality. Dentists find that some children, even if they are very careful, still get cavities. Others get few, no matter how careless they are. This is because some people have inherited a protective mechanism that discourages decay. Dentists advise parents who have had many cavities themselves to be especially careful to teach their children good tooth care.

Tooth Decay

Tooth decay affects almost everyone at some time during life. Decay is caused by harmful bacteria in the mouth. The bacteria are constantly forming a sticky, colorless film called **plaque** (PLACK). The plaque reacts with leftover food particles and liquids in the mouth—especially sugar—to produce acids. These acids dissolve the hard tooth enamel and a cavity begins. The decay spreads throughout the tooth and gradually destroys it unless corrective measures are taken.

How can tooth decay be prevented? Diet is of major importance. The acids are produced immediately after eating. They remain active for about twenty minutes, or until saliva naturally cleanses the mouth. Several sweet snacks a day expose the teeth to a twenty-minute acid attack after each snack. Sweets (such as hard candy) that remain in the mouth for a long time and soft, sticky candies are particularly bad for the teeth. You can see it is better to avoid sweets. If they are eaten, it is best to have them with a meal or all at once to cut down on the acid-producing time. Parents who avoid the habit of giving their children sweets as treats will help them have fewer cavities.

Dentists feel another particularly bad children's food is sugar-coated cereal. The cereal sticks between the teeth. Unless the child brushes right away, cavities are more likely. Children who cannot brush after eating sweets should be taught to rinse out their mouth immediately after eating.

Although many children are given sweet treats on special occasions, parents should avoid making them part of the daily diet. Why?

Motor Skills

In Chapter 6 you studied the patterns of physical development. It proceeds from head to foot, near to far, and simple to complex.

When you compare the skills of children at age one and at the end of the third year, these patterns are easy to see. Hand skills are a good example. At thirteen months, a child only stacks about two blocks. By the fourth birthday, however, the same child uses blocks to make high towers, houses, and roads.

Motor skills are often divided into two types. **Large motor skills** are those that use the large muscles of the back, legs, shoulders, and arms. Walking, running, and throwing balls would all be examples of large motor skills. **Small motor skills** involve the finer muscles of the wrists, fingers, and ankles. Many small motor skills, such as building with blocks, require eye-hand coordination—the ability to precisely move the hands in relation to what is seen.

Children ages one to three do not acquire physical skills as predictably as during the first year. Most children learn some skills earlier than "average" and others later. Such variations can be caused by differences in the child's size, health, interests, opportunities, and many other factors. They do not necessarily indicate intellectual ability. As you study about average development for a particular age, remember that many children develop more slowly or quickly.

Both large and small motor skills become increasingly well developed as children grow. Which type of motor skills do you see each of these children using?

Large Motor Skills

Physical exercise and repeated practice of actions are necessary for the development of motor skills. Improvement in any one skill is slow, but steady, and follows a predictable pattern.

As you learned earlier, most children begin to walk shortly before or after their first birthday. This is an important accomplishment. It gives the child a feeling of independence and much more mobility for exploration. At first, the toddler walks by holding on to furniture. The first steps alone are wobbly, with toes pointed outward and arms held out for balance. After a few shaky steps, the child collapses into a sitting position. It is constant practice that brings improvement in steadiness, balance, and body control.

Climbing skills follow a similar sequence. Even children who have learned to walk continue to climb stairs on their hands and knees for a while. Then they begin walking up stairs with help, placing both feet on each step. Next, they try this on their own, holding on to a railing. Both feet are still placed on each step. Alternating feet on stairs does not begin until about age three.

Climbing is not limited to stairs. Nothing is safe from the toddler—furniture, counters, ledges, and sometimes even people are conquered like mountains! Safety is an obvious concern for caregivers. The chart on page 244 gives safety tips.

A toddler who has just learned to walk may still need a little help to stay steady.

How to Toddler-Proof the Home

Falls

- Keep floors and stairs clear of toys and other objects.
- Wipe up spills immediately.
- Use a rubber mat or adhesive strips in the tub or shower.
- Use expanding gates at stairways to keep young toddlers from falling. (Do not use older expansion gates with wide openings. These are dangerous because a child's head can get caught in the opening.)
- Use the seat belt in a high chair.
- Windows that open should have secure screens. Windows in high-rise buildings pose a particular danger. They need special safety latches.

Burns

- Teach children as early as possible that the stove is hot and should be avoided.
- Turn pot handles toward the center of the stove.
- Check the water temperature of the hot water. It should be no higher than 120°-130°F (49°-54°C) to prevent burns.
- Unplug appliance cords after use.
- Put safety caps on electrical outlets when they are not in use.

Other Hazards

- Keep all dangerous items such as cleaning supplies, medicines, paints, and insecticides out of reach. When children begin climbing, these should be stored in locked cabinets or containers.
- Keep sharp knives, razor blades, scissors, and matches out of reach.
- Lock unused refrigerators or remove their doors.

Small Motor Skills

Between their first and second birthdays, children learn to feed themselves and to drink from a cup fairly well. At first, poor eye-hand coordination causes many spills. Neatness improves with practice. Toys such as blocks, large pop beads, and pyramids of different-size rings help develop small motor skills.

Two-year-olds show improved **manipulation** (skillful use of the hands and fingers). They can turn the pages of a book one at a time, peel a banana, and turn on faucets. Crayons are used with happy abandon, the strokes running haphazardly over onto the table or floor. Towers of blocks rarely exceed five or six in height before being toppled.

Three-year-olds show considerably more skill. They can take lids off of jars and screw them on again. (They love to take things apart and put them back together again.) Children this age can draw rough circles and horizontal and vertical lines.

The chart on page 246 shows average large and small motor development between the first and fourth birthdays.

Check Your Understanding

1. How is a toddler's posture related to body proportions?

2. List at least ten foods you feel are bad for teeth. Explain the reasons for your selections.

3. Give at least five examples of activities using large motor skills. Do the same for small motor skills.

4. Explain why two-year-olds can't build block towers and draw with crayons as well as four-year-olds.

As small motor skills improve, a child's random scribbles gradually become more recognizable lines and shapes.

Average Motor Skills Development
Ages One to Four

Age	Large Motor Skills	Small Motor Skills
1 to 1½ YEARS	■ Improves from walking a few unsteady steps to walking well. ■ Slides down stairs backwards, one at a time. ■ Stoops to pick up toys.	■ Turns pages of a book, several pages at a time. ■ Picks up small objects easily using thumb and forefinger. ■ Scribbles.
1½ to 2 YEARS	■ Runs fairly well. ■ Can stand on one foot. ■ Learns to walk up and down stairs, holding on, both feet on each step. ■ Throws objects overhand.	■ Buttons large buttons. ■ Pulls down zippers. ■ Turns doorknobs. ■ Stacks several cubes to form a tower.
2 to 2½ YEARS	■ Walks with more coordination and confidence. ■ Climbs, even in unsafe places. ■ Jumps off bottom step. ■ Pushes self on wheeled toys.	■ Turns pages of a book one at a time. ■ Screws lids on and off containers. ■ Builds towers of about six blocks.
2½ to 3 YEARS	■ Runs, but cannot stop accurately; runs into things. ■ Alternates feet going up stairs, but not going down. ■ Throws ball overhand, but inaccurately. ■ Kicks balls.	■ Builds towers of about eight blocks. ■ Draws horizontal and vertical lines, circles. ■ Strings large beads.
3 to 4 YEARS	■ Jumps up and down. ■ Skips and hops. ■ Balances on one foot. ■ Walks on tiptoe. ■ Rides a tricycle. ■ Catches a ball with arms straight.	■ Builds towers of about nine or ten blocks. ■ Makes a bridge of three blocks. ■ Cuts with scissors. ■ Draws recognizable pictures. ■ Uses a fork and spoon with little spilling.

Providing Care

Caring for a one-, two-, or three-year-old is quite different from caring for a baby. By their first birthday, children are already beginning to do things for themselves. They are starting to feed themselves and may help a bit with dressing and undressing. For caregivers, these attempts to "help" actually make most tasks more difficult. But children can only learn self-help skills through practice. Two-year-olds can do a number of things for themselves, with some supervision. They can feed themselves, put on some clothes, and make attempts at washing themselves. Most become toilet trained during this time. Three-year-olds are capable of a surprising amount of self-care.

Feeding

Between the first and fourth birthdays, food remains an important part of children's lives. Nourishing food is essential for proper growth. It is during this time that children acquire food habits and attitudes that influence their eating throughout life. They also learn to feed themselves. This both depends on and improves small motor skills. Toddlers often use mealtimes to assert their independence.

- **The one-year-old.** The one-year-old eats a variety of baby foods and many simple foods from the family table. Family foods may include such things as mashed or boiled potatoes, cooked vegetables, soups, fresh fruit pieces, and puddings. In the early months, most foods should be chopped finely. As more teeth come in and chewing ability improves, they can have a coarser texture.

Feeding herself is a way for Andrea to show that she is a big girl now.

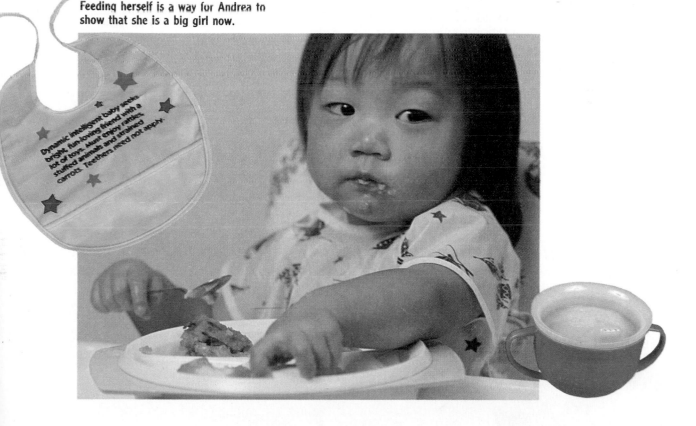

Finger foods are popular with most young children. For one-year-olds, they both improve coordination and encourage self-feeding. Appropriate finger foods include cheese chunks, peas, thin carrot or celery slices, melon or banana pieces, and sections of hard-cooked eggs.

The transition from being fed to self-feeding is a long one. Babies begin to try to use a spoon before their first birthday. However, it is not until eighteen months or later that self-feeding is accomplished with little spilling. By the end of the second year, most children can drink from a cup fairly well.

During the second year, meals can become a battle of wills between parent and toddler. One-year-olds want to not only try to feed themselves, but also choose what they eat. They develop strong food dislikes, but these usually don't last long. Rather than forcing the child to eat a food, it's better to just substitute another similar food at the next meal. In a few weeks, the sweet potatoes that were dumped on the floor three meals in a row will probably be a favorite food again.

Close-up

At age fourteen months, mealtime was Kristin's favorite time of the day. But her mother, Sue, had come to dread the struggle and mess. One night at dinner she described that day's lunchtime to her husband, Tom. "It all started out peacefully enough except that Kristin didn't want to sit in her high chair. You know how she always wants to stand up to eat."

"I sure do," replied Tom. "I never did get her into the high chair yesterday for breakfast."

"For Kristin's lunch," continued Sue, "I fixed her favorites — turkey, peas, mashed potatoes, and melon balls. When I tried to feed her some turkey, she took a few bites and then grabbed the spoon. Instead of eating her peas with her fingers like she usually does, she kept trying to get them onto her spoon. Whenever she did succeed in corralling one, she would usually turn the spoon over on the way to her mouth and lose it. She finally lost interest and started eating her mashed potatoes — with her hands! I tried to distract her with a few more bites of turkey, but she pushed me away with her mashed potato hands. Finally, she started eating the melon balls. When one rolled off the high chair tray and I bent to pick it up, she laughed. That must have given her the idea because she began to push the rest off, one by one. When she ran out of melon, she started on the peas. I grabbed the bowl of turkey just before that went on the floor, too. I was just getting ready to yell at her when I happened to glance at the mirror. There Kristin and I were, covered with food. I had to laugh instead."

Tom chuckled. "You must have had quite a clean-up job."

"Even that had its moments," replied Sue. "Kristin's bath water looked like turkey-vegetable soup!"

What reasons can you give for Kristin's behavior?

How might other parents have reacted to the same situation?

Suggest some ways Kristin's parents could minimize mealtime problems.

Should Sue be worried that Kristin didn't eat much lunch? ∎

■*The two-year-old.* Two-year-olds vary greatly in their eating habits. Some are easy to please. Others are very finicky eaters. Most, however, do have specific likes and dislikes. They often refuse to eat some foods.

Two-year-olds can usually feed themselves without any help. Some are neat, but others are quite messy. At this age, a child can be taught to use a small fork and to use a knife to spread or cut soft foods.

Some children are inclined to dawdle over their food. (Don't confuse dawdling with the longer time it naturally takes a small child to eat.) Conversation distracts the toddler. Many families solve this problem by feeding the child before the family meal. Others feel that the socialization at meals is important. They try to minimize the distractions while allowing the child to eat with the family.

■*The three-year-old.* By three years of age, a child can eat the same foods as the rest of the family. With a full set of baby teeth, chewing foods is not a problem. However, meats and other tough foods should still be served in small pieces.

Three-year-olds are very active and need food for both growth and energy. They should have three meals a day plus nutritious snacks. The amount children eat will vary considerably from day to day depending on the amount of activity they have had.

At this age, it is still best not to make an issue of food likes and dislikes. Children should try new foods, but not be forced to eat large amounts of those they dislike. Substituting similar foods still works. A child who refuses milk for a time will probably eat it in cereal, soup, and pudding.

By age three, children can take part in the regular family meals. A booster seat makes it easier to reach the table.

Meals need to be nutritious, appealing, and easy for a youngster to eat. How does this meal satisfy those requirements?

Choosing Foods for Children

Parents and other caregivers must consciously choose the proper foods for young children. Like adults, children need a variety of nutritious foods daily. The best way to make sure that they get them is to plan meals using the Basic Food Groups. The chart on page 98 shows the food groups and the number of servings from each that young children should eat each day. The size of the serving will vary according to the child's age, health, and activities. However, a good rule of thumb is to serve about 1 tablespoon (15 milliliters) of meat, fruit, and vegetable for each year of life.

While many meals are nutritious, some are more appealing than others. What kinds of things make eating more interesting and easier for young children?

■ *Color.* A variety of bright colors adds interest to a meal. What's wrong with a meal of broiled chicken, mashed potatoes, buttered cauliflower, milk, and vanilla pudding? What foods might you substitute to make it appeal to a three-year-old?

■ *Texture.* Think of all the adjectives you might use to describe foods. Ice cream is smooth, a cracker is crunchy, and a blackberry is grainy. Within each meal, children should have a variety of food textures. Analyze the meal described above. What foods might improve the texture?

■ *Shape.* Children find foods of different shapes more interesting. They also help them to learn to identify shapes. Is there any reason sandwiches need to be square or rectangular? Why not cut them in triangles or strips? Try using a cookie cutter to cut shapes from the bread before assembling the sandwich. (The scraps of bread have a variety of uses—dry bread crumbs, stuffings, croutons for salad.) Can you name three foods suitable for young children that have unusual shapes?

■ ***Temperature.*** Small children are very conscious of the temperature of food. Most do not like most foods that are very hot or cold. Wait until food cools or warms to the right temperature before serving it.

■ ***Ease of eating.*** Some foods are difficult for children to eat. Ground beef is easier to handle than steak. Spaghetti is fine, but it should be cut in short pieces for easier handling. Rich or fried foods may be difficult for small children to digest.

You can see that choosing food for children is a challenge. It must be nutritious, suitable, and interesting. Use your imagination! Read the "Mealtime Tips" chart for additional guidelines for feeding young children.

Mealtime Tips

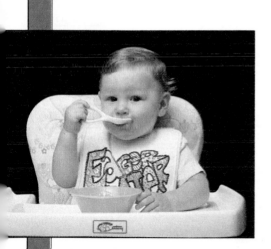

- Keep mealtimes on a regular schedule. It is difficult for children to wait to eat.
- Keep the atmosphere at meals pleasant. Avoid constant criticism. Table manners will improve with age.
- Use a sturdy, unbreakable dish or plate with sides. This helps self-feeding efforts. The child can scoop food against the sides.
- Choose a cup that does not tip easily and is easy to hold.
- Provide child-size eating utensils. A young child can't handle a full-size fork or spoon well.
- Feed a young toddler in a high chair. When the child starts sitting at the family table, use a high stool with a back or a booster chair on a regular chair.
- Never use food as a punishment or a bribe. Eating good food should be considered expected behavior. If you say, "You can't have a cookie until you finish your vegetables," you give the impression that vegetables are bad and cookies are good.
- Remember that children imitate others. Set a good example in food choices and table manners.

Bathing

Personal habits established early affect future attitudes about cleanliness. Caregivers need to help children develop good attitudes as well as cleanliness skills.

At this age, most children are bathed in the family tub. The bath is usually given in the evening before bed. Most children like baths, but more for play than for getting clean.

One-year-olds begin to try to wash themselves. At first this merely means rubbing the washcloth over their face and stomach. By age two, however, most children can wash, rinse, and dry themselves fairly well—except for the neck and back. By age three, children can bathe themselves with a minimum of supervision.

Children under age two and one-half should never be left alone in the bathtub. Even a minute away to answer the phone or get clean clothes can have disastrous results. As one mother relates, "I just left the bathroom for a second to get Denny's shoes. He was bathed and fully dressed for the day. When I came back, he was sitting in the tub again—with all his clothes on—playing with his toys in the bath water!" This situation is funny, but the child could have drowned just as easily.

By three years of age, children are old enough to accept cleanliness routines. They can wash before and after meals and after toileting.

As children grow older, they need less adult help while bathing. However, for safety's sake, a young child should not be left unattended in the bath.

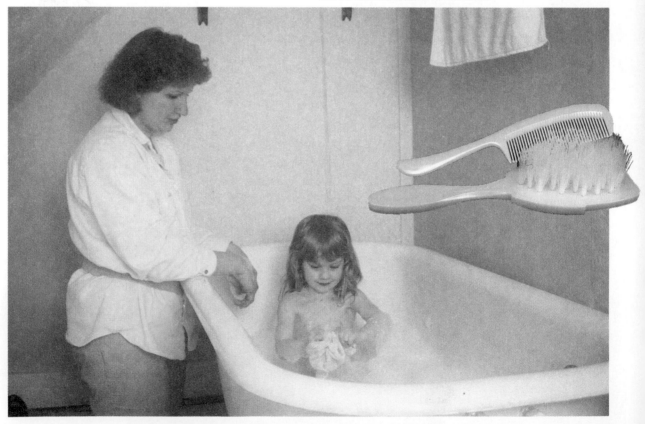

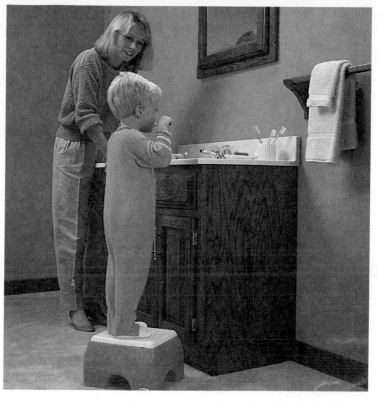

Most toddlers like to brush their teeth because they want to imitate other family members. Provide a stepstool so that the child can reach the sink more easily.

Caring for the Teeth

Tooth brushing should begin as soon as there are enough teeth to brush—around eighteen months. Give the toddler a small, soft brush and a bit of toothpaste. First attempts will not be very effective, but it is important that children try. Even three-year-olds often only swish the front teeth a few times with the toothbrush. They still need adult help. Parents should also begin teaching how to floss between teeth to remove food particles.

Dressing

Toddlers are eager to learn dressing skills. Unfortunately, they learn how to take off clothes before they learn to put them on! Self-dressing should be encouraged when a child begins to show interest. However, the large and small motor skills involved must be learned one step at a time. Patience is important during this long process.

Soon after the first birthday, the child begins pulling clothing off. At first it may just be a sock or hat. Between eighteen and twenty-four months, the toddler learns to undress completely, unless clothes have difficult fasteners.

First attempts to help in dressing begin at about thirteen or fourteen months. The child may hold out an arm or leg, if requested. Next the child may thrust an arm through the sleeve of a shirt or a leg into pants. By two years the child can pull up pants, but shirts are still difficult. Garments are often put on inside out or backwards. At age three, the child can dress independently except for some help with buttons, difficult fasteners, and shoelaces.

To encourage interest in dressing, clothing should be easy to put on and take off. Self-dressing helps develop independence, responsibility, and cooperation. This period calls for patience on the part of the caregivers. With a relaxed attitude, they can share the child's fun and satisfaction in learning. See pages 310–311 for specific suggestions on encouraging independence and self-care.

What signs did Michael give that he was ready to learn to dress himself?
Why do you think he learned so rapidly once he was given the opportunity? ■

Close-up

Three-year-old Michael could not dress himself. It was not because he didn't want to or was unable to learn. He simply had no opportunity to do so.

Michael had three older sisters. To make the household run smoothly, each family member had assigned tasks. Dressing Michael was one of twelve-year-old Linda's duties before she left for school each morning.

Linda had taken over this job when Michael was still a baby. She learned to dress him quickly and efficiently. When Michael attempted to put on his own shoe, it was taken from him, slipped on and quickly tied. Linda did not let him pull up his pants or try to button his shirt either. She could do it much faster herself.

Michael finally learned to dress himself when a new baby joined the family. Mornings were hectic with tending the baby, eating breakfast, and getting the family off to work and school. Linda occasionally helped by dressing the baby, too. Busy with this task, Linda discovered that when she directed Michael's own efforts at dressing, he could do much of the work himself. She was surprised and delighted with his rapid progress.

Young children take pride in being able to dress themselves. Avoid clothing with difficult fasteners or tight openings—they will only frustrate the child.

Choosing Clothing

Comfort, durability, and economy are the most important characteristics to look for in clothing for young children.

■*Comfort.* Clothes that allow freedom of movement are the most comfortable. Knit clothes that stretch with movement are good choices. Avoid stiff or scratchy fabrics.

Clothing size affects both comfort and movement. Clothes that are too small restrict movement. Pants that are too long can cause a toddler to trip. A long-sleeved shirt that covers the hands makes play difficult. All clothing that is the same size does not fit the same way. It is best to have children try clothes on before buying.

■*Durability.* Children's clothes must withstand both hard wear and repeated laundering. Durability is influenced by the construction of the clothing. Look for close, even stitching with strong thread. The stitching should be reinforced at points of strain. All fasteners and trims should be firmly attached.

Cotton is a good fabric choice, especially for jeans, T-shirts, and underwear. It wears well, launders well (though some cotton fabrics shrink), and does not irritate the skin. Since it absorbs moisture, it is also comfortable to wear.

Fibers such as polyester, nylon, and acrylic are often included in children's clothes. They are **synthetic fibers**. That means they are manufactured from chemicals. (Cotton, wool, silk, and linen come from plants or animals and are called **natural fibers**.) Fabrics made from synthetic fibers have many advantages. They are durable, wrinkle-resistant, and quick-drying. They require little or no ironing. However, unlike natural fibers, they do not absorb moisture well. Heat and perspiration are held against the body.

By law, all clothing must have a label that shows the fibers it is made of. By checking clothing labels, you can determine how clothing will wear and feel.

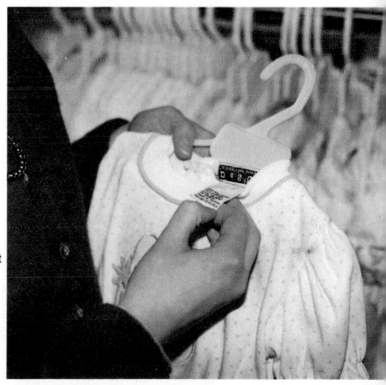

Clothing labels tell you not only the fiber content of the garment, but how it should be cared for. Why is care an especially important consideration for children's clothing?

Since children's clothing is outgrown so quickly, secondhand items often show little wear.

■*Economy.* Since young children continue to grow rapidly, they need larger clothes often. Many parents exchange outgrown clothes to cut costs. Children's clothes are also plentiful at yard sales, tag sales, and thrift stores.

Children's clothes are most economical when they can expand a bit to allow for growth. Look for deep hems or cuffs that can be let down. On overalls or jumpers, the straps should be long enough to allow the buttons to be moved. Large seam allowances allow garments to be let out as the child grows.

Allow a child some choice in clothing selection. Children love bright colors. In fact, children choose their clothes more by color than anything else. They also love "picture clothes"—fabrics printed with animals, toys, or story characters, or garments with a picture on the front.

Sleeping

As the second birthday approaches, sleeping habits undergo a change. Children require less sleep and may not sleep as easily or as willingly.

By age two, most children no longer take a morning nap. They do sleep all night plus take an afternoon nap. Most three-year-olds sleep slightly less and may not nap at all.

Emotionally, the two-year-old appears more dependent on adults than during the previous year. Parents are often called back at bedtime. What the child really wants is someone near. Endless excuses are used—a drink of water, another trip to the bathroom, a second story. Self-comforting techniques like thumb-sucking, rocking the crib, or cuddling a favorite blanket or soft toy are common.

Love and understanding are essential during this period. At bedtime, parents should be sure the child's physical needs have been met. Then gentle firmness and consistency give the most positive results. Impatience only makes the situation worse.

Waking in the middle of the night and even getting out of bed are not uncommon at age three. Emotional experiences of the day, excitement at bedtime, or nighttime fears may cause insecurity at night.

Fear of the dark is common during this period. There are many possible causes. Sometimes, children overhear talk of prowlers or fires. Some children are placed in a dark room as punishment. Such fears are very real to a child. Unfortunately, there is rarely a quick solution. A calm discussion of the problem may help some children. For others, a night-light helps. Ridicule or shaming the child only makes the problem worse.

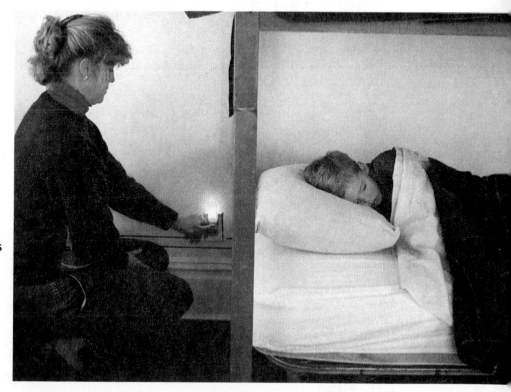

Forcing a child to sleep in the dark is not likely to eliminate fear. A night-light may be needed, along with the caregiver's patience and reassurance.

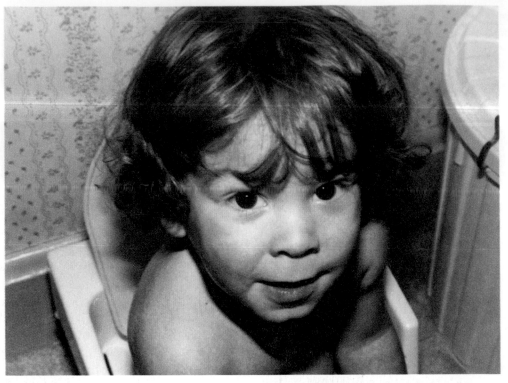

Once the child is physically ready for toilet training and shows an interest in it, the process can usually be accomplished with little trouble.

Toilet Training

In order for toilet training to be successful, the **sphincter muscles** (SFINK-ter) which control elimination must mature. The child must also recognize the body sensations that precede elimination. Then the child must learn how to control and release the sphincter muscles.

There is no set age at which a child should be toilet trained. Children reach the needed physical maturity at different ages. The time at which they are emotionally ready is also highly individual. However, most children are toilet trained between eighteen months and three years of age.

Bowel training usually comes before bladder training. Children who give some sign of a bowel movement are probably ready to begin being trained. The caregiver should note the approximate time of bowel movements each day. Then, a few minutes before that time, place the child on a sturdy child's seat on the adult toilet or on a potty chair. Children who follow a regular pattern of elimination usually are more easily trained than those who do not.

Even experts disagree on whether a special child's seat on the toilet or a potty chair is better. Using the adult toilet has the advantage that it already has a specific association for the child. It also eliminates adjustment to another seat later. However, a child-size potty chair allows more independence. With the adult toilet, a longer period of adult help is required because the child must be placed on the seat. Later, a small box or stool for the child to reach the seat can be used. It also will provide a place for the child's feet and improve balance. Some children are frightened by the flushing water of a toilet. They may fear that they will go down the drain and disappear, too! It is better at first to flush the toilet after the child has left the bathroom.

Parents' attitudes toward toilet training are important. An overly strict attitude can make training more difficult and cause long-lasting emotional problems for the child. Interest and calm encouragement are more effective. When beginning toilet training, it is important never to force the child. If the child resists, abandon attempts for several weeks, then try again.

Even after bowel training is fairly well established, accidents should be expected. In addition, new foods added to the diet and sickness tend to make bowel movements irregular.

Parents should let other caregivers know about the child's progress so that toilet training is consistent. This mother is explaining the potty chair that will be placed on the floor for the child to use.

Bladder training is usually begun several months after bowel training. (Some children learn both at about the same time.) Again, wait for signs of readiness. Less frequent need to urinate, sometimes as long as from one meal to the next, is a sign. So is the child's indication that diapers need changing or that he or she is the cause of the puddle on the floor.

A child's urination habits are often irregular. They are affected by liquid intake, weather, temperament, and excitement. However, the parent or caregiver should take note of the pattern and try the youngster on the potty or toilet for short periods at specific times. These times should include before and after meals, bath, and sleep.

Substituting **training pants** (heavy, absorbent underpants) for diapers during bladder training eliminates much dressing and undressing. The novelty also intrigues a youngster and instills the desire to begin self-help.

By three years of age, toilet accidents are infrequent for most children. By this time most also stay dry all night. Some may still awaken once to use the bathroom.

Check Your Understanding

1. Describe a nutritious, appealing meal that you would prepare for a two-year-old.

2. Describe an entire outfit you would buy for a three-year old that would encourage self-dressing, be comfortable and durable, offer growth features, and be appealing to the child.

3. Name two bedtime problems common with one-to three-year-olds and tell what you would do to cope with them.

4. What are the advantages of using a potty chair for toilet training? Can you think of any disadvantages?

Chapter Review

To Sum Up

- Physical growth slows for children ages one through three.
- Posture improves as body proportions change.
- By age three, most children have a full set of baby teeth.
- Both large and small motor skills improve greatly during this period.
- Children this age are developing lifetime eating and cleanliness habits.
- Children gradually learn to feed and dress themselves.
- Bedtime problems are common during this stage.
- Toilet training should not be started until children are physically and emotionally ready.

To Review and Remember

1. When does a baby become a toddler?
2. Compare the growth of children ages one to three to that of infants.
3. Explain how diet affects the teeth.
4. What is plaque and what effect does it have?
5. What is the difference between large and small motor skills? Give one example of each.
6. List five safety guidelines for small children.
7. Name the food groups and tell how many servings children need from each daily.
8. List five factors you should consider when planning an appealing meal for young children.
9. At about what age do most children begin to try to "help" with dressing?
10. What are sphincter muscles? What is their role in toilet training?

To Discuss and Discover

1. Observe how two children of different ages between one and three do the same thing (such as run, climb stairs, or feed themselves). Write down what you saw and discuss the reasons for the differences you noted.
2. In small groups, make a list of activities for one- to three-year-olds to promote one of the following: large motor skills, small motor skills, eye-hand coordination. Make charts of your lists.
3. Check several stores or catalogs that carry toddlers' clothes. Make a list of "growth" and self-help features available on different types of clothing.

10 Emotional and Social Development from One to Three

To help you to . . .

- Describe the general patterns of emotional and social development in children ages one to three.
- Identify the common emotions of young children and the changes in how they are expressed.
- Describe how young children gradually learn to play with each other.
- Explain the importance of a positive self-concept and identify ways it can be developed.
- Describe effective discipline techniques.

Terms to Learn

cooperative play	parallel play	separation anxiety
discipline	positive	sibling rivalry
negative	self-concept	socialization
self-concept	self-centered	temper tantrum
negativism	self-discipline	

Scene: A long checkout line in a busy supermarket. A tired-looking mother has a baby in the seat of the shopping cart and a boy age two and one-half at her side.

Son: (Tugs at his mother's coat.) "Mommy, I want some candy."

Mother: "No, Jeff. It's almost lunchtime."

Son: (Whining) "I'm hungry, Mommy!"

Mother: "Just be patient a few more minutes. See, the line is finally moving. Pretty soon they'll put all our groceries in bags and we can go home."

Son: (Grabs a handful of candy from checkout display.)

Mother: "Jeff, I said no." (Puts candy back.)

Son: (Sits down on the floor in front of the cart—out of his mother's reach—and starts to scream.)

Mother: "Jeff, stop that! Come back here by me!"

Son: (Screams more loudly and kicks at the cart.)

Baby: (Begins to cry.)

Other shoppers. (Stare at scene, most looking annoyed and disapproving.)

You have probably seen something like this happen. What causes a problem like this? An undisciplined child? An ineffective parent?

In this chapter you will learn about the emotional and social characteristics of children from one to three. Some of what you learn about the causes of and cures for situations like this one may surprise you.

Emotional Development

Emotional development is easier to observe in early childhood than at other stages in life. Children develop new emotions, such as jealousy, that they did not feel as young babies. They display their emotions very clearly, first through their actions and later through their words. At the end of this period, they also begin to learn to control their emotions or show them in more socially acceptable ways.

General Emotional Patterns

The time between the first and fourth birthdays is one of emotional ups and downs. There are periods of contrariness and rebellion, but there are also ones of happiness and affection.

Throughout childhood, emotional development tends to go in cycles. This seems particularly true of one-, two-, and three-year-olds. There are predictable emotional stages most children go through. However, it is important to remember that each child is an individual. Manuel may not go through the usual "contrariness" of age two and one-half until age three. Janey, with her calm and sunny disposition, may not seem to go through it at all. Generally, however, you would probably find the following characteristics at about the ages given.

Toddlers show their feelings by their facial expressions and their actions. Both smiles and tears are common.

Eighteen Months

Eighteen-month-old children are still primarily **self-centered**. (They think about their own needs and wants, not those of others.) This is not surprising. As a baby, needs and desires are promptly met by parents. At eighteen months, however, parents are beginning to teach the child that some desires won't be met immediately, and others will never be met. This is a difficult and long-term lesson for a child. An eighteen-month-old is only beginning this process.

Parents' spoken instructions are usually not very successful at this age. The toddler is more likely to do the opposite of what is wanted. This child's favorite response is "no." A request to "give it to me" usually prompts the child to run off with the object instead.

Negativism (doing the opposite of what others want) is a normal part of development for the toddler. This has a number of causes. One is the child's desire for independence. Saying "no" to parents is merely a way of saying, "Let me decide for myself sometimes." Often the child really wants to do what he or she says "no" to.

Another cause of negativism is simply the frustration that toddlers feel. Their bodies are not developed enough to obey their wishes and they don't have sufficient language skills to express their feelings. The result is anger or frustration.

At this age, children also finally realize that they are a separate person. This is both exciting and frightening. They like the power, but miss the close bond with their mother or other primary caregiver.

It is important to remember that this is just a normal stage in emotional development. Understanding its causes makes it easier to deal with. One of the best ways to combat negativism at this age is simply to eliminate as many restrictions as possible. It is unreasonable to expect an eighteen-month-old child not to touch things in a room. Reduce the problem by moving things that are valuable or dangerous. As the child becomes older, things can gradually be returned.

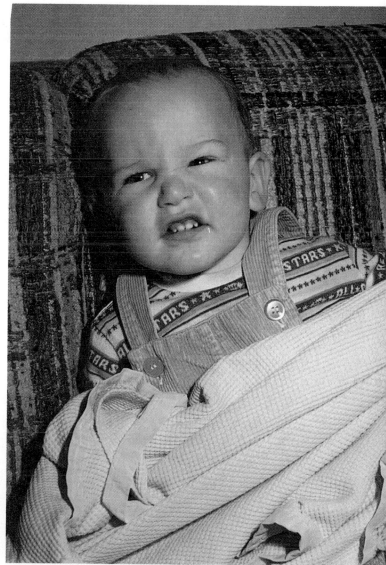

Being "contrary" is a way for toddlers to prove that they don't always have to follow along with the desires of others.

At this age, distraction is another effective technique for coping with misbehavior. Try, for example, opening a picture book and talking about what you see. Or noisily arrange the child's blocks in an interesting pattern. The toddler will soon leave the undesirable activity to join you.

It also helps to give the child reasonable choices whenever possible. If the child can choose between pears and a banana for lunch, it won't matter quite so much that there

is no choice about taking a nap. It is best to limit choices to two alternatives, however. Toddlers cannot think about three or four things at the same time.

Temper tantrums, another common problem, often start at this age and may continue until about age three or four. In a temper tantrum, children release anger or frustration violently by screaming, crying, kicking, pounding, and sometimes even by holding their breath. Even minor frustrations can cause temper tantrums. For example, Sara had one when her ball rolled behind a chair where she couldn't reach it. Pages 312–313 give tips for understanding and handling temper tantrums.

Young children don't yet have the skill to do things as well as they want. They must also cope with restrictions from caregivers. Temper tantrums are a typical result of such frustrations.

Two Years

Emotionally, the two-year-old is less at odds with the world than at eighteen months. Speech and motor skills have improved, eliminating much of the previous frustration. The child understands more and makes fewer demands.

The two-year-old expresses love and affection freely and actively seeks approval and praise. Emotional outbursts are less frequent and intense. The child is easier to reason with. Relationships with parents and other children have improved, for the two-year-old tends to be outgoing, friendly, and less self-centered.

Two and One-Half Years

Just as parents have relaxed with their two-year-old, the child enters a new stage. Toddlers of this age are even more difficult to live with than at eighteen months because they are not as easily distracted.

At two and one-half, children are learning so many things that it overwhelms them. Their comprehension and desires exceed their physical abilities. They want their blocks and dolls placed just so, but they only partially succeed before they accidentally knock them over. They work hard at talking. They know what they want to say, but do not always succeed in making themselves understood. If caregivers answer with an absentminded "uh-huh" or ignore them, they become even more frustrated.

Two-year-olds lose some of their preoccupation with themselves and are better able to get along with playmates.

Toddlers' drive for independence causes them to resist pressure to conform. They are sensitive about being bossed, shown, helped, or directed. Independence and immaturity clash head-on at this age. At two and one-half, children are often stubborn, demanding, and domineering. But they are also lovable at times.

One characteristic of this age is the child's desire for sameness. This is the child's way of coping with a confusing world. The child insists that routines be carried out without variation. Tasks must be done in exactly the same way. Objects must always be in the same places. Going along with the toddler as much as possible helps build feelings of security and confidence.

At two and one-half, toddlers are part baby, part child. Sometimes they seek comfort and help, while at others they assert their independence. Parents can help children of this age most by giving them much love and a great deal of patience—especially when they are neither lovable nor patient. They need loose bounds rather than hard and fast rules.

Three Years

Most three-year-olds have made remarkable strides in emotional development. They are again generally sunny and cooperative. They are also learning to be considerate. Since they are now more physically able to do things, their frustrations are lessened.

Three-year-olds take directions from others with little of their previous resistance. They follow orders and take pride in tasks performed for others. Praise and affection are eagerly sought. Temper outbursts are less frequent and not so violent.

At three, children love to talk and are much better at it. They talk to their toys, playmates, imaginary companions, or to themselves. They can be reasoned with and controlled with words. They derive emotional pleasure from talking.

Three and One-Half Years

The self-confident three-year-old is suddenly very insecure at three and one-half. To parents, it may seem that their child is going backward rather than forward emotionally.

Fears are common at this age. The child may be afraid of the dark, lions and tigers, strangers, or loud noises—even though none of these were frightening before.

Emotional tension and insecurity often show up in physical ways, too. Tensional outlets such as thumb-sucking, nail-biting, and nose-picking are common. Other children may stumble or stutter.

At three and one-half, children try to provide security by controlling their environment. "I want to sit on the floor to eat lunch" might be an insistent demand, or "Talk to me!"

At two and one-half, children sometimes want to be grown-up but aren't sure of their ability to do so. At other times, they look for reassurance that they can still be babied when they want.

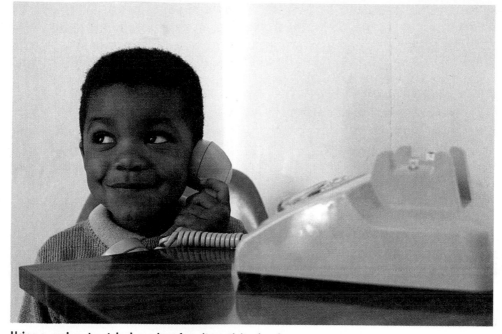

Using a real or toy telephone is a favorite activity for three-year-olds. Children this age are finally able to express themselves clearly by talking.

Age three and one-half often brings fears and insecurity, such as a fear of the dark. Parents should be calm and reassuring.

Close-up

Andy, age three and one-half, had been staying with his grandparents while his parents were out of town. The surroundings were familiar and, aside from an uncharacteristic quietness, he seemed to be coping well. However, near bedtime one evening his grandparents had visitors. Andy buried his head against his grandmother, covered his eyes, and cried, "I don't want to see anybody!" While his behavior is funny, it is also understandable. He was simply trying to control his environment by covering his eyes. He was feeling tired and abandoned, and strangers were more than he could cope with emotionally.

Why might a child have more difficulty coping with a separation from parents at age two and one-half than at three and one-half?

How can parents help a child cope with such a separation?

If you were Andy's grandmother, how would you react to his outburst?

Why? ■

Specific Emotions

Children express their emotions openly until the age of two or three. With more maturity, our culture demands more control of direct expression. The three-year-old begins to learn socially acceptable ways of displaying feelings. For example, three-year-old Jonathan expresses his anger through words. His fifteen-month-old sister, Marta, expresses hers by screaming and kicking.

Children's emotions become more specific as they grow older. Some of the common emotions of this period—anger, fear, jealousy, affection, and sympathy—are discussed here.

Anger

The crying and screaming of temper tantrums is most common at about eighteen months and then begins to decline. During this period, the child is not hostile toward any particular person or thing, just angry. Between ages two and three, the object or person responsible for the anger comes under attack. For example, a ten-month-old who is intent on obtaining a ball is concerned only with the ball. However, a two-year-old may attack the person who has the ball.

Outgoing, confident children tend to display their anger more aggressively, such as by hitting and kicking. Timid youngsters are more likely to cry and seek adult comfort.

These primitive expressions of anger gradually disappear if they do not bring the desired results. Reactions become less violent and explosive. Physical attacks begin to be replaced by threatening, name-calling, pouting, or scolding.

Even though the frequency of anger lessens with age, the anger lasts longer. Children become capable of lasting hostility. Three-year-olds think about "getting even" when someone makes them angry.

A number of factors can cause a child to be angry more often than normal. Anger is more frequent in anxious, insecure children. The child who has not learned self-control also tends to have frequent outbursts. Children whose parents are overly critical or inconsistent become frustrated easily and show anger. You have probably witnessed the more common temporary causes of bad temper. A child who is sick, uncomfortable, tired, or hungry will become angry much more easily than one who is not.

Frequent, intense outbursts are destructive and disturbing to both parent and child. Parents should recognize the child's bewilderment and anxiety rather than react angrily themselves. They should make sure demands on the child are both limited and reasonable as they teach self-control.

Fear

Every phase of a child's development has its particular fears. For a one-year-old it may be high places, strangers, and loud noises. A three-year-old might be afraid of the dark, animals, and storms. Some fears are helpful since they keep the child from dangerous situations. Others must be overcome for proper emotional and social development.

Some children have more fears than others. This depends on such factors as the child's physical condition, mental development, feeling of security, and ability to cope with life. Thoughtless adults sometimes build fears to insure obedience. They may say, "You stay on the sidewalk or the police will get you."

People often communicate their own fears to a child. Even if the fear is never discussed, the child senses it. For example, a child may pick up fear of dogs simply from the alarmed call of a parent whenever a dog comes near.

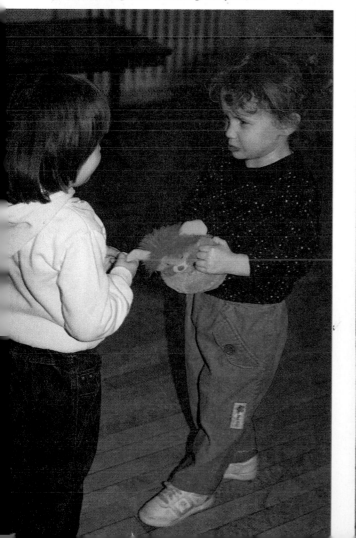

As children get older, their anger becomes focused on the person or thing that is causing the problem.

Fears depend a great deal on individual experience. A child with a pet cat will probably not be afraid of other cats. However, unfamiliar situations are likely to prompt fears at first.

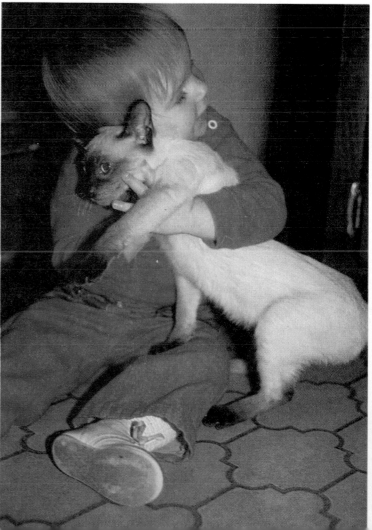

Many one- to four-year-olds suffer from **separation anxiety** at one time or another. Separation anxiety is fear of being away from parents, familiar caregivers, or their normal environment. It's common, for example, for a child to cry when left with an unfamiliar babysitter.

Some fears are based on real experiences. A toddler who is frightened by a bird may remain afraid of all birds. When a situation occurs that seems likely to produce fears, it is best to try to talk to the child about it right away. Otherwise, the child's imagination may blow the experience out of proportion.

Close-up

Traci, age three, attended preschool two mornings a week at Jackson High School. The Child Care class there ran the preschool program to gain experience working with young children.

One day while the children were finger painting, the school's fire alarm rang. As prearranged, each teen took charge of leading one child out of the building. Stephanie, who took Traci's hand, couldn't get Traci to move. Traci just stood there with a look of horror on her face. Stephanie explained that the loud siren was a fire alarm and that everyone needed to walk quickly to the parking lot. That just seemed to make Traci more afraid. Stephanie finally picked Traci up and carried her out of the building. It turned out that there was no fire, just a problem with the alarm system. The children were soon able to return to their room. Traci seemed fine by the time she left for home.

It soon became apparent, however, that Traci's fears had not gone away. The next week she did not want to come to preschool and didn't participate in activities when she was there. She just sat in the corner and sucked her thumb. Both Stephanie and Ms. Lee, the Child Care teacher, talked to her but got no response. Finally, Ms. Lee called Traci's parents to discuss the problem.

Traci's mother had also been puzzled about her reluctance to go to preschool. Normally, Traci could hardly wait from one session to the next. But when Ms. Lee asked if the fire alarm might have been the cause, Traci's mother immediately understood the problem.

"A month ago," she explained, "the house across the street burned in the middle of the night. The older man who lived there was killed. Traci was awakened by the fire engines and saw the fire. Mr. Schultz, the man who was killed, always talked to the kids in the neighborhood and Traci's had a hard time understanding his death. I suppose the fire alarm brought all these fears to the surface and now she is afraid there will be a fire at school. She hasn't said much at home, but I knew she was upset about something. What do you think we can do to help her?" Traci's mother asked.

How might Traci's fear have been avoided or lessened?

What could be done at this point to help Traci cope with her fear? ■

It is never a good idea to shame a child for fears or to treat the fears lightly. Listen to what the child has to say and give honest, understandable explanations. Children overcome their fears without too much trouble if they have help and support from a considerate adult. See the chart on page 273 for additional tips for handling the fears of children this age.

Tips for Handling Toddlers' Fears

- Set an example by not showing fear yourself.
- Encourage children to talk about their fears. Recognizing and admitting them may lessen their impact.
- Nightmares are common at this age. Help the child separate reality from fantasy.
- Make unfamiliar situations more secure with your presence. The first visit to the dentist, for example, goes more smoothly with someone familiar there.
- Being unprepared for a situation is one of the chief causes of fear. If a child knows what to expect from a strange babysitter, necessary hospitalization, or a move to another house, coping is less difficult.
- Teach children how to control frightening situations. A child who is afraid of the dark can be taught how to turn on the light. A child can be taught how to take a breath and put his or her face in the water. This avoids panic if the child slips underwater in the bathtub or wading pool.
- Give support and understanding, not ridicule or punishment for fears.

Jealousy

Jealousy becomes a recognizable emotion sometime in the second year. The one-year-old shows no such reaction, but by eighteen months jealousy is very pronounced. It reaches its peak at age three, then declines as outside relationships begin to replace the close ties to home and parents.

Resentment of affection between parents is one of the most common causes of jealousy in early childhood. The very young child may not understand that parents have enough love for everyone.

Sibling rivalry, or competition between children for their parents' love and attention, is another common cause of jealousy. This is often particularly evident when there is a new baby in the family. Suddenly, all the attention is focused on the baby rather than the older child.

Jealousy of a new baby can lead an older child to return to babyish habits.

Children between eighteen months and three and one-half seem to be most jealous of a new baby. They may try to hurt the infant or demand that the baby be "taken back." Some children respond by trying to get attention. They do so by showing off, being naughty, or resorting to babylike behavior such as bed-wetting, thumb-sucking, or baby talk.

If parents act shocked or threaten not to love the toddler anymore, they worsen the problem. The feeling of loss of love was the cause of the behavior to begin with. Instead, the older child needs more affection and reassurance.

Wise parents prepare older children ahead of time for the mother's absence and the arrival of the new baby. The chart on page 274 gives suggestions for dealing with this problem.

Promoting Good Sibling Relationships

- Prepare the older child for the baby's coming. Instill the feeling that the new baby is the youngster's, too, and that parents need the older child's help.
- If the older child must change bedrooms, this should be done months in advance.
- Arrange special time alone with the older child.
- Ask the child to help with small tasks in caring for the baby. An older child can run errands or help with feeding and dressing. Such positive tasks make the child feel like a useful part of the family.
- Compliment the youngster's good behavior whenever possible.
- Point up the advantages of not being a baby.
- Give the older child extra love and sympathy.

Love and Affection

The capacity for love and affection in later life stems from relationships in the early years. Children must learn to love.

First comes "love" of those who satisfy the baby's physical needs. If one person is the baby's primary caregiver for the first year, he or she is preferred above all others. Gradually, the baby's affection expands to include both parents, siblings, favorite toys, pets, and people outside the home.

Relationships between parents and children should be strong, but not too binding. A child who is overly dependent on parents has difficulty forming other relationships.

Sympathy

Most children show little evidence of sympathy until about age two. The child must be able to understand that a situation can be upsetting for another even though not for himself or herself. The youngster must also be able to relate to others emotionally. A well-adjusted, happy child is more inclined to be sympathetic than one whose relationships are less satisfactory. Why do you suppose this is true?

The first sympathetic responses are limited to crying when another cries. At about age three, the child attempts to comfort someone else and remove the cause of distress. The child may pat and talk to an unhappy baby. All the child's toys may be pushed into the crib of a crying brother or sister. Actually understanding the feelings of others does not come until later.

Older toddlers may try to comfort someone who appears distressed. However, they don't always know the best way to go about it. Why not?

Evaluating Emotional Adjustment

How can parents tell whether their child is developing well emotionally? Between the first and fourth birthdays, the single most important clue is the smoothness of the parent-child relationship. The early pattern that becomes established between parents and children is never outgrown. It will have great influence on the youngster's later relationships in life, with a spouse, children, co-workers, and friends.

A good relationship exists when a child:
- Seeks approval and praise from parents.
- Turns to them for comfort and help.
- Tells them about happy events so they may share the joy.
- Accepts limits and discipline without too much resistance.

The second area of importance in emotional adjustment is in relationships with brothers and sisters. Friends and outside relationships are more significant when the child is slightly older. Quarreling with brothers and sisters is not always a sign of poor adjustment. Bickering is a normal pattern in some families. But the child who is continuously and bitterly at odds with brothers and sisters, in spite of parents' efforts to lessen the friction, needs professional help.

Check Your Understanding

1. Briefly describe the most common emotional pattern at each of the following ages: eighteen months, two, two and one-half, three, and three and one-half.

2. How does the way anger is expressed change from age one to age three?

3. Imagine you are babysitting for a boy age three who refuses to go to bed because he is afraid of the dark. What would you do?

A warm positive relationship between parent and child will foster the child's ability to form good relationships with others.

Social Development

Between the ages of one and four, many of a person's lifetime social attitudes and skills are developed. Early experiences in the family must teach a child how to cooperate and adapt to the needs of others. This is the process of **socialization**—learning to get along with others.

General Social Patterns

Social development is also related to emotional, intellectual, and physical development. Certain social characteristics and tasks can be expected at different ages. Remember that individual differences may influence these general patterns.

Eighteen Months

The primary socialization goal of children at eighteen months is to begin developing some independence from the family. For most children, closest relationships are with family members and will remain so. But toddlers need to begin to learn about the outside world. This may mean trips to the playground or other opportunities to be with children and adults who are not part of the family. Children who remain too dependent upon their parents find normal social development difficult.

At about eighteen months, children begin to notice the presence of other children in play situations. But there is little real interaction. **Parallel play**—playing beside, rather than actually with, another child—is characteristic of this age. Participation between children varies. One child will merely watch another play with a toy. Another child will grab the toy away. A third child may seem to pay no attention to other children at all.

The younger the children, the less likely they are to interact while playing.

Children this age often treat people more as objects. The toddler is intent on satisfying strong desires at the expense of anyone who interferes. There may be conflicts over toys that result in screaming, hitting, or hair-pulling.

At eighteen months, many children are still afraid of unfamiliar adults. This generally decreases as they have more experiences outside the home.

Two Years

By age two, children already have an impressive list of social skills. They are especially good at understanding and influencing their primary caregiver, usually their mother. They can read her moods and what she will let them get away with. As their speech develops, they are increasingly able to influence the behavior of others.

Two-year-olds find it is fun to have someone to play with. They enjoy being with other children although most play is still parallel.

Sharing and taking turns is still beyond two-year-olds. However, they like to please others. Occasionally, they will put someone else's wishes (usually an adult's) above their own.

Two and One-Half Years

The negativism that is characteristic at age two and one-half carries over into children's social relationships. They may refuse to do anything for one person, but perform tasks willingly for another. It is often impossible to understand their reasoning.

At this age, children are beginning to learn about the rights of others. Social play is still parallel and works best with only two children. Squabbles are frequent, but brief. Children forget about them quickly and resume play.

Between eighteen months and two years, children gradually begin to enjoy the company of playmates.

By age three, children are able to play together, not just next to each other. This is called cooperative play.

Three Years

Most three-year-olds are relatively sunny and agreeable. This shows in their relationships with others. People are important. Three-year-olds will share, help, or do things another's way just to please.

At this age, children make friends more easily and are more willing to give and take. Conflicts and temper displays are short-lived.

Cooperative play—actually playing with other children—begins. Sand castles are built together, tractors use the same roads, and cars can share the same garage without friction. Building blocks, doll families, and puzzles can be used by several children at once.

Parents are no longer the center of the world for three-year-olds. Most children this age seek friends on their own. They may prefer some companions over others.

At three, children are more sure of themselves. They are less easily frustrated. Experience gives them confidence in themselves and their relationships with others.

Three and One-Half Years

Cooperative play improves and includes much more conversation. Disagreements with playmates are less frequent. Because youngsters like companionship, they realize that they must share toys and put up with some things they do not like.

There is an increasing ability to evaluate friendships. "I don't like Kevin to come over here. He doesn't play nice." Close friends begin to exclude others, although friendships are not always long lasting.

Friendships help young children learn to enjoy companionship, consider other people's desires, and handle disagreements.

Making Friends

Friendships are important to normal social development. They may also be a sign of good social progress. A child who is comfortable and friendly with others and has at least one friend at a time is usually developing normally. However, if a child is unable or unwilling to make friends, it is important to find out the cause and take steps to help. Remember that this is a crucial stage for developing lifetime social skills.

It is important to expose even very young children to other people. The give-and-take of socializing is needed throughout life. Children who begin to play with others early are not likely to be afraid of other children. They learn to cope with the occasional blows and snatching of other one- and two-year-olds.

Parents may have to make a special effort to arrange playtimes with others for a first or only child in a family. Children who grow up with only adults for companionship may have problems with normal social development. Adults are more polite and considerate than children. If the child does not learn the rough-and-tumble companionship of other children until school age, it is more difficult. At five or six, the child's feelings are hurt more easily and the socialization process takes longer.

What about the child who does not get along with playmates? Remember that all children sometimes have disagreements and arguments. Whether or not a caregiver should step in depends upon the situation. Children need to learn how to solve such disagreements. If two children are relatively evenly matched and there is no physical or emotional harm being done, the caregiver can simply observe the situation. But if this is not the case, the caregiver may need to step in and help the children solve the problem. Talking about the feelings of others, seeking options, and urging compromise teaches problem-solving skills children will need in social situations throughout life.

Giving children your attention and praise helps them develop a good self-concept.

Developing a Good Self-Concept

Your self-concept—the way you feel about yourself—affects your relationships with other people. The formation of self-concept begins at birth and continues throughout life. But your basic attitudes about yourself are formed in early childhood. If you see yourself as a good, worthwhile person who is capable of many things, you have a **positive self-concept**. People with a **negative self-concept** see themselves as bad, unimportant people who are not able to do things well.

Children form their self-concept according to what they feel others think of them and how people treat them. Parents usually spend the most time with the child, so they have the most influence on the child's self-concept. Children who are treated with love and respect generally view themselves positively.

Most parents do not think of a newborn as forming a self-concept. However, the process is beginning. If the infant cries and the parents respond quickly with food or comfort, the baby begins to feel like a worthwhile person.

Soon the baby begins to explore the surroundings. These explorations give the child a chance to experience different sights, sounds, smells, tastes, and feelings. This helps the child to learn and gives a sense of accomplishment.

Many parents discourage their baby's early attempts at exploration. Instead of making their home safe for exploration, they keep the baby confined to a playpen. This limits the baby's opportunities to successfully experience the surroundings and develop a positive self-concept.

As children begin to understand language, they are more influenced by what others say to or about them. Children also reveal their image of themselves in what they say and do. For example, three small boys were playing together at a neighborhood playground. Two of them scrambled to the top of a log fort. They called to their friend still on the ground, "C'mon up here, Teddy. See how high we are!" But Teddy only watched them. "I can't. I'm too little to climb. Mom says I'll fall and get hurt."

Too many "don'ts" hurt a child's self-confidence. Sensible limits protect children, help them learn what they are able to do, and encourage success.

Some parents unintentionally hurt a child's self-concept by their actions, not their words. Let's say Jackie sets the table. Her mother smiles and says, "You did a very nice job!" Then she proceeds to move the dishes and silverware to their correct places. This tells Jackie her efforts weren't worth much, in spite of her mother's compliment. A better approach would have been for Jackie's mother to avoid making any changes. At dinner she might say, "Jackie set the table tonight. Didn't she do a nice job? She knows where the knives and spoons go. Soon she will learn where to put the forks, too."

Children who have a positive self-concept get along better with others. They don't have to show off or boss other children to prove themselves. They are more confident and outgoing. When they need help, they accept it more readily.

Establishing a positive self-concept early in life is essential. Young children accept what others say about them as being true. If they believe they are good, they try to act the part. However, if they constantly hear that they are "bad" or "stupid," they will live up to that image, too. It is not until children are older and can judge their own actions that this is less of an influence. By that time, however, the self-concept and matching behavior are already well-established.

Check Your Understanding

1. Compare the social relationships of children at ages eighteen months, two years, and three years.

2. How should caregivers decide whether or not to become involved in toddlers' quarrels? Describe a situation that calls for interference.

3. What is self-concept? Give some suggestions for helping build a positive self-concept in a small child.

Personality Patterns and Behavior

You will remember from Chapter 7 that an individual's personality is the combination of all the behavior characteristics usually shown by the person. Everyone has a unique personality (unlike that of anyone else), but general personality types can be identified. The sensitive child, the placid child, and the aggressive child are discussed in this book. Personality type may not remain the same from infancy through adulthood.

It is important for parents to recognize and respect their child's individuality. Parents often want their child to be like themselves. Outgoing, aggressive parents may attempt to make their shy child more outgoing. This doesn't work. Remember that a child's self-concept depends on how well the child is accepted by others.

Parents do have a responsibility to guide their children. A sensitive child needs experiences that will encourage adapting to new people and situations. An aggressive child needs to learn consideration for others.

Descriptions of three basic personality types follow. Remember that they show children who are extremely sensitive, placid, or aggressive. Most children show characteristics of more than one type.

The Sensitive Child

Sensitive, self-restrained toddlers prefer to be alone much of the time. Their attention span (the length of time spent on one activity) is longer than that of other children. The sensitive child rarely asks, "What can I do now?"

Sensitive children often lack the assertiveness to stand up for their own rights and desires. They tend to be dominated by others. They are less adventurous and hold back from new experiences, watching until they feel more sure of themselves. They also seem to have less tolerance for conflict.

Caregivers must help sensitive children meet new situations with less reluctance. Overprotecting them makes life easier, but does not encourage independence. Such youngsters must be allowed to explore and achieve slowly. Small tasks that can be successfully achieved help build confidence. When possible, tell the sensitive child what to expect from a new situation. If, for example, the child has learned about the animals and the sounds they make, a trip to the zoo will be more successful.

Sensitive children need opportunities to become more independent. How can parents and other caregivers help make sure that these experiences are successful?

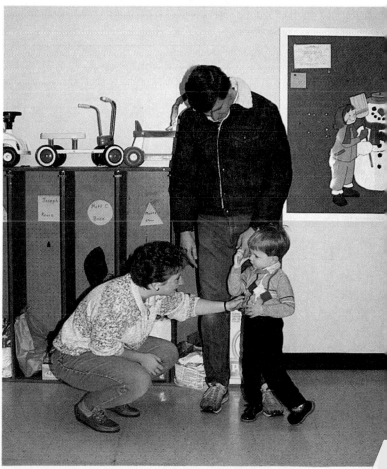

Give new experiences as these youngsters can accept them. Do not hurry them into feeding themselves, toilet training, or dressing. Substitute goals within their ability. One playmate at a time is best until they learn to cope with a group. They will also play best with children their own age or younger.

Some sensitive children are especially frightened of strangers. Such children need to gradually learn to do without their parents or customary caregivers. The transition should be gradual, not forced. Prepare them for an outsider's care by emphasizing the enjoyment that can be expected. "Sally is going to help you make soap bubbles while I'm gone." "Jeff is bringing a new story on dinosaurs with him. He's going to read it to you this afternoon."

The Placid Child

The placid toddler takes things as they are. Such children are most often at peace with their world.

Placid children play more happily with brothers, sisters, and friends. They are outgoing and respond easily to others. They are inclined to make games of eating, dressing, and bathing. They take guidance well and invite love. Parents find these children easiest to live with.

Placid children usually play well with others, but are also content to amuse themselves.

Children with an aggressive personality are even more active and adventurous than most toddlers. They need to be kept within the bounds of safe, acceptable behavior without being punished for their natural assertiveness.

The Aggressive Child

Aggressive toddlers are usually energetic and noisy. They are inclined toward active, physical play. They rarely take time for quiet activities such as coloring or "reading" books.

Aggressive youngsters often simply take the toys they want from others. If caregivers make them return the toys, they soon learn to trade toys rather than grab them. They often kick, bite, or hit to get their own way. As a last resort, they cry or have a temper tantrum.

Praise is useful for guiding aggressive toddlers. When the child misbehaves, point out the bad effects of such actions. Excessive aggression is actually encouraged by too much physical punishment. It may stop the immediate behavior, but it generates more hostility.

Self-assertive children are usually leaders rather than followers. They set examples—either good or bad—for other children. Parents need to make very clear what behavior is desirable and acceptable.

Discipline

Discipline is the task of helping children learn to behave in acceptable ways. It is a subject that worries most parents. They realize the need to teach their children to control their behavior, but worry about how to handle discipline effectively.

Most experts agree that the long-range goal of parental discipline is to help children develop **self-discipline**—the ability to control their own behavior. There will not always be someone around to tell children what is right and wrong. They must acquire and follow their own standards of responsible conduct.

The most effective method of discipline depends upon the individual parent and child. It also depends on the child's personality and age level. Different methods work best at different ages.

■ *Eight to twelve months.* Children can usually be controlled by distraction. If the baby is chewing on a newspaper, jingle a bright rattle in front of the child. As the rattle catches the baby's attention, the newspaper can quietly be removed.

■ *Twelve to fifteen months.* Remove as many problem or unsafe objects as possible from the baby's reach. Distraction and physically removing the child from forbidden activities or places work best at this age. For example, Jason was fascinated by the lawn mower and tried to follow it around the yard. His older sister Jan picked him up and took him in the house saying, "Let's go see if we can find the book about the teddy bear."

Discipline—or establishing some limits on behavior—is often necessary to keep children out of danger. How would you handle this situation?

■*Fifteen to twenty-four months.* Children this age require distraction, removal, and spoken restrictions. Two-year-old Richard is playing with toy cars on the driveway where a television repair truck is parked. Richard's father says, "Let's take your cars into the backyard for a while. You can play there until the truck is gone. If you stay here, the man in the truck might not see you playing when he is ready to leave. We don't want you to get hurt. After the truck leaves you can play on the driveway again."

■*Two to three years.* Two-year-olds are better at responding to spoken commands and explanations. With their improved knowledge, they can more easily understand adults' reasoning. Caregivers who explain reasons get better results than those who give only sharp commands. "Kari, you need to get dressed now because Grandma is coming to go shopping with us. We can't go unless we are ready."

■*Three to four years.* Three-year-olds take reasonable, loving discipline more readily than other ages. They like to please and may remind a parent that they are obedient. "I remembered to wear my boots today, didn't I? See my clean shoes? I'm a good boy, aren't I?"

In the long run, desired behavior can best be taught through example. Parents and caregivers who serve as positive role models in their daily lives have the most lasting influence on children. The chart on page 288 gives additional suggestions for disciplining children effectively. See Chapter 16 for a more complete discussion of guidance and discipline.

Once children are old enough, simple explanations can help them understand why they must follow rules.

Check Your Understanding

1. How do the personality differences between sensitive and aggressive children affect the ways their parents must guide them?

2. Give four guidelines for using discipline effectively.

3. Why would giving a two-year-old an explanation of desired behavior probably be more effective than giving a command?

How to Use Discipline Effectively

- Make relatively few and only reasonable demands.
- Let the child know you mean what you say. Carry out threats and promises, but keep both reasonable.
- Look at things from the child's point of view. When three-year-old Lisa pulls up the tulip plant out of the garden, she may just be trying to find out what makes it grow.
- Respond to misbehavior by telling the child:
    What he or she is doing wrong.
    Why it is wrong.
    What should be done instead.
- Keep explanations simple and brief. Remember that a child's vocabulary and attention span are limited.
- Be prepared to repeat over and over again. Toddlers have difficulty transferring learning. They don't realize that what applies to one situation also applies to similar ones.

- Be consistent. Don't laugh at the child one day and punish for the same thing the next day. Parents should agree on methods of discipline.
- Discipline should not be an outlet for an adult's anger, but should be relevant to the misbehavior.
- Remember that the difficult, hostile child is the one who needs love and guidance the most.

Chapter Review

To Sum Up

- The time between the first and fourth birthdays is one of emotional ups and downs.
- Negativism is a normal part of toddlers' development.
- Children's emotions become more specific as they grow older.
- The parent-child relationship is a clue to a child's emotional development.
- Many lifetime social attitudes and skills develop between one and four.
- A positive self-concept is needed for good emotional and social development.
- Children with different personality types need different types of guidance.
- The best method of discipline depends on the individual parent and child.

To Review and Remember

1. What is negativism? Name two causes of it.
2. Why might a child insist on unchanging routines?
3. Give three reasons a child might be angry more often than normal.
4. Why are some fears helpful? Give an example.
5. What is sibling rivalry?
6. What is the difference between parallel and cooperative play? At what ages is each found?
7. Give two ways a person with a positive self-concept differs from one with a negative self-concept.
8. What is the long-range goal of parental discipline?
9. What is the best way to teach a child desired behavior?
10. What three things should you tell a child who is misbehaving?

To Discuss and Discover

1. For several days watch the young children you come in contact with. (You may need to look for them while shopping or at a playground.) Describe two situations when you saw children express emotions. For each, tell the approximate age of the child, how the specific emotion was expressed, and what prompted it.
2. Discuss the advantages of a toddler having an older brother or sister. Are there any disadvantages? Does the age of the older child make a difference?
3. Observe parents with small children in a store or park. Describe an episode when the child's self-concept was positively reinforced by a parent's actions. Did you see any situations that parents seemed to handle poorly? What might they have done instead?

11 Intellectual Development from One to Three

To help you to . . .

- Describe various methods of learning.
- Explain how children develop concepts.
- Explain the seven basic elements of intellectual activity.
- Suggest ways to encourage young children to learn.
- Select safe, appropriate toys that promote learning as well as physical and social skills.
- Describe how children develop speech patterns and identify common speech problems.

Terms to Learn

articulation	flammable	speech therapist
concepts	imitation	trial-and-error
creativity	incidental learning	learning
directed learning	intelligence	

Have you ever watched the activity in a day care center or nursery school? Or have you ever stopped to watch a group of young children playing together? If you have not, do so sometime.

It is quite fascinating to watch children in the one- to three-year-old range. This is a time when children express their feelings easily—and often loudly! It is also a period when children begin to learn to play with each other. When you are observing children rather than interacting with them, you can see this more clearly. You can observe not only distinct personalities but also many stages of emotional and social development.

Have you ever considered what your own actions reveal to those who might observe you and your friends? Many signs of your own emotional and social development could be noted just by watching you carefully.

Understanding Learning

Learning occurs long before a child starts school. If it didn't, children would begin school unable to sit or walk, to feed themselves, or to talk or understand language. Learning begins on the first day of life and never ends.

Parents are a child's most important teachers. In early childhood, they must provide children with learning opportunities and encouragement. Other caregivers also play a role in intellectual development. Understanding how children learn will help you to help them learn more effectively.

The Role of Intelligence

You already know that intelligence means the capacity to learn. However, a more precise definition is helpful as you read about intellectual development between ages one and three. **Intelligence** can be defined as the ability to interpret or understand everyday situations and to use that experience when faced with new situations or problems.

A person's intelligence is determined both by heredity and by environment. Everyone is born with certain possible limits of intellectual development. Some people have more intellectual potential than others. However, the amount of that potential that is actually developed is greatly influenced by a person's environment.

As you read in Chapter 8, environmental experiences (such as home, family, toys) are especially important in the early years of life. It is then that the foundation for later learning is formed. Children also develop good or poor attitudes toward learning at this time. However, most people, even with a good home and education, never come close to using their maximum intellectual potential.

Methods of Learning

Children learn in a variety of ways, some rather unexpected. It is easy to see learning when you sit and teach a child to stack blocks or count. But children don't just wait for others to teach them. They learn on their own through everyday experiences and through play.

Although toys can aid learning, the encouragement of caregivers is far more important.

Unexpected events often lead to learning. Not all of them are as unusual as the chance to see a baby bird up close for the first time.

Incidental Learning

Incidental learning is unplanned learning. A small baby happens to push both feet against the bottom of the crib and discovers that action moves his or her body forward. When this happens accidentally a number of times, the baby finally understands and repeats the pushing on purpose. A two-year-old who sits on a balloon will probably remember the "pop" for a long time.

Trial-and-Error Learning

Pete is trying to put together a puzzle with four pieces. He picks up the first piece and tries to fit it into each hole in the puzzle board until he finds the right one. Janet wants to play with the truck her younger brother is using. First she takes it from him, but he screams and her mother makes her give it back. Next she tells him to go outside and play, but he doesn't want to. Finally, Janet offers to let him play with her clay if she can play with his truck. He agrees and Janet gets what she wants.

In both cases, the children had to try several solutions before finding out what worked. This is called **trial-and-error learning**.

Imitative Learning

Have you ever been annoyed by a younger brother or sister who copied everything you did? **Imitation** is really a method of learning. Children (and adults) learn by watching and imitating others. A three-year-old pretends to give a doll a bath because that's what parents do with the child's younger brother or sister. Both skills and behavior are learned by imitation.

Directed Learning

Directed learning is really another name for being taught, either formally or informally. A six-year-old is taught to read in a step-by-step way at school. Showing a two-year-old how to point to her nose, mouth, and eyes is also directed learning. It's just a less formal process. Directed learning begins in the early years at home and continues throughout life.

It took Colleen many tries before she found where to put all the puzzle pieces. What type of learning does this illustrate?

You might not think "pretending" is an example of learning, but it is. Much of a child's behavior comes from watching and imitating others.

"Here's how the record player works." Both caregivers and playmates can act as teachers in the process of directed learning.

Concept Development

In order to think effectively, children must learn to organize the information that they receive from their senses. This is done by forming **concepts**, general categories of objects and information. Concepts range from categories for objects such as "fruit," to qualities like color or shape and abstract ideas such as time.

As a child matures and learns, concepts become more refined and more accurate. At first, a baby is able to make only broad distinctions between people or things. For example, all women are "Mama" and all men are "Daddy." Later, "man," "woman," "girl," and "boy" begin to have meaning. Similarly, the child learns that this is a table and that is a chair. Tables have flat surfaces and no backs. They may be small or large and vary in color. They are used to eat from or to put things on.

Children also learn to categorize objects by shape, color, and size in early childhood. Balls are round, and so are biscuits and plates. Grass and trees are both green. When shown balls of three different sizes, most two-year-olds cannot recognize the middle-size ball. But at age three, they can do so easily. However, the relationship between two items, "biggest" and "littlest," may be recognized as early as eighteen months. At that time, the larger cat in the picture is called the "mama kitty" and the smaller one the "baby kitty."

Concepts of life and time are not learned until later. A young child believes that anything that moves or works is alive. This includes clouds, mechanical toys, dolls, and the washing machine. Later the child will realize only plants, animals, and people are alive.

Concepts of time improve slowly during the second and third years. Two-year-olds may be more patient than before because they know "soon" means something will happen. They know the difference between "before" and "after." However, "today," "tomorrow," and "yesterday" continue to be confusing until about age three.

What concepts is Ramona learning through this activity?

The Mind at Work

Intellectual activity is a complex process that coordinates the many elements of the mind. The most basic elements—attention, memory, perception, reasoning, imagination, creativity, and curiosity—are discussed here. Each of these is continuously developing.

Attention

Every moment the five senses are bombarded with information. Right now as you are reading is a good example. You see the words on the page. At the same time, you are also aware of such things as the size, shape, and color of the book and the amount of light in the room. You can probably hear pages being turned and perhaps someone walking in the hall, or a fly buzzing around the room. You may be able to smell lunch being prepared in the cafeteria or fresh wax on the floor. Your skin is telling you that the paper of the book is smooth and perhaps that you have a small rock in your shoe.

Fortunately, you are able to block out most of this sense information and focus only on the book. You can concentrate. A baby is not able to do so. The infant's attention flits from one thing to the next.

As children mature, they begin to be able to ignore most of the information their senses provide and concentrate on one item of interest. One- to three-year-olds have short attention spans. However, a three-year-old can focus on one activity for much longer than a one-year-old.

Memory

Without memory, there would be no learning. If an experience left no impression, it could not improve future behavior. A child reacts to a situation by remembering similar experiences in the past. A one-year-old who was frightened by a dog may be afraid of all animals for a time. A three-year-old can remember the particular dog and compare it with others to judge their character.

Memory begins with the routine of a baby's life. The comfortable familiarity of parents is one of a baby's earliest memories.

By age two, a toddler has a fairly good memory. A two-year-old can deliver simple messages. The child remembers a parent who has been absent several weeks, repeats bits of favorite stories, and can relate experiences after returning from a walk.

The three-year-old remembers simple commands, uses numbers as if counting (though fourteen may come directly after six), and names most colors.

Perception

Perception is the ability to receive and use information from the senses. This ability develops gradually throughout childhood.

A newborn receives a great deal of sensory information but is unable to interpret much of it. Gradually, a baby is able to make broad distinctions between people. These become more refined with experience.

Two- and three-year-olds are particularly known for their endless questions: "Why?" "What's that?" "How does this work?"

Perception improves and learning is more rapid if such questions are answered cheerfully and accurately. When passing a store window, you might say, "Look at the blue coat. Your shirt is blue, too. So is the sky." Such extra effort is certainly not a waste of time. It improves perception and aids concept development.

Adults often turn away a child's questions with an absent-minded "uh-huh" or "Don't bother me right now. I'm busy." Learning opportunities are lost. If these are the usual answers, the child eventually stops asking questions.

Reasoning

Reasoning is basic to the ability to solve problems and to make decisions. It is also important in recognizing relationships and forming concepts.

Babies show the beginnings of problem-solving ability at about four to six months of age. At this time the child pushes away one object in order to get at another.

Later, the child solves problems by actually trying out all possible solutions. For example, a box in which objects of various shapes are dropped through matching holes is a popular toy. The fourteen-month-old child will pick up a triangle and try to fit it into all the holes until one works.

By about two or three years of age, problem-solving becomes more mental. The child can think through possible solutions to a problem and eliminate those that won't work without actually trying them.

Decision-making is closely related to problem-solving. A decision is a type of problem. In making a decision, a child must learn to follow a logical process. The child might mentally ask the following questions:

1. What is the problem?
2. What do I already know about it?
3. What are possible solutions?
4. Which is the best solution?
5. Did I make the right choice?

Parents can help a child learn to make good decisions. One way is to give the child a chance to actually make decisions. At first, those decisions should be limited and a poor decision should not cause any harm. "Would you rather wear your yellow shirt or the green striped one with your brown pants?" "Would you like chicken soup or vegetable soup for lunch?" Eventually, the child will learn how to make decisions and avoid snap judgements if given opportunities to learn.

If a difficult situation is beyond the toddler, give just enough help to prevent discouragement. Show the child a possible solution and then allow the child to continue. "Let's see. This piece of puzzle has green grass on it. Maybe it fits on that side of the picture where everything is green." Children need successful experiences to gain perseverance, self-confidence, and the willingness to test their own reasoning ability.

Can you explain how playing this "piano" involves attention, memory, perception, and reasoning?

Imagination

Imagination begins to show itself at about two years of age. Actually, babies may also have active imaginations, but there is no way of knowing since they cannot speak. An active imagination is an important part of learning.

Unfortunately, imagination is often stifled early in life by the lack of understanding in adults. For example, when a three-year-old makes up a story, the youngster is not lying. Until about five years of age, a child simply is not sure where reality ends and imagination begins.

Imagination allows the child to try new things and be different people—at least in the mind. Chairs become trains, boxes are buildings, and closets are caves. The child becomes a ferocious lion or a mail carrier. Imaginary playmates are common at this age.

Children use their imagination to connect what they see and hear with themselves. An airplane may lead them to ask, "Will I fly in one someday?" They hear about death and ask, "Will I die, too?"

Parents who understand the reason for imaginative stories don't accuse the child of lying. They realize that time will usually take care of such exaggeration.

Children can be and do almost anything through imagination. An empty box makes a good house. Another day it might become a spaceship or a fort.

Close-up

Jane Brown was expecting several people for a neighborhood association committee meeting. Three-year-old Jessica was underfoot, so her mother suggested she let the neighbors in as they arrived. Jessica greeted each person politely and proceeded to tell about her upcoming trip to see her grandmother.

"This is my suitcase with my clothes. I am taking the bus that leaves at 3:30. Mommy and Daddy are taking me to the bus. They will put my suitcase on the bus and put me in a bus seat and then go home. I'll go on the bus alone 'til I get to Grandma's house."

Surprised, each adult asked the same question. "Are you really going alone?"

"Yup. I'm going all by myself. I'm big enough now. I can do things by myself," she answered confidently.

The details were so complete that the puzzled adults accepted Jessica's story. But as they gathered around the table for their meeting, one said doubtfully, "Jane, are you sure you want Jessica to go on a bus to Granite City by herself? She's only three! I wouldn't even let my ten-year-old do that!" The other adults agreed.

Jessica's mother laughed in surprise. "Oh, you mean Jessie's trip to her grandmother's! Of course, she's not going. She's just pretending she is. Two days ago, we sent Jenny, Jessica's twelve-year-old sister, on the bus to visit her grandmother. It's a nonstop ride. Her grandmother was there to meet her. Jessie heard all the planning and instructions we gave Jenny. She also went with us when we took Jenny to her seat on the bus. Jessie likes to imitate Jenny, so she thinks she can go on the bus by herself, too.

"Next week Jessie will probably be a karate expert. We're all going to Todd's karate tournament on Saturday. That will keep Jessie's imagination busy for a few days, too."

How do imaginary experiences help children at this stage?

Would you have handled the situation differently than Jessica's mother did? Why or why not? ■

Creativity

Imagination and **creativity** are closely related. Creativity means that imagination is put to use to produce something. The product is usually something others can see, such as a finger painting. But daydreams are also products of creativity.

Creativity is an asset throughout life. It is in early childhood, however, that it develops most—if children are given opportunities and encouragement. Here are some ways to promote creativity:

- Encourage play activities that depend on imagination and creativity. Drawing, playing with clay, building things, and telling stories are opportunities for creative expression.
- Don't insist on conformity in every aspect of life. The message that being different is always bad stifles creativity. You might respond, "My, Martin, I've never seen a cat with three eyes before or a purple cat. Purple is such a pretty color. Wouldn't it be fun to have a purple cat?"
- Praise the child's efforts. Display that new picture of a three-eyed, purple cat on the refrigerator.

Creative activities are a way for children to express themselves. They also help children feel good about their accomplishments.

Curiosity

Babies are curious about the world around them. That curiosity is the source of learning and should increase with age. However, parents sometimes stifle a child's curiosity by overprotecting the child—or the home—from harm. They don't realize that children are educating themselves while creating clutter.

Young children seem to be into everything. They poke into every corner and closet. They handle and examine everything within reach. It is impossible for caregivers to anticipate what a two- or three-year-old might do next. Surprised parents may find a doll or truck in the washing machine because "It was dirty." A plastic horse stands in the center of the mashed potatoes as the child explains, "Horsey eat too."

Caregivers need to remember that curiosity stimulates learning, but it can also be dangerous. Keep children safe by removing hazards from their environment and checking on them frequently. Don't totally limit their freedom to explore. You may wish to review the safety tips on page 244.

Check Your Understanding

1. Give three examples of how children can learn on their own through everyday experiences and through play.

2. Make a list of ten concepts. Which three would be easiest for a child to learn? Which three would be most difficult? Why?

3. Explain this statement: "Without memory there would be no learning."

4. If you were caring for a three-year-old, what activities might you use to encourage the child to use his or her imagination?

Encouraging Learning

Parents and other caregivers have either a positive or negative effect on a child's learning. Providing a relaxed atmosphere and a variety of experiences encourages children to learn. However, adults who are overly harsh and those who show children they do not really care discourage learning.

Children learn each skill only when they are physically and intellectually ready. It would be a waste of time to try to teach a three-month-old to ride a tricycle—the baby has neither the physical nor intellectual ma-turity necessary. Children who are pushed too early may also feel a sense of failure. This often causes them to learn more slowly rather than more rapidly.

Some parents cause the opposite prob-lem. They are unwilling to give their child the opportunity to learn when the child is ready. For example, one mother discovered that put-ting on her youngster's shoes every time he struggled with them caused problems later. When he was well past the age where he should have succeeded, he continued to bring his shoes to her to put on. He was impatient with the effort and anxious to be off to play.

Learning should be fun. Sharing new experiences with caregivers helps give a child confidence.

Here is a list of things to keep in mind when guiding the learning of young children:

■*Give your time and attention.* Children learn best when encouraged by someone who cares about them. That doesn't necessarily mean actively teaching them lessons. Going places together or sharing a game teaches, too. All children like to be read a story. See pages 314–315 for tips on having fun with books.

■*Allow time for thinking.* Time means little to toddlers. Do not hurry them in decisions.

■*Give only as much help as needed to succeed.* Instead of putting on a sock for a toddler, just help slip it down over the heel before it gets caught.

■*Encourage children to draw their own conclusions.* "Let's find out," is better than an explanation. Seeing and doing helps reinforce learning. For example, let a child help prepare muffin batter. Explain why ingredients are added. Then let the child watch (if the oven has a glass window) as the muffins rise and bake.

■*Show how to solve problems.* When blocks keep toppling, show how placing them directly above each other balances them better. Serve as a role model in teaching children how to solve problems.

■*Maintain a positive attitude.* Encourage learning by letting the child know you have confidence in his or her abilities.

■*Keep explanations simple and on the child's level.* You might say, "The fish are in the tank because they live in the water. People live outside the water. We need air to breathe."

■*Allow children to explore and discover.* Let them occasionally roll in the grass, climb trees, and squeeze mud through their fingers and toes. This is a part of learning, too. Let children live in their own world, not an adult's. Can you remember the fun of wading in puddles despite your parents' disapproval? Constantly saying "Don't do this" and "Don't touch that" inhibits sensory and motor experiences.

■*Help youngsters understand the world and how it works.* Take them along whenever possible. Places like the library, supermarket, and gas station can all be learning experiences. Talk about what is happening in those places and why. Let children snap string beans for dinner; call attention to the snapping sound and the seeds inside. When painting the steps, let the child "paint" the sidewalk with an old brush and water. Children draw on these kinds of experiences for conversation and for understanding other experiences.

It doesn't take much effort to turn everyday activities into learning experiences. These children are finding out about where the food they eat comes from and how it grows.

Play Activities and Toys

Through play with toys and other children, a child develops physically, intellectually, socially, and emotionally. A child's play can be compared to an adult's work—it is the basic task of that stage of life.

Toys are an important part of play. They allow children to experience imaginary situations and play different roles. They encourage the development of both large and small motor skills. They also help children learn to share and cooperate with others. Today, with thousands of toys to choose from, it is important to know how to choose wisely. This requires a knowledge of both toy safety and child development. The "Toy Selection Checklist" on page 305 will help you choose toys wisely.

Safety should be the most important consideration in choosing toys. This is especially true for toddlers. Remember that toys receive hard use. They should not break easily, have any sharp edges, have small parts that a young child could swallow, or be **flammable** (easily burned). Be sure no lead-base paints are used on the toys, because they are poisonous. Read all labels carefully before buying. The Food and Drug Administration and the Consumer Product Safety Commission have the power to recall toys that are unsafe. However, sometimes the danger is not known until a child is seriously injured or killed by a toy.

There is nothing more discouraging to a child (or an adult) than to have a toy break the first time it is used. When buying a toy, think about the child or children who will be using it. How will the toy be used? Is it made of materials that will withstand children's play? Are all parts firmly attached? Choose only toys that will give good value and service for their price.

Many people do not think about care when selecting a toy, but it is an important consideration. A stuffed bear that takes a ride through a mud puddle may be ruined unless it can be cleaned. Books with wipe-clean covers are much more practical for small children.

Many toys for sale today do everything for the child. They do not help the child develop an imagination. Simple toys that can be many different things or can be used in a variety of ways are better. A doll that talks may be able to say five phrases. But a doll that cannot talk can say anything desired through the child. Toys that lend themselves to many uses allow toddlers to work out their own ideas and develop self-confidence.

A shovel, a pail, and sand are simple toys, yet think of how many areas of development they benefit: creativity, motor skills, cooperative play. What else would you add to the list?

Colorful toys are important. Children—especially young children—respond more readily to colorful objects. Later, bright toys encourage children to learn color names.

Sometimes those buying toys fail to take the size of the child into consideration. A toy that is too large for the youngster to handle alone cannot be played with easily. The excitement of a new tricycle is quickly lost if the child's legs are too short to reach the pedals. A wooden baseball bat may be too heavy to swing, but plastic ones are lightweight and easy to handle.

Similar problems occur when toys are not appropriate for the child's age. Baby toys are not challenging enough for a three-year-old. Neither will an older child's toy amuse a fourteen-month-old for very long. It is important to know the capabilities and interests of children at various ages in order to choose appropriate toys.

Three- and four-year-olds need safe opportunities to run, jump, and climb.

■*One to two years.* A child practices body control and learns through exploration. Many toys during this period can be items found in the home. Anything that allows the child to use large muscles is usually popular. This includes swings, small wagons, rocking horses or riding toys with wheels, balls, boxes, and low furniture. At this age, children also like small dolls and animals, sturdy books, and containers of all sorts. Stacking toys, simple puzzles, and toy cars are also popular. Small toys or ones with parts that fit in the mouth should be avoided to prevent children from swallowing them.

■*Two to three years.* A child's coordination and understanding improve markedly. In addition, the child wants to do what he or she sees adults doing. This desire to imitate suggests a variety of toys: a child-size broom, shovel, plastic or wooden tools, play dishes, and empty food containers to name a few. Crayons, clay, beads to string, books, large blocks, and blunt scissors are popular. A sandbox can provide hours of enjoyment, and some children are ready for a small tricycle.

■*Three to four years.* At this age, children still enjoy many of the same toys. Their improved motor skills and imagination increase their interest in toys requiring the hands. Dolls to dress, trucks, trains, and similar toys are enjoyed. Children this age love to color, paint—especially finger paint—and play with clay. The three-year-old also spends longer periods with books and likes to listen to records. Puzzles that are not too difficult are worked over and over again. Gym equipment such as ladders, swings, and slides get enthusiastic use. Most three-year-olds love the freedom and mobility of a tricycle.

Toy Selection Checklist

√ Is the toy safe?
√ Is it well made and durable?
√ Will it be easy to care for?
√ Will it encourage the child to use his or her imagination?
√ Is it colorful?
√ Will it be easy for the child to handle?
√ Is it appropriate for the child's age?

Speech Development

In Chapter 8 you read that babies learn words by repeating sounds. Gradually, they learn that some combinations of sounds—words—have specific meanings. Now you will learn how one-, two-, and three-year-olds acquire speech patterns and grammar just by listening to others.

Speech depends on all areas of development—physical, social, emotional, and intellectual. A problem in any one area can slow or prevent speech development. However, even children without such problems vary greatly in learning to speak.

Between their first and second birthdays, children work at learning new words. They like to learn the names of everything and listen to the sounds the words make. During this period, most children use one word rather than a whole sentence to express a thought. "Water" means "I want a drink," when the child holds out a cup.

How adults and other children speak to a child has a significant effect on the child's language development. For example, Helen Collins always spoke baby talk to her son, Jason. "It's time for my itsy, bitsy baby to go nightnight." At three-and-one-half, Jason still cannot speak plainly enough for others to understand. Jim Standard rarely talked to his infant daughter, Amy. When someone asked him why, he replied, "I'd feel silly doing it. She can't understand anything anyway." Amy started talking much later than average. Each of these parents probably contributed to their child's speech difficulties.

You can encourage or discourage language development and learning in children this age just by the way you talk to the child. You can, for example, describe what the child is seeing or doing. "My, Cindy! Look at the big bite you've taken out of that shiny red apple. Can you hear the crunch it makes when you put your teeth into it?" "Jake, can you point to the white chicken in the story? What sound does a chicken make? Let's count the eggs in the chicken's nest. You had an egg for breakfast this morning, didn't you?"

You can see how Cindy and Jake will learn much more quickly. They hear correctly spoken English that tells them the words for what they are experiencing.

At about age two, the child will combine two or three words to make short sentences: "Doggie bark," "Jimmy fall down." The child calls himself or herself by name.

Children often find pronouns (such as I, you, me, and they) confusing at first. Two-year-old Katie spent several weeks demanding, "Help you!" and "Change you!" For months she has been listening to her parents say, "I'll help you," and "I think it's time to change you." She logically thought "you" was another word for "Katie"!

At about age two and one-half, children begin to learn some of the rules of grammar. They learn by listening to others talk rather than by any formal teaching. For example, a child will begin putting an "s" on words to make them plural. The rule is applied to all words. At two and one-half, "foots" and "tooths" make as much sense as "fingers" and "flowers." It is the English language with all its exceptions that doesn't follow the rules rather than the child. Gradually, the child will learn the right words by hearing older children and adults use correct English.

Speech Difficulties

Many parents are concerned about "late talkers." Delayed speech isn't considered a problem before age three if the child understands what is said and other areas of development are normal. Some parents make the mistake

"The *sun* is in the *sky*. Can you make a 's-s-s' sound?" Some words and sounds are difficult for young children to articulate. With time and practice, however, most children eventually master them.

of pressuring the child who talks late or unclearly. Most often, this just makes the child aware of the problem and exaggerates it.

Children who do not seem to understand what is said and who do not speak or speak very little should have a thorough physical examination. If there is a problem hindering language development, it is important that it be caught early. Poor hearing is one physical problem that obviously would interfere with speech development. Mental retardation, learning difficulties, and emotional problems may also slow speech.

Many children continue to have problems with **articulation**—the ability to use clear, distinct speech—until at least age three. Sometimes it is only certain sounds that cause difficulty. Other children skip syllables or leave off the endings of words. These problems usually correct themselves as the child grows older.

Avoid correcting pronunciation too often. Instead, set a good example with your own careful speech. If the toddler says, "ba" and reaches for a bottle, hand it over saying, "Bottle. Tommy wants his bottle."

Other early speech difficulties may be more serious. Many children between two and five years stutter or lisp.

Some children repeat whole words or phrases: "Johnny . . . Johnny . . . Johnny. He . . . he . . . he hit Sally! He hit Sally!" This is not true stuttering. The child's speaking and thinking abilities are still immature. The youngster simply cannot get the words out as rapidly as necessary. The same thing happens when a child says, "I ah . . . ah . . . ah . . . I ah . . . I want this green one," when offered a choice of colored balloons. The child is thinking and waiting for the right words to come. Some hesitation and repetition are common to all preschool children and they are not a sign of real stuttering.

A true stutter is recognized by the rhythm, pitch, and speed of speech. It is rapid, forced, and short and sharp in sound. Usually, only the beginning of a word is repeated: "I c—c—c—can't g—g—g—go outside." The child usually shows tenseness in some way—gasping, sputtering, or rapid blinking.

The cause of stuttering is still not clearly understood. Most children outgrow it with no outside help. Some, however, need the help of a speech therapist. (A **speech therapist** is a professional trained to diagnose and help correct speech problems.) Patience and understanding are very important.

Many young children also lisp to some degree. It takes a while to learn to place the tongue correctly to produce desired sounds. True lisping usually results from two main causes: a tight muscle beneath the tongue or the inability to clearly distinguish between sounds. A doctor should be able to determine the cause and suggest treatment.

No matter what speaking difficulties any child may have, parents must let the youngster know that it does not affect their love. Such an attitude will help the child cope with the problem, if not overcome it.

Check Your Understanding

1. How is it possible to give a child too much help? What effect does this have on a child's learning?

2. Explain ways in which a trip to the supermarket could be made into a good learning experience for a young child.

3. Explain how the ways adults and other children speak to a child can affect the child's language development.

Most children eventually grow out of their minor speech problems. Sometimes, however, an examination reveals a physical problem affecting speech. The help of a trained professional may be needed.

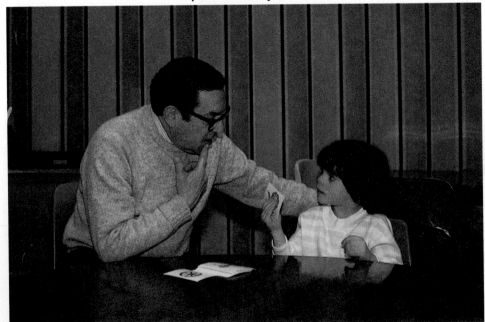

Chapter Review

To Sum Up

- Intelligence is determined by both heredity and environment.
- Children learn on their own, as well as by being taught.
- Children learn to organize the information they receive from their senses by gradually developing concepts.
- Many elements of the mind are continuously developing.
- Play and toys promote all aspects of development.
- Toys should be safe, appealing, and appropriate to a child's age.
- The rate of speech development varies greatly.
- How adults and other children speak to a young child greatly affects the child's language development.
- Some young children have difficulty with articulation, stuttering, or lisping.

To Review and Remember

1. What is intelligence?
2. Describe how heredity and environment affect learning.
3. What are three methods of learning, other than being taught?
4. Name seven basic elements of intellectual activity and give an example of each.
5. Why is the ability to reason important?
6. Give two ways to promote creativity.
7. Give five guidelines for encouraging learning.
8. What are three reasons that toys are important?
9. List six toys appropriate for a two-year-old.
10. Name two possible causes of delayed speech development beyond age three.

To Discuss and Discover

1. Plan an intellectual development activity for two-year-olds in a day care center. Include exactly what you will do and any materials needed. Explain how your activity will help intellectual development and why it is appropriate for that age level.
2. While shopping (or in any situation where there are young children), look for signs of children trying to learn. Keep track of youngsters' comments and questions and their parents' responses. Then, in writing, give examples of parents encouraging learning and of parents discouraging learning.

Encouraging Independence

Children, ages one to three, both want more independence and are afraid of it. Caregivers must help them develop a sense of independence and learn self-help skills.

As you interact with toddlers, you will see that age, personality, and environment all affect how independent they feel. But children this age are also unpredictable. One morning Josh, age two and a half, insisted on dressing himself without any help. He was a "big boy now." But at breakfast, Josh grabbed his baby sister's bottle and started sucking it. The comfort of babyhood still has a strong pull.

You will probably never understand such changes in mood. But you can help children develop independence. Here are some tips:

- Be sure the child is comfortable. For eating at the table, a high chair with the tray removed or a booster seat helps raise a toddler to the right height.

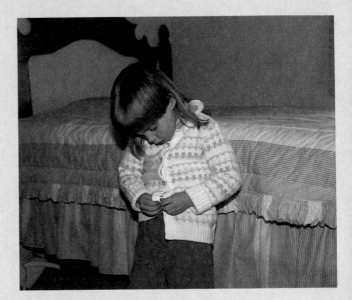

Self-Dressing

- Choose clothes that are easy to put on and take off. Look for roomy shirts that slip on quickly. Pants, skirts, or shorts with elastic waistbands are good. Front openings are easier to handle than those down the back.
- Fasteners often cause problems. Self-gripping fasteners, large buttons, and zippers that don't come apart at the bottom are easiest for toddlers to manage.
- If a dressing task is too difficult for the child to do completely, let him or her do one part. Pulling up a zipper or slipping a foot into a shoe can be the first step to learning a more complex task.
- Praise effort as well as accomplishment.

Self-Feeding

- Don't expect a child just learning to feed himself or herself to be neat. Minimize the mess with unbreakable dishes and a child-size spoon and fork. A cup with a spill-proof lid helps during the learning stage.
- Choose foods that are easy to handle and eat. Cut food into bite-size pieces before serving. Remember that attractively served food encourages interest.

Grooming Skills

- Children should have their own towel, wash-cloth, brush, comb, and toothbrush within easy reach.
- A small stool can help toddlers cope with adult-size bathrooms.
- Establish grooming routines and follow them daily.
- Set a good example yourself. Children are more likely to wash their hands before eating, for example, when they see that you do, too.

Helping Others

- Putting away toys can start as a game and be encouraged with praise. Be sure there is adequate storage space within the child's reach.
- Toddlers love to imitate. Let them help with simple chores like sweeping, carrying or folding laundry, or setting the table.
- Keep directions short and clear. Younger children can remember only one step at a time.
- Be patient. A child's efforts will always be slower and less efficient than your own. But learning can't take place without practice.

Coping with Temper Tantrums

Nothing makes most caregivers feel more helpless than a child's temper tantrum. But if you understand what causes tantrums, you can cut down on their frequency. And when they do occur, knowing how to respond can minimize frustration for both you and the child.

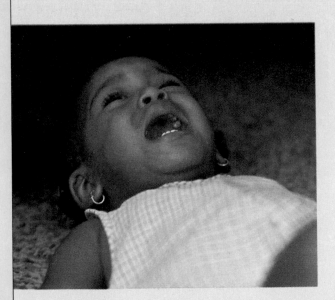

What Triggers Tantrums?

Temper tantrums occur most frequently at ages two and three. But even older children sometimes have them.

Basically, tantrums are a sign of a child's struggle for control and independence. When they don't get what they want, children express their anger by crying, kicking, screaming, or even biting or breath-holding.

Why does this happen in some situations, but not others? Child development specialists have identified a number of common triggers for temper tantrums:

- Being overly tired.
- Disruption in normal routine.
- Too much excitement or activity.
- Frustration from having too many restrictions and too few choices.
- Lack of firm, realistic limits.

Responding Appropriately

A tantrum is upsetting to both the child and the caregiver. There's no magic formula for turning a screaming child into a happy one. But as a caregiver, you can lessen the impact of the tantrum by responding appropriately.

In handling a tantrum, there are two main goals. First, you must prevent the child from being hurt or hurting anyone else. Second, you must enforce the limits you have set. If you give in to the child's demands, tantrums are more likely to be repeated because the child thinks they work.

If a tantrum occurs at home, the behavior can sometimes simply be ignored. Putting the child in his or her room or in a chair away from others often helps. These techniques remove the child's audience.

When a tantrum occurs in a public place, it's natural to feel embarrassed. But it is still important not to give in to the child's demands. Move the child to a quiet spot to cool down, or just go home.

Screaming at the child is never effective. Spanking merely makes the child angrier. It's important to remain calm. Acknowledge the child's feelings while reemphasizing the reason his or her demands can't be met. "I know you are upset that you can't go outside and play. It's getting dark now and you can't play in the yard after dark. Tomorrow morning you can go out and play." Sometimes offering an alternative helps. "When you stop crying, we can put this puzzle together."

Occasionally, a child must be restrained to prevent harm. When this happens, keep the period of restraint as short as possible. The child will naturally be even more frustrated by it.

Temper tantrums are always unpleasant. But through appropriate responses, you can help children learn more acceptable ways to deal with anger and frustration.

Fun with Books

Books are wonderful learning tools. But reading to a child also nourishes close relationships, encourages language and listening skills, and helps the child separate reality from fantasy. And children who learn early in childhood that books are fun are more likely to remain readers throughout life.

By age three, children can enjoy longer stories (up to 10 or 15 minutes) with more of a plot. They like realistic stories about children, but also ones that help them use their imagination. Look for books that help them learn how things work and why things happen.

Choose Appropriate Books

Children of different ages respond best to different types of books. Understanding their interests will help you choose books they will like.

One-year-olds need short, simple books with large, uncomplicated pictures. They like picture books with objects they can name. Books with rhymes and rhythms are also popular. Some books have different textures on each page to stimulate the toddler's sense of touch.

Two-year-olds prefer simple stories they can relate to. Books about families and familiar experiences are good choices. Like one-year-olds, they never tire of hearing their favorite stories again and again.

Become a Master Storyteller

Reading a story is much like putting on a play — but you are all the characters. Create excitement as you read. Give each character a different voice. A bear can be low and growly. A princess can be shy or commanding. Reinforce what the book says with gestures and facial expressions.

If you are reading to one or two children, snuggle up close and hold the book so they can see. If you are reading to a group, the children should be in a semicircle facing you. Read loudly enough for everyone to hear. And learn the story beforehand so you can keep the pictures facing the children.

Encourage Participation

Long before they can read, children can participate in stories. Active involvement helps increase learning and fun.

- Even very young children can turn the pages. This gives practice in eye-hand coordination.
- Relate the action and pictures in the book to the child's own life. "You have a red ball, too, don't you?" "In the story, Peter has a baby sister. You have a baby brother."
- Ask questions as you read. "What do you think Melissa will find when she opens the box?" "What color is the dog?" "How would you feel if you were lost in the store? What would you do?"
- With familiar books, let the child play the part of one character. Don't look for word-for-word accuracy. Provide clues, when necessary, to keep the story moving.
- With older children, practice recognizing letters and the sounds they make. Point out the words for familiar objects.
- Have a puppet show to dramatize a story, or draw a picture of it.
- Remember that interaction with the child and enjoyment are more important than finishing the story.

Chapter 12: Physical Development

Chapter 13: Emotional & Social Development

Chapter 14: Intellectual Development

W hat is it like to be a child four, five, or six years of age? You already have some first-hand knowledge. Your earliest clear memories probably date back to around this time.

Perhaps you remember how proud you were when you learned to print your name or do a somersault. What did you like to eat? Did you have a favorite outfit to wear? Topics such as physical skills, clothing, and eating habits are discussed in Chapter 12. As you will see, children this age are practicing and refining their physical abilities. They learn to be responsible for most of their personal care.

The beginning of school is a major milestone of this stage. It brings many adjustments and rapid development in the emotional and social areas. The child must also learn to cope with new fears and emotions, as Chapter 13 explains.

How well children adjust socially and emotionally to school affects how well they learn. But learning also continues to come from everyday experiences and the encouragement of care-givers. In Chapter 14, you will see evidence of the four- to six-year-old's increasingly refined thinking processes. You will also read about the needs of children with special problems or potential.

Think of the remarkable changes that take place between a child's birth and seventh birthday. Of course, development does not stop at that age. But after reading this unit and the ones that precede it, you should agree that the early years of life are in many ways the most important.

12 Physical Development from Four to Six

To help you to . . .

- Describe normal physical growth for children ages four to six.

- Describe motor skill development for this age group.

- Explain the importance of good nutrition for children this age and tell how it can be encouraged.

- Explain how to help children develop good self-care habits.

- Identify the possible causes of enuresis and how the problem should be handled.

Terms to Learn

ambidextrous	enuresis	preschoolers
dexterity	group identification	secondary teeth

Five-year-old Kimberly skipped across the driveway to her neighbor's door.

"Hi, Kimberly," said Mrs. Horton.

"I just went to my first ballet lesson. I get to take ballet lessons because my mommy said that when I learned to tie my shoes all by myself, then I could take ballet lessons, and I can tie my shoes all by myself so now I take ballet lessons." Kimberly was so excited that she talked very fast.

"Why, that's wonderful," replied Mrs. Horton.

"Watch this," said Kimberly. "This is first position." She stood with her heels together and her toes pointed outward. "And this is fifth position." Kimberly struggled to slide one foot in front of the other.

"That's very good," said Mrs. Horton.

Kimberly, like other children her age, is growing physically. Not only is she growing in size, but she is developing the skills that allow her to skip, tie her shoes, dance, and do many other things.

Physical Growth and Development

Children ages four and five are often called **preschoolers** (Sometimes three year olds are included, too.) Actually, many preschoolers are in some type of a school or day care program where they are learning some school skills. Still, they have not started the formalized learning of first grade.

Children of four, five, and six are known for their activity. They run instead of walk and wiggle when they sit. Yet behind all this activity is a purpose. This period is a time of practicing and refining physical skills.

Height and Weight

The rate of physical growth from ages four to six is only slightly slower than at ages one through three. The average yearly increase in height at ages four to six is 2½ to 3 in. (6.4 to 7.6 cm). You may remember that, as a general rule, children double their birth length in five years. Thus, a shorter-than-average baby may still be shorter than most children at age five. Height and weight charts give averages. Many children are smaller or larger, but are still considered to be developing normally.

At this age, children seem to be always in motion.

Differences in height and weight increase as children grow older. Note the differences in size among a group of kindergartners or even among those in your own class.

In general, there is a tendency for children to be taller and heavier than their parents. Improved diet and health habits, enriched foods, and advances in medicine have combined to make this generation the largest and healthiest in history.

Average heights and weights for this period are given in the chart on page 316. Most children gain about 4 to 5 lb. (1.8 to 2.3 kg) per year during this period. However, larger or smaller gains are quite common. Boys are often slightly taller and heavier than girls. As a child grows, height and weight charts become less reliable guides.

Proportion and Posture

Between a child's fourth and seventh birthdays, the body becomes straighter and slimmer. The protruding abdomen of babyhood flattens. The shoulders widen and are held more erect. The chest, which was round at birth, remains so until about age three. Then it broadens and flattens. The neck also becomes longer.

The legs lead in development during this period. They lengthen rapidly, growing straighter and firmer. Because their balance and coordination have improved, children hold their arms nearer the body when walking or running.

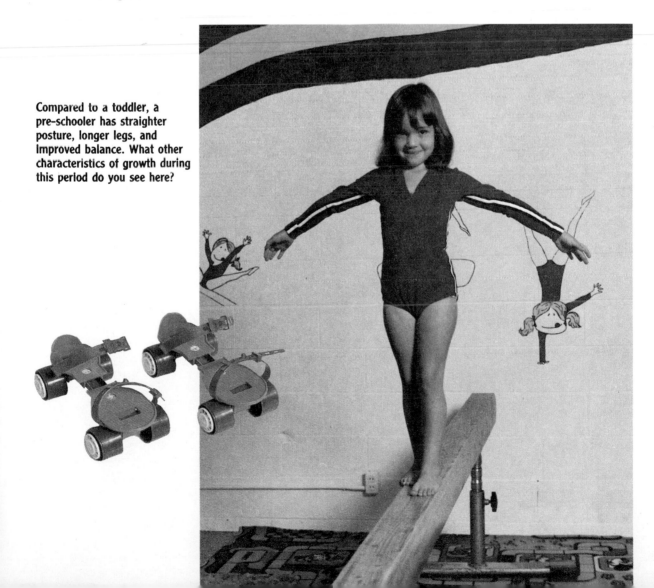

Compared to a toddler, a pre-schooler has straighter posture, longer legs, and improved balance. What other characteristics of growth during this period do you see here?

Average Heights and Weights
Ages Four to Six

Age	Height		Weight	
	Customary	Metric	Customary	Metric
4	40.7 in.	104 cm	36.0 lb.	16.4 kg
5	43.5 in.	110 cm	40.5 lb.	18.4 kg
6	46.0 in.	117 cm	45.0 lb.	20.5 kg

Missing teeth are a sign of leaving babyhood behind. Speech may be affected until the gaps are filled in.

Teeth

At about age six, children begin to lose their primary teeth. They are gradually replaced with secondary teeth, sometimes called "permanent teeth."

The six-year molars or "first molars" are the first of the secondary teeth to appear. There are four of these—two upper and two lower—positioned in back of the twenty baby teeth. They appear before the front teeth are replaced and act as a lock to keep all teeth in position. Later, as front teeth are replaced by new and larger teeth, the molars prevent the new front teeth from pushing other teeth farther back in the jaw.

In general, the primary teeth are lost in approximately the same order as they came in. The two lower front teeth are usually the first to be replaced, followed by the two upper front teeth, and so on.

Thumb-Sucking

Some four-, five-, and six-year-olds continue to suck their thumb. As in earlier years, this is a self-comforting technique. Most children learn that this is not socially acceptable. They give up the habit entirely or limit it to home.

Thumb-sucking can cause other problems. Heavy or strong sucking several times a day or all night can affect the position of the permanent teeth and the shape of the jaw.

Only a professional can diagnose the seriousness of the child's sucking. A dentist should be consulted. Several positive methods may be suggested to stop the habit. Scolding or punishing the child usually only prolongs the habit rather than stopping it.

Motor Skills

During this period, most basic large motor skills such as walking, running, and climbing become well developed. Small motor skills also show significant improvement.

Four- and five-year-olds are very energetic. Favorite activities are usually physical—jumping, climbing, rapid tricycling, and turning somersaults. At four, children are learning to throw and catch both large and small balls. Five-year-olds have improved speed and coordination in all these activities.

Learning to bat a ball requires large and small motor skills, eye-hand coordination, and lots of practice.

Writing the alphabet is not only an intellectual skill, but a physical one. Can you explain why?

Dexterity (skilled use of the hands and fingers) is improved in four- and five-year-olds. They build towers and buildings of blocks with steady hands. Four-year-olds lace their shoes, but most cannot tie them until about age five. Children this age can pour liquids from a pitcher into a glass, showing improved eye-hand coordination. They like to cut and paste and can print some letters, but often not words.

The motor activities and interests of six-year-olds remain much the same but are done with greater ease and skill. Movements are smoothly coordinated. Increased mental ability lends judgement to throwing, catching, building, and drawing. Six-year-olds enjoy balancing activities such as walking a curb or riding a two-wheeled bicycle. Rhythm intrigues them. They like to keep time to music and jump rope to chanted jingles.

Once in school, children have greater opportunity to practice and improve small motor skills. Emphasis is placed on coloring, drawing, cutting, and writing.

The chart on page 321 summarizes average motor abilities by age. Timing may vary because of a child's abilities and interests.

Close-up

Joanne Simons teaches kindergarten at Monroe Elementary School. Today, she is the guest speaker on motor skills development in the Child Development class at Big Springs High.

"You only have to look at my class," said Ms. Simons, "to realize that motor skill development varies greatly from child to child. The children range in age from four and a half to five and a half. However, you can't necessarily tell which are older by how well they cut or color or jump."

"I have one child in class who is among the youngest, but who has excellent coordination and concentration. He likes to put together puzzles with 75 or 100 pieces. Another child is almost a year older but can't put together a 35-piece puzzle or draw a very good circle. There's just a lot of individual variation."

"If you think back to your own kindergarten days, you will remember that many of the class activities are designed to help children improve their small and large motor skills. Painting is not only fun and creative, but it also helps eye-hand coordination. Cutting and coloring do, too. We play games that involve running and jumping and climbing — all large motor skill activities."

Jennifer raised her hand and asked Ms. Simons, "Why are these skills emphasized so much in school? I would think kids would learn them on their own at home. Shouldn't school concentrate more on things like reading and writing and thinking?"

"That's a good question," replied Ms. Simons. "There are really two reasons for motor skill emphasis. First, we know that children who have good motor skill development will be more successful learning to read and write. Think about writing for a moment. Forming letters takes the same kind of small muscle control and eye-hand coordination as coloring, doesn't it? The second reason we emphasize these activities is that they provide a transition between home and first grade. They resemble the play activities children are accustomed to, but they are somewhat more structured or controlled. It helps children prepare for the more formal learning of first grade."

"Your teacher is planning to bring you to observe my kindergarten class next week. I think you'll find the kids interesting and very much individuals. If you look closely, you will also see lots of learning going on — whether they are jumping rope or listening to a story. I will be back to answer your questions after you have observed the class."

How many kindergarten activities can you list that give practice in small or large motor skills?

Do you think children who have poor motor skill development should be promoted to first grade or spend another year in kindergarten? Why?

What other factors might be considered? ■

Hand Preference

By about age five, most children consistently use either their right or left hand for most activities. The hand that is used most often becomes the most skillful. A few people can use both hands with equal skill. They are described as being **ambidextrous** (am-bih-DECK-struss).

Actually, preference for the right or left hand begins before the second birthday. It is not known exactly how this happens. Recent studies point to heredity as a probable source. Other people think it depends on which hand parents usually put objects into during the first several years.

It is not a good idea for parents to try to change their child's hand preference. It doesn't really matter whether a child is right- or left-handed, except for the inconvenience of being left-handed in a world made for right-handed individuals.

Check Your Understanding

1. What are some of the reasons a group of five-year-olds will differ significantly from each other in height and weight?

2. Explain why thumb sucking might be a problem at age five or six.

3. Name at least six games for four- to six-year-olds that make use of their enjoyment of large motor skills.

4. Describe at least three games or other activities that children ages four to six would enjoy and that would help develop their dexterity.

Forcing a child to switch from the left to the right hand can cause problems. It is better not to try to alter the child's natural hand preference.

Average Motor Skills Development Ages Four to Six

Four Years

- Skips and hops.
- Laces shoes.
- Dresses and undresses self.
- Cuts on line with scissors.
- Can jump forward as well as up and down.
- Throws overhand with less body participation.

Five Years

- Ties shoelaces.
- Draws recognizable person.
- Skillfully picks up very small items.
- Draws alphabet letters.
- Stands and balances on tiptoe for short period.
- Buttons, snaps, and zips clothes.

Six Years

- Throws and catches balls with more ease and accuracy.
- Builds block towers to shoulder height.
- Cuts, pastes, molds, and colors skillfully.
- Writes entire words.

Providing Care

Four-, five-, and six-year-olds need less actual physical care than younger children. Parents and other caregivers must still remind children and direct their self-care efforts.

The biggest change in schedule during this period is the addition of school. Some four-year-olds go to preschool programs. Most five-year-olds go to kindergarten for a half or full day. Six-year-olds are often in school for a full day.

Feeding

Food provides energy to run the body, something like the way gasoline runs a car. The amount of food needed depends on many factors—activities, height, weight, and temperament of the child. For example, running requires much more food energy than watching TV. Even the time of year can make a difference. More food is needed in cold weather to keep the body warm.

A child who is overweight is eating more food than can be used by the body. This extra food is stored as fat to meet future energy needs. A child who is underweight is not eating enough to supply bodily needs. Neither of these conditions happens suddenly (except, perhaps, due to illness). They result from long-term eating habits that are not right for the individual's needs. Children must learn to balance the amount of food they eat with what their body needs.

Snacks

Few children grow up without snacks between meals. Actually, snacks are not bad—if they contribute to the child's daily nutritional needs. Some snacks such as candy, cake, and soft drinks provide the body with some energy. However, they do not supply many of the nutrients (such as protein, vitamins, and minerals) necessary to keep the body healthy. Advertising encourages children to ask for snacks like these. Children who are given too many sweets at an early age often develop a "sweet tooth." On the other hand, children who are given nutritious snacks like fresh fruit and raw vegetables continue to enjoy them as snacks when they are teenagers and adults.

Nutrition is important for preschool youngsters, whether meals are eaten at home or away from home.

An apple makes a tasty, healthy, and portable snack. Children who learn to enjoy nutritious snack foods when young will still have these habits as adults.

Growing vegetables is a good way to learn to enjoy eating them. It also teaches children about nutrition and science, and makes them proud of their new skill.

Poor Nutrition

Poor nutrition has many causes. Lack of money to buy healthful food is not the most common cause. Many children in families with sufficient money have poor diets. Sometimes parents do not understand good nutrition or they do not care enough to make sure their children are eating well. In other cases, children are responsible for their own meals. The choices they make are often not the best ones.

Poor nutrition can have a number of bad effects. Children with inadequate diets have less resistance to colds and infections. They also may find learning more difficult. Poorly nourished children are easily distracted and often lack motivation to learn.

Teaching Children About Good Nutrition

The best way to make sure children have a proper diet is to teach them about good nutrition early in life. Both home and school are part of this educational process. In our society, many meals are eaten away from the family. That means children regularly choose which foods they will eat and which they will not.

One study at Washington State University showed how better eating habits could be successfully taught to four- and five-year-olds. Vegetables were chosen for the study because many children dislike most vegetables. First a survey was taken to find out the vegetable likes and dislikes of children. White potatoes and carrots (both mild-flavored vegetables) were liked best. Green peppers and cauliflower were liked least.

The University nursery school was used for the educational part of the project. Five of the less popular vegetables—asparagus, broccoli, rutabagas, spinach, and turnips—were used. The children helped clean, chop, and prepare these vegetables for their own meals. They learned about growing, harvesting, and preserving them. Most importantly, they learned how each vegetable helped them to grow and stay healthy. After the three-month experiment, most children accepted the vegetables at school. In addition, their parents reported that they were more willing to try new vegetables and other foods at home.

Similar learning projects can be carried out at home. Four- to six-year-olds love to help in the kitchen. Everyone gains from such a project. The child learns about new foods, improves motor skills, and usually is more willing to try new foods. Parents have a chance to spend time alone with the child, improve eating habits, and help the child become more self-sufficient.

Eating balanced meals is important for good health. Do you recall what foods are in each of the Basic Food Groups? If not, review the chart on page 98.

What kinds of things can children this age do? They love pulling the husks from ears of corn or tearing lettuce for salads. An egg beater helps develop small motor skills and can be used for instant pudding, eggs, or batter. Rolling and cutting out biscuits or cookies is fun. How about flattening biscuits, spreading on tomato sauce, and sprinkling on toppings for mini-pizzas?

It is important to teach preschoolers good food habits because lifetime eating habits are being formed at this age. They learn quickly. As one four-year-old said as he waved his carrot stick during lunch, "This gives me good eyes, Grandma."

Once children start school, many take a packed lunch. Lunches should be nutritious, but there's no need to fall into a peanut butter sandwich and apple routine. Look on page 332 for tips for keeping packed lunches interesting and fun to eat.

Tips for Packed Lunches

- Spruce up that brown bag. A funny face or quick drawing will delight a young child.
- Kids like finger food. Cut chicken, cheese, or meat into bite-size pieces for easier handling.
- Sandwiches don't have to be boring. Use a variety of breads and fillings. Cut them into squares or triangles or make fancy shapes with cookie cutters.
- Insulated containers make it possible to keep foods hot or cold until lunchtime. Soup, casseroles, or salads are interesting alternatives to sandwiches.
- Muffins, biscuits, rolls, and breadsticks are all good substitutes for slices of bread.
- Pack fruits and vegetables ready to eat. Peel and cut them at home, if necessary. Vegetables can be cut into strips, chunks, or flowers.
- Extras don't have to be cookies or candy. Raisins, peanuts, popcorn, or pumpkin or sunflower seeds are fun to eat and have more nutrients.

Bathing and Dressing

Decreased interest in washing, bathing, and dressing is common during this stage. Performing these tasks has lost its novelty. The three-year-old's satisfaction of accomplishment gives way to reluctance to perform a task that has to be repeated frequently.

Children need help in maintaining cleanliness habits. Poor habits acquired at this time can continue into adulthood. It is important for the rest of the family to set a good example and provide encouragement.

It is best to set up and maintain routines for bathing, washing hands, and other cleanliness habits. It helps children accept them as expected behavior, just like bedtime. Praise works better than nagging or scolding. A caregiver might say, "You always smell so good after your bath!" or "We'll let dinner wait until you've finished washing because it's much nicer when we all sit down together." When the task is done, a "My, you do look nice!" makes children feel good about themselves.

Four-, five-, and six-year-olds are able to dress themselves. Some may need help with complicated fasteners such as buttons down the back or shoelaces. Many children have difficulty figuring out which clothes "match." It's not unusual for them to choose combinations of prints and plaids or colors that clash.

Choosing Clothes

The guidelines for choosing toddlers' clothes —comfort, durability, and economy—remain important at this age. Knit shirts and jeans are popular and practical for everyday wear.

Four- to six-year-olds have definite likes and dislikes in clothing. Some become as attached to a favorite garment as they do to a particular toy.

Group identification—the need for a feeling of "belonging"—also begins to be important. Clothing and following clothing fads are an important part of belonging to a group. Within reason, it is important to allow children to make their own clothing choices. Children who are happy with their clothing are more self-confident.

Children can be taught at an early age to take pride in their appearance. They will benefit from both good grooming habits and a good self-concept.

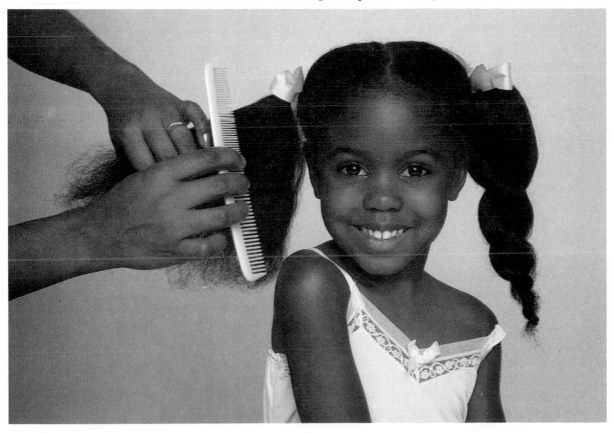

Taking care of clothes, like anything else, can become a habit if caregivers provide praise and encouragement.

Caring for Clothes

As soon as children begin to care about what they wear, they can learn care habits. It is a long process. Parents will probably still find it necessary to remind Bobby to pick up or put away his clothes as a ten-year-old.

Children frequently are careful of dress-up or favorite clothes, but may never routinely hang up their pajamas or put their dirty clothes in the hamper or laundry bag to be washed. Consistent guidance and patience are essential.

Parents who continue to pick up after their child should not wonder why the child fails to care for clothing as a teenager. Good habits must be taught early.

It is important to provide adequate storage that the child can reach. Otherwise, the child will lose interest. Low hooks and rods and handy shelves encourage a child to put things where they belong.

Sleeping

Sleeping arrangements after the third year should provide separate rooms for boys and girls, if at all possible. An individual bed for each child is also best.

Most four-year-olds do not take an afternoon nap, though a few continue to do so until they begin a full day of school.

Reluctance to go to bed lessens about this time. A few children still use delaying tactics, but many ask to go to bed! After saying good night and perhaps looking at a book awhile, most go to sleep easily. At six, bedtime resistance is infrequent. Some children may need conversation, companionship, or a stuffed toy before going to sleep. Bedtime stories continue to be popular.

Toileting

By the fourth birthday, most children have few accidents. When they do occur, it is usually because concentration on a particular activity has postponed elimination too long. Sickness—even as minor as a cold—is another common cause.

Some children may suffer from constipation or occasionally wet their pants when beginning school. In strange surroundings, these children cannot relax sufficiently. The length of time for adjustment depends on the child. Most will adjust within a few months. For some, the problem may reoccur at the beginning of school for several years. Parents can help by developing a morning schedule that allows enough time for relaxation and bathroom use before school. A calm, secure home atmosphere is also important.

Enuresis

A lack of bladder control is called **enuresis** (en-you-REE-sis). This is not considered a problem until after the third or fourth year. If the situation remains, steps should be taken to determine the cause. In the meantime, accidents should be treated casually. Humiliation only aggravates the problem. Enuresis may be caused by physical or psychological factors, or result from poor training.

While most children have gained both day and night bladder control by the age of five, 10 to 15 percent of normal five-year-olds wet their bed. Even at age nine, 5 percent have an occasional accident.

A medical examination will determine if the reason is physical. Bed-wetting is most frequent in the child who has a small bladder and is also a heavy sleeper. When a child sleeps too soundly, the youngster cannot respond to the bladder's "warning signal" that says it is time to urinate.

In a new situation, such as attending a child care center, it is important to help the child feel secure about toileting routines.

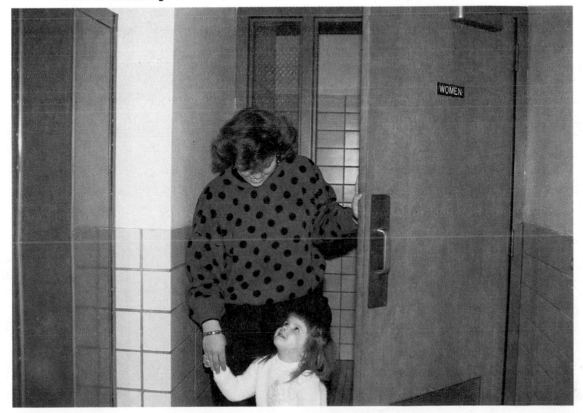

If sound sleep is the cause, the doctor may suggest that a parent wake the child for a trip to the bathroom an hour or two after bedtime. There are also effective conditioning devices available. These are battery-operated buzzers that go off at the first drop of urine. Within a few months, the child awakes naturally as the bladder fills.

The doctor may ask if either parent was slow about nighttime toilet training. Delayed maturity of the bladder can be inherited.

Parents may need to take a child to the bathroom during the night.

Psychological reasons for enuresis or bedwetting are as varied and individual as the children themselves. The cause may be difficult to determine. It may be jealousy of a new baby brother or sister, the start of school, or tension in the home. It may stem from problems with other children, general immaturity, or a nervous and high-strung temperament.

Whatever the cause, caregivers should never resort to shame, scolding, or punishment. This only increases the youngster's anxiety. In the words of one specialist in children's kidney diseases, "There is no point in punishing a child who is a bed-wetter or rewarding such a child for staying dry at night. Bed-wetting is entirely out of the control of the bed-wetter." The most helpful treatment parents can offer is cheerful patience and an abundance of love.

Check Your Understanding

1. How can snacking be both good and bad?

2. Plan an appealing, nutritious lunch to pack for a six-year-old.

3. Suggest three ways parents might encourage children to care for their clothes.

4. Why is it important for children ages four to six to be able to make their own clothing choices?

Chapter Review

To Sum Up

- Growth in height and weight remains steady from ages four to six.
- Primary teeth begin to be replaced by secondary teeth at this age.
- This is a time for practicing and refining motor skills.
- Establishing good eating habits is an important goal at this age.
- Children this age can help and care for themselves and their clothes.
- Enuresis may still be a problem for some children this age.

To Review and Remember

1. Describe four changes in proportion and posture that take place at this age.
2. What are the first secondary teeth to appear? What function do they serve?
3. What is dexterity? Give three examples of a five-year-old's improved dexterity.
4. Why is it important to balance the amount of food eaten with the body's needs?
5. Describe two effects of poor nutrition.
6. Name four benefits of letting children help prepare meals.
7. What are three ways to help children develop cleanliness habits?
8. What is meant by "group identification"? What is one important way children can achieve this?
9. What is enuresis? Name two possible physical causes and two possible psychological causes.
10. Should caregivers punish a child for bed-wetting? Explain.

To Discuss and Discover

1. Many common items such as watches and can openers are designed for right-handed people. Name some other items that cause problems for those who are left-handed. Suggest ways to help a child cope with these difficulties.
2. Write a commercial to promote healthy snacks.
3. Look in several catalogs and check stores for children's clothes. Make a list describing a complete outfit you would choose for a six-year-old. What characteristics did you look for? Compute the cost of this outfit.

13 Emotional and Social Development from Four to Six

To help you to . . .

- Describe general patterns of emotional and social development of children ages four, five, and six.
- Give examples of the causes of and responses to anger, fear, and jealousy in children ages four to six.
- Discuss the good and bad effects of competition.
- Tell how school affects a child's emotional and social development.
- Describe a child's relationship to family at ages four, five, and six.
- Explain how children develop a sense of right and wrong.

Terms to Learn

conscience	peers
moral development	self-esteem

John and Derek were playing in John's basement. The two four-year-olds had put all the toys in a pile and were sitting inside the toy box.

"Now, this is our ship," said Derek. He threw one end of a jump rope onto the floor. "You be the pirate, and I'll be the captain."

"No, I want to be the captain," said John.

"No, I want to," insisted Derek. "I said so first."

Derek gave John a shove. John bumped his head and began to cry. He grabbed Derek's shirt with one hand and the jump rope with the other. "Gimme that rope," he screamed.

John's father came down. "He grabbed me," yelled Derek. "He hit me first," John replied.

Learning to play together is not always easy for four-year-olds. They want to do things their own way. They also lack many of the social skills older children use to get along with each other. But through play, they develop both emotionally and socially.

Emotional Development

Four-, five-, and six-year-olds must cope with many changes in their lives. Most begin regular school attendance during this period. School takes children away from the comfortable familiarity of their home and into a world of strangers. In addition, children this age must assume the responsibilities of childhood and leave babyhood behind. These big steps require many emotional adjustments. In this chapter, you will learn how children's emotions develop during this age span.

General Emotional Patterns

Like the children from one to three, children ages four to six often go through characteristic emotional stages. However, each child will be somewhat different from others. Remember that emotional development depends on each individual's personality, family, and experiences.

Four Years

Most four-year-olds are not as pleasant to live with as they were at three. They are more selfish, impatient, defiant, and boastful. They argue, compete, and are bossier than in the past.

Yet four-year-olds can be loving and affectionate as well. They need and seek parental approval. One minute they stamp their feet and say they "hate" their mother or father. The next minute they return with a present of a shiny stone or a flower plucked from someone's garden.

Four-year-olds are increasingly independent. They are responsible for their own care. They are proud of their abilities, possessions, and creations.

At this age, children often deny responsibility for their actions. It is common to hear, "A big dog came by and knocked it over," or "Joe made me hit her."

Most children are both excited and apprehensive about starting school. Entering kindergarten or first grade opens the door to an entirely new phase of childhood.

Four-year-olds use their language ability with enthusiasm. Parents are often dismayed with some of the additions to their vocabulary. They use silly names and enjoy a play on words. "Antsy-Wantsy-Nancy," or similar nonsense, often sends them into hysterical laughter. They want to talk like older people, but do not know enough to do so. They boast, tell tall tales, and tattle on others. Four-year-olds have difficulty separating fact from fantasy. Parents should treat exaggerations with humor since they are not deliberate lies.

Although four-year-olds like people to laugh at their jokes, they do not like them to laugh at their mistakes. They do not want to be a "baby" anymore. Until this time, they thought people were just having fun when they laughed.

Why are four-year-olds this way? It is just a phase of emotional development. Adults should respect the youngsters' need to explore and test themselves and should try to treat them less like babies. Flexible rules seem to work best.

Four-year-olds can sometimes be difficult. But when they are lovable, it's hard to resist them.

At age five, children are usually willing to cooperate with parents and follow reasonable rules, such as putting away toys. They can stick with a task until it is done.

Five Years

Five-year-olds enter a quieter period much like that of age three, but at a higher level. Children of five are more practical, sympathetic, and serious. Their improved attention span allows them to finish what they have started, rather than move from one thing to another. Also, they can go back to finish uncompleted tasks.

Five-year-olds have learned that others will not accept tall stories and lies. Therefore they are increasingly realistic. They still enjoy slapstick humor. They are able to carry on a discussion and ask meaningful questions.

At this age, children conform to rules more easily. They like supervision, accept instruction, and ask permission. They willingly mind parents—for the most part! However, adult criticism is very hard for five-year-olds to take.

Emotionally, children age five are more patient, generous, persistent, and conscientious than they were earlier. Occasional anxiety is usually caused by a desire to achieve acceptable results rather than by general insecurity.

Six Years

In the up-and-down stages of emotional development, six is once more a "down" phase. Like children of four, six-year-olds are stubborn and quarrelsome. They resent directions and "know everything." They are the center of their own universe and are often at their worst with their parents.

At six, children have rapidly changing moods. They love and hate, accept and reject, smile and storm—sometimes for no apparent reason. Even their favorite playmate is likely to get a swift whack before being informed, "You bumped into my truck." But a playmate who is also six will probably deliver an immediate blow in return!

Six-year-olds are learning to appreciate humorous situations and jokes. They throw themselves into their fun with the abandon that characterizes all they do.

It is easy to understand why six is a difficult age for children. Many are beginning school full-time and must develop their status outside the home. Both are difficult transitions. It is all different from what youngsters expected it to be. Six-year-olds want to be grown-up, but often feel small and dependent. They crave praise and approval. They are easily hurt, wilt under criticism, and are easily discouraged.

The acceptance of family members is very important to six-year-olds. Caregivers need to offer more encouragement and reassurance than criticism.

Specific Emotions

Pleasant emotions are rarely discussed simply because they don't cause problems. Children in this stage can be delightful. But if you understand the reasons for their negative emotions, you will be able to deal with them more effectively.

Anger

Anger shows more distinct changes during childhood than any other emotion. Young children show their anger freely, without any attempt to restrain themselves. But as children grow older, more subtle expressions are used:

■*Age four.* Four-year-olds may still engage in physical fights. Their anger lasts longer than before. They threaten and attempt to "get even."

■*Age five.* Five-year-olds often attempt to hurt other children's feelings rather than hurt them physically.

■*Age six.* Six-year-olds are even more stinging with words. They tease, insult, nag, and make fun of others.

The frequency of anger declines during this period. However, the effects are longer lasting. There are a number of reasons for this. Tolerance for frustration increases as children grow older. Four- to six-year-olds have a better concept of the property rights of others. Improvement in motor skills eliminates earlier physical frustrations. Children this age are also learning about the personalities of others.

The most common cause of anger is disagreement with other children. While quarrels are still loud and verbal, school-age children begin to conceal and disguise their feelings.

As children grow older, they find new ways to vent their anger. How might a two–year–old have reacted in this situation?

Sometimes their methods of revenge are indirect. They may pretend indifference, sneer, or make sly remarks. Often they make exaggerated threats. Occasionally, they take their anger out on a scapegoat such as a younger sibling, a pet, toy, or the furniture.

School-age children begin to understand that sometimes others try to provoke their anger. One particularly imaginative five-year-old scored a crushing defeat with his reply to a kick. "Aw, that just felt like a little minnow swimming by me!" He recognized his opponent's intent to hurt and the frustration that accompanied the obvious failure to do so.

Parents are often on the receiving end of a school-age child's anger. To children, parents are the source of rules. Often in their anger they will "punish" a parent by breaking yet another rule. For example, when six-year-old Cindy was told to go to her room for telling a lie, she retorted, "Okay, I'm not going to hang up my clothes for a week, or maybe a year!"

Children vary greatly in the amount of anger they show and the ways in which they show it. Some of this depends on each child's personality. However, parents' own examples and the way they handle the child's anger are also important. All caregivers should set an example by not easily giving way to anger and by providing a happy and orderly environment for the child. They should also help teach the child self-control early in life before anger becomes a habit.

Fear

Children from four to six have well-developed imaginations, and many of their fears center on imaginary dangers. They may be afraid of ghosts, robbers, kidnappers, or vampires. Sensitive and insecure children are more prone to fears. Fear of the dark is common. The possibility of being left alone or abandoned worries some children.

A naturally active imagination, combined with things children have seen or heard about, results in many fears at this age.

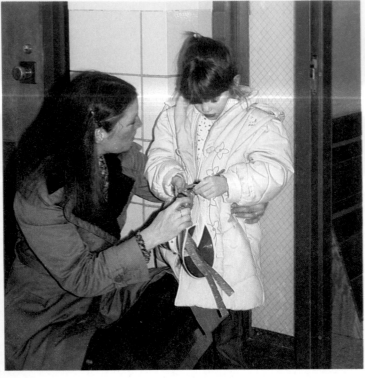

Anxiety about school is common. Parents or caregivers should be sympathetic, but must help the child understand that going to school is necessary.

Children this age do not show their fear as openly because they do not want to be ridiculed. Instead, the child may act aggressively, pretend indifference, or deliberately try to distract himself or herself. This type of coping is a sign of the child's increased maturity.

For more tips on understanding and handling the fears of four- to six-year-olds, see pages 376-377.

Jealousy and Sibling Relationships

Jealousy of brothers and sisters, or sibling rivalry, is common during this stage. Some parents increase such problems, often without meaning to, by showing favoritism to one child. Another common mistake is trying to improve behavior by comparing one child to another. "Why can't you be neat and clean like Jeff? I never have to tell him to wash before meals." Such comparisons rarely improve behavior, but they can damage a child's self-concept and family relationship.

At this age, jealousy often takes the form of tattling, criticizing, or even lying. Some children react to jealousy by boasting, while others pretend there is no rivalry. Jealousy may also result in tensional outlets such as nail-biting, bed-wetting, or tantrums.

Normally, early childhood jealousy fades as the child matures and develops interests outside the family. However, some children never seem to outgrow it and are jealous even as adults. In such cases, jealousy is often a part of deeper emotional problems.

Many children fear school, but there can be a number of causes. Some children are afraid of being without the protection of parents. Others may fear a bully at school, a stern teacher, or "hard" school work. Whatever the reason, the troubled child needs reassurance and support. Taking the youngster to school, talking about the problem, and an understanding explanation may be all that is needed. "Daddy and Mommy go to work. We don't always feel like going, but that's our job. Going to school is your job, unless you are sick."

Special fears also arise in four- to six-year-olds. Social acceptance is very important at this stage. The threat of its loss is a continual source of anxiety. Children fear ridicule.

Children and Stress

Stress among teens and adults is a well-recognized problem. But many people don't realize that children, too, lead stressful lives. They may worry about everything from fires to being unpopular, grades at school, or news about missing children.

As with adults, emotional stress can lead to physical symptoms. Stomachaches, headaches, moodiness, irritability, and trouble eating or sleeping may be caused by stress, as well as by purely physical ailments.

What should parents and caregivers do? Hugs help. So do careful listening, a relaxed manner, and building up a child's self-confidence. Talking through problems with the child helps reduce stress.

Close-up

It seemed that every day when Janie came home from school she had a list of complaints. Several times, when her mother asked her about her day, she burst into tears. "The kids don't play with me." "I can't run fast — I'm always last." "Jimmy calls me 'Freckles' and now the others do, too."

Fortunately, Janie's mother took her child's unhappiness seriously. She didn't simply pass the complaints off with a casual, "Oh, the kids will get over it. They'll like you when they get to know you." Instead she put aside her work and said soothingly, "I think I'll have some milk and apple slices while you have yours and we'll talk about it."

Two friends had indeed rejected Janie's attempts to enter their game that day. Her mother hugged her and said, "Well, Honey, maybe they already had enough players. It's not that they don't like you. When it happens again, ask someone else to play another game. Other kids like to be asked to do things just like you do."

Janie's complaint of not running fast was due to the fact that the swings were all taken by the time she got to the playground after lunch. "You run as fast as most of your friends. I've seen you do it. Maybe you're taking too much time taking your tray back after lunch. You can always play on the climbing platform for a while if the swings are all full. The swings will soon be empty and you can take your turn."

The nickname "Freckles" prompted this reassuring comment from Janie's mother: "I think your freckles are beautiful. Your father has freckles, too. That's one of the things I liked first about him. He's so proud that you look like him. And he loves you very much. Besides, people with freckles have the very nicest complexions — just like yours. I wouldn't change one of your cute freckles for the world!"

Janie's unhappiness soon faded, but her mother decided to make the after-school talks part of their daily routine. She soon realized it gave them a special time together to talk, solve problems, and develop a special closeness.

What effect do you think these early sessions between Janie and her mother will have on Janie as she grows older?

Do you find talking with someone helps ease stressful times for you? ■

Competition — Good or Bad?

People have different views about the role competition should play in children's lives. Some believe that it helps children excel and prepares them for the competition of the adult world. Others feel that competition discourages cooperation. And since there are more losers than winners in competitive situations, competition can damage children's **self-esteem** or positive sense of self-worth. The chart below summarizes the advantages and disadvantages of competition.

Sometimes parents' feelings about competition are based on their desire to see their child excel or do things the parent did not. Monica Spalding couldn't play on the Little League team as a child, so she pressures her daughter Sara into joining. Jack Parker was an "A" student in school. His six-year-old son Joe works hard but is an average student. Mr. Parker constantly "encourages" his son to do better. "Don't you want to be at the top of your class?" he asks. Neither parent has really considered the child's interests and abilities.

Most four-, five-, and six-year-olds prefer cooperative play to competitive games. Older children are more likely to be competitive at play.

Competitiveness, often spurred by sibling rivalry, is likely to show up at home. "Holly gets to stay up until eight o'clock. Why can't I?" "Why can't I cross the street by myself? You let David!"

Children differ in their responses to competition. Some who constantly lead come to think of themselves as superior. Losers may develop a harsh, unpleasant attitude to cover their feelings of inferiority. Many, though, find it a continual challenge and suffer no harmful effects.

Advantages and Disadvantages of Competition

Advantages of Competition

- Gives a realistic estimate of one's own ability in relation to others.
- Promotes higher standards.
- Stimulates and adds zest to otherwise dull tasks.
- Encourages speed in accomplishment.
- Creates interest in finishing a task.
- Stimulates individual effort.

Disadvantages of Competition

- Instills the idea that success depends on the ability to outdo others.
- Leads to hostile relationships with others.
- Defeat may provoke a desire for revenge.
- Those who never win may lose incentive or quit.
- Points up inadequacies.
- Lowers the status of those who lose.

All children need to be encouraged and praised for their own unique abilities.

Personality and Behavior

By age four, the basic behavior pattern of most children is clear. Children will have many of their same characteristics as adults. Other characteristics will change in response to new experiences. For example, a rejected child may learn to love in a caring family situation. The suspicious preschooler can acquire trust. At any age, positive or negative changes in personality can occur. This is one reason that adults should not label a child while discussing the youngster's behavior. Children tend to live up to others' ideas of them. They may become lazy or unfriendly simply because everyone tells them they are.

A successful businessman recalled that as a child his father had continually lectured him about his poor management of his paper route. He was "irresponsible, stupid, and never did anything right." As an adult, he realized that he had actually handled his responsibilities with better than average efficiency. However, years of hearing about his shortcomings made him think he was a failure. He developed a realistic view of his abilities only when his own judgement and values matured. Many children continue to believe others' false evaluations, even as adults.

The understanding and guidance of children are as important in this period as in earlier years. The individual child—whether aggressive, sensitive, placid, or a combination of many traits—needs individual treatment.

Social Development

School brings four-, five-, and six-year-olds in contact with many new people. They must learn how to meet strangers, make friends, work and play in a group, and accept authority from new people.

General Social Patterns

During the preschool and early school years, social skill development is a major task. As children move outside the home, they learn to get along with children their own age—their **peers**. Not all children learn social skills at the same rate, but there are general patterns common at each age.

Four Years

Four-year-olds are much more interested in their friends than they are in adults. At this age, children spend more time in cooperative play than in playing alone. They seem to play best in groups of three or four.

By age four, most children begin to share their toys and take turns. However, they are still often bossy and inconsiderate, and fighting is common.

Though friends are important to four-year-olds, the family is still most important. Children this age continually look for approval with remarks such as, "I'm a good builder, aren't I?" or "Look how high I can climb!" If things go wrong, they still look to adults for comfort.

Five Years

Most five-year-olds are more outgoing and talkative than at age four. They play best in groups of five or six, and their play is more complicated. They prefer friends of their own age. Quarreling is less frequent. When it does occur, the five-year-old resorts to name-calling and wild threats.

At age five, children have more respect for things belonging to others. This does not mean that a five-year-old will never snatch a toy from another child. Such behavior, though, is not as common.

As children begin school, social acceptance by peers becomes more important. They are concerned about what their friends say and do. They don't like to be different.

The preschool years bring more opportunities to develop social relationships outside the home.

At age five, most children are able to play together with a minimum of conflict. They are willing to pool their toys with the understanding that each will be returned to its owner when the game is over.

Close-up

Tim, the youngest of three children, could read before he started kindergarten. His parents didn't make any special effort to teach him. He just enjoyed the attention when his sister Marta played school with him. Of course, she was always the teacher and he was the student. Even though he only played at being the student, he learned quite a bit.

"Tim, what letter is this?" she would ask.

"An *O*?" Tim answered hopefully.

"No," Marta responded. "It's like an *O* but it has a bite out of the side. It's a *C*."

Tim soon learned to recognize all the letters and then a few simple words. Marta had him reading her easiest books by the summer before he started kindergarten. She was as proud of his accomplishments as he was.

Tim's parents talked to his kindergarten teacher, Mrs. Cole, several months after school began. They asked her if Tim read in class.

"I've suspected he knows more than he lets on," she replied. "We've been learning our letters in class. Tim always does well on his papers, but he doesn't volunteer in class. Several times I've asked him if he can read a word from one of the signs I've posted in the room — things like 'door' or 'fish.' He'll just shake his head no."

In the weeks after the conference Mrs. Cole tried to find out just how well Tim could read. She soon discovered that asking him to read for the class did no good. But one day she sat with him in the story corner while the other children were busy finishing a project. She started out slowly, asking him letters they learned in class, then some they hadn't yet discussed. She went on to a simple book about cars — his favorite subject.

"Tim, what's this word?" she asked.

"Car," he answered.

"Can you tell me what that one is?" Mrs. Cole went on.

"Truck," he answered. "The tow truck pulled the car," he read. "It went up, up the hill."

Just then, one of Tim's friends came to join them and that put an end to Tim's reading. He wouldn't answer any more questions.

When she talked to Tim's parents again, Mrs. Cole said, "I think I've solved the mystery. Tim simply wants to fit into the group. Being able to read in a class of nonreaders would make him just as different — in his eyes — as wearing a dress-up suit to class. He's at that age where conformity is important to him. He will read to me, but not if any of the other kids are around."

Why do you think Tim learned to read so early?

Could (and should) every child do so?

Why might conformity be so important to children this age? ■

Six Years

At age six, social relations with family and friends are often characterized by friction, aggression, threats, stubbornness, and rudeness. Six-year-olds want everything and want to do things in their own way. When playing with other children, they may not want to share their own toys but are jealous of the toys of others.

Best friends are usually of the same sex, although six-year-olds play readily in mixed groups. Friendships are closer and longer lasting now than at age five. However, six-year-olds tend to form groups that exclude other children.

At this age, children like the group play and organized teams of school games. As soon as they tire of playing, though, they will drop out without regard for the team effort.

Six-year-olds form close friendships, usually with others of the same sex. However, boys and girls still play together in groups.

Family Relationships

During the infant and toddler years, children learn to get along with others by forming strong relationships with their family. They must learn cooperation, fair play, and respect for others. In the preschool and early school years, children must put these social skills to work in social situations outside the home.

Four-year-olds have a strong sense of family and home. They want to feel important to the family. They are proud to be able to do tasks to help. However, they are also apt to quarrel and bicker with brothers and sisters at this age.

In many ways, the family relationships of five-year-olds are similar. They are proud of their parents and delight in helping. Now, though, they play much better with younger brothers and sisters. They are usually protective, kind, and dependable with them.

Six-year-olds are less in harmony with their family. One reason is that children tend to be more self-centered at age six. Their own opinions and needs come first. Arguing with parents is common. They are often rough and impatient with younger brothers and sisters and may fight with older ones.

School attendance diminishes the family's importance in the eyes of the child. Peers and teachers take on more influence. This tension between family and outside influences continues through the school and teen years.

Relationships with parents, brothers, and sisters are the foundation for social relationships outside the home.

Moral Development

Moral development—gradually learning to base your behavior on what you believe is right and wrong—begins early in life. Parents have a responsibility for helping their children develop a moral sense that will guide their behavior.

As toddlers, children begin to learn the rules their parents and other caregivers set. At this age, though, they can't understand the reasons behind the rules or the difference between right and wrong. They just know that some actions—such as hitting a playmate—cause caregivers to be unhappy with them. They learn to avoid such behavior because they don't want to lose love and approval.

Between ages five and seven, children gradually develop the beginnings of a conscience. A **conscience** (KAHN-shens) is an inner sense of right and wrong that prompts good behavior or causes feelings of guilt for bad behavior. The rules learned in early childhood form the basis of the conscience in the early school years.

At this stage, children begin to know the difference between truth and lies. However, that understanding is not very accurate. For example, a mistake may be considered a lie and therefore worthy of punishment. On the other hand, youngsters don't always realize that their tall tales are fantasy, not reality. Caregivers need to help children separate fact from fiction rather than punish them for using their imagination.

At about ages seven to ten, children accept the authority of their parents, teachers, and other caregivers. While they don't like or understand all the rules they must obey, they don't question the right of those in authority to make them. Children still follow rules mainly because they fear punishment. They don't consistently control their own behavior based on personal beliefs about what is right or wrong.

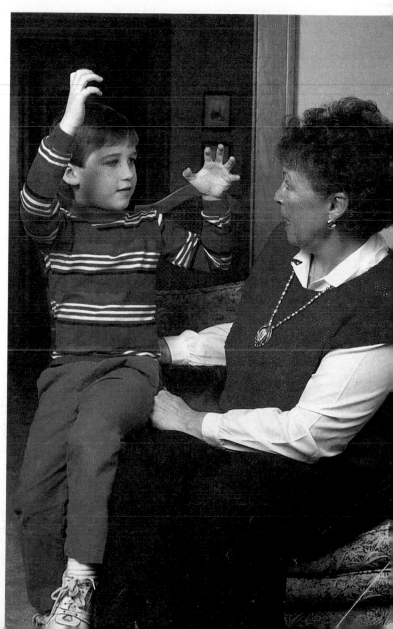

How would you react to this child's story of how a polar bear came in his bedroom window? Remember that the story is probably very real to the child, not a deliberate lie.

Guidelines for Moral Development

Most parents take their responsibilities for moral development seriously. However, it can be difficult to know how to help children learn right from wrong. Here are some guidelines:

■*Consider the child's age and abilities.* Toddlers can't be expected not to touch anything in a room simply because they are told "no." They have a driving need to explore in order to learn. And they don't remember well. It's better to remove breakables and give only a few rules needed to keep the child safe.

■*Remember that parents and caregivers teach most effectively by example.* A child who is told that lying is wrong but listens to parents lie gets a mixed message. If you are around children, you must behave the way you want them to behave.

■*Understand that the process of learning to monitor one's own behavior is a lifelong task.* It is unfair to expect perfection from children. Help them learn from their mistakes.

■*Don't withhold love because of misbehavior.* It is important for children to know that you don't like what they did, but that you still love them.

Chapter 16 gives additional suggestions for guiding children effectively.

A developing moral sense helps older children understand the importance of being dependable. Parents can set a good example by the way they approach their own responsibilities.

Check Your Understanding

1. Discuss the general social development of four-, five-, and six-year-olds.

2. The chapter explains the general social development of children at different ages. Why might the five-year-old you know differ from the description given?

3. Compare the family relationships of four-, five-, and six-year-olds.

4. Explain why a child might have a poorly formed conscience.

Chapter Review

To Sum Up

- Beginning regular school attendance requires many emotional adjustments and brings about rapid social development.
- Although four-, five-, and six-year-olds have better emotional control, emotional development still alternates between positive and negative stages.
- Expression of anger becomes more subtle and less physical at this age.
- An active imagination, school, and the need for social acceptance can lead to a variety of fears.
- Competition can have both good and bad effects on children.
- As children spend more time with their peers, the family gradually loses some of its influence, as well as its importance, in the eyes of a child.
- Conscience and moral values are developed during this period.

To Review and Remember

1. Why does beginning school cause so many emotional and social adjustments?
2. Why are tall tales more common to four-year-olds than five-year-olds?
3. What is the most common cause of anger in children ages four to six?
4. What are three things that can contribute to children's fears at this age? Name some common fears.
5. Name two ways parents contribute to sibling rivalry.
6. How can caregivers help relieve a child's stress?
7. Name three advantages and three disadvantages of competition.
8. Why shouldn't parents or caregivers label a child while discussing the youngster's behavior?
9. What is a conscience? What forms the basis of the conscience of children four to six?
10. Define moral development. Give three guidelines for helping children in this area.

To Discuss and Discover

1. Discuss how anger, fear, and jealousy for four- to six-year-olds are different from the same emotions at ages one to three. Explain why they are different.
2. Divide your class into teams and debate whether competition is good or bad for a child.
3. Discuss ways in which parents serve as role models for their children.

To help you to . . .

- Describe the characteristics of intellectual development of children four to six.

- Explain what IQ tests are and their advantages and disadvantages.

- Give examples of ways children can learn from everyday experiences.

- Explain how parents and caregivers can encourage children's interest in reading, art, and music.

- Explain what learning disabilities are.

- Identify the effects of learning disabilities and giftedness on school experiences.

- Describe the speech development of children this age and identify possible speech problems.

Terms to Learn

- dramatic play
- dyslexia
- finger plays
- gifted children
- hyperactive
- intelligence quotient (IQ)
- learning disability
- vocabulary

Remember those days of early childhood? Call them up from your memory. Think of the sights and sounds and feelings you experienced . . .

- Fingerpainting.
- Your first day of school.
- Learning to tie your shoes.
- Trying to sit still in class.
- Singing "I'm a Little Teapot."
- Having fun at recess.
- The smell of chalk and erasers.
- Trying to stay within the lines as you colored.

Memories like these can help you as you read about how four-, five-, and six-year-olds learn. Your own joys and fears, successes and failures are much like those of children today.

How Intelligence Develops

In Chapter 7 you learned that Jean Piaget described the time between ages two and seven as the preoperational period. Four-, five-, and six-year-olds show by their thinking and actions that they are still in this period. Here are some signs of preoperational thinking:

■*Using symbols.* Children learn that objects and words can be symbols—that is, they can represent something else. A box wrapped in colorful paper with a bow on top may mean "present" or "birthday" or "Christmas."

■*Make-believe play.* Children continue to learn through fantasy and through creative and dramatic play. **Dramatic play** is imitating real-life situations, such as playing house or school.

■*Egocentric viewpoint.* At four, five, and six, children continue to view the world in terms of themselves. Their words and actions show their self-centeredness.

■*Limited focus.* In the preoperational period, children find it difficult to focus on more than one characteristic at a time. For example, you might place ten tennis balls in front of a four-year-old. Three of the balls are white and seven are yellow. If you asked the child whether there are more yellow balls or more tennis balls, he or she wouldn't know what to answer. The child can't focus on both the color and the type of ball at once. An older child would know immediately that all the balls are tennis balls but only some of them are yellow.

Between the fourth and seventh birthdays, children make significant gains in intelligence. It is easy to see these changes, but it is not easy to judge how the intelligence of one child compares with another.

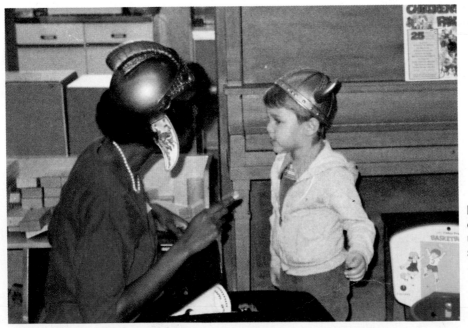

Fantasy play is a way for children to learn. How does the use of these helmets show symbolic thinking?

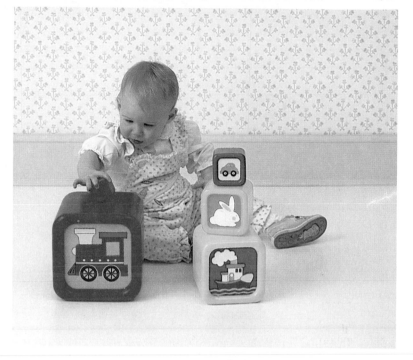

Intelligence testing is simply a way to compare a child's abilities with those of others the same age. The skills tested in infancy—stacking blocks, for example—are very different from those tested in later life.

Measuring Intelligence

Children are often labeled as intelligent or unintelligent by adults who are influenced by observations that have nothing to do with intelligence. Maria is considered bright. She has a dimpled smile, dark curls, and appealing manners. People seem inclined to think well of her. Jack is considered slow. He is large for his age and is often compared with children several years older. He is actually of average intelligence. Traci is so shy that few people ever see her true ability. It is difficult to objectively separate a child's intellectual ability from such characteristics as curls, shyness, and size. Everyday observations rarely provide an accurate guide for judging abilities.

Educators use formal intelligence tests to more accurately determine the intellectual abilities of children. The test results help determine students' educational needs.

The first intelligence test was developed by a French psychologist, Alfred Binet, in 1905. In 1916, Dr. Lewis M. Terman of Stanford University made a major revision of the Binet test. Today the test is known as the Stanford-Binet and it is widely used to test children from age two to sixteen.

Dr. Terman devised a way to give a person's intelligence a numerical score. He did this by having many children take the test. Eventually, he was able to determine how well the average child of a particular age would do. Using a simple mathematical formula, a number representing the child's intelligence can be determined. This **intelligence quotient** (more often referred to as IQ) is simply a number that tells whether a child shows intelligence that is average, or above or below average for his or her age. With this method, the average child of any age has an IQ between 90 and 110.

Intelligence tests are composed of tasks and questions. These correspond to the expected abilities at various age levels. Two-year-olds, for example, cannot read. An IQ test for them might include building a tower of blocks, identifying parts of the body, and fitting simple geometric shapes into corresponding holes.

Disadvantages of IQ Tests

Many types of intelligence tests are used today. However, no one test gives an absolutely accurate estimate of an individual's mental ability. Many things can influence test results. The child's physical or emotional state during the test, limited experiences, or unfamiliarity with the language can all have an effect.

Most tests depend a great deal on language ability and the experiences of a particular culture. This may penalize those who speak another language at home or have different cultural traditions.

Another problem with IQ tests is that they do not tell much about specific abilities. Two people with the same IQ may have very different strengths and weaknesses. One person may be very good at science and math, but poor in language skills. Another may have the opposite strengths and weaknesses. Also, two different tests administered to the same child sometimes show a wide difference in scores.

Unfortunately, some parents and children become too concerned about IQ test scores. The Rockefeller Foundation report on quality in education made a good point: "Tests are effective on a limited front. We cannot measure the rarer qualities of character that are a necessary ingredient of great performance. We cannot measure aspiration, purpose, courage, vitality, determination." Nor do tests measure such positive qualities as originality, creativity, self-confidence, and independence.

If a child's test score seems unreasonable compared to the child's behavior and achievement, parents can ask that the child be re-tested. An individually administered test (rather than one given to a group) may give more accurate results.

Everyday Learning Opportunities

No matter how busy their lives, parents need to spend time with their children each day. Parents who work full-time outside the home must make a special effort. Even a short but regular time together is important to the child.

Four-, five-, and six-year-olds learn from a wide variety of experiences. However, these experiences provide more learning if a teen or adult shares them. You can try techniques like those mentioned here whenever you are with children.

Look for opportunities to talk with children about what they are doing. A few positive comments can encourage interest. Questions help children think about what is happening in new ways and organize their thoughts into answers. Ask questions that require more than a "yes" or "no" answer. Questions like "Where does the rain come from?" or "Why did the rock fall faster than the feather?" encourage learning.

Suggestions or explanations can also be helpful. You might explain in simple terms why water turns to ice. Or if a child is trying to lift a box full of toys, you could suggest that pushing it might be easier.

Asking a child's advice is another effective technique. For example, you might ask how the carrot sticks and radishes should be arranged on the plate. Following through on such advice gives the idea that the child's opinions are valued. It improves the child's self-esteem.

Although books and television programs can be educational, it's always more exciting to learn about the world first-hand.

Recreational activities are important to learning. On short car trips, the child can follow the progress on a map if the route is clearly marked. A bus, subway, or plane ride can be an exciting adventure. Nature walks are fun and free. The whole family can learn by looking closely at leaves, flowers, and birds.

Children need to be included in household tasks such as shopping, cooking, and keeping the house clean. Besides the learning involved, sharing activities strengthens family bonds. Children develop responsibility, maturity, and independence.

Parents and other caregivers should also take time to help their children learn and explore. Even preschoolers can participate in experiments. Finding out what magnets attract, determining what floats, and learning why a candle goes out when covered with a jar are just a few possibilities. Other activities can encourage creativity and curiosity. The sound of a watch ticking is magnified when you listen through an empty paper towel tube. Oil floats on top of water, but food coloring mixes with it. Learning should be an everyday, family-centered event.

Children of this age are curious to learn more about their bodies and where babies come from. Answer their questions in simple terms they can understand. Help them learn the correct terms for body parts. Encourage children to have positive attitudes by answering their questions in an unembarrassed, natural way.

Appreciating Reading, Art, and Music

Whether or not children enjoy reading, art, and music depends largely on the attitudes of their parents. For many people, these are hobbies which bring them pleasure throughout their life. It is in this beginning school stage that many children develop an interest in one or more of these areas.

Reading

Young children love books and stories. If this interest is encouraged and adults take time to read to them, they are more likely to enjoy reading as they grow older. This is important. Books provide an opportunity to learn about and understand the world and the people in it. Children who like reading will find learning easier.

Four- to six-year-olds like stories about things that are different from their own experiences. Children who live in the city need to know about farms. Children who live far from a large city can "experience" buses, apartments, skyscrapers, and other things common to city life through books.

Children this age also appreciate humor and unusual situations. They giggle over the picture of a horse in the bathtub or a dog wearing a hat. This shows they are beginning to be able to separate reality from fantasy.

The chart below gives guidelines for choosing books for children. You may also wish to review the suggestions on pages 314–315.

Children need to have some books of their own, but books can be expensive. You might try making one for a child you know. It can be fun! Cut pictures from old magazines or newspapers or draw your own. The story can be simple, or even rhyme if you write poetry. Children love to have a story about their own family.

Another way to provide children with a variety of books is to use the public library. In most cities and towns you can borrow books free. Many libraries also have story hours for young children.

Checklist for Choosing Books for Children

√Are the pictures colorful, interesting, and easy to understand?
√Will the story appeal to the child's interests?
√Will the child understand most of the words?
√Does the book use descriptive language that brings the story alive?
√Is the story the right length to keep the child's attention?
√Is the book well-constructed so it will stand up under hard use?

Children love to express their artistic talents on paper — as well as on their fingers, arms, and smocks!

Art

Art helps children express their feelings, learn to control their body, and show their creativity. Parents should supply a variety of art materials. Clay, crayons, paper, paste, and scissors with rounded points are good supplies for four- to six-year-olds.

Children should be allowed to experiment with art materials. Don't offer corrections, ridicule, or "lessons." Eventually, scribbles will turn into recognizable shapes and the frogs will be green instead of pink.

Instead of guessing what a child's picture represents, ask the child to tell you about it. Also try to praise the child's actions rather than the artwork produced. For example, you might say, "I really like the bright colors you used for the flowers," instead of "That's a good picture."

Music

A baby beats a rhythm with a spoon, enjoying the sound. A boy holds a stick against a fence as he walks, listening to the rhythm. A little girl listens to the beat of her footsteps as she runs. All children imitate the sounds they hear around them. They naturally respond to rhythmical sound, which is part of music.

Singing and rhythm games are fun, especially for four- to six-year-olds. Many children are introduced to singing by **finger plays**. These combine a simple song or chant with hand motions. Don't be surprised if a young child's song doesn't sound very much like the original. Most children cannot carry a tune at least until age three or four.

Simple instruments develop an interest in rhythm. Bells, a drum, a tambourine, or almost anything that makes a noise will do. Kitchen pans, and mixing spoons provide good substitutes for purchased instruments.

Check Your Understanding

1. Identify at least eight circumstances that could alter a child's intellectual development.

2. Do you think the advantages of IQ tests outweigh their disadvantages? Defend your position.

3. Imagine you are responsible for two children, ages four and five, for the afternoon. Describe at least two learning activities you could plan for them that would also be fun. Be sure to keep your ideas practical.

Early, positive experiences with music can lead to a lifetime of enjoyment. Children should have opportunities for creative experiments with sound and rhythm.

The School Experience

Although a child learns from the moment of birth, many people connect learning with school. Most children begin school between the ages of four and six. Some have their first experience when they go to nursery school or a preschool program. Others start by going to kindergarten.

Since children will attend school for many years, it is vital they develop a good attitude at the beginning. Children who have a bad experience with classmates or a teacher can develop a negative feeling about school. This keeps them from learning as well as they might.

There are many things parents can do to help make sure their child adjusts well to school:

- Make certain the child has a complete medical and dental examination. Vision and hearing tests are especially important since problems with sight or hearing can severely handicap a child's learning.

- Children need self-help skills. They should be able to put on and fasten their own outer garments and shoes. Of course, such tasks as blowing their nose and taking care of toileting needs are essential.

- Children should know their full name, address, and phone number.

- They should also be able to follow simple directions.

- Children who know what to expect will be less fearful. Many schools hold open house days for children starting school.

How well children do in school depends partly on how well prepared they are for the experience.

Although most children learn well in school, some have special educational needs. Two common causes—learning disabilities and exceptional intelligence—are discussed here. You will learn about the needs of children with physical, mental, and emotional handicaps in Chapter 17.

Learning Disabilities

Not all children learn easily. You may have heard the term "learning disability" or know a child who has one. A **learning disability** is a communication problem within the brain that prevents a person from using information received through the senses in a normal way for learning. The New York Institute of Child Development defines a learning disability as a complicated disorder that generally falls into four basic areas of difficulties:

1. How a child receives information from his or her senses.
2. How the brain puts such information together.
3. How the information is stored in the brain as memory.
4. How the information is expressed as written or spoken language.

Most experts would not say someone with a severe physical handicap, such as blindness, has a learning disability. Obviously, lack of sight makes learning more difficult, but the problem is in the eyes. A person with a learning disability would be able to see the writing in a book, but, for example, the brain might register every sentence or some letters backwards. This would be like trying to read a book by looking in a mirror. In this case, the problem would be a learning disability because the brain is not functioning normally.

In the past, little was known about learning disabilities. Children who had them were simply labeled as "dumb" or "lazy" or became "troublemakers" in school. You can imagine the discouragement of these children. They tried as hard as they could, but were still unable to keep up with their classmates.

Actually, IQ has nothing to do with learning disabilities. Some children who have a very low IQ also have a learning disability. However, so do some children with average or above average IQs.

There are many types of learning disabilities. Some are easier to recognize than others. For example, **hyperactive** children cannot concentrate on anything long enough to learn effectively. Such children are usually constantly active and may seem uncontrollable. Some error in their brain keeps them from focusing their attention and controlling their actions.

Other children cannot understand the relationship between objects. They may not understand the difference between "under" and "over" or between "near" and "far," for example. Some children cannot understand what words mean and others cannot form their own thoughts into speech or cannot write properly. If these and similar problems come from an error in brain processes, they are learning disabilities.

Dyslexia (dis-LEX-ee-uh) is a learning disability that prevents a person from handling language in a normal way. This usually causes problems with reading, writing, spelling, and math. Children with dyslexia are often intelligent, but information—especially visual information—is not processed normally by the brain. Researchers have found that children with dyslexia have difficulty processing a series of instructions, such as "Add one to three and then divide by two." They have trouble sounding out words and often have a short attention span. Such children need special help, especially during the early school years.

Many of the causes of learning disabilities are not known, though research is yielding some answers. Many children with such problems are never identified or helped. Sometimes, too, the label of "learning disabled" can be as harmful as the problem itself. People who do not know what the term means may say cruel things to such children. Sometimes learning disabled children are treated as if they cannot learn. In fact, they can learn— but somewhat differently from most children. They must also work much harder to grasp things that others learn easily.

Gifted and Talented Children

It is estimated that 3 to 10 percent of the nation's children have an IQ of 130 or above. They are often described as **gifted children**. But children may also be gifted in an area that does not show up well on IQ tests. Ramon, for example, has exceptional musical ability. Jennifer, even as a preschooler, shows remarkable artistic talent. Neither has an IQ over 130.

It was once thought that gifted and talented children would thrive in any environment. It is now known that they have special needs that must be met. Among these are the need for recognition and acceptance and for challenging pursuits in which they can be successful. They need to be free from feelings of inferiority, superiority, or "being different." They benefit from play with a variety of children, but also need time with other gifted learners.

Parents, teachers, and others should not overwhelm gifted and talented children with unrealistic expectations or goals. They need encouragement and opportunities for leadership and creativity.

Children with above-average ability—like all children—need challenging opportunities, but should not feel pressured.

When children "act up" in school, it is sometimes because they find the classroom work too easy. How might the teacher find out whether this is the case?

Gifted children can easily become bored and frustrated in school. They are sometimes labeled as problem children because they may not conform to classroom procedures and often come up with unexpected answers. Some gifted children who lack challenges at school become poor students.

Most bright children exhibit recognizable signs by age two. They may talk early, using complete sentences, and know many words. Many read before school age, some by age two and a half. Gifted children are highly curious and ask challenging questions.

Close-up

Eric and Josh were three-year-old cousins. Because they lived near each other, they were frequent playmates.

Eric was bright and quick and constantly active. Josh was quieter and more easily directed into activities. He was content to watch many of Eric's accomplishments.

Eric asked questions constantly. Many showed surprisingly advanced thought. "Won't that airplane hit birds up there?" "Why does soap make me clean?" He was particularly fascinated when he heard his voice played back on a tape recorder, asking, "How can I say those things in there?" Josh's questions were more general and typical of a three-year-old. He might ask, "Why does it do that?" or "How does this work?"

It seemed that Eric was always taking toys apart. One day he proudly showed his mother that he had "snow tires" on a toy car. He had placed the larger wheels of a truck on the back of the car!

Eric was inclined to be more restless than Josh and easily became bored with routine play. He loved to operate the calculator, soon learning to punch the numbers he recited. He knew all his colors. Once when naming the colors of objects, he corrected his aunt's suggestion of "light brown." "No, that's tan!" he insisted.

Josh was less inquisitive and did less exploring. He could name most of the bright colors and loved listening to stories. He seldom took toys apart, but was conscientious about keeping them in their box when not in use. He was assigned household tasks and performed them proudly. He tended to take things as they came with easy-going acceptance.

One morning, both youngsters were seeing another cousin off on a bus trip. Josh stood nearby, waving enthusiastically. Eric, after pacing nervously near the bus door, finally tugged at his departing cousin's sleeve to get her attention. He asked worriedly, "How do you know this bus will take you where you want to go?"

We do not need tests to know that Eric displays behavior that may indicate above-average intelligence. However, Eric and Josh are too young for us to be able to predict their future achievement. Both need experiences that will challenge them and help them reach their potentials.

How might the boys' personalities affect our view of their intelligence?

If you were a preschool teacher, what are some ways you might keep both boys interested in activities? ■

Most schools have special educational programs for gifted students. In small schools, enrichment programs within regular classes are often offered. Large school systems usually have special classes or even special schools.

A gifted child may benefit from learning through independent activities, as well as in school. However, intellectual enrichment should be balanced with physical, emotional, and social needs.

Speech Development

By school age, language ability is one of the most dependable indications of intelligence. What children say tells much about the way they think. Speech also reveals each child's interests and personality. Remember, however, that there are exceptions. Some children who speak poorly or cannot speak at all are quite intelligent.

By the time they start school, children generally have learned most of their language just by listening. They probably do not know what adjectives are, but they use them correctly. As they grow older, their **vocabulary** (the number of words they know) will increase. The sentences they use will also become more complex. However, all the basic language forms have already been learned in the preschool period.

Articulation (clear, distinct speech) improves dramatically between ages three and six. At age three, children can say about 30 percent of their words correctly. By age six, that has increased to 90 percent.

Much of the improvement depends on physical development. Some sounds are more difficult to make than others. For example, "b," "m," and "p" are made simply by moving the lips. By three years of age, most children can make these sounds. Sounds such as "f" and "v" involve both the lips and teeth. Children may not master them until age five. "J," "ch," "st," "pl," and "sl" are the most difficult sounds. They require the smooth coordination and timing of the lips, tongue, and throat muscles. Some children may be six or seven before "p'wease" becomes "please" and "shicken" becomes "chicken."

A child's vocabulary should increase rapidly during this period. A normally developing six-year-old knows about two and one-half times the number of words a three-year-old knows. This means a six-year-old will understand and use approximately 2,500 different words!

Speech Difficulties

Often young children seem to talk all the time. However, many kindergarten and first-grade teachers complain that some children do not talk enough. Children who are unable to handle language well have difficulty with reading and cannot keep up with the class.

Close-up

Jill is an attractive and polite five-year-old. Her parents both work and Jill spends much of her time with a babysitter. The babysitter spends her day watching television and rarely plays with or talks to Jill. In the evenings, Jill's parents are tired, so she plays alone in her room or watches TV.

Jill rarely talks. The words she does use, she pronounces poorly. For example, she says "wery" for "very" and "thed" for "said." Jill's speech is not due to a physical problem or lack of intelligence. She simply has no incentive to talk. She has found that she pleases her parents and babysitter most when she is quiet. No one has ever taken the time to talk with her and listen to her.

Why does clear speech depend on practice? In what other ways might Jill's lack of playmates and attention from adults influence her intellectual development? ■

If you were the caregiver in this situation, what could you do to enrich Allison's speech development?

Some children are language-poor in another sense. Although there is plenty of talk at home, only simple words are used. No one ever says, "That cookie is sweet," "The cereal is crunchy," "The teddy bear is fuzzy," or "The sun is hot." Young children know the word "run," so all animals and people "run." They are not encouraged to say that a boy *races*, mother *jogs* every morning, a horse *gallops*, a deer *dashes*, and a bug *crawls*.

Children from families who speak a foreign language at home often experience problems when they begin school. They must learn English language skills and at the same time keep up with their classes. Children who move from one part of the country to another may have difficulty because of differences in pronunciation.

In all these cases, children may suffer from a communication problem in school. They may not be able to understand the teacher or may have difficulty making themselves understood. Consequently, learning suffers.

Difficulties in school may arise when a child's family speaks a foreign language at home. However, talking with and listening to classmates can help improve the child's English skills.

Sometimes the emotional damage of such an experience can be worse than the intellectual. Classmates are often unkind to a child whose speech is different.

Of course, not all language-poor children are handicapped because of speech patterns in the home. Some have physical problems preventing normal speech. Some are mentally retarded. Others may be emotionally immature. Such children require help, preferably before they begin school.

Overall, parents are a child's most powerful teachers. Children whose parents spend time with them talking and listening are more likely to speak and read well.

Check Your Understanding

1. How could undetected vision or hearing problems cause learning difficulties for a child entering school? Include all areas of development.

2. Explain the difference between a learning disability and a physical disability.

3. Why might a hyperactive child have difficulty in school? A gifted child?

4. Compare the speech development of a three-year-old with that of a six-year-old.

Parents and other family members can make a tremendous difference in a child's development through their positive interaction.

Chapter Review

To Sum Up

- Children ages four to six are in the preoperational period of thinking.
- Intelligence tests can help determine a child's intellectual abilities.
- Parents and caregivers who listen, explain, answer questions, and provide learning experiences help children learn better and faster.
- Children should be encouraged to develop an interest in reading, art, and music.
- Children who are properly prepared for school adjust more easily.
- Learning disabilities result from a communication problem within the brain.
- Gifted children need opportunities that will challenge, but not overwhelm, them.
- Speech develops rapidly at ages four to six, especially vocabulary and articulation.
- Some children have language problems that hinder learning.

To Review and Remember

1. What are four signs of preoperational thinking?
2. Define intelligence quotient.
3. What are two ways children can benefit from helping with household tasks?
4. What are two ways parents could encourage an interest in reading without buying books?
5. Name three skills a child should master before beginning school.
6. What is a learning disability?
7. What four basic areas of difficulty are considered learning disabilities?
8. Describe a hyperactive child.
9. What is meant by the term "gifted children"?
10. Give four possible reasons for speech or language difficulties.

To Discuss and Discover

1. In a catalog, advertisement, or store, find a toy that is appropriate for a four-, five-, or six-year-old. Explain why you think this is a good choice, linking your reasons to what you know about children at this stage of development. Include a photo or drawing with your report and indicate the price of the toy.
2. Find out how your school system identifies and helps children with learning disabilities. Identify other sources of help for children and parents.
3. Discuss the emotional damage that can be caused by speech problems.

Handling Fears

Older children are more imaginative and so are likely to have new types of fears. By about age four, children are able to imagine dangers that they have not actually experienced. They question all that they see and then try to relate it to themselves. For example, when children this age hear that someone has died, they may become preoccupied with death. They ask many questions and become fearful that they, too, will die.

These worries and fears are often more intense if children have been overstimulated by scary stories or TV violence. Caregivers need to learn the cause of the fear, offer reassurance, and then help the child overcome the fear.

When a child is fearful, be calm and understanding. This helps the child talk out his or her fears. Never argue with the child, become impatient, or make fun of a fear. To the child, it is very real.

Children over the age of three can be reasoned with, so explaining a fearful situation may also help relieve fears. For example, if a child is afraid of the dark, turning on the light in the room helps show there's nothing to fear. The room is the same whether the light is on or off, and the scary things imagined are not real.

Forcing a child into a situation he or she is afraid of will not eliminate a fear. The more a caregiver pushes the child, the stronger the fear is likely to become. For example, a caregiver who throws a child into a swimming pool to "cure" a fear of water will have little success. A better approach would be to start in a wading pool with the comforting presence of an adult. Gradually teach the child how to put his or her head underwater. Eventually you can help the child to float in the shallow end of an adult pool. Such a process is likely to take weeks or months, but can't be hurried.

Sometimes children can conquer fears through the use of make-believe play. For example, if the child is afraid of dogs, you might suggest pretending a toy dog is injured and needs the child's help. In this way, the child feels in control of the situation and may work out the fear by himself or herself. Coping skills can also be practiced this way. "What would you do if a dog in a fenced yard barked at you?" you might ask. Discussing possibilities before they happen helps build self-confidence.

Never ignore a child's fears. If they aren't dealt with and overcome, they don't disappear. They may pile up and create emotional problems. A happy, active life and understanding adults can help keep childhood fears to a minimum.

Make-Believe Play

Between the ages of two and nine, children often engage in make-believe play. Such play is important to a child's development because it helps make sense of the adult world. In fantasy play, children themselves choose what to play and create a situation over which they have full control. The real world is brought down to a manageable size. In their pretend world they can be successful, feel important, and gain confidence in their abilities. They make up their own rules and can try out new activities without fear of failure or ridicule.

In make-believe play, children often reenact situations they observe in the adult world. After watching an adult bake a cake, a child may pretend to bake one for a favorite stuffed animal. Old pots and pans, wooden spoons, toy tools, child-size benches or tables and chairs, and plastic or toy dishes are good props for make-believe play.

Pretend play provides endless opportunities for trying out different roles. A chalkboard and some books can turn a room into a school. Old clothes, jewelry, and shoes for dressing up can make playing house more fun. Many throwaway items can become make-believe treasures.

Fantasy play also helps children understand and express their feelings and may help them cope with negative emotions. Stuffed animals, dolls, toy figures, and puppets can all act as good friends (or perhaps enemies) to talk to and act out feelings with.

When invited, the caregiver can take part in fantasy play — by being an audience, by playing a minor role, or even by sampling a piece of pretend apple pie. But as soon as possible, the caregiver should leave the play area, allowing the child to control and create the fantasy.

Within reason, caregivers should not limit negative fantasy play. They can, however, let children know how they feel about it. Caregivers can tell children engaged in "shooting" each other with pointed fingers or toy guns that they don't like to shoot people or be shot at. In this way, a set of values are presented without stopping children from learning about aggressive behavior.

Television and Kids

Whether TV viewing is good or bad for children depends largely on what they watch, how much, and with whom.

Television can help with many types of learning. Shows like *Sesame Street*, for example, have been specially developed to make learning fun and easy for children. Such shows may teach the alphabet and numbers, help children learn about different cultures, and help them understand their feelings. Nature shows are both entertaining and educational. Programs on space exploration or other special events help children develop a sense of history.

To a busy caregiver, the TV can be a tempting solution to the problem of keeping a child occupied. Unfortunately, this electronic "babysitter" may not be a healthy influence. The more a child watches TV, the less time he or she has for other activities important to physical, social, and intellectual development. Negative effects of television include:

- Children learn to expect to be continually entertained. This may make adjustment to school more difficult.
- Children become less active and physically fit.
- Television can stifle imagination and creativity. Children find it difficult to amuse themselves.
- Children who are overdependent on television don't develop the social skills learned through play with other children.
- Children often have trouble distinguishing between reality and fantasy. They are misled into thinking everything they see on TV is true.

Not all TV programs are suitable for children to watch. Some frighten or confuse them. Other programs present topics that are too mature for them to understand or deal with. One particular problem is the amount of violence depicted on television, even cartoons. Research is still being conducted on the effects of such violence. Check your library for the latest findings.

Television watching can be an asset or a liability to a child's learning and development. Caregivers should select shows that are appropriate for the child — musical entertainment, children's stories, or programs that present reassuring images of family life. Whenever possible, adults should watch along with the child to explain things that may be confusing and to help differentiate between what is real and what is fantasy. If violence or other inappropriate behavior is shown, the caregiver and child can discuss ways it could have been avoided and better ways of handling the situation. In these ways, watching TV can be an enjoyable, shared activity.

15 Health and Safety

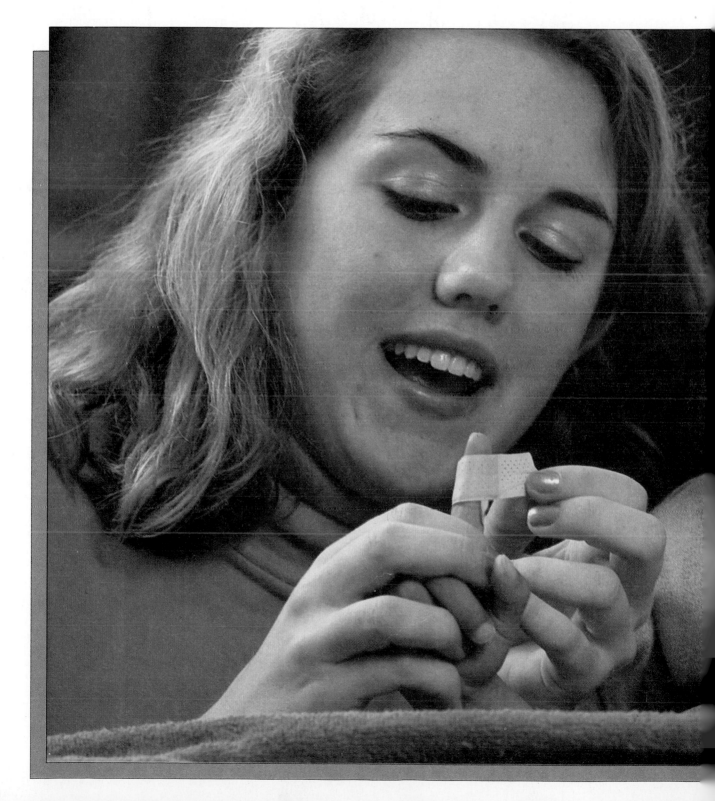

M ost of the earlier chapters of this book are designed to help you learn about what children are like at particular ages. This unit is different. It includes some special topics that will enhance your understanding of children of all ages.

Would you know what to do if a medical emergency arose while you were caring for a child? Sooner or later this can happen to anyone. Chapter 15 will help you be prepared to treat an injury or care for a sick child. You will also learn how accidents and illnesses can be prevented.

Chapter 16 addresses some common concerns of parents, such as: "How can we help our child's development?" Even if you never become a parent, what you learn can help you expand your own child care skills. This chapter also takes a look at single-parent families, adoption, and other special situations.

Some children must cope with personal or family difficulties. Chapter 17 tells how caregivers can help meet the special needs of children with handicaps. It also explores the serious problem of child abuse. And it discusses how to help children deal with stressful events.

Do you wonder how you can possibly decide what career is right for you? If so, Chapter 18 should be of special interest. It will make you aware of many careers that relate to children. In addition, you will find helpful pointers on choosing and preparing for a career in any field.

To help you to . . .

- Identify safety hazards for children of different ages.

- Explain the part immunizations and health checkups play in the prevention of illnesses.

- Recognize emergency situations and plan appropriate responses.

- Demonstrate appropriate first aid for common ailments.

- Give basic guidelines for caring for children who are ill.

Terms to Learn

allergy	convulsion	nontoxic
artificial	fracture	poison control
respiration	Heimlich maneuver	center
cardiopulmonary	immunize	sprain
resuscitation	infant mortality	vaccine
(CPR)	rate	
communicable		
diseases		

In the seventeenth century, 67 percent of all children in the American colonies died from childhood illnesses before age four. Almost all families experienced the death of a child. In other countries, the problem was the same if not worse.

Two hundred years ago, life expectancy at birth for Americans was 35 years. Infectious diseases killed many who did survive infancy. Smallpox and yellow fever were most feared. Tuberculosis, cholera, dysentery, typhoid, diphtheria, measles, and mumps were a constant threat. Malaria was common. Modern medicines and techniques were unknown. Home remedies were often based on custom or superstition.

Cleanliness and bathing were considered by many as unnecessary and even harmful. In 1799, one woman wrote in her diary that she "withstood" a shower bath "better than I expected, not having been wet all over at once for 28 years past."

By the eighteenth century, the **infant mortality rate** (percentage of deaths during the first year) was still almost 40 percent. Today, it is less than 2 percent.

Many medical advances were made during the nineteenth century. Deadly smallpox epidemics were controlled. Surgery improved as surgical instruments were perfected. Antiseptic techniques controlled infection. The use of ether as an anesthetic to produce a sleeplike state without pain was demonstrated in 1846. By 1900, the average life expectancy had increased to 50 years. Today, the average American can expect to live 74 years or longer.

Prevention of Accidents and Illness

You have probably heard the saying, "An ounce of prevention is worth a pound of cure." This means it is much easier to prevent many illnesses and accidents than to cope with their effects.

Safety

The safety of the child is the most important responsibility of the caregiver. Keeping a child safe requires:
- Knowledge of child development.
- A safe environment.
- Alertness to safety hazards.
- Teaching the child safe habits.

Early in this century, babies were always born at home. In this 1910 scene, a visiting nurse checks a newborn and gives the mother advice on health care.

Although infant walkers are commonly used, they can lead to injury, They can easily tip over or roll down a flight of stairs.

Every age has its particular hazards because children of different ages have different abilities and interests. What you know about child development will help you anticipate hazards to children.

Infants

Falls cause the most injuries among infants and account for many deaths. Even before the infant can crawl, his or her wriggling can produce enough movement to cause a fall from a bed, dressing table, or infant seat placed on a table. Such accidents are particularly dangerous since babies tend to fall headfirst. This can result in brain damage or other serious injury.

Babies like to suck and chew on objects, and they may choke on small ones. Objects that could be swallowed must be kept away from infants. (The information on page 388 gives tips on how to prevent choking in children.) All objects that can be placed in the mouth (even the edges of furniture) must be **nontoxic** (not poisonous). Some paints that contain lead are particularly dangerous for children. Plastic bags can cause suffocation, and no child should be allowed to play with them. Never use them in a crib or playpen.

A small child should *never* be left alone near water. Drownings can happen quickly—even in the time it takes to answer the door or telephone.

Automobile accidents cause the most deaths among young children. In spite of that fact, many loving parents allow their children to sit or stand in a moving vehicle without any protection. An accident or sudden stop can throw the child against the windshield or instrument panel. More and more states are passing laws that make child safety restraints mandatory. Check your own state's laws.

Not all car seats or restraints are equally good. Regular adult safety belts are not suitable for young children. See the information about car seats and restraints on pages 390-391.

Tips to Prevent Choking

Teach children to:

- Stay seated while eating.
- Always take small bites.
- Swallow what is in their mouth before taking another bite.
- Not talk or laugh with food in their mouth.
- Chew all food thoroughly.
- Avoid putting small toys or objects in their mouth.

Caregivers should:

- Cut foods into small pieces (no more than ½ in. [1.3 cm] square).
- Avoid serving peanuts, grapes, popcorn, or hot dogs to children under age three.
- Always hold a baby's bottle, never prop it.
- Always keep an eye on a small child who is eating.
- Keep small objects out of infants' reach.

Ages One to Three

Once children are able to move around with ease, they seem to be into everything. One- to three-year-olds need particularly careful supervision. Check the surroundings for safety and avoid leaving the child alone for any length of time. Review the information on page 244 for tips for making a home safe for toddlers.

Ages Four to Six

Young children from four to six spend more of their time in unsupervised play. They need to learn good safety practices. However, children often forget. Frequent reminders and watchfulness are essential.

Outdoor play equipment, such as swings, should be anchored firmly so it does not tip over. Set play rules, such as only one child on a swing at a time.

Children should be taught how to telephone for help before they need to do so in an emergency.

As soon as they are old enough, children should be taught their address and telephone number and how to reach the telephone operator in an emergency. Some communities have a special emergency number that is easy to remember. Keeping important numbers by the telephone, including parents' numbers at work, can help a child in an emergency.

Young children are often fascinated by fire. Even those who have been taught that matches are unsafe may sometimes play with them. As the match burns closer to the fingers, the child often becomes frightened. Sometimes children drop the match or throw it in a wastebasket to hide the evidence. This is how many fires start. Children's activities still need to be watched carefully.

Keeping a smoke detector in the home (more than one if the home is large) can alert the family to fire. Children should be taught ahead of time what to do in case of a fire. Plan escape routes from various places in the home and practice escape routines. The child who knows what to do in a fire emergency is much more likely to escape from a burning building safely.

When young children begin school they still face many of the safety hazards already mentioned. They also encounter many new dangers.

Keeping their children safe from crime is an increasing concern among parents. It is important to talk to children honestly and openly about crime. However, it is also important not to frighten them unnecessarily.

Parents need to set up safety rules for their children. They may make it clear, for example, that they will *never* send a stranger to pick the child up. If the child walks to school, point out the safest route. If possible, arrange for older children to walk with younger ones. Children need to understand caregivers must know where they are at all times.

Some school children must return to an unsupervised house after school. This is never a satisfactory situation. If the child must occasionally stay alone, establish special rules. These should cover keeping keys secure, dealing with strangers, keeping doors locked, and deciding whether friends can visit.

Many communities offer safety programs sponsored by the police, fire department, or civic groups. Children can learn traffic rules and other ways to stay safe.

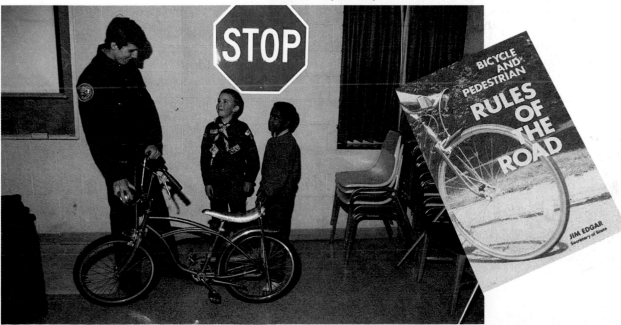

How to Choose Car Safety Restraints

You are on your way to the store with your sister and month-old niece. Your sister is driving. You are in the passenger seat holding the baby in your arms. Suddenly, a car pulls out in front of you from a side street. Your sister slams on the brakes. Fortunately, she's only going 35 m.p.h. and stops in time to avoid a collision. But the force was enough to tear the baby from your arms and crush her between you and the dash. She is seriously injured. The doctors are unsure if she has suffered brain damage.

Everyone needs to be buckled up in a moving vehicle. But because of their size, children under age four need special safety restraints. Regular adult seat belts do not fit or restrain young children properly.

There are many types of car safety restraints designed especially for infants and toddlers. Those manufactured since 1981 must meet federal safety standards. The best choice depends on the size of the child and how the restraint will be used. Some restraints require special installation, so check before you buy.

Infants

Babies need a bucket-type carrier. The infant should face backwards in a reclining position. A harness in the carrier holds the baby in position and the carrier is secured with a car seat belt.

Toddlers

At about age nine months, children are ready for a toddler seat. Some infant carriers can be converted to toddler seats, but a variety of other types are also available.

- **Seat with harness.** A harness comes over the child's shoulders and up between the legs. The seat is secured by the car safety belt. The child faces forward.

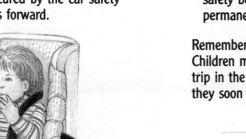

- **Seat with protective shield.** A padded surface protects the child who is thrown forward by impact or sudden braking. Look for seats with extended, padded shields around the head. The child is held in place by the car safety belt and sometimes by a harness as well.

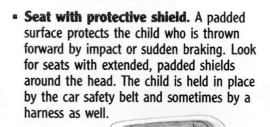

- **Booster seats.** These are strong seats without a back. They are used with the car safety belt and a special harness fastened permanently to the car.

Remember that accidents are never planned. Children must wear safety restraints for *every* trip in the car. When everyone else wears one, they soon accept this as expected behavior.

Health Care

Everyone, especially children, should see a doctor regularly. A physician can often catch health problems in their early stages. Early treatment can help prevent serious illness or permanent damage to health.

Newborns should be examined frequently during the first year. The physician or clinic will recommend how often. After the first year, healthy children need checkups less frequently, but at least once a year. Most cities have free or inexpensive clinics for those who cannot afford a private doctor.

Remember that infants can become seriously ill very quickly. If any health problems develop, consult a doctor. Symptoms of possibly serious illness in older children can include fever, persistent cough or vomiting, severe headache, fatigue, and dizziness.

Dental checkups are also an important part of health care. Although children lose their "baby" teeth, their adult teeth can be affected by poor dental care during childhood. The family's dentist should be consulted and a schedule of regular checkups arranged.

Immunization

To **immunize** is to protect the person against a particular disease. People can be protected from many **communicable diseases**—diseases which are easily passed on from one person to another—by being immunized against them. Unless people are immunized against them, many communicable diseases can easily turn into serious epidemics.

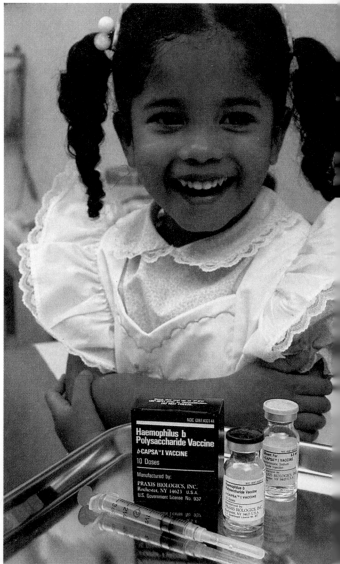

Immunizations have helped many youngsters lead healthier lives.

Vaccines are given to help people build up a resistance to particular diseases. A **vaccine**, usually given by injection, contains a very small amount of the disease germs. The person's body then produces antibodies that fight off the germs. Later, if the person is exposed to the disease, he or she will either not catch it at all or only in a mild form.

You have read that babies are born with temporary immunity against some diseases. However, doctors are uncertain how long this protection lasts. Therefore the first immunizations are usually given at two or three months of age.

Every child needs protection from seven serious diseases: tetanus, diphtheria, whooping cough (pertussis), polio, measles, rubella (German measles), and mumps. All can cause serious illness or even death. The chart on pages 408-410 gives information on the immunizations recommended by the American Academy of Pediatrics and the National Center for Disease Control. Parents should keep a record of each child's immunizations. Do you know which diseases you are immunized against?

Many states now require certain immunizations for all school children. (Exceptions are made for those who object on religious grounds.) However, preschool youngsters are the ones most likely to develop complications, so parents should not wait.

Allergies

An **allergy** is an oversensitivity to one or more common substances. The substances may cause a reaction when eaten, breathed in, or touched. About 50 percent of children in the United States develop some form of allergy. Allergic tendencies may be inherited. If both parents have allergies, the chance of their child developing one is about 70 percent.

While allergies cannot be cured, their effects are often preventable. If a certain food causes an allergy, it can be avoided. Common foods causing allergies in babies and children include milk, cereal grains, eggs, shellfish, nuts, fresh fruit juices, chocolate, and food additives.

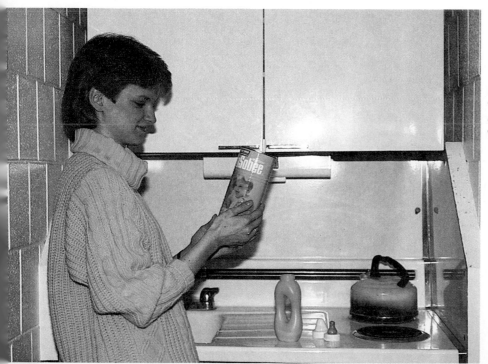

Special formulas are available for infants who are allergic to cow's milk. A doctor can advise whether these are necessary.

A child who is sensitive to animal hair may still be able to have a pet, as long as it is kept outdoors.

Dust and other substances in the air are also common causes of allergies. The bedroom of an allergic child can be kept clear of allergens (allergy-causing substances) in the air by filtering devices and air conditioners. Dusting and vacuuming frequently also helps minimize problems. Bedding can be made of allergy-free materials. Pets can be kept outside the house.

A doctor may prescribe medication to help control an allergy. If the allergy causes severe problems, allergy tests can be given to find out specifically what a person is allergic to. Then the person is gradually desensitized to those substances that caused a reaction.

Check Your Understanding

1. Pretend you have a four-year-old brother or sister. What would you teach the child about safety in case of fire? Consider your own home in your answer.

2. Why do you think it's important to keep records of a child's immunizations?

3. Why aren't regular car seat belts suitable for young children? Why does the type of restraint they need depend on their age and weight?

Handling Emergencies

Someday you may have to take care of a child in an emergency. You, then, may have to make decisions and take action that will affect the child's health—and perhaps life. That's quite a responsibility! You can prepare yourself by knowing how to act in an emergency, and how to give first aid and use rescue techniques.

Guidelines for Fast Action

In spite of careful supervision, children do get hurt. Accidents often happen because children do not recognize danger or their own limitations. These guidelines will help you make good decisions during an emergency:

1. *Above all, try to remain calm.* A quiet, soothing approach will help reassure the child. It will also help you think more clearly.

2. *Evaluate the situation.* What seems to be wrong? Is the child burned, bleeding heavily, or unconscious? Does the child have an arm or leg in an awkward position?

3. *Make the victim comfortable.* If the injury is serious, keep the child warm with a blanket, jacket, or other covering.

4. *Call for help, if indicated.* If you are not certain what the problem is or how to care for an injury, call for help. Contact the child's parents, a neighbor, a doctor, the emergency room of the hospital, or call for an ambulance.

   What you say on the phone is as important as making the call. Give the facts as clearly and concisely as possible. Having a list on hand of the phone numbers you might need and the address of where you are can save valuable time.

5. *Give the minimum necessary first aid treatment.* Knowing what you *should not* do in an emergency situation is as important as knowing what you should do. For instance, some injuries can be made worse just by moving the patient. If you are in doubt about how to handle an injured person, give only the most necessary first aid treatment and seek help from someone better trained.

No one can predict an emergency. However, it is possible to prepare yourself so that you can act quickly if an emergency occurs.

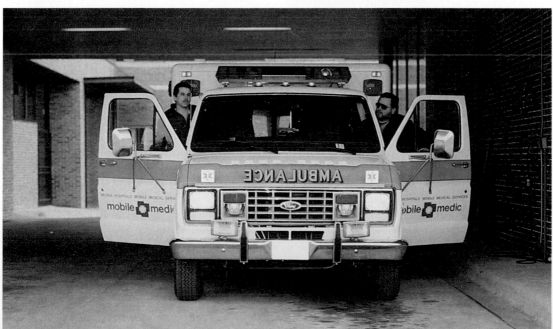

First Aid

The following first aid procedures are meant only as very general guidelines. For more information, contact the nearest office of the American Red Cross about first aid training classes.

Animal Bites

Wash the area with soap and running water. Try to have the animal caught so that it can be tested for rabies. (Wild animals are most likely to have rabies.) The victim should be checked by a doctor.

Bleeding

Stop the bleeding by placing a clean cloth over the wound and pressing hard for about 10 minutes without releasing. If the bleeding is severe, send for help.

■*Minor cuts or scrapes.* Clean with soap and warm water. Apply a mild antiseptic and cover with a bandage.

■*Deep cuts or wounds.* These may be severe. If the child is pale or bluish and skin is moist or if breathing is shallow and rapid, send for help. Continue to try to stop the bleeding until medical assistance arrives. Elevating the affected area may help. Do not apply a tourniquet. (A tourniquet is a tight bandage that cuts off the blood supply to a portion of the body.) An improperly applied tourniquet can further harm the victim.

■*Nosebleeds.* Nosebleeds may result from an injury or may have no apparent cause. Usually a small blood vessel inside the nose has broken. The child should sit down and lean slightly forward over a basin or sink. Squeeze the nose firmly with your thumb and forefinger just below the bones in the nose. Continue this for at least several minutes, then check to see if the

To stop a nosebleed, have the child lean forward slightly. Firmly press the nostrils shut and hold for several minutes.

bleeding has stopped. If not, reapply pressure for five to ten minutes. Sometimes applying cold packs to the nose and forehead will also help. If bleeding cannot be stopped or the child becomes dizzy or pale, seek medical help.

Bumps and Bruises

Treat bumps and bruises with a cold cloth or ice pack to minimize swelling. An injured arm or leg can be elevated. If pain persists for more than a day, call a physician.

A fall or bump on the head can be serious. The doctor should be called if the child loses consciousness, is drowsy or irritable, complains of headache, or vomits.

Burns

How you treat a burn depends on how it was caused and how bad it is. All but small surface burns are serious because they may cause scarring, infections, or shock.

Burns are classified by degree:

■*First-degree burns look red and slightly swollen.* They are caused by such things as too much sun, hot objects, hot water, or steam. First-degree burns heal rapidly.

■*Second-degree burns are deeper, redder, and blistered.* They remain swollen and somewhat moist for several days. They are caused by such things as very deep sunburn, hot liquids, and flammable products like gasoline. Second-degree burns should be treated by a physician.

■*Third-degree burns destroy the skin.* The burns look white or charred or may resemble second-degree burns at first. There may be little pain at first because the nerve endings have been destroyed. Third-degree burns can be caused by flames, burning clothing, hot water, extremely hot objects, or electricity. The skin is lost and will not grow back. Only scar tissue covers the area. Third-degree burns are extremely serious and require emergency medical attention.

Treat small, surface burns where the skin is not broken with a cold, wet cloth. Apply several times for short periods to take the heat out of the burn. A burned hand or foot may be placed in a basin of cold water. Then cover the area with a clean, loose cloth. Never apply butter or grease to a burn.

If the skin has been broken or the burn looks serious, call for help. Cover the burn with a clean cloth and keep the patient warm. To lessen pain, elevate the burned area slightly. The patient should be taken to a hospital as soon as possible.

Household products, such as toilet bowl and drain cleaners and disinfectants, can cause chemical burns. Using protective gloves or a towel, wash off the affected area immediately and completely with water. Remove any clothing with the chemical on it, unless it is stuck to the skin. Apply a clean bandage and call a doctor.

Electrical burns may be deep, but appear minor, leaving only a small black dot on the skin. Cool the burned area with cold water and cover it with a clean, smooth cloth, such as a handkerchief. Then the patient should lie down with legs elevated and head turned to one side. This prevents shock (see page 402). Take the child to a hospital emergency room or call an ambulance.

Minor burns should be treated with a cold, wet cloth then covered with a clean, dry cloth. More serious burns require professional medical help.

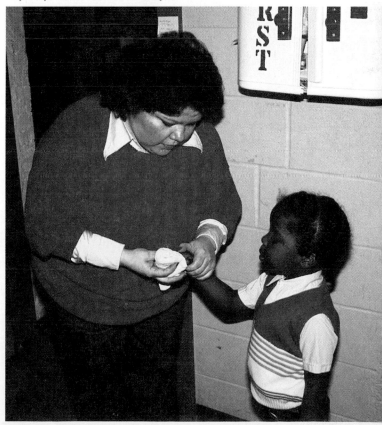

Choking

Choking occurs when something is caught in a person's throat. With a child, this may be food or a small object. The danger is that choking can cut off the supply of air. Brain damage can occur within a few minutes.

First, look in the child's throat to see if you can see anything caught. Next, see if the child can cough up the object. A small child can be held upside down across the lap with head lowered. This often helps get the object out. If these methods do not work, the **Heimlich maneuver** can be used. Basically, this procedure relies on the air within the body to force the object out. The diagrams on this page and the next show how to administer the Heimlich maneuver to infants and to older children and adults.

Keep in mind that the amount of pressure to use in the Heimlich maneuver depends on the age of the victim. Too much pressure, especially on a young child, can be harmful. It is best to be trained to do this procedure correctly before you need to use it.

If nothing else works and the person is not breathing, use your thumb and index finger to try to locate and remove the object from the throat. Call for emergency medical help and begin artificial respiration immediately (see page 404). Continue until help arrives.

Heimlich Maneuver for Infants and Toddlers

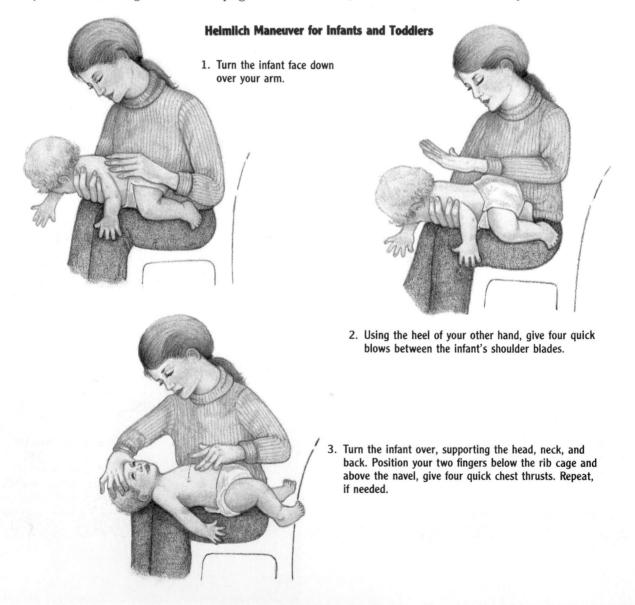

1. Turn the infant face down over your arm.

2. Using the heel of your other hand, give four quick blows between the infant's shoulder blades.

3. Turn the infant over, supporting the head, neck, and back. Position your two fingers below the rib cage and above the navel, give four quick chest thrusts. Repeat, if needed.

Heimlich Maneuver for Older Children and Adults

If the victim is standing or sitting. . .

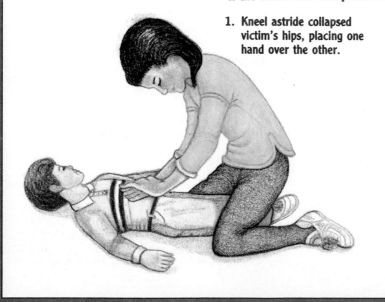

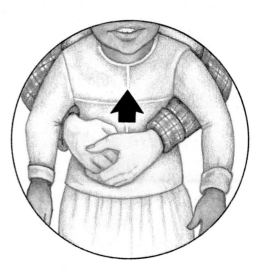

1. Stand behind victim and place fists just below rib cage.

2. Press fist into victim's abdomen with quick upward thrust.

If the victim has collapsed. . .

1. Kneel astride collapsed victim's hips, placing one hand over the other.

2. Place heel of bottom hand slightly above navel and below rib cage. Press with quick upward thrust. Repeat, if needed.

Convulsions

A **convulsion** is a period of unconsciousness with uncontrolled jerking or twitching of the muscles. There are many causes. Convulsions occur most often in infants, usually as a result of high fever.

If a baby or young child has a convulsion, place the child on his or her side on the floor. Move any hard objects out of the way. Don't attempt to hold the patient down or force anything between the teeth. After the convulsion stops, be sure the patient's head is turned to one side. Check with a doctor for further directions. If the convulsion lasts more than 15 minutes, take the person to a hospital emergency room or call an ambulance.

Fainting

Fainting is loss of consciousness. The person may collapse without warning or may first experience sweating, cold skin, nausea, or dizziness. People about to faint often look pale or bluish. A person who feels faint should lie down or sit with the head between the legs.

If a person has fainted, loosen any tight clothing. Position the person's head to one side. If breathing has stopped, begin artificial respiration (see page 404). If the patient does not quickly revive, call for help.

Fractures and Sprains

A **fracture** is a break or crack in a bone. A **sprain** is an injury caused by sudden, violent stretching of a joint or muscle. Both may cause pain, swelling, and bruising. It is often difficult to tell a sprain from a fracture without an X ray.

Do not move the injured person until you know how serious the injury is. This is extremely important for back, rib, neck, or collarbone injuries. You can cause further damage (even paralysis) by moving the person. Call for qualified medical help and use artificial respiration, if necessary.

Mild sprains can be treated by elevating the area. Cold packs help reduce swelling. If the pain persists, check with a doctor.

A broken bone must be set by a doctor so that the fracture will heal properly.

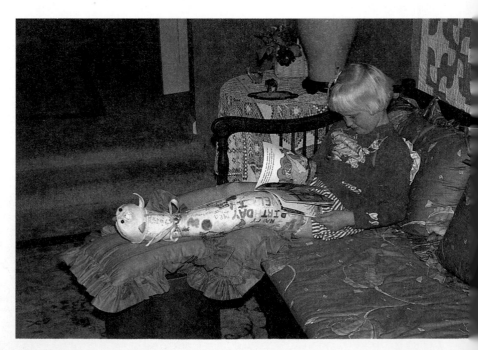

Insect Bites

In case of a bee, wasp, hornet, or yellow jacket sting, remove any stinger. Apply an ice pack or ice water to the affected area. Then the area can be covered with a baking soda and water paste.

Some people are very allergic to insect stings and can even die from them. The person must be taken to a hospital or doctor immediately. Anyone who becomes dizzy, faint, or perspires heavily after a sting needs prompt medical attention.

Ticks are small insects that cling to the skin or scalp. They are dangerous because they carry diseases. Don't pull them off. Cover the tick with heavy oil, such as cooking oil, until it comes loose. Then carefully remove it with tweezers, taking care that the entire tick is removed. Wash the area well with soap and water.

Mosquito, ant, and chigger bites are annoying but usually not dangerous. A baking soda paste or coating of witch hazel or rubbing alcohol will give relief.

Poisoning

Poisons are one of the greatest hazards for young children. Many caregivers leave poisonous products within a child's reach around the house. Part of the problem is that so many common household products are poisonous. The chart on page 403 lists common household poisons. These should be kept out of reach of children, preferably in a locked cabinet.

If you suspect poisoning, call for help right away. Be prepared to tell what you think caused the poisoning and how much was involved. Have the container with you when you call.

If a toddler is holding a bottle of vitamins and has a mouthful of pieces, it is clear you have a poisoning problem. Often, it is more difficult to tell. Here are some symptoms that may indicate poisoning:

- Difficulty breathing, unconsciousness, fever, burns in the mouth and throat, and vomiting from swallowed poisons or chemicals.
- Burns or rash on the skin.
- Burning or irritation of the eyes or blindness.
- Choking, coughing, nausea, or dizziness from fumes, sprays, and poisonous gases.

In case a poisoning does happen, know what to do:

1. Keep emergency phone numbers and addresses posted by all telephones. Include the doctor, hospital, police, rescue squad, and poison control center. **Poison control centers** are special hospital units that are equipped to advise and treat poison victims. If you care for children in someone else's home, take a copy of your emergency number list with you.

2. Determine what has poisoned the child. If it is a swallowed poison, estimate how much was swallowed.
3. Phone the poison control center or your doctor. (The emergency procedures listed on product labels are not always accurate.) Have the product container at hand as you call.
4. Follow the directions you are given quickly and calmly.

Anyone who has been poisoned must be checked by a physician, even if emergency treatment has already been given or there are no symptoms. Be sure to take the poison container or a sample of the poison substance with you. This helps the doctor to give proper treatment.

Shock

When a person's body is threatened such as by an injury, loss of much blood, or poisoning, the body goes into shock. Important body functions such as breathing and heart action are impaired. Symptoms can include a pale or bluish skin color, rapid pulse, clammy skin, shallow breathing, enlarged pupils, a glassy stare, and nausea. Sometimes the person loses consciousness.

Shock can be serious and medical help should be sought immediately. In the meantime, keep the patient warm and lying down.

Splinters

Although splinters are not dangerous, they hurt and can become infected. They may be tiny pieces of wood, metal, glass, or thorns.

If part of the splinter is above the surface of the skin, it can be removed with tweezers. Sterilize the tweezers in boiling water or in a flame. If the splinter is just under the skin surface, it can be carefully taken out with a sterilized needle. Numb the skin over the splinter first with a piece of ice to help dull the pain. Afterwards put antiseptic on the wound and cover with a sterile bandage.

Large or deep splinters and those caused by glass can be more serious. They should be removed by a physician.

Remove splinters carefully to avoid pushing them further into the skin. Be sure the tweezers have been sterilized to reduce the chance of infection.

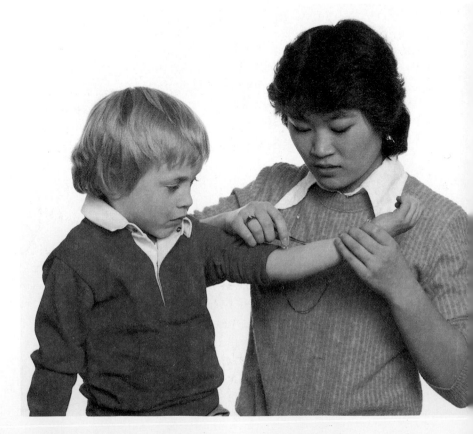

Common Household Poisons

■**Swallowed poisons.** Can cause many different symptoms such as breathing difficulty, unconsciousness, fever, burns in mouth and throat from chemicals, and vomiting.

■**Skin contact poisons.** Can cause burns, rash, or other allergic reactions.

■**Eye contact poisons.** Many substances can cause burning, irritation, or blindness when they come in contact with the eyes.

■**Inhaled poisons.** Chemical sprays, fumes, and poisonous gases can cause suffocation or brain damage.

Kinds of Poisons	Examples	Type of Contact
MEDICINES	■ Sleeping pills ■ Aspirin ■ Tranquilizers ■ Vitamins ■ Cold preparations	■ Swallowing
CLEANING PRODUCTS	■ Ammonia ■ Laundry detergents ■ Bleach ■ Drain and toilet bowl cleaners ■ Disinfectants ■ Furniture polish	■ Swallowing ■ Skin ■ Eyes ■ Inhaling
PERSONAL CARE PRODUCTS	■ Shampoo ■ Soap ■ Nail polish remover ■ Perfumes and after-shave lotions ■ Mouthwash ■ Rubbing alcohol	■ Swallowing ■ Skin ■ Eyes ■ Inhaling
GARDENING AND GARAGE PRODUCTS	■ Insecticides ■ Fertilizers ■ Rat and mouse poisons ■ Acids of all kinds ■ Gasoline ■ Paint thinner ■ Charcoal lighter fluid ■ Antifreeze	■ Swallowing ■ Skin ■ Eyes ■ Inhaling
PLANTS	■ Mushrooms ■ English ivy ■ Daffodil bulbs ■ Rhubarb leaves ■ Holly berries ■ Poinsettias ■ Poison ivy and oak	■ Swallowing ■ Skin

Rescue Techniques

When emergency situations cause the victim to stop breathing and perhaps even the heart to stop beating, immediate action is vital. You should become familiar with rescue techniques that will enable you to respond quickly to the life-or-death situation.

Artificial Respiration

Artificial respiration means forcing air into a person's lungs when breathing has stopped. It is a procedure that is called for in many emergencies. The technique for giving artificial respiration to infants and small children is slightly different than for adults. It is shown below. A rescue training class can give you practice in, and more information about, the proper way to give artificial respiration.

Cardiopulmonary Resuscitation (CPR)

Cardiopulmonary resuscitation (**CPR**) is a technique used when both breathing and heart action have stopped. Special training from a certified instructor is needed to perform CPR, and many communities offer training programs. Find out if CPR training is offered in your area by calling the American Red Cross or the American Heart Association.

**Artificial Respiration
for Infants and Small Children**

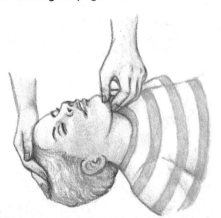

1. Turn the child's head to one side. With your finger, carefully clear the child's mouth of any foreign objects or fluid. (Do not try this on a young baby.) If there is an object caught in the throat, or to clear the mouth of a young baby, follow the instructions for choking on pages 398-399.

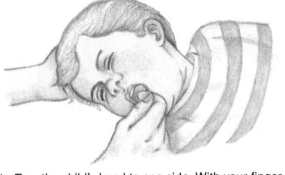

2. Tilt the head back slightly. Put two fingers just under the chinbone and lift the jaw into a jutting-out position. Check for breathing.

3. If the child is not breathing, take a deep breath. Seal your lips around the child's mouth and nose. (If you can only cover the mouth, pinch the nostrils shut with your fingers.)
4. Blow into the mouth and nose. (For an infant, use gentle puffs of air.) When you see the chest lift, remove your mouth and let the air come out. Then blow in again. Repeat 15 to 20 times per minute for a child and 20 times per minute for an infant. Continue until the child resumes normal breathing or until help arrives.

Check Your Understanding

1. Why do you think it's important to remain calm in an emergency?

2. Pretend you have just seen a three-year-old girl burn herself on a hot pan from the stove. What would you do to help the child?

3. What is shock and why is it dangerous?

Infants may need comforting and quiet play to distract them from their illness.

Caring for a Sick Child

It is never easy caring for a child who is ill. Normal routines are upset. The child may cry often, demand attention, and have a short temper. However, the attitude of the caregiver can be as important in restoring good health as the medical treatment. If you remember how it feels to be ill yourself, you will have more patience.

A caregiver should maintain a calm, efficient, confident, and cheerful attitude. Treat the illness matter-of-factly, and discuss it as little as possible.

Kindness and good care differ from over-protectiveness. Paying *too* much attention to a sick child can prolong the illness and make the child more demanding. Children who are ill should be encouraged to do as much as possible for themselves. They should be helped to consider the comfort and welfare of other members of the family.

Another responsibility of the caregiver is to entertain the child. When children are very ill they do not have much energy for play and may spend much of their time sleeping. However, during mild illness or the recovery stage of a serious illness, the child may be easily bored.

■*Infants.* Infants who are ill sleep much more than usual. They tend to be cranky and may want a lot of physical comforting. Comforting is important because the small child cannot understand what is wrong. However, no caregiver can be with the child constantly. Remember that a very young child cannot focus on more than one thing at a time. A baby who is happily engrossed with a new or interesting toy will temporarily forget about the illness.

■*Ages one to three.* Young children need more help than older children in keeping cheerful and occupied. They are more physically active, and staying in bed is difficult for them. Doctors often do not insist on keeping preschoolers in bed, unless there is a good reason. A child who is dressed warmly can play quietly around the house. Preschoolers like stories and simple games. A variety of odds and ends and art materials can keep the child occupied for a long time. The child can also help with simple household tasks.

■*Ages four to six.* Older children handle ordinary illnesses much better. They help care for themselves and may like to make schedules for such things as medication. They may be more conscientious about these things than their parents. If medication is ten minutes late, they show real concern. Storybooks, stickers, puzzles, and games can entertain them.

Because of medical advances, childhood illnesses are viewed differently today. One hundred years ago people took longer to recover from illness. Today, however, antibiotics and other medical treatments prevent many illnesses from becoming serious. Children are usually up and about in a few days. Often recovery involves no more than keeping the child inside and quiet for a while.

Of course, serious illnesses or injuries may need additional treatment and a long period of recovery. This requires the understanding and cooperation of the entire family. The child needs to remain as much an active and contributing part of the family as possible.

The chart on pages 408–410 lists symptoms, immunization, and care for common childhood diseases.

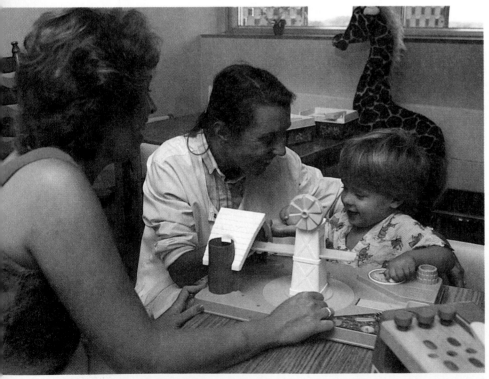

Medical treatment keeps many childhood illnesses from becoming serious. Having companionship and fun things to do helps the child feel better, too.

Sick children are usually thirsty. Plenty of liquids, such as fruit juices, should be offered.

Nutrition During Illness

Unless the doctor prescribes a special diet, small amounts of regular foods are suitable for the child who is ill. Lack of appetite is common during illness and the child should not be forced to eat.

Children should be offered extra liquids between meals. They frequently crave water, particularly if they have a fever. However, if the stomach is upset, water may cause vomiting. If this happens, give the stomach a rest of several hours, then give liquids in small amounts—only a sip or two at first. One consolation for sick children is the chance to drink more fruit juices and carbonated soft drinks. Sometimes clear carbonated soft drinks stay down best. They help relieve stomach gas by causing burping.

The doctor may advise a bland diet or a liquid diet. A bland diet is one of soft, smooth, mild-flavored foods. This might include soups, hot cereals, casseroles, puddings, gelatin desserts, eggs, and mild cooked vegetables and canned fruits. A bland diet should not include fried foods, spicy or salty foods, rich pastries, candy, raw fruits or vegetables, or pork.

A liquid diet is prescribed to ease digestive problems. Foods in liquid form can be used more easily by the body. If there is a fever, liquids also help regulate body temperature and elimination. Depending on the type of illness, a liquid diet may include such foods as fruit juice, carbonated soft drinks, milk, thin cooked cereal, broth, cream soup, ice cream, and pudding.

Common Childhood Diseases

Disease	Immunization	Symptoms	Home Care
CHICKEN POX ✓	None available.	A rash of tiny red, raised pimples or blisters appears first. In a day or two, scabs form which fall off in 7 to 10 days. The rash affects the whole body. Fever is either absent or no higher than 102°F (39°C). Rash is irritating but child usually does not feel ill otherwise.	Rest in bed during feverish stage. Fever control is recommended but do not use aspirin. The child shouldn't scratch; this spreads the rash. Keep the child cool in loose clothing. Apply talcum powder or calamine lotion. Medicine to prevent itching may be needed. Recovery is usually within 7 days. Once scabs form, and no new pox have appeared for 2 days, the disease is no longer infectious. Consult a physician if vomiting or a change in personality occurs.
DIPHTHERIA	DPT shots against diphtheria, pertussis (whooping cough), and tetanus are given at 2, 4, and 6 months of age. Booster shots should be given at 18 months and between 3 and 6 years. A combined tetanus and diphtheria shot should be given at age 12 and every 10 years thereafter.	Sore throat, pain in limbs, loss of appetite, swollen neck glands, difficulty breathing.	Child should be under close medical supervision. Hospitalization is usually necessary.
HAEMOPHILUS INFLUENZA (HIB)	Vaccinations are given at 2 years of age. Children 18–23 months of age who attend day care facilities should be vaccinated, as the disease is easily spread. Children should be revaccinated 2–12 months later, but not before 24 months of age.	Most common cause of bacterial meningitis. Symptoms include sudden onset of fever, nausea, vomiting, and intense headaches.	A doctor's care is essential. Patient will need immediate hospitalization. Disease is fatal in 5 percent of meningitis cases in children less than 5 years of age. Causes long-term neurological problems in many others.

(Continued)

Common Childhood Diseases (Continued)

MEASLES ✓	Vaccination at about 15 months. Combination vaccines (a Measles/Rubella and a Measles/Mumps/Rubella) are available.	Usually fever, sometimes as high as 105°F (41°C). The child may also cough, have a runny nose and inflamed, watery eyes. About 4 days later a blotchy, dusty-red rash appears, often seen first behind the ears or on the forehead and face.	Occasionally complications occur; therefore, child should be under a doctor's supervision and kept in bed for the duration of the fever. The disease is most contagious during the few days before and after the rash appears. If patient's eyes are sensitive, the child should be kept in a darkened room and not allowed to read or do other close work. In most cases the rash fades, temperature drops, and patient begins to feel more comfortable 3—5 days after the rash appears.
MUMPS ✓	Vaccine is given at 12 months or thereafter. A parent who has not had mumps may be immunized if his or her child contracts the disease.	Sudden fever, occasional nausea, abdominal pain, and swelling of one or more salivary glands, most commonly those located at the angles of the jaws. Swelling reaches maximum within 24 hours and may last 7—10 days. In boys, infection may also cause painful swelling in the testicles.	A hot-water bottle and analgesics may ease pain. Fluids are easiest to swallow. Mumps is usually a mild disease, leaving no ill effects. However, sometimes deafness occurs.
POLIOMYELITIS	The Sabin vaccine is given orally at 2, 4, and 18 months of age and again at 4 or 5 years. Immunization of adults is not recommended unless the individual has been (or might be) exposed to polio.	Sudden fever, headache, vomiting, stiffness of neck. In paralytic cases, the muscles become painful and tender; paralysis follows.	A doctor's care is essential. Patient must be isolated and kept in bed during acute phase. In paralytic cases, even partial recovery takes many months.
RUBELLA ✓ (German Measles)	Vaccination between 12 and 15 months of age or thereafter.	Similar to those of a head cold. Mild fever and joint pain are often the first signs, followed by rash on face and head, and later on neck and body. Lymph nodes at back of neck may become tender and swollen.	Child should be kept at home until recovery. The disease is dangerous only for women during pregnancy. It can cause defects in the unborn child. A blood test which indicates whether or not a woman is immune should be taken before pregnancy.

(Continued on next page)

Common Childhood Diseases (Continued)

SCARLET FEVER and STREPTOCOCCAL SORE THROAT	No prevention. Penicillin or erythromycin helps prevent such complications as rheumatic fever.	Sudden onset, with headache, fever, sore throat. Lymph nodes usually enlarged. In scarlet fever a rash appears, usually within 24 hours, as fine red dots. The rash is seen first on the neck and upper part of the chest, and lasts 24 hours to 10 days. When it fades, skin peels. The rash is the only symptom that differentiates scarlet fever from "strep throat."	Because strep throat and scarlet fever can be followed by or reactivate rheumatic fever, a physician's care is needed. The child should rest in a warm, well-ventilated room. Patient usually recovers in a week's time, but parent should watch for such complications as earache or inflamed neck glands.
SMALLPOX	Smallpox vaccinations are no longer recommended.		
WHOOPING COUGH (Pertussis)	See Diphtheria section.	Begins with cough that is worse at night. Symptoms may at first be mild. Characteristic "whooping" cough develops in about 2 weeks, and coughing spasms sometimes end with vomiting.	Child should take antibiotics under a doctor's care. Hospitalization is often required for infants. Rest is important, as is a diet that will not irritate the throat. The doctor may prescribe breathing exercises. Patients should be isolated from other children until antibiotics have been taken for at least 5 days.

Alan R. Hinman, M.D., Director of Division of Immunization, Center for Prevention Services, National Center for Disease Control.

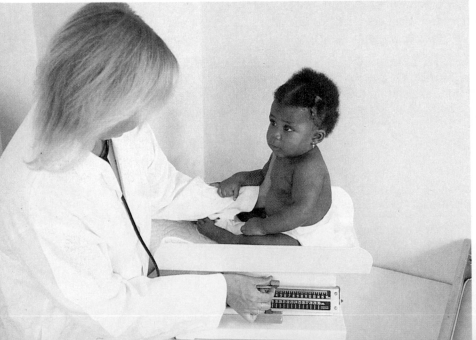

Regular checkups and immunizations help insure good health.

Hospitalization

A hospital stay is an emotional crisis for almost every child. Child psychologists agree that no experience is more emotionally upsetting to a child than suddenly being separated from home and family. In the hospital the youngster finds unfamiliar people, unusual routines, strange smells, and frightening machines.

Hospitalized youngsters often fear that their parents have abandoned them. They may be frightened that they will be hurt or mutilated or will die. Some think they are being punished. This is because children do not really understand what is happening to them.

If it is known in advance that a child will be hospitalized, helping the child prepare for the event is extremely important. The parents or doctor should explain to the child in simple words just what to expect. A visit to the hospital ahead of time is helpful. Many hospitals have special tours for children. These tours include a look in the patients' rooms, operating and recovery rooms, and sometimes a puppet show or movie. Some have play rooms where children can play with stethoscopes, masks, identification bracelets, and other equipment. When the child is admitted, these things are less frightening.

Most hospitals realize that children recover better if a parent is allowed to stay in the hospital with them. Sometimes a cot is moved into the child's room. Other hospitals have rooms with space for both the child and a parent. Even where this is not available, visiting hours are usually quite flexible for parents. Many minor procedures are performed in the hospital but the child is allowed to go home the same day.

Parents should be truthful when a child asks, "Will it hurt?" Some parents are tempted to give a reassuring, "No." A far better response is, "Yes, it will hurt for a while, but then you will feel much better. It is all right for you to cry when it hurts, if you feel like it."

Studies show that with good preparation, hospitalized children do not become as frightened or as withdrawn. They eat, sleep, and recover better from their illnesses.

Visits from parents and other family members can help a hospitalized child keep from feeling frightened and alone.

Close-up

Three-year-old Alex had to go to the hospital to have his tonsils removed. His family chose a hospital that encouraged family support.

Ahead of time, Alex went with his parents to see the hospital and meet several friendly nurses. Later at home, his parents explained everything that would happen to him, using hand puppets for doctor-patient stories.

Along with his toothbrush, robe, and pajamas, Alex was allowed to take along several favorite books, small toys, a stuffed animal, and his cuddly blanket.

After Alex's surgery, his parents took turns staying with him so someone was always there. The parents bathed Alex, fed him, and were present during all medical checks. His father slept by his bedside during the overnight stay.

Back home Alex recovered quickly and was soon his old self. He told his brother and sister all about his operation and how he got to ride on a bed with wheels.

What special arrangements are offered at your local hospital for parents of hospitalized children?

Were you ever hospitalized when you were younger?

Was your experience as positive as Alex's? ■

Check Your Understanding

1. How could you entertain a sick child for an entire evening? Give at least three suggestions.

2. Why do school age children handle illness better than infants and toddlers?

3. Plan one day's meals for a four-year-old on a bland diet.

A hospital tour can help eliminate fear for a child scheduled for hospitalization. Do hospitals in your area offer this service?

Chapter Review

To Sum Up

- It is easier to prevent illnesses and accidents than to cope with their effects.
- The safety of the child is the most important responsibility of the caregiver.
- Children need regular medical checkups and immunizations for childhood diseases.
- Emergencies must be dealt with quickly and calmly.
- Artificial respiration and cardiopulmonary resuscitation are rescue techniques used when breathing and heart action have stopped.
- The attitude of the caregiver toward a sick child can be as important to the patient as medical treatment.
- A hospital stay is usually an emotional crisis for a child.

To Review and Remember

1. Define infant mortality rate. Why has this rate changed so drastically in the past 200 years?
2. What four things are needed to keep a child safe?
3. What is the leading cause of death among children?
4. Describe five ways to make a home safer for young children.
5. What are communicable diseases? How can they best be controlled?
6. Name seven serious diseases children should be immunized against.
7. What are the five steps for dealing with an emergency?
8. Describe the three categories of burns and give a possible cause for each.
9. Name four types of common household products that can cause poisoning.
10. Describe a bland diet.

To Discuss and Discover

1. List six or more safety hazards for children that exist in your home. How might each be corrected?
2. Design a poster to make parents more aware of one aspect of child safety.
3. Check your own home for fire safety. Are there smoke detectors? If not, where should they be placed for best protection? Plan escape routes from each room in case of fire. Draw a diagram of your plan.
4. Plan a series of activities that will keep a sick three-year-old quiet and entertained while recovering from an illness.

To help you to . . .

- Describe how parents and other caregivers can encourage a child's development.
- Explain the importance of giving children love and support.
- List techniques for communicating positively with children.
- Discuss characteristics of good discipline.
- Explain the need for substitute care and the types available.
- Describe how single parents, stepparents, adoptive parents, and teen parents can meet their special challenges.

Terms to Learn

blended family	Montessori	play group
child care aide	preschool	positive
day care center	nanny	reinforcement
deprivation	negative	preschool
family day care	reinforcement	single parents
Head Start	nursery school	time out
latch-key children	parent cooperative	

arol Cheng watched with a smile as her older brother Paul held his eight-month-old son. Paul was wiggling little David's toes. "Are you ticklish? See your funny little feet. Yes, you are ticklish, aren't you! I'm going to get you for that!" The baby chuckled happily as his father's fingers crept up to his chin.

Just then David's three-year-old sister Cindy came into the room. "Aunt Carol, do you want to play outside with me?"

"Okay," Carol said. "Let's get our coats on."

"Don't want to wear a coat!"

"Cindy, it's cold out. You must wear a coat or stay inside," Paul said. "Do you want to wear your blue jacket or the red one?"

"I want, um, the red one," Cindy said and ran to her bedroom. She returned in a few minutes, struggling to put her arms in the sleeves. "Can we make piles of leaves and jump in them?"

"Yes, you may," Paul said as he handed the baby to Carol. "Just remember to stay in our own yard." He hooked the jacket zipper and let Cindy pull it up herself. "Bye, Peanut. Have fun," he said and gave Cindy a kiss.

Carol handed David back to his father. As she went to get her own coat, she thought back to when she and Paul were kids themselves. It didn't seem that long ago. "Now here Paul is with two kids of his own," Carol thought. "How did he ever learn to be such a good parent? I sure hope some of it rubs off on me."

Parenting: A Learning Process

People aren't born with parenting skills. But as you probably know by now, many people have need of these skills—not only parents, but anyone who cares for a child.

Parenting is a complicated task. It requires an understanding of the child's needs in all areas and the family leadership to meet those needs. It involves providing physical care, encouragement, love, support, and guidance. All this is done with the goal of helping the child develop to the fullest.

How do people qualify to do all these things? No one has to pass a test to become a parent. There is not even one right method of parenting. But in order to care for children well, many different parenting skills are needed. Effective caregivers continue to develop these skills all their lives. They learn by:

- Asking the advice of friends and family members.
- Reading books and magazine articles about parenting.
- Observing other parents and children.
- Attending parenting classes.
- Gaining experience with children.

Skills needed also change as the children in the family grow up. Infants' needs are different from those of preschoolers or teens. Parents continue to need new parenting skills at each stage of development. The chart on page 417 shows the life cycle of a typical family.

It's true that parenting doesn't "come naturally" to everyone—and perhaps not to anyone. Like any other skill, it must be learned.

The Family Life Cycle

Beginning Stage
A couple works to establish a home and a marriage relationship.

Childbearing Stage
The couple prepare for and adjust to parenthood.

Child-Rearing Stage
As children grow, the parents work to meet their children's changing needs and help them develop independence.

Retirement Stage
The couple adjust to the aging process. They may develop new interests or renew old ones.

Launching Stage
Children gradually leave home to support themselves. Parents help their children adapt to life on their own.

Empty-Nest Stage
After the last child has left home, the couple renew their relationship and adjust to the change in their parenting role.

Variations in the Family Life Cycle

Any of the following situations may change the pattern of the family life cycle or the characteristics of each stage:

- Single adulthood
- Divorce
- Single parenthood
- Remarriage
- Couples without children

The trend in society today is toward more formal training in parenting for those with children of all ages. Parents can be trained at hospitals, schools, through community organizations, or in private classes. Most communities have a variety of options for parents who want to learn more about children.

Most of the groups that offer parenting courses do so because they are interested in the healthy growth and development of children. They work to ensure that parents respect the rights of children and know how to nurture, discipline, and guide children in ways that respect these rights.

Nurturing Children

Nurturing is an important part of parenting. A parent nurtures a child by providing encouragement and enriching experiences. Nurturing also means showing love, support, concern, understanding—all the things that are part of the special closeness between parent and child.

Understanding Children

Have you ever heard an adult tell a child, "Act your age"? Children usually *do* act their age. The trouble is, caregivers do not always understand what to expect from children. This basic knowledge is the first step in helping children develop.

It takes a good understanding of how children develop to provide them with activities that are challenging, but not overly difficult.

Caregivers need to be realistic about what children are capable of. Giving a preschooler a puzzle that is too difficult will make the child frustrated. An understanding parent can help guide the child toward a more suitable activity.

Parents who are aware of the difficult stages children go through are better able to handle them when they occur. For example, Liz was bewildered at first by her nine-month-old daughter's crying whenever a stranger approached. As the crying episodes continued, Liz became more and more impatient. Then she learned from her own mother that all babies go through a stage of "stranger anxiety." From then on Liz looked at the situation as a sign of healthy development rather than as a problem.

It is also important to understand and respect the differences between children. Some will learn to walk earlier than others. Some children need more encouragement to make friends. The more time parents spend talking with and observing their children, the better they will be able to meet each child's individual needs.

Providing Enrichment and Encouragement

Part of the job parents do is to teach children. They do this whether they realize it or not. Children naturally learn by exploring their world, trying new things, and imitating others. Nurturing parents give children the freedom they need in order to learn. They provide positive examples, encouragement, and enriching experiences.

As much as possible, caregivers should eliminate barriers that might otherwise prevent children from discovering things on their own. For an infant or toddler, this means putting away breakable objects, covering up electrical outlets, locking up poisons, and so on. For a preschooler, it might mean letting the child dig for worms without worrying about dirty hands and clothes.

The activities that provide the most learning, creativity, and fun are often the messiest.

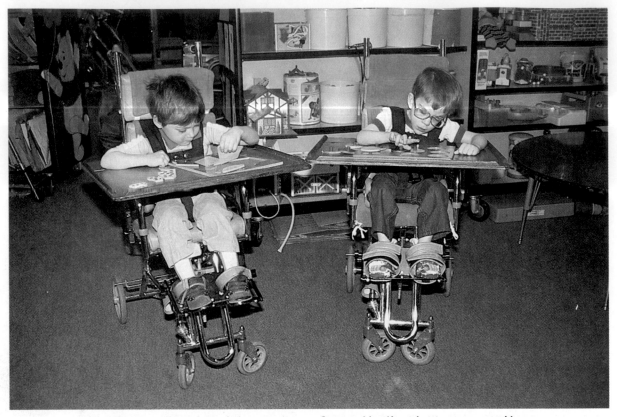

All children need a variety of play experiences. Can you identify at least one way working on these puzzles together benefits each area of development?

Enrichment can come through everyday objects and experiences. An infant is stimulated by being held, talked to, played with, and given safe objects to look at and handle. (See pages 228-229 for specific ideas.) Daily routines can become learning experiences for a child of any age. In the supermarket, for example, you can help a three-year-old name objects and colors, smell a ripe pineapple, and learn about how onions grow. An older child can help steer the shopping cart and count change.

Parents should not push children beyond what they are ready for. Nor should children be held back from an activity just because parents are afraid they may fail. Trying and failing are part of learning about life. Successes should be rewarded by praise. Mistakes should be met with understanding and patience. In this way children are encouraged to try again no matter what the outcome.

The Importance of Play

Play is an important part of a child's development. Consider all the ways that play benefits children:

■*Physically.* Activities such as running, climbing, jumping rope, and riding a tricycle help the large muscles of the arms and legs develop. Strength and balance improve as a result. Puzzles, finger painting, and stringing beads help develop control of the small muscles.

■*Intellectually.* A toy or game does not have to be "educational" to promote intellectual development. What might a child learn from singing nursery rhymes? Stacking blocks? Sorting through a box of buttons?

■*Emotionally.* Play can help children work through life's challenges and problems. For example, acting out the role of parent, firefighter, or jungle explorer can lessen the frustrations of being a small person in a big world.

■*Socially.* As children grow, they progress from playing alone to playing beside one another. Gradually they learn to get along with others, share, and take turns. Leadership, friendly competition, and cooperation are some of the valuable social lessons taught by play.

Parents can encourage development by letting children have the time, space, materials, and freedom for safe, creative play. Children should have opportunities to play alone, with other children, and with caregivers. Playthings can be as simple as a plastic spoon or an empty box big enough to crawl inside. In other chapters you can find specific guidelines about toys and play for children of various ages.

When Children Are Deprived

By age four, children raised in homes where the parents lack parenting skills and do not encourage learning are far behind other children in development. These children suffer from **deprivation**—the lack of a healthy, nurturing environment.

The words "deprivation" and "poverty" are sometimes wrongly used to mean the same thing. The child of a millionaire can be just as deprived as the child of a poor family. A poor child can get a rich variety of knowledge if the parents have the know-how and concern and take the time for teaching.

Fortunately, the effects of deprivation are not irreversible as once thought. The child's development can be improved provided the environment is enriched.

Having fun with other children is an important part of social development.

Close-up

Nicholas was adopted by the Waldens when he was fourteen months old. He came from the Philippines. His parents had taken him to an orphanage there because they could no longer afford to feed him and had no hope their situation would improve.

When he was adopted, Nicholas was thin, sickly, unresponsive, and far behind in both physical and intellectual development for his age. JoAnn Walden said, "When we picked up Nicholas at the airport, he was the most forlorn little creature I'd ever seen. The big, brown eyes in his little face just stared blankly. He couldn't feed himself, walk, or talk. In fact, he barely moved at all when placed on the floor. The orphanage assumed Nicholas was retarded."

Had the Waldens not adopted Nicholas, he probably would have remained far below average in development. As it was, they took him into a loving home. Slowly, Nicholas's health problems improved. He gained weight. His abilities — both physical and mental — gradually increased to the level he would have reached had his early life been different. Everyone in the family talked to and played with Nicholas. He was surrounded by love and seldom alone. Today Nicholas is a bright first-grader, secure and happy.

Do you think Nicholas's problems when he came to this country resulted solely from his lack of physical health?

How do you account for the difference in his responsiveness at fourteen months and as a first-grader? ■

Providing Love and Support

In many ways, nurturing is the same as loving. Love is the total of the caring and positive things we do for the benefit of others. Children need love just as much as they need food to eat and a place to sleep.

Parents can show children their love in many different ways. Hugs, kisses, and smiles are worth more to a child than piles of expensive gifts. Listening patiently and attentively is another way to show love. This lets children know that parents respect their feelings and are concerned about their well-being. The parent who takes time to help a child fix a broken toy or think of a way to get along better with a playmate is also giving support.

Some parents have difficulty showing affection for their children. They may be embarrassed or feel that it will make their children "too soft." But without a loving parent's recognition of their accomplishments, children feel insecure and worthless. They may resort to poor behavior just to get attention. It is difficult for such children to form any social relationships because they have never learned how to give and receive love.

Overparenting

It's not really possible to give a child too much love. However, some parents become overprotective and overattentive. They tend to shower the child with too much attention, too many toys, and too many treats. Such a parent makes excuses for the child's poor behavior and tries to shield the child from difficult or unpleasant experiences.

The overprotective parent forgets that children learn from trial and error and that mistakes are a part of the growth process. The child who has been overparented always seeks out adult help. He or she lacks the initiative to try out new things independently. Because parents have always made choices for them, such children have difficulty making decisions on their own.

Parents show love for their children by giving help when it is needed.

Communicating Positively

Good communication is an important part of the relationship between children and caregivers. As you already know, being a good listener is one way to show children that you respect them. The way that you talk to children is equally important. Speaking in a kind, respectful tone and using simple words and language works best.

Techniques for good communication depend somewhat on the child's age. The chart on page 424 gives general suggestions.

Using good communication skills has many benefits. It helps you avoid conflict and misunderstanding. When communication is based on mutual respect and love, children learn to value their own thoughts and ideas. They also learn to respect other people's opinions. Open, trusting communication is the foundation for a good lifelong relationship between parent and child.

Check Your Understanding

1. What is the importance of understanding what to expect from children?

2. Give an example of a play activity. In what way does it benefit the child? How could a parent encourage this type of play?

3. Why is it important for parents to show affection for their children?

4. Describe how you would explain the process of brushing teeth or making a bed to a four-year-old.

Tips for Communicating Effectively

- **Get on the child's level.** Sit or kneel so that you are eye-to-eye, not towering over the child.

- **Be simple.** Use words the child can understand. Long, complicated sentences are confusing. If you must give a child a long set of instructions, break it into steps and give one direction at a time.

- **Be clear.** Think in terms of the child's point of view. A four-year-old told to "settle down" will have little idea of what that means. Avoid such vague statements.

- **Be timely.** Young children shouldn't be expected to remember instructions given to them far in advance. Give directions at the time you want them carried out.

- **Use action words.** Put them near the beginning of the sentence. "Please pick up your toys" is much easier to understand than a statement like this: "I need to get this room cleaned up, so wouldn't you like to help me?"

- **Be positive.** Hearing a constant series of "don'ts" and other negative messages is discouraging. Instead of "How many times do I have to tell you — don't slam the door!" try saying, "Please shut the door quietly."

- **Give praise and love.** Everyone needs to hear good things about themselves, but especially impressionable young children. Remember, too, that a smile or a hug can often say more than words.

- **Be open to enjoyable, rewarding communication.** Although communicating with young children often involves telling them what to do, it should not be limited to that. Children need to express their thoughts and feelings to someone who will listen to and respect them. Give children your attention and attune yourself to what they are trying to say. You will find that talking with and listening to children is often delightful and fun.

Guiding Children's Behavior

One of the most challenging aspects of a parent's job is discipline. As discussed in Chapter 10, discipline is the task of helping children learn to behave appropriately. In this sense, guidance and discipline mean the same thing.

Some people think of discipline only in terms of punishment. Actually, punishment is just a small part of effective guidance. It should be used only when necessary and in specific ways, as you will learn. Furthermore, discipline does not mean "making children behave." Children cannot be forced to act according to adult standards. But when caregivers combine firmness with understanding, children can learn to control their actions.

This learning process is a very important part of a child's development. It relates to emotional and social development. Effective guidance helps children learn to get along with others and to deal with their own feelings in acceptable ways. It promotes security and a positive self-concept.

Guidance is also part of moral development. Very young children only understand right and wrong in terms of being scolded or praised. Gradually, children begin to see *why* certain actions are right or wrong. They develop a conscience, or an inner sense of what is the right thing to do.

When children have developed the ability to direct their own behavior in a responsible way, they have acquired self-discipline. Effective guidance helps children reach this goal. In the process, they learn how to make decisions and take responsibility for their actions. You can see that discipline is very important to the child's task of gaining independence.

Three keys to effective discipline are:

- Encouraging good behavior.
- Setting and enforcing limits.
- Dealing with misbehavior in appropriate ways.

Self-discipline develops gradually. It shows whenever a child behaves appropriately without having to be told how by a caregiver.

Encouraging Good Behavior

Put yourself in the place of child. Suppose no one ever explained what they wanted you to do or praised you for being good. Every so often you are punished for something. Perhaps it is for talking too loudly in a movie theater one day, and for pulling someone's hair the next. What would the results be? You would not be able to learn much from the situation. You would have trouble understanding why what you did was wrong, and what you should do instead.

Discipline that is practiced only after the child has done something wrong has little chance of success. To be effective, discipline should begin with encouraging good behavior through examples, explanations, and praise.

Setting a Good Example

Children are great imitators. If they see a parent acting in a certain way, they want to act that way too. They learn best by being shown what to do rather than just being told. Parents who want their child to talk nicely to others should talk nicely to others themselves.

The desire to imitate applies to all the examples set for children, not just the good ones! For example, three-year-old Mark sees that his parents and his older sister have dessert every night, no matter how much of the rest of the meal they finish. Is it any wonder that Mark rebels at having to clean his plate?

Telling What Is Expected

Children need to be told what is expected of them in a way they can understand. At first it is not necessary to explain the reasons behind good behavior. For a one-year-old, "pat the doggy" combined with a demonstration of gentle handling is enough.

Somewhere around age three, children begin to understand simple reasoning. "It hurts the dog when you pull his tail. If you want to play with him, you will have to be gentle." Understanding why the behavior is necessary makes it easier for children this age and older to follow the rules.

Matthew needs to be shown—not just told—that a real dog should be handled more gently than a stuffed toy.

All children need to hear good things about themselves. Make your praise specific and sincere.

Praising Good Behavior

Giving praise is an excellent way to provide encouragement. Praise helps children feel good about themselves. It also makes them want to continue the desired behavior. This is an example of what researchers call **positive reinforcement**—something that acts to encourage a particular behavior. When children associate their actions with a reward, such as attention and praise, they are likely to repeat those actions.

When giving praise, follow these guidelines:

- *Be specific.* Focus on what the child is doing appropriately. "You remembered to brush your teeth, didn't you? I'm proud of you!"

- *Be sincere and positive.* Children are quick to sense when praise is false or halfhearted. A mumbled "That's nice" or "Well, you didn't mess up *too* much this time" is not very encouraging, is it?

- *Give the praise as soon as possible.* A compliment given for something done the previous day has little meaning for a child. When praise is given soon after the desired behavior, the child is able to associate the two.

- *Tailor the praise to the needs of the child.* For example, the child who sits quietly and listens to stories being read, but also remains silent during a sing-along, doesn't need constant praise for being quiet. Observing children can help caregivers know what behaviors need to be encouraged.

Food, especially sugary treats, should not be given as part of praise. Using food as a reward for punishment can lead to poor eating habits.

Offering Choices

As children become more mature, they should be allowed to make some decisions related to their behavior. This helps them learn that they are really responsible for their own actions. It also minimizes feelings of frustration. The parent, instead of making demands of the child, offers a choice and respects the child's decision.

For example, a two-year-old boy sometimes hits his year-old sister. To encourage good behavior, the parent can say, "You seem to be angry with Mary. I know sometimes she wants to play with the same toy you do, and that makes you angry. I cannot allow you to hurt her. Would you like to choose one of your toys she can play with, or would you like me to sit down and build a house with both of you?"

The caregiver should offer only alternatives that are readily available and should make sure they are carried out. Whatever choice the child makes, it must be honored. If not, the child will lose trust in the parent.

When examples, simple instructions, praise, and choices are combined, efforts to improve the child's behavior are likely to succeed. The following situation illustrates this.

Being told that you can't do something isn't quite so bad if you can choose what to do instead.

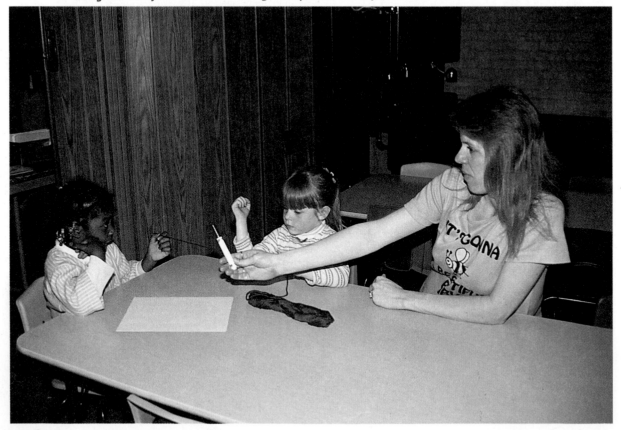

Close-up

Becky was frustrated because her four-year-old son Christopher never put his toys away after playing with them. Sometimes Becky put them away herself. Most of the time, however, she was too busy to worry about the toys, and they were simply left out until the next playtime. When friends or relatives came by, Becky was embarrassed by the mess. Her scoldings upset Christopher but did little to solve the problem.

Finally, on the advice of her older sister, Becky tried a new approach. One evening before bathtime, she sat down with Christopher as he played. She explained, "Christopher, if you pick up your toys after you've finished playing with them, they won't become lost or broken. I'll help you put the toys away and show you where they go. Should we start with the blocks or the train set?"

Though reluctant at first, Christopher soon became interested in this new game. When they were finished, Becky said, "Thank you for helping me, Christopher. You did a good job."

This scene was repeated on the following evenings. Christopher was more than willing to please his mother once he had been shown how. After a few weeks, he was able to put the toys away all by himself. Occasional reminders were all that was needed.

Becky also found that handling the situation this way reduced her own frustration. Although the house was indeed much neater now, she no longer got upset if things were not perfectly orderly at all times. Both she and Christopher were much happier.

What techniques did Becky use to encourage Christopher to put away his toys?
How did this solution benefit Christopher?
How did it benefit Becky? ∎

Setting Limits

Setting limits is another way to guide children toward good, safe behavior. The term "limits" may refer to physical restrictions, such as not allowing the child to cross the street. Another kind of limit is a rule of behavior: "We play nicely with others. We don't hit them."

Children both want and need limits. They lack the maturity to make good judgements in all areas of their life. Limits help them know what is acceptable, appropriate, and safe for them to do.

What Should the Limits Be?

In general, a good guideline is that limits should keep children from hurting themselves, others, or property. The specific limits needed will vary depending on the individual child. Children will respect and follow limits if they are few and reasonable. When setting limits, parents should keep in mind:

- Does the limit still allow the child to learn, explore, and grow? Too much restriction will hinder development.
- Is the limit fair and appropriate for the child's age? A toddler might be restricted to a fenced-in yard. By school age, the same child may be permitted to walk to school alone and call on a friend who lives down the street.
- Does the limit benefit the child, or is it merely for adults' convenience? Sometimes the only thing threatened by a child's behavior is an adult's orderly routine.

Making Limits Clear

Limits should be simple and briefly stated. For example, "We walk inside the house. Running is done outside." Be prepared to repeat the limits or rules several times. Young children, especially toddlers, do not realize that the same rule applies to different situations.

Telling three-year-old Julie she can splash her sister "only a little" during pool playtime is a limit someone her age will find difficult to follow. More than likely, "a little" will soon become "a lot" without her realizing it. A better limit would be "no splashing." What methods would you use to encourage Julie to play constructively with her sister?

As children grow older they need fewer restrictions, especially when they show they will follow rules.

When you explain limits to a child, use language that is simple and clear. Although you should be firm, avoid scolding or belittling the child.

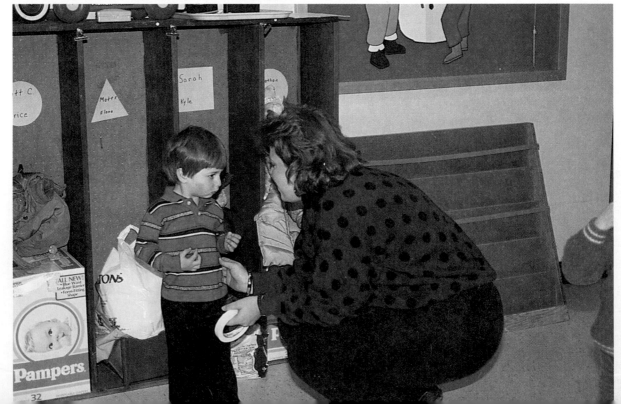

Limits should be presented to the child in a calm, direct tone of voice that indicates the limit is real and to be respected. When introducing a limit, it is best to follow these steps:

- Be understanding of the child's desires. "I know you think it's fun to write on the wall."
- Set the limit and explain it. "You may not write on the wall. We use paper to write on."
- Acknowledge the child's feelings. "I know you may not be happy with this, but sometimes I must make rules."
- Give alternatives. "You may draw on this piece of paper, or you may play with your blocks. Which would you like to do?"

Once established and explained, limits should be firmly and consistently enforced. Children respect their parents more if they know parents will stick to the rules. Parents who give in teach their children that they do not mean what they say.

Dealing with Misbehavior

No matter how much is done to encourage good behavior, all children sometimes misbehave. Caregivers must be able to deal with these situations appropriately and effectively.

Part of what determines how the caregiver should respond to misbehavior is the child's age. A one-year-old that bites another child can be told, "No! Don't bite," but should not be expected to understand the meaning of his or her actions. Behavior at this age can best be controlled by distraction. On the other hand, a four-year-old is capable of understanding that biting is an unacceptable behavior. The questions that the caregiver should ask, then, when responding to misbehavior are:

- Does the child understand that the behavior is wrong?
- Was the behavior intentional (done on purpose), or was it simply beyond the child's control?

Unintentional Misbehavior

With children of any age, misbehavior is sometimes unintentional. For example, a three-year-old may cry or whine if forced to wait a long time for food at a restaurant. This is a natural reaction to being hungry, not deliberate misbehavior. A child simply does not have the patience of an adult in that situation. Similarly, a child may drop a glass of milk that is too heavy to handle, or accidentally break a vase that should have been put out of reach. These examples of misbehavior, because they are unintentional, should go unpunished.

To this child, a cat's tail looks like a convenient handle to grab. Would this be intentional or unintentional misbehavior?

Another example of unintentional misbehavior is if the child had no way of knowing the behavior was wrong. For example, while playing in the park Tyler picked a flower and brought it to his father. Tyler's father did not get angry or scold him. Instead he explained that the flowers in the park were for everyone to look at and enjoy, not to pick. Since this limit had never been given to him before, Tyler was not deliberately misbehaving.

Using Punishment Effectively

When children deliberately do something that they know is wrong, some form of punishment may be necessary. Punishment acts as a **negative reinforcement**. That is, it tends to discourage the behavior with which it is associated. Punishment should not take the place of encouragement and clearly stated limits. But when used with good judgement, it can be a part of positive and effective discipline.

The first time a child breaks a rule, the parent or caregiver may choose to give a warning rather than punishment. Even a child who usually has good self-control may occasionally make mistakes. This is especially likely under unusual circumstances, such as the excitement of a birthday party.

Punishment should be in proportion to the seriousness of the misbehavior. A relatively minor offense, such as forgetting to put away a bicycle one time, does not deserve a severe punishment. In this case, it would be fair for the child to have to give up using the bicycle for one day, but not for a whole week.

All children are occasionally forgetful. However, some form of punishment may be needed when misbehavior is repeated or deliberate.

If parents have established positive, mutual feelings of love and respect with their children, they need not fear that punishment will cause resentment. This is especially true when parents make it clear that they disapprove of the behavior, not the child as a person. Children must be assured that their parents love them and want to help them learn how to behave properly.

Following are some useful techniques for dealing with misbehavior. They can be effective in many situations.

■ *Natural consequences.* Sometimes it is punishment enough for a child to suffer the consequences, or natural results, of his or her own misbehavior. For example, after having been called to dinner more than once, Sandra arrives late at the table. Rather than reheating her food, Sandra's grandmother tells her she must eat her dinner cold. Next time, Sandra will be more likely to come when called.

■ *Removal of privileges.* In some cases the natural consequences of a child's actions are not appropriate to use as punishment. For example, suppose a five-year-old keeps running into the street while playing. The natural consequences may be that the child gets hurt. A good way to deal with this situation might be to give a warning that if the child runs into the street again, there will be no more play outdoors that day. This type of punishment is most effective for children age five or older. The privilege that is taken away should always be related to the misbehavior so that the child associates the two.

■ *Ignoring misbehavior.* Sometimes a child misbehaves simply to get attention. As long as the behavior is not harmful, the best "punishment" is to ignore the child. Any other reaction will give the child the desired attention and make it likely that the behavior will be repeated.

For example, Tony had several times asked if he could have some candy. His mother firmly explained that sweets were not allowed between meals. Tony brought some blocks into the kitchen and began loudly dropping them on the floor, watching for a reaction each time. When he saw that his mother was ignoring him, Tony

Being careless near traffic is an example of misbehavior that can be dangerous. In this situation, letting the child suffer that natural consequences is not an appropriate means of discipline.

stopped the annoying behavior. Soon he went into the living room and played quietly. His mother then took a moment to admire the tower Tony was building and praise him for playing nicely. Thus Tony saw that it was his good behavior, rather than his misbehavior, that got his mother's attention.

For older children, "time out" might mean going to a quiet place to think about what happened and why what they did was wrong.

isolation. For example, the caregiver can say, "You are angry and not acting properly. You need time to calm down. You may return to playing with the others when you can do so without hitting." **Time out** is an effective method of discipline because it reinforces the idea that the child must learn to control his or her own behavior.

Poor Disciplinary Measures

Some methods of punishment should be avoided. They are not effective in helping children learn self-discipline.

■*Don't rely on spanking and physical punishment.* Most child care experts recommend that spanking be used sparingly, if at all. While spanking may stop poor behavior for the moment, it doesn't help the child learn proper behavior. It is also demeaning for both the parent and the child. Parents sometimes use spanking as a way to vent their anger and frustration. This sets a poor example. The child only learns that it's all right to use hitting and fighting instead of learning how to control strong emotions.

■*Time out.* Another way to respond to misbehavior is to remove the child from the presence of others or from the center of activity. An example of this is the "time-out chair." This is a place where the child must sit for a short time until he or she can settle down enough to return to playing. It is important to explain the purpose of this

■*Don't threaten to withhold love.* When a parent says, "I won't love you anymore if you don't stop hitting your brother," the child is left with a fear of being rejected and abandoned. Withholding love doesn't show the child how to correct misbehavior. It merely fills the child with needless anxiety.

■**Don't offer bribes.** Bribing a child with a special treat if he or she stops misbehaving is not an effective method of discipline. Instead of learning self-control, the child will always look for an outside reward for good behavior.

■**Don't make the child promise to behave.** In the process of learning to control their behavior, children will naturally make mistakes. When a promise is made, the child may feel forced to lie about misbehavior rather than disappoint someone he or she loves.

■**Don't try to control the child through shame or guilt.** When a child misbehaves, it is natural for the parent to feel anger and disappointment. These feelings should be expressed, but calmly and reasonably. Parents should not use statements such as, "How could you do a thing like that?" or, "If this keeps up, you'll never amount to anything." Similarly, parents should not ridicule the child's mistakes.

Parents who know how to discipline effectively usually experience less conflict and enjoy their children more.

Handling Conflict

Discipline can create a conflict between parents and children. When they don't succeed in breaking a rule of behavior, children may become angry. Parents must be ready to deal with this. They should not make children feel bad or guilty about their anger. Anger is a normal emotion.

Parents should instead give children an opportunity to discuss the conflict and express their anger. It may help to talk over the misbehavior and punishment some time after the incident. The child can be helped to understand why the misbehavior occurred. The parent can explain what should have been done instead and offer reassurance and encouragement.

It may take time for children to get over being angry and to understand why punishment was necessary. Talking things over helps reassure them that they are still loved and accepted.

Consistency Is the Key

The secret to guiding children's behavior is being consistent. Consistency helps children learn the limits of behavior. Children who know what is expected of them and what to expect of the parents feel more secure.

Children lose trust and confidence in a parent who constantly changes set limits or fails to enforce them in a consistent manner. If a parent laughs at a child's behavior one day and punishes the same behavior the next day, the child will only be confused. When more than one person is caring for a child, limits and methods of enforcement should be agreed on in advance. Otherwise children quickly learn to use the inconsistency to their advantage. They may always go to one parent if the other will not give them what they want.

Check Your Understanding

1. Suppose you are the parent of a four-year-old who bullies other children on the playground. What could you do to correct this behavior?

2. What might be appropriate limits for a one-year-old? A three-year-old? A five-year-old? Give three examples of each.

3. Why is it important to distinguish between intentional and unintentional misbehavior?

Providing Substitute Care

One of the responsibilities of parents is providing quality substitute care when they must be away from their children. In some families, substitute care is needed only occasionally. However, an increasing number of parents depend on others to care for their children on a regular basis.

Those who are faced with finding substitute care must choose wisely from the many types available. Child care facilities range from a babysitter in the home to large group child care centers. Caregivers also differ. Those who care for children must know about their physical, emotional, social, and intellectual needs. Caregivers should also have attitudes and skills necessary for working with and caring for young children. This section will help you understand the different types of substitute care available and how to choose good ones.

The Need for Substitute Care

There are many reasons for the trend toward placing children in substitute care:

- Many children live in one-parent homes. In such cases, the parent who cares for the child usually has a full-time job. This brings the additional problem of finding adequate child care.
- In many two-parent families, both parents work to provide income. Unless the parents have different work schedules, the children will probably need care.
- Some parents who do provide care for their own children at home feel that some outside care can be beneficial for the child. For example, an only child may live in a neighborhood with few children. That child might profit from the social aspects of a nursery school. In such situations, the child usually attends a child care facility only two or three times a week.

Parents who work outside the home must often depend on substitute caregivers on a regular basis.

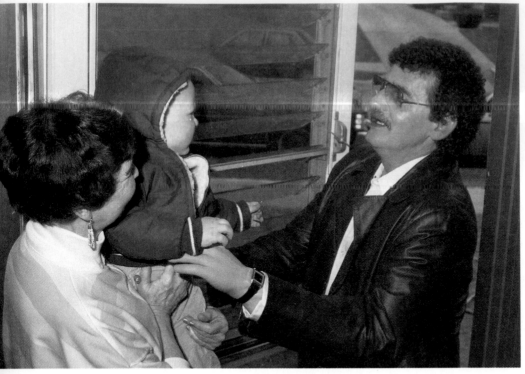

A parent's employment can have a major effect on a child's life. The child has to adapt to the people and schedules involved in the child care chosen by the parent.

Some parents take turns providing care in their own home for a small group of children.

Types of Substitute Care

Many types of child care services are available. All provide some type of physical care and a place to play. Some also include planned activities to encourage the child's physical, emotional, social, and intellectual development. A few also provide health and social services for the child and often the family as well.

Child care services also differ in the type of setting. Some are offered in someone's home. Others are provided in a child care center. Within these two basic categories, each type of child care has its own advantages and disadvantages. Finding the best type of care for the child is extremely important for the child's future and the parents' peace of mind.

Home-Based Care

Many children are cared for in their own home or another family's home. Care in a home setting may be easier for the child to get used to because the surroundings are familiar. This type of care may also be more readily available and convenient for the parents. Usually it involves smaller groups of children than center-based care. This makes it an especially good choice for infants and other children who need a great deal of individual attention. There are three main types of home-based care.

■ *Care in the child's own home.* Many parents prefer their child to be cared for by someone who comes to their own home. In-home care is convenient. Almost all parents make use of this type of care occasionally, as for an evening out. Many parents also use it on a regular basis. However, care in the child's own home can be costly. Usually it does not provide an opportunity for play with other children outside the family.

The caregiver may be an extended family member, friend, or babysitter. A less common alternative is to employ a live-in caregiver. Although a live-in arrangement is much more costly, it has the advantage that reliable care is available at almost any time of day or night.

The need for quality substitute care has even revived the 19th century tradition of the **nanny**. Today nannies are professionally trained, live-in caregivers. Many have completed a course of academic study in all areas of child development and care. They may have also completed a period of supervised on-the-job training. Among those who can afford their services, nannies are in high demand.

■ *Family day care.* When the child is taken to a caregiver's home, the arrangement is referred to as **family day care**. Usually this type of care involves a small group of children. It combines the familiarity of a home setting with opportunities for social play and learning. Since the group size is small, individual attention can be given. The cost is usually less than for care in the child's own home.

■ *Play groups.* A **play group** is similar to family day care, except that it involves a number of different homes and caregivers. Parents simply take turns caring for each other's children on certain days. The children are brought to the home of the parent providing care. Most play groups involve no fees. They are often a good choice for parents who do not work full-time.

Quality home-based care includes a daily routine of quiet and active times. Both planned activities and informal play are included. Caregivers participate with children in activities. At other times, the children play by themselves. Children should not simply be placed in front of the television set or left unsupervised for long periods of time.

Child care centers often provide children with opportunities that they might not otherwise have. They can play with other children their age and take part in a variety of planned learning activities.

Center-Based Care

In many communities, facilities are available in which a staff of several adults cares for one or more groups of children. These child care centers vary widely in hours of operation; the size, training, and experience of the staff; the ages of children accepted; activities, equipment, and play areas; and fees.

Some child care centers are businesses run for a profit. Others charge fees to cover expenses, but do not try to make a profit. Still others are funded by the city, state, or federal government. They may be offered free or at a reduced cost to those who qualify.

Child care centers must meet minimum health and safety requirements in order to be licensed. Their license also limits the number of children they may accept depending on space, facilities, and size of staff.

Some common types of child care centers include:

■*Day care centers.* A child care facility that provides all-day care for children of working parents is usually referred to as a **day care center**. A variety of activities may be offered. Some day care centers emphasize specific learning activities, while others allow more informal play. Usually there is a daily routine with time set aside for indoor and outdoor play, meals, and naps. Most day care centers are designed for children age two years and up. Some provide care for infants.

Nursery schools. This type of child care center provides an educational program, usually for ages three to five. A **nursery school**—sometimes called a **preschool**—typically offers activities designed to enrich the child's development in all areas. For example, there may be games to help children improve motor skills, language skills, and social skills. Art, music, and science activities may be included. The staff usually includes one or more teachers and a number of aides. (A **child care aide** helps the person in charge of the program provide care for the children.)

Usually, a nursery school operates half-day sessions two or more days a week. Some centers combine nursery school and a day care program as a convenience for working parents.

Parent cooperatives. Some nursery schools or day care centers are run as **parent cooperatives**. This means that parents take turns helping provide supervision for the children at the center. The parents are guided by a preschool teacher or other qualified caregiver who organizes the program. Working at the center helps parents understand their child's development. Another advantage is the lower cost of the program. Of course, this type of care is rarely suitable for the parent who works full-time.

Head Start centers. In the 1960s, the federal government began a program called **Head Start**. Its purpose is to help lower income and disadvantaged children function effectively in the home, in school, and in the community. The government provides funding for locally operated Head Start centers. The program at these centers usually includes three- to five-year-olds.

Besides a variety of activities to improve development, Head Start children receive one-half to one-third of their daily nutritional needs. Health care is provided and social services, such as counseling, are available to both parents and children. Parents are expected to become actively involved in the program.

At Head Start centers, children are given nutritious meals, as well as enriching learning opportunities.

Montessori preschools. Some child care centers provide a specialized program of learning that is different from the traditional nursery school. An example is **Montessori preschools** for children ages three to six. This type of educational program is named for Dr. Maria Montessori, the founder of the methods used.

Many children go home to an empty house or apartment after school. What alternatives does your community offer?

Specially designed learning materials are provided in the Montessori classroom. The children are encouraged to explore the materials on their own, moving from one activity to another as they wish. The teacher demonstrates activities and observes the children, but does not participate often with the youngsters.

What About Older Children?

So far, child care has been discussed in terms of infants, toddlers, and preschoolers. However, some school-age children also regularly need substitute care. For many, there is a gap of several hours between the time school lets out and the time parents arrive home from work.

Some children do not receive substitute care during these hours. Often this is because affordable care is not available. It is estimated that at least two million children across the country are home alone after school. Because they let themselves in with their own key, they are sometimes called **latch-key children**. If parents leave for work early, these children may also be alone before school.

Many child care experts advise against leaving children without adult supervision before the teen years. An increasing number of schools, community groups, and nonprofit agencies are arranging activities to fill the parenting gap for latch-key children. These programs include supervised recreation such as games, films, and art projects. Children may also do homework, read, or rest. Some programs provide before-school supervision, including breakfast.

Choosing Substitute Care

There are no easy answers as to which type of child care is best for an individual child. Parents must consider many factors. The types available, the costs, the convenience, and the individual needs of the child will all influence the decision.

A personal visit to the home or child care center being considered is essential. The child should be taken along because the child's happiness and well-being are among the most important considerations. Some things to look for during such a visit are listed on page 444.

Once a child care facility is decided upon, the parent should drop by unexpectedly from time to time. This helps make certain that the care is and remains as it was promised. After the child has attended the program for two or three weeks, the parent can ask the child how he or she feels about it. Whether the child is happy is the most dependable indicator of quality in child care.

Is Substitute Care as Good as Parental Care?

Professionals in all areas of child care and development agree that emotional and intellectual development are directly influenced by a child's environment and experiences, beginning at birth. These professionals consider parents to be the child's best source of love and learning.

Many child development specialists advise that a parent should stay at home to provide child care, if possible, for as long as possible. For many working parents, however, an extended maternity or paternity leave isn't possible. Does this mean that parents must choose between having an income to pay bills and giving their child a good start in life?

No matter what type of substitute care is being considered, the quality of the caregiver is the most important factor.

Checklist for Substitute Care

The Caregiver

√ How many children are there for each caregiver? Do the caregivers seem to have time for each child?

√ What type of training or experience has the caregiver had?

√ Is the caregiver warm and loving toward the children? Calm and patient?

√ Does the caregiver provide and direct activities well?

√ Does the caregiver participate with the children frequently and respond to their questions?

√ Do you agree with the caregiver's child-rearing attitudes and with the methods of discipline used?

√ Does the caregiver seem to understand children's individual needs?

√ Does the caregiver regularly take time to talk with parents about their children?

The Program and Facilities

√ Where do the children eat, sleep, and play? Are the areas safe, comfortable, and sanitary?

√ What kinds of social and learning opportunities are provided?

√ Are books, toys, and large-muscle equipment available?

√ Are children encouraged to participate in a variety of activities?

√ Is there enough indoor and outdoor space for children to play without crowding?

√ If meals or snacks are provided, are they nutritious?

√ Are the rules and routines that are followed reasonable? Are they easy for children to understand?

√ What arrangements will be made if the caregiver is away or ill? What arrangements are made for children who are ill?

Overall Impressions

√ Do the children seem to be involved and happy?

√ If you were a child, would you like to stay there?

Parents Magazine reported that thirty studies conducted over fifteen years found no adverse effect on children's intellectual or emotional development in good substitute care. The key is the quality of the child care service. By far the most important part of the decision is to carefully select the parent-substitute. The best caregiver is someone who enjoys the child and spends time playing with him or her. In a group facility, there should be a warm, caring atmosphere and enough staff to give individual attention.

Quality child care programs recognize the need they are filling and the influence they have on the physical and emotional development of children. Parents can improve the quality of child care by making their needs and wants known. Active involvement helps parents and other concerned individuals insure that their expectations for quality child care are being met.

Special Parenting Situations

All parents have many things in common—the responsibilities that come with their role, and the satisfaction they may gain from it. However, in some situations parents also face unique concerns and challenges. These situations include single parenting, stepparenting, adoption, and teen parenting.

Single Parents

Single parents include divorced, widowed, or single people with children. The number of single parents has increased dramatically in recent years. There have always been some people who are single parents because of the death of a spouse. Rising divorce rates have placed millions more in this category. In addition, many unmarried people become parents through birth or adoption.

In many homes, one parent must take on all the responsibilities of raising a family, managing a household, and earning a living.

Children growing up in a single-parent home should spend time with adults of both sexes.

the youngster what a mature man or woman is like. This is especially important for boys who are being raised by single mothers and girls who are being raised by single fathers. Adult friends or relatives can often provide a positive example of male or female behavior and relationships. In addition, many cities have programs such as Big Brothers–Big Sisters and scouts to help fill this gap.

The parent and child should both maintain interests outside the family. Some single parents become totally immersed in their children's lives. Children, too, can become overly concerned about the private life of their parent. Many children of single parents react negatively when the parent goes out socially. The child fears someone is taking away the only parent he or she has. The child feels left out and is afraid of a loss of love. In such situations, the parent must try to reassure the child, but maintain the right to develop friendships with others.

Single parenting puts many demands on the parent. He or she has a great deal of responsibility, little free time, and no spouse with whom to share problems. Many communities have organizations for single parents. They provide emotional support and social opportunities.

Stepparents

When a single parent marries, his or her new spouse becomes a stepparent. In some marriages both the husband and the wife already have children from previous relationships. Each becomes a stepparent to the other's children.

In situations like these, a **blended family** is created. Both the children and the parents may experience problems in establishing a new family unit. Everyone has to learn about a new person while living with him or her. Even food likes and dislikes have to be learned.

Although a two-parent family is considered the ideal, the love, care, and security children need can be provided in a one-parent home. Some single parents may do a better job of child-rearing than couples.

One special concern that faces single parents is the need for their children to develop positive relationships with adults of the opposite sex from the parent. A close and meaningful relationship with such a person can show

Often, members of a blended family find that they have different ways of doing things when it comes to mealtime, chores, and other daily routines. All members of the family must be prepared to give up some of the customs they are used to. Eventually they may combine old and new systems into one that works for everyone.

Many times, children feel that the new parent and his or her children are invading their lives. Each family member must learn to respect the possessions and privacy of others. Because there are more family members, parents may find that they have less time to spend with each other, as well as with children and stepchildren. It is important that parents make all the children in the family feel secure and loved during this time.

Stepparents often find that discipline is a problem. Both husband and wife must agree on how discipline will be handled. Children should not feel that their stepbrothers or stepsisters are being given any special favors or privileges.

It takes time for members of a stepfamily to learn to build bonds of trust and love with each other. Several years may be needed for the new family to establish a firm foundation. At the same time, relationships children have with former family members should be maintained. In the case of a divorce and remarriage, for example, children should be encouraged to remain close to the natural mother or father and other relatives. Stepparents should recognize that they are an additional parent, not a "replacement" for one separated from the child by divorce or death.

Stepparenting brings many challenges. However, when all family members work together to overcome problems, the results can be rewarding. Both stepchildren and stepparents can benefit from the new perspectives and resources that are brought to the family. The important thing in any family is not how its members are related, but whether they are able to provide each other with love, caring, and support.

Remarriage may bring children of different parents together to form a new, blended family. Habits and customs may have to be adapted to fit the new situation.

Adaptation

Adoption was a favorite theme of fiction and movies years ago. The young hero or heroine found out, with great horror, that he or she was adopted. Life and reputation were ruined. This theme resulted mainly from the secrecy which surrounded adoptions in the past.

Today, this attitude has changed. Most people accept adoption as a logical way to give children without natural parents the love and care they need.

In the past, most parents adopted only healthy babies. Children were always matched as closely as possible to their adoptive parents. Characteristics matched included race, ethnic and religious background, and physical characteristics. Interracial adoptions were rare and frowned upon.

Now, the emphasis is on finding good homes for children without them. Matching of characteristics is not considered as important. Older children, handicapped children, children from other countries, and those of mixed race are more frequently adopted.

Some people still find it difficult to accept the adoption of a child into a family of a different race. The success of such adoptions depends greatly on the parents. If they are mature, flexible, and loving, they can give the child a positive self-image. This minimizes the influence of unkind remarks by others.

Experts advise parents to tell children they are adopted as soon as they can understand. It can be very upsetting to a child to find out later that parents are not his or her biological parents. The parents should not make a big thing of the information. It should come openly and comfortably in conversation.

As adopted children get older, they will want to know about their biological parents. This is only natural. You have probably wondered about your grandparents or great-grandparents whom you did not know. Instead of feeling hurt or avoiding the issue,

Handicapped children often accomplish more than expected when they have the security of a loving adoptive home.

The bonds between an adoptive parent and child are as strong as those between biological parents and children.

parents should be as truthful as possible. Of course, what the child is told will depend on his or her age and ability to understand.

It is rarely a good idea for parents to say the biological parents did not want the child. A simple "I don't know, honey, but I'm glad it worked out this way," accompanied by a hug, is better. This helps avoid the feeling of rejection that some adopted children have. Showing adopted children that they are loved and wanted helps them realize that they truly belong and will not be given up again. Children need to understand that it is often difficult, but necessary and unselfish, for natural parents to give up a child.

When there are both adopted and biological children in a family, parents should give plenty of reassurance that all are loved and wanted equally. Adopted children should not be made to feel "second best." On the other hand, stressing that an adopted child is "special" or "chosen" may lead to resentment on the part of others in the family.

Sometimes, relatives cause problems by favoring natural children over adopted children. Playmates, on the other hand, usually take adoption in stride. They may be curious at first, but then forget about it. If teasing does occur, the parents can help the child deal with it.

Adoption, although it may involve some problems, provides homes for thousands of children each year. It gives them a loving family and normal home life.

Teen Parents

If you have read earlier chapters of this book, you know by now that becoming a parent during the teen years presents special problems. Most people are not emotionally or financially prepared for the responsibilities of parenthood before their twenties. In addition, teen pregnancy poses a health risk for both mother and baby. Review the information on pages 49–50 and page 86. All teens should be aware of these facts so that they can make responsible decisions.

Teens who do become parents need to learn how to be good ones. The help of family members, social workers, and parent education classes is especially valuable in these situations. Young parents who marry must also learn to handle the give-and-take that is part of a stable relationship. At stake is not only their own happiness, but the well-being of their child.

When they learn they are pregnant, many teenage girls drop out of school. Other teen mothers and fathers drop out after the baby is born. Many will not return to finish their education. This lack of education makes it difficult for young parents to find a well-paying job. They may be unable to support themselves and their child. Even if a job is found, quality child care may not be available or affordable.

To combat these problems, many schools now have special programs for teen parents. Some even have in-school child care programs. Children are cared for during the day while parents attend classes. These programs make it possible for young parents to finish their education.

Teen parents face many more difficulties than most other parents. Their success at meeting these challenges depends greatly on their own maturity and the resources available to them.

Check Your Understanding

1. Compare the advantages and disadvantages of home-based and center-based substitute care.

2. Why is it important for a single mother to make sure her children have a positive relationship with a male adult?

3. Give an example of a conflict that might arise in a blended family. How could the problem be avoided or solved?

4. Should parents try to hide the fact that their children are adopted? Explain.

Many teen parents know that finishing school is worth the effort because it opens up job opportunities.

Chapter Review

To Sum Up

- Acquiring parenting skills is a lifelong learning process.
- Caregivers who understand children and their individual differences are better able to promote healthy development.
- Children need encouragement, enriching experiences, love, and support.
- Communication skills can help caregivers talk with and listen to children.
- Good behavior should be encouraged through examples, simple explanations, praise, and reasonable choices.
- Children want and need reasonable limits on their behavior.
- Misbehavior should be handled calmly in a manner appropriate to the situation.
- Many different types of substitute care are available.
- Single parents, stepparents, adoptive parents, and teen parents face special challenges, but all can be good parents.

To Review and Remember

1. Name three ways of how parenting skills can be learned.
2. What is deprivation? What effect can it have?
3. Name four guidelines to follow when communicating with a young child.
4. What are three keys to effective discipline?
5. What is positive reinforcement? Give an example.
6. What is meant by limits? Why are they needed?
7. Name three possible situations in which substitute care would be needed.
8. What is family day care? Name two of its advantages.
9. Explain the difference between a play group and a parent cooperative.
10. Give three examples of resources teen parents can turn to for help.

To Discuss and Discover

1. Discuss the stages of the family life cycle. What particular problems or stresses might occur at each stage? How can family members handle these stresses? Discuss how situations such as single parenting and stepparenting affect the family life cycle.
2. Find out what community resources are available to help parents in your area. Describe the agencies (or other resources) and how parents can contact them. What types of help are provided? Are there fees involved? Present your findings to the class.

17 Problem Situations for Children

To help you to . . .

- Describe the needs of children with physical, mental, and emotional handicaps.

- Tell how parents and other caregivers can assist and encourage handicapped children.

- Explain what is meant by child abuse, why it happens, and what can be done about it.

- Describe the emotional effects on children of stressful family situations such as divorce and death and tell how to minimize them.

Terms to Learn

child abuse	empathy
crisis nurseries	therapist

Jim is a successful electrical engineer with a large company. He also happens to have a physical disability. He was born with a left arm that ends just below the elbow.

"I guess my parents were ahead of their time," he remarked. "When I was born, a lot of people told them I should be placed in an institution. They said I'd never lead a 'normal' life.

"My parents resisted the idea and brought me home. From the very start, they encouraged me to try everything. It's not that they ignored the fact I have a disability. They just helped me understand I could do most things if I put my mind to it. Of course, sometimes I have to be a bit creative to figure out a way to do two-handed jobs with only one!

"It's never really bothered me to meet strangers—I guess because I had lots of practice as a kid. Most people are curious or don't know what to say to someone with only one hand. But that's natural. I just try to get them to see me instead of my arm."

Helping Children Face Problems

Many problems children face are more publicly recognized today than they were in the past. Some trends in our society, such as child abuse and divorce, create problems for children.

Children have a right to help in facing problem or crisis situations. How they cope depends on many factors. The most important are the attitudes and actions of parents and other caregivers. They can help or hinder a child's adjustment.

This chapter discusses some of the most common crisis situations for children. These include handicaps, child abuse, and family stresses such as the death of a loved one.

Handicaps

Handicaps—physical, mental, emotional, or any combination of the three—present special problems for children and their parents. In the past, babies with problems often died at birth or soon after. A child with a disability was often hidden away at home or sent to an institution. Fortunately, there is much more awareness of the needs and potential of handicapped, or exceptional, children today. Medical science saves the lives of many infants with physical problems. Doctors are also able to treat many handicaps to make them less severe. Children can often be taught to compensate for their disabilities. With proper care and treatment, most can lead happy, productive lives.

Of course, not all handicaps are present at birth. Injury or illness can cause a handicap at any time of life.

Children with disabilities have the same basic needs as other children. Their most important need is to feel loved and accepted by their families and by society.

The attitude of parents toward a handicap can make a big difference to the child's future. Parents can teach their child to be as independent as possible and to accept those limitations that cannot be overcome. Parents who pity, resent, or coddle a child with disabilities hinder good emotional development. The child may become angry and self-pitying. Such a child will have difficulty functioning in society. A child with a positive attitude will have a happier life.

Helping out with tasks at home makes the handicapped child feel worthwhile and needed. Of course, the jobs given must fit the abilities of the child. Setting the table, helping with dishes, dusting, folding laundry, and similar tasks can all be considered. This helps the child's social and emotional development while improving physical skills.

Parents of handicapped children should contact national or community agencies that can offer information and support. Many states now require that public schools provide programs for handicapped children and their parents from the time of the child's birth. Many others provide preschool experiences for these youngsters from the time of their third birthday. Studies have shown that many children do best when placed in regular preschool programs. Both the children with handicaps and those without benefit. They grow intellectually, develop social skills, and learn to feel **empathy**—to understand and share each other's feelings.

Physical Handicaps

Leg braces or a missing arm are obvious indications of a physical handicap, but many handicaps are not so apparent. Such things as hearing loss or a heart defect are also physical disabilities.

Special preschool programs give handicapped children a chance to be like everyone else. They also boost readiness for kindergarten.

For a child with a physical handicap, exercise sessions are often part of the daily routine. Though sometimes painful, exercises are necessary to maintain and improve the child's physical abilities.

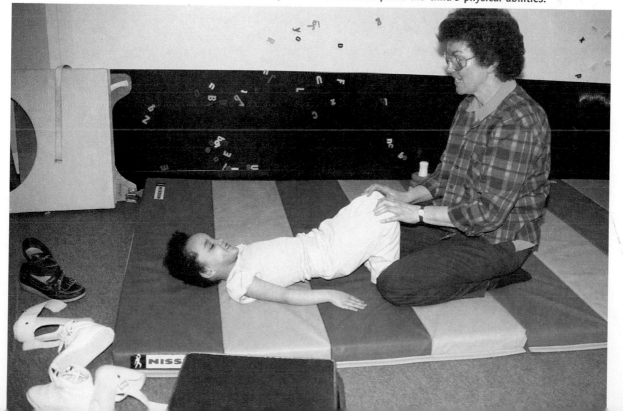

Diagnosis of a physical handicap should be sought as soon as a problem is suspected. Treatment should begin as soon as possible. Today, through early diagnosis and treatment, many children born with physical handicaps are able to lead fairly normal lives. Even infants benefit from learning to use their remaining physical abilities to the fullest.

Each physically handicapped child has individual care needs. These will differ somewhat from those of the average child. Routines that others take for granted can be difficult or impossible. For example, a three-year-old with poor coordination may be unable to dress or eat without help.

Special exercises, special equipment, understanding, and patience are the keys to helping children with disabilities be as independent as possible. Independence is essential, not only for future living, but for development of a positive self-concept. Self-care skills such as eating, dressing, bathing, and using the toilet are fundamental to this independence.

Bathing is a good example. Many handicapped children need to be lifted in and out of the tub. Even children who are able to bathe themselves may need special attention.

The child must feel secure during the bath. This means at least a nonskid mat in the bottom of the tub. Some youngsters need an inner tube or inflated cushion to keep their head above water. For those who cannot sit, water levels must be kept low for safety.

Children with good balance and coordination can often help wash themselves. A washcloth made into a mitt is easier to handle and less likely to be lost in the water. Soap worn around the neck on a string helps keep it from slipping away. Towels with a hole cut into the middle so they can be slipped over the head make drying off easier.

Similar techniques may need to be developed for eating and other activities. Some children need special help with only a few tasks. Others have very limited abilities.

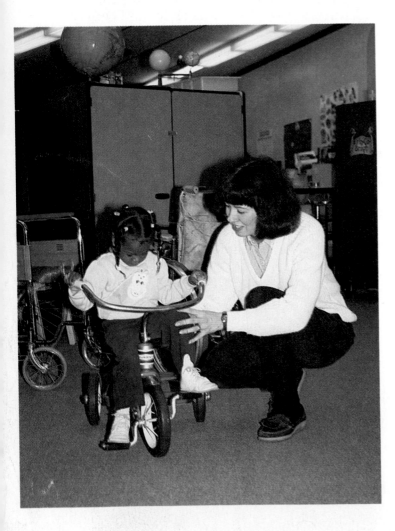

Many fun activities also help develop physical skills. Why might riding a tricycle be good for a handicapped preschooler?

Mental Handicaps

Mentally handicapped children grow just as other children do. The major difference is that mental development is slower and stops at a lower level. There are many degrees of mental retardation. Some children are only a little slow. Others remain like babies for life and need constant care.

Medical professionals can usually diagnose mental retardation early and determine its cause. They can also advise parents about the child's learning potential. Education and treatment must begin early to achieve the greatest results. Often doctors recommend special programs for mentally handicapped children. These usually begin in infancy.

Mentally handicapped children do best with a regular routine. They must know what to expect. Directions should be simple and direct. Example and demonstration along with constant repetition seem to teach best.

The long-range goal for children with mental disabilities is that, as adults, they become as independent as possible. Many can learn living and job skills that enable them to live alone, support themselves, and perhaps marry and raise a family. Others need more care and support. Many communities have sheltered care homes that offer supervised group living for those mentally handicapped adults who need it. These adults can usually work under supervision. However, some mentally impaired people remain totally dependent on others throughout their life.

Social acceptance is essential to the mentally handicapped. Part of the child's training should focus on grooming, manners, and acceptable social behavior. However, society must also learn to accept those who are different.

Not all mental handicaps are caused by retardation. See Chapter 14 for information about learning disabilities.

Many mentally handicapped children will continue to need special supervised home and work situations as adults.

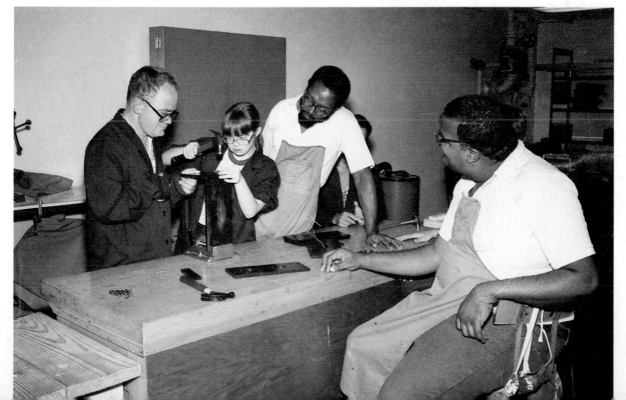

Children with emotional handicaps have difficulty coping with the stresses of life.

Emotional Handicaps

Everyone has trouble dealing with his or her emotions once in a while. For most people, the trouble is resolved with time and adjustment to whatever is causing the stress. For some people, however, the stress is too great or goes on for too long a time and their emotions become seriously disturbed. Others are simply unable to cope with the strain of everyday life.

How do parents know when children are emotionally troubled and need professional help? The child's behavior is the best indication. However, there is no clear-cut line between normal and emotionally disturbed behavior. Some troublesome behavior is natural. It may result from the need for a little special attention or may just be a normal stage of development. However, when behavior prevents normal development or disturbs the lives of family members, a serious emotional problem should be suspected.

Nervous habits, loss of appetite, sleeplessness, excessive fear, withdrawal, aggressive or violent behavior, and failing grades may be signs of emotional disturbance. Keep in mind, however, that other causes for such behavior must be ruled out first.

At age two, Terry began to rock his crib constantly and bang his head over and over against the headboard. He was late in becoming toilet trained and had frequent accidents even after he reached school age. His speech was rapid, breathless, and hampered by stuttering. He fought with other children and disrupted classes with his outbursts. He entered third grade unable to read or write. At this point, the school recommended Terry receive psychological evaluation.

Even when a child's behavior clearly indicates serious emotional problems, some parents are reluctant to ask for help. They are ashamed to admit they cannot handle the problem themselves. But parents can't be expected to have all the answers.

When a child does need help, the parents will need to find a **therapist**—a professional trained in helping people work through emotional problems. Pediatricians, school counselors, or members of the clergy can usually recommend a therapist. So can the local office of the Mental Health Association. Therapists ask the family for background information on the problem, get to know the family better, observe the child in various situations, and plan treatment. Sometimes a few changes in how the family interacts are all that are needed.

Some emotional problems may be due to physical causes. In this case, the therapist may recommend medical evaluation and treatment. One mother learned that her child had a brain impairment that caused some of his actions to be beyond his control. A behavior management program combined with medication produced marked improvement.

Much emotional therapy involves improving the person's self-image. Therapy can change the way children view themselves and, consequently, the way they behave.

The results of therapy greatly depend on the parents. They must believe in and support the therapist's work. They must be available to listen and talk when the child is ready. They need to accept the resulting changes. Sharing children's personal feelings, learning to understand them, and accepting them for what they are—not what parents expect them to be—are ways parents can help children overcome their problems.

It takes time for therapy to change deep-seated emotional problems. Relapses should be expected, but it is important for parents to see the treatment through to the end. Good emotional health in childhood prepares a person for a happy adulthood.

Parents of children with similar handicaps can provide valuable support for one another.

Raising a Handicapped Child

For a parent, the responsibilities and demands of raising a handicapped child can often seem overwhelming. Most parents experience a grief process that includes guilt, sadness, anger, and frustration. Though there are times of happiness and contentment, there is always underlying sadness.

Support groups for parents of handicapped children serve a valuable function. They help parents explore and accept their feelings. They also help parents to better meet the emotional needs of their children. Parents learn to separate the handicap from the child and realize they have a child who happens to have a handicap. Children who receive strong emotional support are better able to develop the inner strength, patience, and courage necessary to cope with their disabilities.

Parents can also get together with other parents of handicapped children to share comfort, advice, and solutions to everyday problems. Groups keep members up to date on research and treatment.

Handicapped children can bring as much joy to a family as children without handicaps. They give parents the opportunity to learn about loving and giving and to appreciate small achievements.

Close-up

Sylvia and Ed Sanchez hurried to the first meeting of a group of parents of infants with Down syndrome. They were scheduled to talk to the group that evening.

After they had been introduced, Sylvia said, "When I look around the table at all of you, I see Ed and myself sitting there just a few years ago. When you have a child with Down syndrome, it seems like your world has shattered. I remember that I cried for weeks. But I want you to know that now I laugh often and rarely cry. Our daughter Rosa has made us a happier family."

Ed continued, "Rosa's now five and we have two other younger children. I'm sure you have been told that Down syndrome results from an accident of genetics. If you want other children, there is no greater risk they will have Down's."

"Sylvia and I have been actively involved in the local organization for the mentally handicapped. At first, we attended meetings because we needed information on what we were up against and we needed to talk to other parents in the same boat. But we've become more involved because we enjoy it and we want to help other parents."

"Rosa's been in the special preschool program since she was two," Sylvia explained. "Before that, trained parent-child educators came into our home on a regular basis to help assess Rosa's abilities and to set up a program of learning and therapy. They taught us how to teach her most effectively. We also learned exercises to enhance her physical development."

"Rosa's such a lovable child. She is usually cheerful and loves to give hugs and kisses. Though we don't know just how much independence she'll be capable of as an adult, each of her achievements is cause for celebration. We really do enjoy her!"

"I am anxious to hear about your own situations," she went on. "Some of you have babies who are more severely retarded. Others may be only mildly retarded. Some probably suffer from physical defects related to Down's. But remember, there are lots of other parents to help you and guide you through the network of government and community programs. Give your children a chance to be the best they can be. And give them a chance to enrich your lives."

How does having a mentally retarded child affect the long-term goals of a family?
What programs are available in your area for retarded children? ■

Check Your Understanding

1. How can parents help a handicapped child develop independence and a positive self-concept?

2. In what ways could placing handicapped children in regular school programs benefit both those with and without handicaps?

3. How can support groups help parents of children with disabilities?

Child Abuse

Child abuse is the physical and/or emotional mistreatment of a child. It refers to more than an occasional scolding or moderate spanking. Physical abuse produces serious injuries such as black eyes, burns, bruises, and broken bones, as well as severe emotional distress. The effects of child abuse, of any type, are long-lasting. It can affect the physical, emotional, mental, and social health of its victims throughout their lifetime.

Many people find it difficult to understand how a person can abuse children. But according to the National Committee for the Prevention of Child Abuse, abuse of children has reached epidemic proportions throughout the world. Every day an average of five American children are abused so badly that they die.

Child abuse may be divided into a number of general categories:

- **Nonaccidental physical injury.** Injury caused by such things as severe beatings, burns, bites, or scalding water.

- **Neglect.** Failing to provide a child with the basic necessities of life, such as food, clothing, shelter, and medical care.

- **Sexual molestation.** Using a child for the sexual pleasure of an adult.

- **Emotional abuse.** Placing unreasonable, unrealistic, and excessive demands on the child. Examples are constant belittling, teasing, or verbal attacks. Some children never receive the love and affection they need for normal emotional development.

A single incident does not generally mean child abuse. It is usually a pattern of behavior. The longer it continues, the more serious the problem becomes for both parent and child.

Any type of abuse prevents a child from developing normally. Children who suffer continuing abuse are also more likely to become abusive parents themselves.

What Are Child Abusers Like?

Contrary to what you might expect, most child abusers are not monsters. They are ordinary people, usually parents, caught in situations they cannot handle emotionally. They are often people who feel lonely and can't cope with their own personal problems. Low self-esteem is a common trait among child abusers. In many cases, they were abused themselves as children. Because this is the only kind of parenting they have known, they repeat it with their own children.

Child abusers come from all income levels, ethnic groups, and religions. Often, only one parent in a family abuses the children. However, if the other parent realizes what is going on, he or she may be reluctant to seek help.

Parents who abuse their children are easily provoked. When irritated, they respond quickly and violently, much like a child does. A three-year-old who is angry responds without thought. The child may kick the cat, smash a toy truck, or throw a doll across the room. The abusive adult displays the same uncontrollable emotions. An argument, a car that will not start—almost anything—can trigger an incident. The child is seldom the cause. But he or she is nearby and a defenseless target for a violent physical or verbal attacks.

Abusive parents generally believe that infants will be spoiled if they are picked up and comforted when they cry. But this is the way newborns develop trust. Abusive parents feel that they must continually show their children "who's boss." They have unrealistic expectations of what children can do. They expect them to be perfect. For example, they may tell a toddler to "sit up and eat right." The child is expected to do so promptly, even though the nature of toddlers makes this almost impossible. Young children are expected to remember commands given only once. But, of course, young children learn only after things have been repeated many times. Abusive parents see the child's failure to obey as stubbornness or meanness—behavior they feel must be severely punished.

Counselors can help abusive parents understand and change their behavior.

Are There Any Answers?

It is against the law in every state to abuse a child. Many states, though, have more severe penalties for abusing animals than for abusing children! States also require by law that people such as doctors, social workers, and child care workers report suspected cases of child abuse. However, many cases are not reported. Child abuse should be reported to the closest social service or child welfare agency.

Once a report of child abuse is received, an investigation begins. If the child is in immediate danger, the court may place the youngster in a foster home. If there is a history of past abuse or the child's injuries are severe, uncooperative parents can be taken to court.

Putting abusive people in jail does not solve the problem. It only temporarily protects children. In most cases, treatment and counseling are used to try to correct the cause of the abuse.

Abusive parents can, in most cases, learn to care for their children responsibly. To help parents there are many types of government, private, and volunteer programs available. Parents Anonymous, one of the best known groups, is made up of parents who help each other gain self-control.

Some towns have **crisis nurseries**—child care facilities where troubled parents can leave their children for a short time. This gives the parents time to cool off and try to cope with their frustrations and anger away from the child. Volunteers or professionals usually work with the abusive parents on a one-to-one basis. They help parents understand their frustrations and resolve their problems. Parents learn how to break the cycle of child abuse.

Many problems are caused by poor parenting skills and a lack of knowledge of child development. Classes like the one you are taking help give future parents realistic ideas of what parenting involves. You know by now that babies are not always clean and happy and that they don't stay babies forever. You also know what normal behavior is at certain ages so you can make better decisions about discipline. Preparing people for parenthood before they become parents and providing them with help when they are parents can help eliminate child abuse.

The temporary child care offered by a crisis nursery can help prevent child abuse.

Family Stresses

Every child is exposed to stress at one time or another. The stress may be fairly mild and short-term, such as when the family moves from one home to another. Or the stress may be severe, such as when someone close to the child dies.

During times of stress, everyone needs support. However, children need more help and support than adults because they are less able to understand and cope with what is happening. They should be encouraged to talk about their feelings. Parents must be careful not to take out their own stress on the children. When parents feel they are up against more than they can handle, they shouldn't hesitate to ask for help. Other family members, the clergy, and professional counselors can help them cope with stressful burdens.

Divorce

Child and family experts generally agree that children should have the influence of both a mother and father while growing up. Normal development may be hindered when one parent is absent. On the other hand, experts also know that a home in which parents continually fight or can't get along can be damaging.

If a family is breaking up, the children need to be told in an honest and reassuring way. Experts advise using the following guidelines for helping children deal with separation or divorce:

When parents divorce, a child's time is often split between two homes. Why should activities with both parents be kept as normal as possible?

■**Truth.** The children should be told the truth about the upcoming changes. If possible, both parents should sit down with the children and discuss the situation. All children, even toddlers, should be included in the discussion. Young children often understand much more than parents realize. Parents can say something like, "We're having a hard time right now. We are going to live apart, for a while at least. No matter what happens, we will both always love you and take care of you."

■**Elimination of blame.** Parents should avoid placing blame on one another for the divorce, at least in front of the children. Children should not be forced to take sides. Parents can ask a counselor or member of the clergy to help explain the reasons behind the divorce if they are not able to do so without placing blame.

Children must be assured that they are in no way responsible for the breakup. Parents should stress that they are separating because of their own differences, not because of anything the children have done. Most children feel guilty when there is trouble between parents. This is because parents often fight about the children, as well as other things.

■**Reassurance.** The children need reassurance that they will continue to be loved by both parents. The children will probably be living with only one parent. They need to know the other parent will still be there for emotional support and companionship.

■**No false hope.** The children should not be encouraged to hope for reconciliation if there is none. Children of divorce usually hope that their parents will get back together again. This only delays adjustment to their new life.

■**Stability and continuity.** The children's lives should be kept as much the same as possible. Brothers and sisters should be kept together, if possible. It helps when schools and homes are not changed. The absent parent should visit frequently. Contact with relatives from both sides—especially grandparents—helps children retain a sense of belonging.

Emotional Effects of Divorce

Divorce requires many emotional adjustments by everyone in the family, but especially children. They need security, stability, and understanding. The new lifestyle that comes with divorce or separation causes new problems and requires many adjustments.

At one time, mothers were almost automatically given custody of children after a divorce. Occasionally, parents were awarded joint custody, in which children divide their time between their two parents' homes. Today, more fathers are given custody of their children than before. Most courts now base the custody decision on which parent can best provide a loving, stable home. However, the courts encourage visitation by the other parent so children can maintain healthy relationships with both their mother and father.

Sometimes children resent the parent they live with and idealize the absent parent. The "home" parent makes the rules and gets all the blame. The absent parent may try to make up for not being there by spoiling the child. Conflict is created and no one wins.

Parents who are caught up in their own troubles can forget that divorce is particularly upsetting for youngsters. Many children, even very young ones, show behavior problems. Even those who appear to adjust well are often hiding their grief and pain. If children have noticeable, continuing adjustment problems, it is wise to seek professional help.

Death

The death of someone close causes special problems for children. The age of the child, however, influences the youngster's reaction.

■*Under age three.* Children this young cannot understand anything more than a brief separation. A toddler will react to a parent's death in the same way as to the parent's week-long vacation

■*Ages three to five.* Children this age think that death is like sleep—you are dead, then you wake up and are alive again. As a result, children of this age may seem unfeeling. They are worried and concerned for a while, but do not understand that death is permanent. One four-year-old said some months after her father's death, "I know Daddy's dead, but when is he coming home?"

■*Ages five to nine.* As children mature, they accept the idea that a person who has died will not come back. However, they do not see death as something that happens to everyone. They especially do not see it as happening to themselves. To them, death only happens to other people.

■*Age nine or ten.* At this age, children finally begin to see death as inevitable for everyone. They realize that they, too, will die. This may make them afraid. They must come to terms with this fear and put it in proper perspective.

By the time they are five, most children have had some contact with death and are curious about it. Perhaps a pet died or they have seen a dead squirrel or bird. Some will have experienced a death in the family. Even the very young realize that death is serious, but misconceptions can cause real problems.

Many children first experience death when a pet dies. True understanding and acceptance may not come until much later.

Close-up

Five-year-old Stephen was brought to a mental health clinic by his parents. They were concerned about his sudden, but continuing, bedtime problems. Until recently, they explained, Stephen had never resisted going to bed. Then he suddenly started crying at bedtimes and refused to settle down. After Stephen finally fell into an exhausted sleep, he was often awakened in the night by nightmares.

Except for this one problem, Stephen's behavior and emotional adjustment seemed normal. Neither parent was able to offer an explanation.

The therapist used a play session with Stephen to try to find out the cause of his fear. During the session, Stephen told the story of a man who " . . . caught a heart attack. He fell out of bed and died." Further questioning revealed that Stephen had overhead his mother telling a neighbor a story. She related that a family friend had suffered a heart attack, fallen out of bed, and died.

Stephen had no idea what a heart attack was or where one came from, but he did understand about falling out of bed. If doing that could make you get a heart attack and die, then no one was going to get him into a bed again!

With this information, the therapist was able to explain to Stephen that he did not need to worry about going to bed. Stephen's parents, in turn, tried to make bedtimes relaxed, happy times for him.

Why would punishment for Stephen's misbehavior at bedtime have been ineffective?

What at-home methods might Stephen's parents have used to discover the cause of his problem?

How can parents help their children develop a realistic, healthy attitude toward death? ■

How Children Cope with Death

Child psychologists believe that children go through a three-step process in accepting death. Parents or other caregivers who understand this process are usually better prepared to help children cope with death. The three steps are:

1. *Disbelief.* At this stage, children may express anger, hostility, and defiance.

2. *Despair.* Later, they are often withdrawn and depressed. Some children go back to babyish behavior.

3. *Reorganization.* Finally, they begin to adjust to life without the person who had died.

If a loved one dies, children should be told in an honest way. They may need an explanation of what death is. Children should be encouraged to talk about their feelings. Parents need to let children know that they, too, miss the person very much. It is often helpful for children and parents to share memories of their loved one.

Children need prompt, direct answers to their questions. A half-truth, such as saying "Grandma went on a long trip" can harm more than help. If the children have been close to their grandmother, they may be hurt that she went away without at least saying good-bye. The real truth will have to be faced sooner or later. Knowing that their parents have not been truthful may shake their trust.

Children, like adults, benefit from taking part in services for a friend or family member who has died.

The words and attitudes used when helping a child understand death are very important. Children understand most things in terms of themselves. If someone has died of an illness, children may think they, too, will die when they get sick. Especially with very young children, using terms like "passed away" or "gone to sleep" only adds to the confusion. It is best to use simple, direct references to death and dying. The type of explanation given must fit the age and understanding of the child, but it should always be honest and direct, no matter how simple.

Some childhood experiences with death will be more upsetting than others. A child whose parent dies needs support for an extended time. The death of a parent is the most tragic thing that can happen to a youngster. Many children react to a parent's death with guilt. The child may think, "I wasn't always good when he wanted me to be," or "I wasn't quiet enough when she was sick." Children need the assurance that nothing they did or said caused the death. They also need help coping with a feeling of abandonment.

Even very young children should usually be allowed to take part in family funerals or memorial services. Children of any age are capable of mourning. Studies have shown that even infants go through a period of excessive crying and searching for a lost parent.

Moving

Moving is stressful to children because they don't know what to expect. Their present home is familiar and safe. They may not want to leave.

Children's fears can be soothed if they are allowed to talk about their feelings. Packing their own things often helps. They feel more a part of what is happening and more in control. If parents stress the positive aspects of the move, such as the child having a room of his or her own, the child may begin to look forward to it.

After the move is made, the parents must help the child get settled. Walking about the neighborhood together, helping the child meet nearby children, and visiting the new school will make the adjustment easier.

Financial Problems

When a family has financial problems, children sense the tensions even though they may not understand them. The parents may be short-tempered or less attentive. The children often believe they themselves have done something wrong.

Even though the children will not understand complex finances, they should be reassured that the problems are not their fault. Parents need to try not to take out their own fears and worries on their children.

If you moved as a young child, you probably still remember the fear and unhappiness you felt. How can talking about these feelings help minimize them?

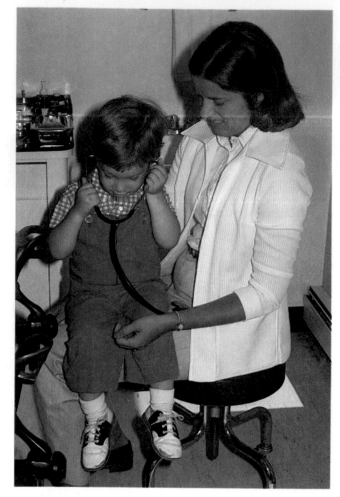

Young children who have long-term illnesses need to understand that doctors and nurses are trying to help them, not hurt them.

Illness

During a family member's illness, the family's routine is disturbed. Parents can help by giving a simple, clear explanation of what's happening. If the illness is minor, the child can be reassured that the person will soon be well and everything will return to normal. If the illness is serious or terminal, the child should be told the truth, but in a calm, reassuring way. Many children worry that similar things will happen to them. They may grow afraid of doctors or hospitals. Parents must be sure to explain the difference between this illness and one the child has or is likely to have.

Check Your Understanding

1. How does child abuse differ from normal discipline?

2. Why may children of divorced parents tend to idealize the parent they only visit and perhaps resent the parent with whom they live? What are some ways this problem might be avoided or handled?

3. Why is it important for even young children to take part in family funerals or memorial services?

Chapter Review

To Sum Up

- Whether or not children cope successfully with problems depends largely on the actions and attitudes of their parents and caregivers.
- Children may be physically, mentally, or emotionally handicapped. Each child has individual care needs.
- Child abuse has severe and long-lasting effects.
- Treatment and counseling can help abusive parents learn to cope with their problems and stop the pattern of abuse.
- When a family is split by separation or divorce, children need to be informed in an honest and reassuring way.
- Children who must cope with family stresses need special support.

To Review and Remember

1. What is the most important need of handicapped children?
2. Why should handicapped children help with tasks around the home?
3. Why is it important for children with physical disabilities to learn self-care?
4. When should serious emotional problems be suspected?
5. Give three guidelines for helping mentally handicapped children learn.
6. Define child abuse and list the four types.
7. List two common traits of child abusers.
8. What is a crisis nursery?
9. Name three ways to maintain stability after a divorce.
10. List the three steps children often go through in accepting a death.

To Discuss and Discover

1. Good listeners are special people. They help others cope with difficult situations. Discuss what qualities are necessary to be a good listener.
2. For one day, pretend that you have a particular handicap. (Simulate the condition as closely as possible.) Report your reactions to the class. What problems did you encounter? How did your experience differ from that of students who are actually handicapped? How could your school be made more convenient and comfortable for these students?

18 Careers Relating to Children

To help you to . . .

- Evaluate your personal interests and aptitudes in light of future career decisions.

- Explain the importance of education and experience to finding and progressing in a job.

- Describe a number of specific jobs in the child care field.

- List the personal qualities needed to be a good babysitter.

- Describe the responsibilities of a babysitter when caring for children of various ages.

Terms to Learn

aptitude test	entry-level job	professional
audiologist	interest inventory	reference
entrepreneur	paraprofessional	

Did you know that just about everything you do is experience that may lead to something else?

Take this course, for example. By learning about child development, you have made one step in the direction of becoming a good parent, aunt or uncle, or friend to children. This course may also be a step toward a career working with children.

Think of other things that you can do to help you decide if you would like such a career. You might take more classes. You could babysit. You might volunteer at a day care center or a hospital. You might work at a summer camp. You could teach classes for children through your church, synagogue, or library.

There are many ways you can gain experience right now. There are even more as you graduate from high school and prepare for college or the work world.

Have you decided on a career? Some people have special talents that help them make career decisions. Others have dreamed since childhood of a particular career and are determined to pursue that dream. You, though, may be one of the majority who find it difficult to decide just what sort of work you would like to do.

Learning about children and how they develop will help you decide whether you would like a career in child care. Careers involving children are not limited to those you might usually think about, such as teaching or working in day care. There are hundreds of jobs that involve children either directly or indirectly. Perhaps one of these is right for you.

Which Career for You?

Different people and experiences have influenced you toward particular careers since early childhood. At five, you may have wanted to be a firefighter. In grade school, liking a certain teacher may have convinced you that you wanted to teach.

Parents are also an important influence. Many children enter the same field as their mother or father, although this is not as common as in the past. Parents may also influence you by encouraging certain interests and discouraging others.

Aptitude Tests

Unfortunately, you can not try out every job you think might interest you. But psychologists have developed tests that give insight into people's strengths and weaknesses. These tests, combined with some thoughtful self-appraisal, can help point you in the right direction. Similar tests are also given by employers. These tests help them know if prospective employees are suited to the job they are applying for.

Taking an aptitude test can help you discover which skills are likely to be your strongest ones.

Chapter 18—Careers Relating to Children   475

An **aptitude test** measures a person's abilities in various skills. The scores help predict how successful a person might be in jobs of a particular type. Aptitude tests are often given to students in high school and college to help them plan careers. Nonstudents can often arrange to take the tests at local colleges or counseling agencies. The following skills are usually checked by aptitude tests:

■*Verbal reasoning.* This is the ability to understand ideas expressed in words and to use words in thinking through your own ideas. Teachers, writers, social workers, and salespeople are among those who should have good scores in verbal reasoning.

■*Abstract reasoning.* Picture a number of objects with different shapes in your mind. Now try to move the objects around to form different patterns. This is an example of thinking logically without using words or numbers. Carpenters, scientists, and computer programmers are among those who need to be good at abstract thinking.

■*Numerical ability.* If you are good at solving mathematical problems and working with figures, you may have good numerical ability. This is important to many careers, including engineering, economics, accounting, and banking.

■*Mechanical reasoning.* Those who understand the mechanical principles involved in motors and tools score highly in this area. Mechanics obviously need these skills, but so do many other workers. They include machinists, medical technicians, television repairpersons, and engineers.

■*Space relationships.* Can you look at a flat drawing of an object and picture in your mind its actual size, shape, and position in relation to other objects? If so, you have an aptitude important to architects, truckers, interior designers, artists, and laboratory technicians.

■*Clerical speed and accuracy.* A high score in this area indicates the good eye-hand coordination needed by people like bookkeepers, bank tellers, and precision assembly workers.

■*Spelling.* Secretaries, editors, writers, and typists are among those who need to be good spellers.

When the results of the aptitude test are evaluated, you may find that you are well suited for a number of specific careers.

■*Language usage.* Putting words together correctly and effectively is necessary for many jobs. Careers using these skills include writing, editing, law, teaching, and sales.

Your score in a single aptitude isn't as important as the pattern formed by your three or four highest scores. Most jobs demand a combination of skills. A good aptitude test can suggest possible careers based on your strong points.

Your Interests

Having the ability to master something doesn't mean you would be happy spending your life doing it. In other words, your interests may differ from your aptitudes. Many people aren't sure how their interests fit in with possible careers. Another type of test, called an **interest inventory**, helps you learn what jobs might fit your interests.

These tests vary, but most examine how you feel about different "themes" related to occupations. For example, if you score highest on the "realistic" theme, you might be interested in work as a mechanic, laboratory technician, farmer, or skilled industrial worker. Other themes suggest different jobs.

Remember, though, tests are only part of the answer. They cannot measure such things as motivation, personality, or ambition. What's more, career decisions are often influenced by other factors, such as job security and prestige. Tests can show fairly accurately what you could do and what you might like doing, but you have to decide what's most important.

Combining information from an aptitude test with that from an interest inventory will help you make a wise career choice. What aptitudes and interests do you think are needed to work in a child care center?

Education and Experience

Having a career is much like climbing a ladder. In every career area, there are many levels of jobs. The more education and work experience you have, the higher you climb the career ladder. However, jobs at any level are important and worth doing well.

When reading about jobs at various levels, you will probably see words like "entry-level position," "paraprofessional," or "professional." Understanding such terms will help you know what qualifications are needed.

An **entry-level job** is one for beginners with limited education and training. As the term indicates, this is where many people enter a career area. Most people, though, don't stay at this level. As they become more experienced and perhaps get more education, they move upward to more responsible and better paying jobs.

A **paraprofessional** is a person with education beyond high school that trains him or her for a certain field. Many paraprofessional jobs require a related degree from a two-year college. The paraprofessional works in a team with more qualified professionals. For example, a paraprofessional might work in a day care center as an assistant teacher.

A **professional** is someone with at least a degree from a four-year college (a bachelor's degree) or a technical school. Many professionals have more advanced degrees—a master's or a doctorate—and years of experience. Professionals may be in charge of programs or supervise paraprofessionals and entry-level workers. The chart below shows various levels of jobs in a child care center.

Typical Jobs and Responsibilities in a Child Care Center

Level	Duties
PROFESSIONAL Director	Supervises other personnel; coordinates program planning; often administers budget, enrollment, staffing, and other procedures. Requires at least two years of professional experience and perhaps an advanced degree.
Group teacher	Teaches 15–25 children; plans learning activities; writes reports on student progress; confers with parents; often supervises paraprofessionals or semiskilled staff members. Generally requires a degree from a four-year college.
PARAPROFESSIONAL Assistant teacher	Helps group teacher in supervising student activities. May need a two-year college degree; usually needs a high school diploma.
Intern	Often works part-time; may be a student completing a degree in early childhood education; may be required to serve as a volunteer; assists group teacher and others as needed.
ENTRY LEVEL Teacher aide	May work full- or part-time; assists group teacher by helping children dress, eat, do art projects, etc.
NOTE: Because of high requirements of state licensing, salaries in public supported facilities are often higher than those in private centers; similarly, publicly funded facilities often have more employee benefits to offer job candidates.	

Education

Have you thought about getting more education after high school? You may not feel you can afford to go on to college or to a technical school, or you may not want to go. But consider carefully before making a decision.

Scholarships and loans are available to those who need financial help. Many schools offer jobs to those who find it difficult to pay for their education. Most areas have community colleges where costs are reasonable. These offer a variety of training programs that take two years or less to complete. Students from two-year colleges can later transfer to a four-year college or university if they wish to continue their studies for a bachelor's degree.

Another possibility is to work two or three years after high school to save enough money to go back to school.

Those who are not interested in education after high school may change their minds after working awhile. They may want a better paying, more responsible job that requires additional education. Or, they may become so interested in their work that they want to take classes to learn more about it.

Experts now predict that most people will have several different careers during their lifetime. Certain jobs will disappear when there is no longer a need for them. Other jobs now performed by people will be done in the future by machines. Also, people's interests

If you want to be a pediatric nurse, you might consider working as a nurse's aide. It can give you valuable experience and help with the cost of nursing school.

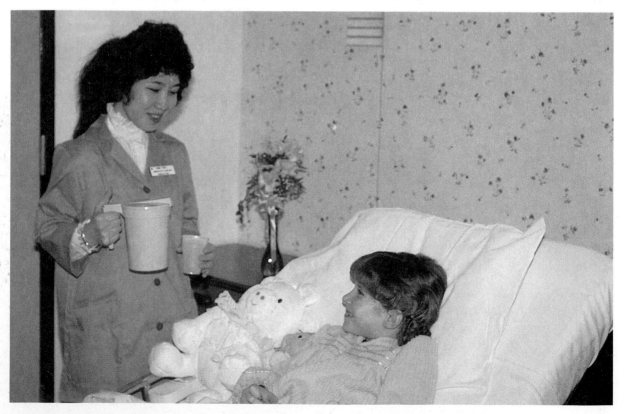

tend to change over time. You may be bored with a job after several years. Getting more education may be something you will want to do in the future.

Experience

If you have ever looked for a job, you know that most employers want to know about your experience. You may wonder how you can get that experience if you can't get a job. That is a puzzle, but not one without a solution.

Too often, people think about experience only in terms of a paying job. But there are many other ways to gain experience. One of the best is through volunteer work. Many programs and agencies depend primarily on volunteer help. In addition to learning the job, there is satisfaction and pride gained in helping others.

Volunteers gain actual experience, build up a good work record, and improve work skills and attitudes. People you work with as a volunteer can be good references when you apply for a paying job. (A **reference** is someone a prospective employer can contact to find out about the applicant's character and skills.)

Another advantage of volunteer work is that you gain experience in securing work. You will learn how important a good appearance is. You can get practice in selling your skills and talents to others. Being able to present yourself well will be a big help when you interview for a job.

Another way to get experience is to create your own job. You can do this by finding a need and filling it. Mowing lawns and shoveling snow are among the more obvious types of "created" jobs. However, other people have become plant-sitters, dog-walkers, and even "human alarm clocks" who call to awaken people each morning. Perhaps your area needs someone to repair bicycles and you know how. Or maybe parents in your neighborhood would pay you to entertain and supervise their children.

Doing volunteer work in a child care center is one way to gain experience with children. What others can you think of?

Close-up

Carolyn Dunn is the successful owner of a day care center. When she was asked what led her to that profession, she said:

"I think mainly it's because I've always loved kids. Even when I was a kid myself, I loved playing with babies. At family picnics I was always carrying someone's baby around.

"I started babysitting when I was pretty young. I was a good babysitter, too. Babysitting wasn't work, it was fun! To be even better at it, I enrolled in all the free babysitting clinics I could.

"When I was in high school, our home economics department had an in-school nursery as part of a child study course. We had about a dozen children at a time, from babies to school-age. After school and during the summer I got a part-time job as an assistant in a real nursery school downtown. I'd dress, feed, and entertain the littlest ones, help the older ones in art projects and games, and answer endless questions.

"By that time, I knew I wanted to make a career of working with children. I enrolled in our local community college for a degree in early childhood education.

"About the time I graduated from college, a computer company in town built a day care center for employees' children. I applied for and got the job as assistant to the director. Within four years, I moved up to director.

"During those early years, I'd often hear friends complain about the trouble they had finding good day care for their children. They'd switch from one center to another, trying to find the right one. They talked about poor food, lack of cleanliness, unhappy kids, and high prices. I decided that I should start my own child care center, giving customers everything I'd want in day care for a child of my own. I knew I'd have no trouble getting clients.

"I started small, renting space in a church basement. Then we moved to larger quarters in a mall. I remodelled the space, hired the best people I could find and here we are today — two years later and going strong. We have a waiting list of parents who have heard about us from satisfied customers."

If you wanted to get a head start on a future career in a child-related field, what would you begin doing today?
What goals might you set for yourself?
Can you think of a need your community has for a child-related business? ■

Careers Related to Child Care

Within the area of child care there is an almost endless variety of careers. Some careers involve working with one child, others with a group. Some require extensive study beyond high school, others do not. Some jobs, such as teaching and day care, involve working with children all day. Others, particularly in health-related fields, may mean less contact.

Brief descriptions of a few child-related careers follow. They will give you an idea of the various kinds of jobs that are available. After reading about these careers you may have a clearer idea of whether you are interested in a child-related career.

All jobs have pluses and minuses. You should be aware of them before you make a final career choice. The chart on page 484 summarizes advantages and disadvantages of child care careers.

Day Care Workers

You have probably noticed an increase in the number of day care centers in your area. This is because in more and more families there is no parent at home during the day to care for the children. Day care workers are in increasing demand.

Many day care facilities are run by government or community agencies. Some large businesses provide day care centers for employees' children. A few day care centers are part of nationwide or regional chains of such centers run for profit. However, most centers are established and operated by individuals.

Because of the great variety of day care centers, educational and personal requirements for workers vary. Some states set requirements for day care workers.

Teachers

Teaching is the largest of all professions. There is a lot of competition for elementary and secondary teaching jobs in many areas of the country. Opportunities are best in nursery school, kindergarten, grades one to three, or in teaching children with mental or physical handicaps.

Teachers are responsible for planning and teaching lessons. What is taught must conform to state guidelines and those of the individual school district. In addition, teachers must take individual students' needs and learning abilities into consideration.

Most elementary teachers instruct a class of 20 to 35 students in several subjects. Some elementary teachers and all secondary teachers specialize in one or two subject areas. They teach these subjects to several grades or classes.

Although being a teacher means working long hours, helping children discover and learn can be very satisfying.

In most states, a teacher must have at least a bachelor's degree from a four-year college in an approved teacher education program. Teaching salaries vary with geographic area, level of education, and experience. Starting salaries are in the low-to-medium range. A common complaint is that, compared to other professions, teachers' salaries do not match the educational requirements and responsibilities of the job. Experience, advanced degrees, and administrative responsibilities can raise salary levels to the middle range and above.

Becoming A Child Care Entrepreneur

An **entrepreneur** (AWN-truh-pruh-NUR) is a person who starts up and runs his or her own business, or who creates and markets a new product. The field of child care is a natural one for those who would like to become entrepreneurs. Setting up a home-based care business or owning a day care center are ways to enter the business world.

Becoming an entrepreneur requires good business management skills and leadership ability. Business owners also need good relationship skills. They must work with customers, suppliers, employees, government regulators, and others like accountants and bankers.

The risk of owning a business is great. Many small businesses fail. While the profits belong to the business owners, so do the losses. Still, many people feel that owning their own business is the best way to participate in our free-enterprise system.

Traits of a Successful Child Care Worker

- **Has Good Work Habits and Attitudes**
  Is dependable
  Arrives on time
  Takes pride in work
  Sees dignity in all work
- **Relates Well to Others**
  Understands good relationships are vital to business success
  Gets along well with the children, peers, and boss
  Supervises others effectively
- **Uses Good Management Skills**
  Plans and organizes work
  Uses appropriate work methods and procedures
  Does job in simplest, most effective way
  Uses time efficiently
  Controls stress through good management
  Balances work and personal life
  Uses management skills to reach business and personal goals
  Has good health

- **Is Emotionally Mature**
  Exercises self control
  Is self-disciplined
  Accepts criticism and uses it to improve
  Understands and accepts authority
- **Has Good Communication Skills**
  Can talk to children (see pp. 423-424)
  Communicates well with peers, boss, and those supervised
  Uses good written language
- **Demonstrates Leadership Skills**
  Takes responsibility
  Is a group leader
  Understands leadership and the role of the leader
  Is a follower when appropriate
- **Shows Ethical Behavior**
  Is motivated by the well-being of children
  Is honest
  Follows the organization's policies and procedures

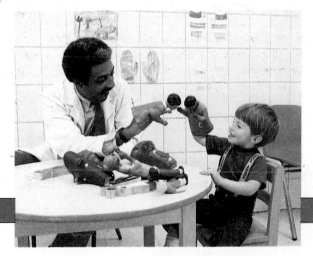

Advantages and Disadvantages of Child Care Careers

Advantages

- Job opportunities at all levels of education, experience, and responsibility.
- Work available in every area of the country.
- Opportunities for both part-time and full-time work.
- Flexible working hours.
- Personal satisfaction for those who like helping others.
- Contact with all age groups from infants to adults.

Disadvantages

- Salaries vary, but often not as high as other careers with comparable educational requirements.
- Work is often emotionally draining.
- May be necessary to work evenings and weekends.
- Great responsibility for the health, safety, and development of children.
- Requires exceptional energy and patience.
- Few periods of relaxation during working hours.

Special Education Teachers

Special education teachers are trained to teach those students with needs beyond the average. This includes students with learning disabilities, mental impairments, social or emotional adjustment problems, or physical handicaps. Sometimes gifted students—or those with above-average potential—also receive special education.

Since students vary greatly in the type and degree of their needs, special education teachers must tailor programs to individuals.

Special education teachers must complete a four-year program at an approved college or university. Some school districts require such teachers to have a master's degree, which means an additional one or two years of study. Special education teachers must be dependable, sensible, patient, and enthusiastic. Salaries may be somewhat higher than those of regular classroom teachers.

Speech Therapists and Audiologists

About ten percent of all Americans are unable to speak or hear clearly. Children who have trouble speaking or hearing cannot participate fully with other children in play or in normal classroom activities.

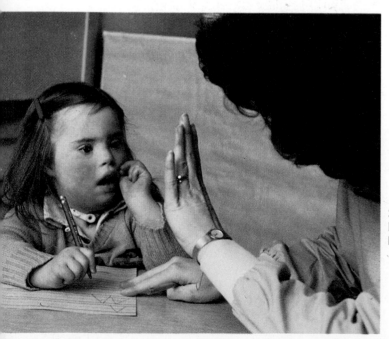

Special education teachers face extra challenges but know they make a difference in children's lives.

A speech therapist works with people who have speech, language, and voice disorders. These may be caused by deafness, brain injury, cleft palate, mental retardation, emotional problems, or foreign languages spoken in the home. Speech therapists are often responsible for both diagnosis and treatment of speech problems. The **audiologist** primarily tests for and diagnoses hearing problems. Speech and hearing, however, are interrelated. A person who is trained in either field must be familiar with both.

Duties vary with education, experience, and place of employment. Speech and hearing clinics—generally held in schools—use special machines, tests, and diagnostic procedures to identify and evaluate disorders. Then, in cooperation with other health professionals, the speech therapist or audiologist plans and arranges for an organized program of treatment.

Persons choosing either of these professions should approach problems objectively and have a concern for the needs of others. They should also be patient because progress is often slow. They must accept responsibility, work independently, and be able to instruct others. Working with detail is also important.

Most states require a master's degree or its equivalent for both professions. Some also require a teaching certificate if work is done in schools. Since educational requirements are advanced, starting salaries begin in the above-average range and tend to be high.

Social Workers

Social workers help people who have social or emotional problems. There are many different jobs within this broad field. Caseworkers help people on a one-to-one basis. Community social workers are involved with groups of people.

Many different types of community agencies employ social workers. This agency helps young parents and their children get off to a good start.

The aim of all social services is to strengthen and improve individual and family life and to protect children. Caseworkers interview individuals or families who need help. They must be skillful at gathering information, getting along with people, and gaining the confidence of their clients. They decide what type of help their clients need—from medical services to psychiatric help—and arrange for it to be given.

Some social workers place children in foster homes or with adoptive families. School social workers help troubled students change classes, receive tutoring, or benefit from special community services.

Social workers must have a bachelor's degree from a school with an officially recognized social work program. A master's degree is necessary for some jobs.

Social work graduates are qualified for jobs in many government and private agencies. Salaries are in the medium range for entry-level jobs and the high range for administrators. Many people find satisfaction in social work because they are helping others. Some, however, find it difficult to cope with the emotional strain.

Pediatricians

A pediatrician's job is the same as your family doctor's, except that the patients are children. Pediatricians generally examine and treat patients in their own offices and in hospitals. Some work full-time in hospitals.

Those who wish to become pediatricians must have a strong desire to serve the sick and injured. They must be willing to study and keep up with the latest advances in medical science. Sincerity and a pleasant personality help gain the confidence of children. Pediatricians must be able to make quick decisions in an emergency.

All states require a license to practice medicine. To qualify, candidates must graduate from an approved medical school. Most medical schools require applicants to first complete at least three years of college education—some require four years. Most applicants have a bachelor's degree. After completing medical school, they must pass a state licensing examination and serve a one- or two-year hospital internship, and usually a hospital residency program.

Medical training is very costly, and it takes a long time to earn a degree. Physicians usually have a high annual income but most work many hours a week and are often on call day and night for emergencies.

Pediatric Dentists

Dentists are responsible for the health and care of the teeth and gums. They take X rays, fill cavities, straighten teeth, and treat gum diseases. Pediatric dentists specialize in the care of children's teeth.

A dentist must be a graduate of an approved dental school and must pass a state examination to receive a license. Dental colleges usually require candidates to complete four years of college. Then dental training lasts another four years.

Dental education is costly and it takes time. Setting up an office and buying equipment are also expensive. However, dentists can expect high earnings after their practice is established. Dentistry, like medicine, is one of the highest paid professions.

Physical Therapists

Physical therapists work with people who have muscle, nerve, joint, or bone diseases or injuries. They help patients cope with or overcome their disabilities.

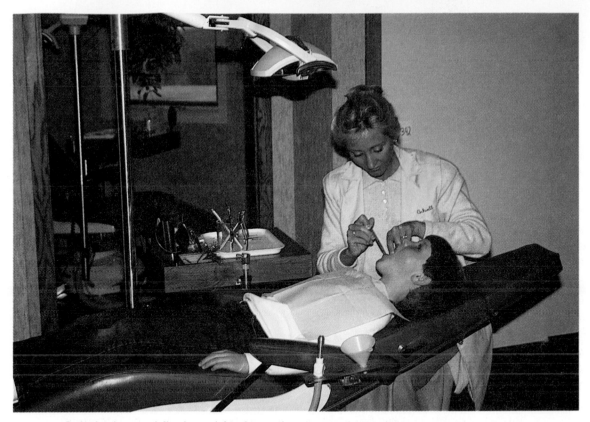

Orthodontists specialize in straightening teeth to improve both health and appearance. Many of their patients are children. The advantages and disadvantages of this career are similar to those of a pediatric dentist.

Physical therapists test patients for muscle strength, motor abilities, and proper body functioning. They develop programs for treatment. They help the patient do exercises to improve strength and coordination.

Physical therapists must have a license to practice. To obtain one, a candidate must have a degree or certificate and pass a state examination. Most approved schools of physical therapy offer bachelor's degree programs. If a person already has a bachelor's degree in another field, a 12- to 16-month course leads to a certificate in physical therapy.

A master's degree in physical therapy, combined with clinical experience, increases opportunities for advancement.

Creative Artists and Designers

Careers in publishing offer creative opportunities for those who enjoy writing or illustrating books, recording stories or music, or designing computer software.

Edautional requirements vary for these careers. However, talent, creativity, and an understanding of what appeals to young children are essential. For the software designer, training in computer science and experience with various microcomputer systems are desirable.

High school classes can give the basics in these careers, but a college degree is best.

Work experience may be gained assisting people already active in the field. Salaries often are paid as royalties—a percentage of the profits earned by the book, tape, or software. Only rarely are salaries very high.

Work hours can be flexible; however, deadlines must be met. Sometimes such a career can be part-time and combined with another job or parenting responsibilities.

Illustrating books for children and teens is just one example of a publishing career. Advantages of working in this field include flexibility and the chance to be creative.

Check Your Understanding

1. Think about your interests. List the three most important to you. How could at least one involve working with children?

2. Think about your abilities. List the three subjects you're best at in school. How could at least one involve working with children?

3. Why can having a career be compared to climbing a ladder?

4. Think of at least three businesses an entrepreneur might create that would involve work with children.

Babysitting

The most common first child care job is babysitting. Actually, "babysitting" is not a very accurate term. It can involve children from infancy through age ten. And, the person who does a good job will probably do very little sitting, unless the children are asleep.

Babysitters have a lot of responsibility. While the parents are gone, they are totally responsible for the safety and welfare of the children. Good babysitters are primarily interested in the children, not just the money they're earning. They have patience, a sense of humor, and an understanding of children's physical, emotional, social, and intellectual stages and needs. They are flexible and can get along with all types of children. They handle unexpected situations well and make sound judgements in emergencies.

Good Beginnings

When you babysit, some families may hire you regularly. However, you will also probably receive an occasional call from families you do not know. If so, find out how they learned about you. If you were recommended by a family you babysit for regularly, you can ask them about the new family, if necessary. You will also want to agree on your charges, learn how long the parents intend to be gone, and make arrangements for getting to and from their home. Be sure your own family is aware of the name, address, and phone number where you will be and the approximate time of your return.

Make arrangements to arrive about twenty minutes early the first time you babysit for a family. This will give the children a chance to get used to you while their parents are still home. It will also allow you enough time to find out any additional information from the parents. Bedtimes, where parents will be, and when they will return are obvious questions that you will want to ask. Also, learning the family's rules and routines will help you do the job better. Knowing that two-year-old Kevin never sleeps without his special blanket just might save a lot of problems at bedtime.

When you start a new babysitting job, the parent should give you a tour of the home and explain the children's routines. Ask about any important points that are not mentioned.

Caring for Children of Different Ages

As you have already learned, children of different ages have different needs. Each age group will require a different type of care.

Babies

Babies need a great deal of physical care and protection. This means a babysitter must have the necessary care skills and understand the characteristics of babies. Review Chapter 9 on infant care.

When handling a small baby, be sure to hold the infant firmly. Give support to the baby's head. Babies can sense nervousness or confidence in caregivers and they will react accordingly.

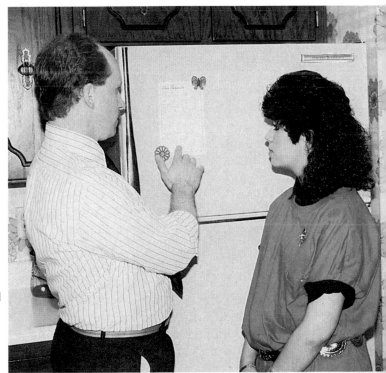

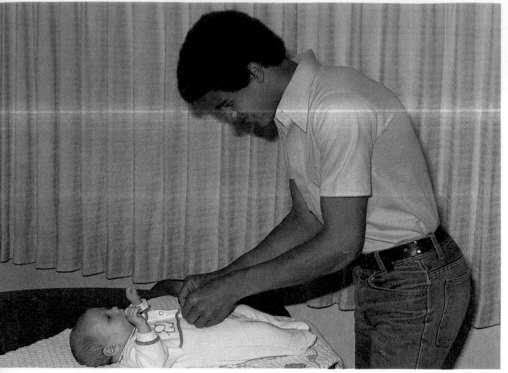

Your confidence shows when you know care skills and genuinely enjoy children.

Never leave a baby on a bed, sofa, or other raised surface. Even tiny babies can wiggle enough to fall off. Be sure to keep harmful objects out of the reach of crawling infants.

Always find out what is troubling a crying baby. Is the child too cold or too warm? Perhaps hunger, sickness, or a wet diaper is the trouble. Except for very young infants, babies do cry when they are lonely. If so, a few minutes of cuddling will help.

Changing diapers is a frequent duty of sitters. Be sure to gather the necessary supplies together before making the change.

Bathing the baby is not usually expected of babysitters. However, a qualified babysitter should be able to do so if asked. Before you try it, learn about and practice bathing a baby under capable supervision.

Some infants sleep the entire time a sitter is there. Check a sleeping baby about every fifteen minutes.

Toddlers and Preschoolers

Young children need different care than babies. They are more sensitive to their parents' leaving and may need comforting. They like being read to, played with, or talked to. Parents are too busy to play constantly, so you can win children's affection just by playing with and entertaining them.

Because preschoolers sleep less and are more adventuresome, they require more watching. Do not leave them alone for a minute while they are awake.

Bedtime can often be a problem. Young children usually don't want to go to bed. Quiet play before bedtime can help. So can following the child's regular bedtime routine. Undressing, brushing teeth, and going to the bathroom prepare children physically and psychologically for bed. Ask the parents in advance about other bedtime activities the child is used to.

Bad dreams wake some children and they will cry. They need to be cuddled and comforted back to sleep. Later, tell the parents about bad dreams or anything else unusual.

Older Children

Older youngsters sometimes give a babysitter a bad time. Some may feel they are too old for a babysitter. Others are jealous of the time and attention given to younger children. Still others try to get away with behavior their parents wouldn't permit if they were home.

Making friends with older children gets the relationship off to a good start. Work at keeping them on your side. If you show an interest in their possessions, games, or activities, you'll win over even the most independent youngsters.

It helps if the parents establish the sitter's authority before they leave. At no time is a babysitter's maturity more important than when a child deliberately misbehaves. You will have better control of the situation if you remain calm. Be fair, but firm.

Should you punish children? The punishment problem is a difficult one, particularly with some children. If a child is consistently too hard for you to handle, do not take the job next time. It is best never to use physical punishment on a child, even if the parents have given you permission. Bribery and threats don't work well either. If you threaten a child you must follow through with the threat when the child disobeys. Be sure to use a reasonable punishment, like no TV. Review the information in Chapter 16 on guiding behavior.

Safety Tips for Babysitters

In Chapter 15 you read about the most common causes of childhood accidents. If you babysit, you will find it helpful to reread that section.

Babysitting requires your full attention. If you are alert and on the scene when something starts to happen, serious problems can usually be prevented. You should never let anything distract you from your primary job, which is watching the children.

Admiring Jennifer's rock collection helped Susan start her babysitting job on a positive note.

One of the most dangerous situations you might encounter as a babysitter is a fire. Fire is fascinating to children, even if they are old enough to know it is dangerous. When you begin a babysitting job, locate all the outside doors. Note escape routes from various parts of the home. Find out if the house has a smoke alarm or fire extinguisher.

Don't let the children wander off alone in the home without checking on them frequently. Matches, cigarette lighters, candles, fireplaces, gas or electric heaters, and burning trash are all possible sources of fire. So are less controllable things such as defective wiring, furnace problems, and lighting.

If a fire does break out, the children are your first responsibility. Lead or carry them to safety. Then alert others in danger and call the fire department. Notify the parents at once.

When you babysit, it's a good idea to ask the parent to point out the location of smoke alarms. What else should you ask about?

How Do You Rate?

Children rate babysitters in terms of how much fun they are. At the same time, they don't really like sitters who let them misbehave. Do you recall from your own childhood a sitter you particularly liked? One you disliked? Why did you feel that way?

Make an effort to know what toys, games, and other activities appeal to children of different ages. Purchased toys are not the only way of keeping children amused and happy. More important are a sitter's interest, imagination, and enthusiasm. The babysitter with a headful of stories, rhymes, songs, tricks, and games is more welcome than toys. These things can make a sitting job a pleasant and worthwhile experience. You will also have a chance to see whether you would like a career working with children.

Check Your Understanding

1. Why do you think it's important for your own family to know whom you're sitting for, where they live, and when you will be home?

2. How does babysitting for infants differ from sitting for older children?

3. What kinds of things would you do with a four-year-old to keep him or her entertained during an evening of babysitting?

Chapter Review

To Sum Up

- Your interests may differ from your aptitudes. Aptitude tests and interest inventories may help you measure each.
- Every career has different levels of jobs. As you climb the career ladder your responsibilities and salary may grow.
- Additional education and work experience help you advance in a job.
- Many career fields include jobs related to children.
- Babysitting is a good beginning job. It not only provides actual work experience, it can help you decide if you're interested in a child care career.
- A babysitter must be a responsible person who can relate to children of different ages.

To Review and Remember

1. What is the purpose of an aptitude test?
2. What is the purpose of an interest inventory?
3. Explain the differences in entry-level, paraprofessional, and professional jobs.
4. What is a reference?
5. Name three advantages and three disadvantages of having a child care career.
6. Explain the difference between a speech therapist and an audiologist.
7. Describe the job of a physical therapist.
8. What are the qualities of a good babysitter?
9. Why should you arrive about twenty minutes early the first time you babysit for a family?
10. What are four important safety tips for a babysitter?

To Discuss and Discover

1. As a class, compile a list of places in your community where students can do volunteer work related to child care careers. Include information on whom to contact. Devise a way to let other students know about these opportunities.
2. Research a career that interests you, but is not discussed in this chapter. Include educational requirements, job responsibilities, salary, advantages and disadvantages of work, and expected future demand for that career.
3. Make a "babysitting bag" of free or found materials that you could take with you on babysitting jobs to keep children entertained.

Experiencing Young Children:

A Handbook for Observing and Participating

As a part of your child development class, you may have an opportunity to observe young children in action and participate in their care and education. Direct experiences with young children will enhance your understanding of child growth and development. You will also learn about and practice providing quality care and education.

The following guidelines will help you observe and participate in a group child care setting. Certain practices and procedures must be followed to ensure that both you and the children will have a safe and meaningful experience.

Observing Young Children

Reading about child growth and development is fascinating. Child development, however, really comes to life when you can observe children in action. Learning how to observe young children is an important skill for both parents and teachers. To be a good observer you need to understand the purpose and importance of observations, how to collect information, and how to use that information.

Why Is Observing Children Important?

One of the most important reasons for observing children is to better understand their growth and development. The sequence of motor development, for instance, that infants progress through in learning to walk is complex. Observing infants at various stages makes it easy to see how each motor skill leads to the next. When you understand this sequence, you can be patient and provide experiences which will promote each skill as it emerges.

Observing young children not only gives you a better understanding of general growth and development patterns, it also helps you learn about individual children. All children progress through similar stages, but each progresses at his or her own individual rate. By observing, you will come to know the skills and needs of individual children and thus be better able to meet those needs.

Another reason for observing children is to gain feedback about your own parenting or teaching abilities. For example, you might be trying to develop the guidance technique of using positive reinforcement (using praise to guide behavior). By observing how children react to your positive reinforcement, you can tell if you are being effective or not.

Taking part in an actual child care situation can be a learning experience for both you and the children. It can be fun for all of you, too!

Finally, observing children's growth and development can help you to identify those children who might have special needs or handicaps. This helps them receive the specific care and learning opportunities they need to reach their potential.

How to Observe Young Children

Observing children means more than just watching what they do and telling what you think it means. Knowing what you want to observe and how to go about it will make your observation more valuable.

Objective vs. Subjective Observations

One of the most difficult aspects of becoming a good observer of young children is learning to separate facts from opinions. Study the following two examples of observations of the same event.

Example 1

Robbie is feeling selfish. He won't let anyone play with the toys in the sandbox. He sure gets mad at Eric a lot.

Example 2

Robbie is sitting in the sandbox. He reaches out and takes a truck away from Eric. Eric grabs for the truck but Robbie pulls it away with a jerk. "It's my turn now," says Robbie, looking Eric straight in the face.

The first observation is **subjective** in nature. Notice that you really cannot tell what happened between Robbie and Eric. The observer in Example 1 is not describing facts, but his or her opinions about what Robbie was feeling and why. The second example is **objective** in nature. The description is factual—it describes what the observer saw and heard and nothing more.

Objective observations are much more valuable than subjective observations. A subjective observation assumes that the observer knows what is going on inside the child's mind, what experiences that child has had, and what motivates that particular child. In reality, no one knows what actually goes on inside the mind of another person. As an observer of young children, you will not always know what other experiences a child has had or why a child acts in a particular way. By separating opinions from factual observations, you can be more accurate. You are also less likely to interpret an event incorrectly. For instance, in Example 2 the observer might have interpreted Robbie's behavior as a positive sign of emerging self-assertion in a child thought to be usually shy. Objective observations can also be studied at a later date or studied by another person. This makes further insights possible.

One tip for making your observations objective is to imagine yourself as a video camera. You are recording (in writing) only what you see and hear. In your written record, avoid using words that are abstract. Terms such as "happy," "sad," "good," or "bad" are difficult to define precisely. You do not actually see happy feelings; you see a smile or hear laughter. These *actions* cause you to make the interpretations that a person is happy. By describing events using only concrete terms for the actions, language, and physical surroundings that you observe, you can be more objective.

Types of Observation Records

Depending on your purpose, there are several types of observation recording methods from which to choose. As a beginning student of child development you will find the running record, the anecdotal record, the frequency count, and the developmental checklist most useful.

■*Running record.*The **running record** involves recording for about an hour everything you are observing about a particular child, a group of children, or a teacher. This recording technique is useful if you are just getting to know a child or are just learning about what goes on in a group child care setting. A running record can also be used for analyzing a certain area of development such as social interaction or motor skills.

■*Anecdotal record.*The **anecdotal record** is similar to the running record in that it involves recording what you observe. However, the anecdotal record is used to focus on particular events or settings. For example, you might wish to learn how a child is adjusting to a new child care setting. Observing arrival time each day is one way to determine a child's adjustment to child care. Over the course of several days, you are likely to see that the separation from the parent becomes easier if the child is adjusting well.

■*Frequency count.*The **frequency count** involves tallying how often a certain behavior occurs by simply making a tally mark on a record sheet each time the behavior is observed. This method of recording behavior is particularly useful when trying to change a child's undesirable behavior. For example, you might notice that a child seems to hit other children quite often. To be objective you would need to have an actual count of how often the child hits. This is sometimes called taking a **baseline**. From the baseline you will be able to determine if the child's behavior changes over time. Because behavior changes slowly, it is sometimes difficult to tell if progress is being made. Taking periodic frequency counts helps you determine if the plan to change a child's behavior is working.

■*Developmental checklist.*The **developmental checklist** is another observation recording method. This method involves the use of a prepared checklist. The checklist identifies a series of specific skills or behaviors that a child of a certain age range should be mastering. The developmental checklist requires the observer to check off those skills or behaviors that are observed.

One advantage of a developmental checklist is that it is easy to use while observing. Less time is needed to check off items than to write a description of what the child is doing.

Sometimes the observer must set up certain circumstances in the environment or interact with the child in some way in order for certain behavior to occur. For example, in the sequence of motor development that leads to walking, one skill is pulling up on furniture to a standing position. This behavior could not be observed if furniture were not provided for the infant to use. Another skill is learning to walk with support while holding an adult's hand. This behavior might not be observed unless the observer were available to give this support. Developmental checklists are especially important in monitoring a child's total development and in the identification of children who might have special needs.

Each of these methods of recording your observations of young children will give you valuable information. The method or methods you select will depend on your purpose for observing. Your purpose for observing will depend on how you plan to use or interpret the information you gather.

Appropriate Behavior While Observing

While observing young children, you want to be as unnoticed as possible. Your very presence can affect the behavior of the children you are observing and make it difficult for you to gather objective information. Observers can also become a source of disruption to the teacher or parent with the children. For this reason, position yourself in such a way that after first interest by the children, you will blend into the background.

To do this, choose a spot that is outside the area in which the children are working or playing. Sit in a comfortable, adult-sized chair. Have your notepad, observation assignment, and pen or pencil ready. Once you are settled, try to remain still. At first the children may come over to you to find out who you are

and what you are doing. Answer their questions politely, but briefly. Avoid encouraging further conversation by asking them questions. If the children need encouragement to return to their activities, tell them, "I am writing a story about how children play. If you go back to playing, I can write about you in my story." If you don't give the children any encouragement, they will soon forget that you are there. Then you can conduct your observations objectively.

A time may arise, however, when you must stop being just an observer and take action. For example, you may see a child get hurt and realize that the child's teacher or parent is unaware of the problem. Though remaining unnoticed is your goal, it should never be at the expense of a child's safety.

As an observer, you don't want to distract children from their activities. Stay in the background, but near enough to see and hear what is going on.

Interpreting and Using Information from Observations

When you set out to observe young children in action, you decide on your purpose, choose the best method of recording or gathering information, and then gather that information. Once you have the information you need, the next step is to interpret and use it. To **interpret** means to find meaning, explain, or make sense of something. Though you made every effort to be objective, recording facts only, it is time now for you to express your opinions about what you observed. An hour's running record of a child's behavior is of little use until you analyze and interpret what you observed. Expressing your ideas about why a child behaved in a certain way is appropriate, so long as they are recorded separately from the factual account of what you observed.

Objective observations, combined with thoughtful interpretations, can be used in a number of ways. Monitoring a child's pattern of growth and development is one of the most important applications of observation information. A teacher or parent who understands a particular child's stage of development can form appropriate expectations of the child. The parent or teacher can also provide an environment and activities which will help that child reach her or his potential. Children who appear to be far behind in certain areas of development can be referred to specialists to identify any special needs early.

Information from observations is also useful in solving problems related to children's behavior or adult-child interaction. Any time a parent or teacher is having a problem with undesirable child behavior, close observation of the situation often reveals the underlying cause and suggests possible solutions. For example, a preschool teacher might be having difficulty keeping the noise level down in the classroom. An objective observation by another person might reveal that the teacher herself frequently uses a loud voice when she speaks to children across the room. This information suggests that the solution might begin with the teacher changing her behavior by using a quieter voice and not shouting across the classroom.

A basic rule in observing children is to maintain **confidentiality**. This means that what you come to know or understand about a child should not be shared with anyone other than the child's parents or your child development teacher.

The children that you will observe and work with as a part of your course in child development will be with you for only a brief time. What you interpret about a child's behavior may not always be accurate because you do not have all the facts. Never, for example, tell one of your friends that you think someone's child is "spoiled" or "a slow learner." Such comments may lead to rumors that could hurt the child and his or her family. If you have questions or concerns about a child you observe or a child care facility you visit, discuss them with your teacher.

It's not easy to be a good observer of young children. But it is a skill that is worthwhile to learn. It will help you become an effective parent or teacher—one who makes a positive difference in the life of a child.

Participating in Child Care and Education

Working directly with young children will greatly improve your understanding of child growth and development. Direct experiences will also help you use your management and leadership skills in a purposeful and positive way.

As a part of your class in child development you may have the opportunity to help your teacher set up an early childhood classroom in your school. The following guidelines will help you get started and suggest ways that both you and the children can learn together. Important issues include organizing the classroom for children, protecting health and safety, planning appropriate activities and a daily schedule, and promoting positive behavior.

The Early Childhood Classroom

Before you can invite young children to your school, you must prepare a place that is especially designed for them. Young children have physical, social, emotional, and intellectual needs that are much different from those of older children and adults. Their environment should be designed to meet these needs and make learning possible.

A classroom for young children must be designed for their activities and their needs. Play equipment and storage areas should be safe, sturdy and child-sized, like this folding jungle gym.

The first requirement is to make everything possible child-sized. Furniture, including chairs, tables, and shelves, should all be of a size and design that is comfortable for young children. For example, when young children sit in a chair, their feet should easily touch the floor. Shelves should be low so that children can get and return materials independently. A child-size environment promotes independence. The more that the surroundings fit the young children, the more capable they are of working and playing without constantly having to ask an adult for help.

Learning Centers

Learning centers are areas of the classroom that are designated for certain types of play, equipment, or learning. Learning centers vary according to the aims of the program and the space and equipment available. A well-equipped program might have the following centers. Examples of supplies and equipment are given with each.

- **Block center.** Small and large blocks, trucks and cars, people and animal figures, flat boards, shelves or bins for storage.

- **Dramatic play center.** Child-size play kitchen, table and chairs, dishes, empty food cartons, dress-up clothes, dolls, play money, telephone, mirror.

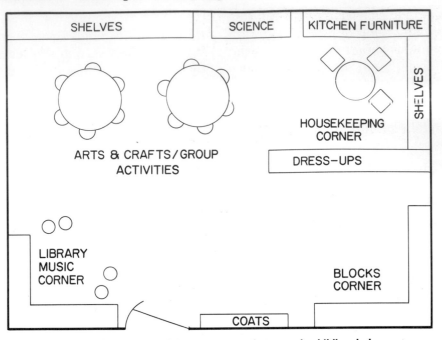

This diagram shows one possible arrangement for an early childhood classroom.

■**Art Center.** Paper, crayons, paints and brushes, markers, paint easel, clay, paste, yarn, felt, scissors, table and chairs, smocks.

■**Library center.** Books, pictures, puppets, low shelves, rug, large pillows.

■**Discovery center.** Plants, small animals (such as a hamster), fish, magnets, magnifying glass, shells, thermometers, scale, soil, seeds.

■**Manipulative center.** Puzzles, beads to string, board and card games, table and chairs.

■**Music center.** Record player and records, drums, shakers, tambourines, triangles, bells, piano, rug.

In smaller classrooms, some learning centers may be combined or eliminated. Much of the equipment can be made instead of purchased.

Each learning center is in some way marked off or distinguished from other centers and others areas of the room. Low, open shelves work well for defining centers. You might also define centers with pegboard dividers, boards stacked between cement blocks (which also act as shelves), fabric panels suspended securely from the ceiling, or even colored tape on the floor.

Other guidelines for setting up learning centers include:
■ Separate noisy centers from quiet centers.
■ Place the art center near water.
■ Keep equipment and supplies neatly organized but within reach of the children.
■ Leave one large, open area for large group activities.

Learning centers offer children learning choices. They can select activities, explore different skills and areas of knowledge, and learn through hands-on experiences.

Learning centers provide areas organized toward specific activities. What is the focus of learning in each center shown here?

Health and Safety

Protecting the health and safety of the children is of greatest importance. While children are in your care, you must prevent illness through health care routines, make sure the environment is safe, and supervise their play.

Health Care Routines

Health care routines for young children prevent the spread of illness. They also help make sure the children are well-nourished and rested. Proper handwashing, though a simple act, is probably the best way to cut down on the spread of illness in a group child care setting. Children must be taught to wash using a brisk, scrubbing motion with warm water and soap, and to dry with a clean paper towel. They should wash after using the toilet or blowing their nose, and before cooking activities, eating, or playing with materials such as clay. You, too, should make a habit of washing your hands frequently while caring for the children. Be sure to do so after helping a child in the restroom or using a tissue to wipe the nose. Always wash after you use the restroom and before handling food.

In addition to handwashing, teach the children how to blow and wipe their nose and dispose of the tissue. They should use their own comb, brush, or headwear—never those of another child. Children should not take bites of each other's food or share the same cup or eating utensils. Finally, children who are sick should not be in a group child care setting.

Children need to feel good before they can participate in learning activities. They should be well rested and have had a good breakfast before coming to your early childhood classroom. They will need a nutritious snack about midmorning or midafternoon, if they are staying half the day. Pace their activities so that they do not become too tired. They need time for both active and quiet play.

By following these important health care routines, you help children stay healthy and feel good. Remember that consistency is important. Both you and the children should make health care routines a habit.

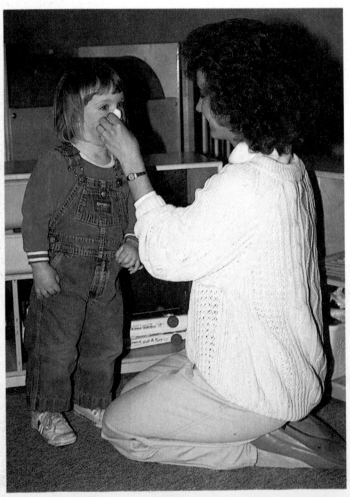

Good health care practices are especially important when caring for a group of children. Always wash your hands after helping a child blow or wipe the nose.

Safety

Safety for young children means checking the environment and making it "childproof." You also need to closely supervise children as they work and play. Check the children's classroom for possible safety hazards. Many of the safety guidelines discussed in Chapter 15 (and in the chart on page 244) also apply to child care centers.

It helps to look at things from a child's point of view. Get down on your knees and look around. What do you see that a child could get into or be hurt by? Check to be sure:

- There are no sharp edges on furniture or equipment.
- Electrical outlets are covered.
- Electrical cords are in good condition and are secured to the walls or floor.
- Poisonous substances, such as cleaning supplies, are not within reach of children.
- Traffic paths around the room are free of clutter.
- Fire exit signs are clearly marked and there is a fire exit plan.
- Dangerous items such as sharp scissors or staplers are not within children's reach.

Check the classroom thoroughly before each visit from the children. While there, the children must be supervised at all times. Children should *never* be left in the classroom alone. In addition, there should be enough teens or adults present to adequately monitor children playing in each area of the room. In case of emergency, someone can stay with the children and someone can go for help. If the restrooms are located outside the classroom, an adult will need to go with the children into the restrooms. Supervision is also important if children go outside to play or on field trips. A little advance planning and alertness on your part will help guard the health and safety of the children in your care.

Planning Appropriate Activities

Advance planning also plays a big role in providing appropriate learning experiences for the young children in your care. Much of the work has already been done by the time you set up the classroom and equip the learning centers. Within the framework of this planned environment, children learn through play. You also need to provide a balanced schedule of activities for individuals and for small and large groups of children. These should focus on each important area of development.

Be sure there is at least one caregiver monitoring each area in which children are playing.

Learning Through Play

As you know, children learn through play. You can observe this as you watch young children in action. For a young child, play means having hands-on experiences that involve the senses and opportunities to talk. It does not mean doing a worksheet or coloring page, or listening to an adult lecture. As you plan activities for young children, remember the more involved that they are and the more realistic the experiences are, the more they learn. For example, a story about a fire truck is not nearly as impressive as a trip to the fire station and a chance to climb on a real fire truck.

Play experiences for young children can be viewed in several ways. One way is to observe how the children are playing in relation to each other. Children may play alone or individually. For example, a child may curl up in a large box with a book and a pillow for some quiet time alone. Children may play individually but alongside one another, as when several children may sit at a table to work puzzles. Children may play in small groups, cooperating in acting out going to the store, for instance. Or, children may play in one large group under the guidance of a teacher, as in a music or movement activity.

Another way to view children's play is by the area of development that is being stimulated. For example, children need many experiences in language. They need opportunities to listen and to speak, to become familiar with written language, and to develop their vocabulary. Learning experiences which stimulate language development include storytelling, open-ended questions, field trips, games, activity records, and cooking activities, to name but a few of the possibilities.

In addition to language, children need play experiences which focus on:
- Thinking and problem-solving.

Play activities can be described according to how children play in relation to each other. Here the children are playing in one large group. Another way to describe play is the area of development being stimulated—in this case, motor skills.

Planning activities for each day will help make your experiences with children more successful. What would happen if you didn't plan ahead?

- Movement or motor skills for both large and small muscles.
- Creativity, including music, dance, dramatic play, and art.
- Themselves and others in the social world.

When planning experiences for young children, keep these types of play in mind. Help children to have individual, small group, and large group activities each day, as well as experiences which focus on each area of development. Children who are actively involved in the experiences you provide will learn more effectively and be better behaved than children who only sit by, watching and waiting.

Writing Learning Activity Plans

Two types of planning forms help you organize learning activities for young children. First is a form based on the daily schedule and the days or sessions that the children are to come. This chart or overview lists the titles of the activities you plan to provide in each learning center and for each time period on your schedule. For example, one part of the schedule might list a period for music and a period for storytime. On the weekly or monthly chart, list the titles of the songs you plan to sing and the books you plan to share.

The second form you might use is one for recording more detailed information about each activity planned. On this form you would include a section for each of the following:

- Title of the activity.
- Purpose of the activity or objective.
- Type of activity (whether for a learning center or group activity).
- Materials needed.
- Procedures listed.
- Evaluation on how the activity went.

The type of form used doesn't matter as much as the fact that you do have written plans.

Writing plans ahead of time helps you think through carefully the appropriateness of each activity. You also have a handy list of everything you need so that materials can be set up before the children arrive. And, just in case you are nervous, your written procedures are handy for quick reference. Written plans are also useful to collect and save for future use or for sharing with others.

The Daily Schedule

Planning the sequence of events is just as important as planning the environment and specific learning activities. The daily schedule is the master plan for how time will be utilized. Schedules vary greatly from program to program. Study the following schedule for a three-hour session:

8:30-8:45	Arrival
8:45-9:30	Small group activities
9:30-9:45	Snack
9:45-10:00	Large group music activity
10:00-10:30	Outdoor play or indoor movement activity
10:30-11:15	Learning centers
11:15-11:30	Large group story

Good schedules for young children in group settings feature a balance of active and quiet, small and large group, and teacher-directed and child-selected activities. Notice in the sample schedule how these elements

A well-planned schedule ensures that children can participate in a balanced variety of activities.

are alternated. The small group activities are learning activities planned and directed by the teaching staff. Snack time allows relaxed conversation with friends. (The children might have prepared their own snacks as a small group activity.) After the snack, the children move to the large, open area of the classroom for group music experiences. After music, the children need brisk physical activity such as outdoor play. Or, if outdoor play is not possible, it is easy to extend the group music session into a session for movement or creative dance. After this period of physical activity, children are ready to return to the slower pace of learning centers. Here, they can select for themselves the centers they want to play in. Finally, the session ends with a group story or language activity. In this way, children will have put away all their learning center materials and be ready to leave on time.

Other features of good schedules include large blocks of time for self-selected activities, shorter periods of time for structured, teacher-directed activities, and allowing time for transitions. **Transitions** are the few minutes between blocks of time during which children must put materials away, use the restroom, and get ready for the next time period.

Often during transition times, teachers lose control over the children. To prevent this from happening to you, always let the children know a few minutes ahead of time that it is almost time for a change. Use songs or games to move children from one place to another. For example, you might sing a special cleanup song as you and the children put away materials after learning centers time. Or, you might play a game where each child wearing the color you name may move to the door before going outside.

Whether you are planning a two-, three-, or four-hour session for the children, plan a schedule carefully to include each of these important features. A well-planned schedule will do much to ensure that the children do not become too tired or bored—both of which result in inappropriate behaviors.

Promoting Positive Behavior

If you have carefully prepared an environment designed for young children, planned appropriate activities, and constructed a well-balanced daily schedule, you have done most of what it takes to promote positive child behavior. Most inappropriate behavior is the result of poor planning on the part of the teacher. However, even the most organized teacher will have times when direct guidance of children's behavior will be necessary. To promote positive behavior, you will need to establish classroom rules, use positive reinforcement effectively, be a positive role model, and develop some strategies for dealing with unacceptable behavior.

Children are usually eager to earn the praise of caregivers. By establishing a way to recognize their positive efforts, you can help them behave well and feel good about themselves.

■*Establish classroom rules.* Classroom rules for young children should be few in number and stated in positive terms. Young children have a hard time remembering more than a few things at a time. If you limit your classroom rules to only three or four important ones, children are more likely to remember and follow them. Rules should be stated in terms of what a child should *do* as opposed to what a child should *not do*. Rules should also have a clear purpose. The most appropriate rules are those that deal with protecting the safety of children and property. Some possible rules are:

1. Use your hands gently.
2. Walk inside the classroom.
3. Put materials away when you are finished.
4. Use an inside voice in the classroom.

Of course, you will have to plan activities to help the children understand the meaning of these rules. For example, you might have a collection of pictures showing gentle, friendly touching and aggressive, hurtful touching. Using an open-ended questioning technique, you could explore the pictures with the children and help them understand what each type of touching feels like. Make it very clear that hurtful touching is not allowed in your classroom.

■*Use positive reinforcement.* Another useful direct guidance technique is positive reinforcement. This means giving children recognition or encouragement for appropriate behavior—in other words, a reward. The reward may be very simple. It might be a smile or hug from you or a comment such as, "I like the way you wipe your paint brush on the side of the jar before you paint." Occasionally, when children are just learning a new behavior, small treats such as a sticker or ribbon are highly effective. However, such material rewards should be used sparingly. Children tend to repeat behaviors that are positively reinforced. Remember, however, that your praise of a child's behavior must be sincere and not given automatically in order for it to be effective.

Smiles and compliments are simple and effective ways to encourage good behavior.

■ *Be a good role model.* Your own behavior in the classroom has a very powerful influence on children. For this reason, you must be especially careful to be a good role model. Children are more likely to do what you do rather than what you say. If you want children to use an inside voice, then you, too, must always use a quiet voice indoors. If you want children to treat each other with kindness, you, too, must do the same. Through your example, children learn how to play and use materials properly and how to treat each other with respect.

Dealing with Misbehavior

When children do behave in unacceptable ways in the classroom, you should have a clear plan of action. Children also need to be clear on what will happen if they behave in unacceptable ways. For the most part, a simple statement of what you want the child to do is effective. If a child is using a loud voice, simply say, "Mary, please use your inside voice. I can't hear well when you are shouting." Or, you may offer the child a choice of more acceptable activities. For instance, if a child is not playing well in the block center, you can say, "Heather, you may choose to go to the dramatic play center or the art center now. I can't let you stay in the block center if you are going to take Ariel's block away from her." Notice that in each statement the teacher gave the child a reason why the behavior was unacceptable.

For some types of unacceptable behavior a stronger response is necessary. Behavior which hurts others or property must not be permitted at any time. Children who break this type of rule must be responded to immediately and consistently. One approach is to have the child sit away from the main activities of the classroom in a place that is sometimes called **time out**. Such a place should in no way be frightening. A small chair placed next to a door or wall, away from the learning centers but still within view of them, would be acceptable. By removing the child from the situation, you are removing him or her from the rewards and pleasures of play. Soon the children will understand that certain behavior will result in being withdrawn from the group.

For example, after a child hit another child with a block, the teacher, Ms. Black, said, "Don, I can't let you hit Mark. It hurts. Go and sit in time out for two minutes." The teacher came over after two minutes and asked Don to choose one of two centers to go to, but not the block center. The teacher did not become angry, nor raise her voice. Time out should only be used for very serious unacceptable behavior or repeated minor unacceptable behavior.

With these basic strategies and skills, you will be able to provide a warm, supportive learning environment for young children. It takes a lot of advanced planning, but you will find that it is all worthwhile.

Glossary

A

adoption. Legal process in which people obtain the permanent right to raise a child not biologically their own as if they were the natural parents.

aggressive. Describes a person who is strong-willed and determined.

allergy. An oversensitivity to certain common substances. The substances may cause a reaction when eaten, inhaled, or touched.

alternative birth center. Home-like facility, outside the hospital, for giving birth.

ambidextrous (AM-bih-DECK-struss). Able to use both hands with equal skill.

amniocentesis (AM-nee-oh-sen-TEE-sihs). The process of withdrawing a sample of the **amniotic fluid** surrounding an unborn baby with a special needle to test for **birth defects** or other health problems.

amniotic fluid (am-nee-AWT-ik). Fluid which surrounds and protects the developing baby during pregnancy.

anecdotal record. A method of recording observations that focuses on a particular event or setting.

anemia. A condition caused by lack of iron that results in poor appetite, tiredness, and weakness.

Apgar scale. Method of evaluating a newborn's physical condition. The infant is rated on a scale from 0 to 2 on five items: pulse, breathing, muscle tone, responsiveness, and skin color.

aptitude test. Test which measures a person's abilities and probable success in various skill areas.

articulation. Clear, distinct speech.

artificial respiration. A procedure for forcing air into the lungs of a person whose own breathing has stopped.

attachment. A strong bond that develops between two people.

attention span. The length of time someone can concentrate on a task without getting bored.

audiologist. A professional specially trained to test for, diagnose, and help treat hearing problems.

B

baseline. A **frequency count** that is taken before trying to correct a particular undesirable **behavior**. The baseline can later be referred to in order to see if the behavior is changing.

behavior. A way of acting or responding.

biological parents. The man and woman who conceive a child.

birth defects. Abnormalities, present at birth, that affect the structure or function of the body.

blended family. A family formed by the marriage of a couple, one or both of whom have children from a previous relationship.

bonding. Process of forming lifelong emotional ties.

budget. Spending plan.

C

cardiopulmonary resuscitation (CPR). A rescue technique used to sustain life when both breathing and heart action have stopped.

caregiver. Anyone who cares for a child, whether on a long-term or short-term basis.

cause and effect. A concept babies gradually learn as they realize that the things they do produce certain results.

central nervous system. The brain and the spinal cord. Sensory impulses are passed to this area and motor impulses are passed back.

cervix. The lower part of the **uterus**.

cesarean birth. Delivering a baby through a surgical incision in the mother's abdomen.

child abuse. The physical and/or emotional mistreatment of a child.

child care aide. An assistant to the person in charge of a child care program.

child development. The study of how children grow physically, mentally, emotionally, and socially.

chorionic villi sampling. (CORE-ee-AHN-ik VIL-eye). A test for detecting certain **birth defects** early in pregnancy.

chromosomes. Threadlike particles in the nucleus of a cell which carry hereditary characteristics.

circumference. Measurement around something roughly circular in shape, such as a child's head or chest.

colostrum. Fluid secreted from the mother's breasts shortly before and after birth. This fluid precedes the milk flow and provides the newborn with nourishment and antibodies to help protect against disease.

communicable diseases. Diseases that can be easily passed from one person to another.

conception. The union of an **ovum** and a **sperm** resulting in the beginning of a new life.

concepts. General categories of objects and information.

concrete operations period. Piaget's third stage of learning, from seven to eleven years of age. Children can think logically, but still learn best by direct experience.

confidentiality. In observing children, refers to keeping observations and findings about a child to yourself, sharing them only with the child's parents or your teacher.

conscience (KAHN-chunts). An inner sense of right and wrong that prompts good behavior or causes feelings of guilt following bad behavior.

consistency. Repeatedly acting in the same way.

contractions. Periodic cramping or tightening of abdominal muscles during **labor**. Contractions open the **cervix** and help expel the baby from the mother's body.

convulsion. A period of unconsciousness with uncontrolled jerking or twitching of the muscles.

cooperative play. Play among children that includes interaction and cooperation.

cortex. The outer layer of the brain which permits more complex learning.

cradle cap. Skin condition common to young babies in which the scalp develops patches of yellowish, crusty scales.

creativity. Putting imagination to use to produce something.

crisis nurseries. Places where, for a short time, troubled parents can leave their children to be cared for while they try to cope with anger or other problems.

D

day care center. A child care facility designed primarily to provide all-day care for children of working parents.

delivery. The birth itself; occurs as the baby is expelled from the mother's body.

deprivation. The lack of healthy, positive influences on development.

depth perception. Ability to recognize that an object is three-dimensional, not flat.

developmental checklist. A list that identifies a series of specific skills or **behaviors** that a child of a certain age range should be mastering. Items can be checked off as a method of recording information when observing children.

dexterity. Skilled use of the body, especially the hands and fingers.

diaper rash. Patches of rough, irritated skin in the diaper area caused by bacteria.

dilate. Widen. The **cervix** dilates during **labor**.

directed learning. Learning from being taught, either formally or informally.

discipline. The task of helping children learn to behave in acceptable ways.

dominant. Describes a **gene** for a particular trait (such as eye color) that is stronger and dictates the outcome of the trait when paired with a weaker, or **recessive**, gene.

dramatic play. Imitating real-life situations, such as playing house or school.

dyslexia (dis-LEX-ee-uh). A **learning disability** that prevents a person from handling language in a normal way.

E

egocentric. Thinking only about oneself.

embryo (EM-bree-oh). The developing cluster of cells in the **uterus** through the seventh or eighth week of pregnancy, after which it is known as the **fetus**.

emotional development. Children's changing feelings about themselves, others, and the world.

empathy. The ability to understand and share another person's feelings.

entrepreneur (AWN-truh-pruh-NUR). A person who creates and markets a new product or who starts up and runs a business.

entry-level job. A position for beginners with limited education and training.

enuresis (en-you-REE-sis). A lack of bladder control.

environment. The people, places, and things that surround or act upon someone and influence how that person develops.

episiotomy (ih-PIHZ-ee-OTT-uh-mee). An incision (surgical cut) that enlarges the external opening of the vagina to make the birth of a baby easier.

eye-hand coordination. The ability to precisely move the hands and fingers in relation to what is seen.

F

family day care. A child care arrangement in which a small number of children are cared for in a person's home.

fetus. Refers to the unborn baby from the seventh or eighth week of pregnancy until birth.

finger plays. Songs or chants with accompanying hand motions that are popular with young children.

fixed expenses. The cost of items such as rent, mortgage payments, taxes, and insurance, which cannot be changed.

flammable. Burns easily.

fontanels. Open spaces, or "soft spots," where the bones of a baby's skull have not permanently joined. These spaces allow the skull bones to move together during birth.

forceps. Special steel tongs which may be used to guide the baby's head during the birth process.

formal operations period. Piaget's fourth stage of learning, beginning about age eleven. Children become capable of abstract thinking at this stage.

formula. Commercially or home prepared mixture of milk or milk substitute, water, and added nutrients to feed to infants.

foster parent. Someone who assumes temporary legal responsibility for a child.

fracture. A break or a crack in a bone.

frequency count. A tally of how often a certain **behavior** occurs.

G

genes. The parts of the **chromosomes** that determine all inherited characteristics.

gifted children. Children with above-average intelligence or talent.

grasp reflex. The automatic closing of a newborn's hand over any object that comes in contact with the baby's palm.

group identification. The need for a feeling of "belonging" to a group.

guardian. Someone appointed to care for a child, usually until the child reaches age eighteen or twenty-one.

H

Head Start. A federal program consisting of locally operated child care facilities designed to help lower income and disadvantaged children function effectively at home, in school, and in the community.

Heimlich maneuver. Using pressure on the air within the body to force an object interfering with breathing from the throat.

heredity. The passing on of certain inherited characteristics from one generation to the next. The characteristics are passed on through **chromosomes** present in the body cells.

hyperactive. Unable to control one's activity or to concentrate for a normal length of time.

I

imitation. Method of learning achieved by watching and copying others.

immunize. To protect a person from a particular disease, usually by giving a **vaccine**.

incidental learning. Unplanned learning.

incubator. A special enclosed crib in which the oxygen supply, temperature, and humidity can be closely controlled. Used for **premature** infants.

infant mortality rate. Percentage of deaths during the first year of life.

infertility. A couple's inability to have children for physical or psychological reasons.

intelligence. The ability to interpret or understand everyday situations and to use experience when faced with new situations or problems.

intelligence quotient (IQ). A numerical standard which tells if a person's intelligence is average or above or below average for his or her age. The intelligence quotient (or IQ) is arrived at through an intelligence test.

interest inventory. A test designed to suggest jobs related to a person's interests.

interpret. To find meaning, explain, or make sense of something.

J K L

labor. The pushing of the muscles of the mother's **uterus** to gradually push the baby out of her body.

large motor skills. Physical skills that use the large muscles of the back, legs, shoulders, and arms.

latch-key children. Youngsters who are unsupervised from the time they come home from school until their parents return from work.

learning centers. Areas of a classroom that are designated for certain types of play, equipment, or learning.

learning disability. A problem within the brain that prevents a person from using information from the senses in a normal way for learning.

M

malnutrition. A health problem resulting from not getting enough food or adequate amounts of needed nutrients.

manipulation. Skillful use of the hands.

marasmus. Physical decline that is caused by lack of love and attention. Marasmus may eventually lead to death.

maternity leave. Time off from a job for a woman to give birth, recuperate, and care for her new baby. This time may range from several weeks to several months.

miscarriage. A pregnancy that ends due to natural causes early in development.

Montessori preschool. An educational facility for three- to six-year-olds that provides special learning materials which children are free to explore on their own. Named for the founder of this method, Dr. Maria Montessori

moral development. Gradually learning to base one's behavior on personal beliefs of right and wrong.

motor skills. Abilities that depend on the use and control of muscles.

N

nanny. A person employed to provide live-in child care services; may have professional training in child development and care.

natural fibers. Fibers from plant or animal sources.

negative reinforcement. Something (for example, punishment) that tends to discourage a particular **behavior** from being repeated.

negative self-concept. Seeing oneself as bad or unimportant.

negativism. Doing the opposite of what others want.

nontoxic. Not poisonous.

nurse-midwife. A registered nurse specially trained to care for women during pregnancy and normal births.

nursery school. A child care center that provides educational programs, usually for children age three to five. May also be called a **preschool.**

nurturing. Providing love, support, attention, and encouragement.

nutrition. A balance of all the food substances needed for health and growth.

O

objective. Using facts, not personal feelings or prejudices, to describe something.

object permanence. Concept that objects still exist, even when not in sight.

obstetrician (OB-stuh-TRISH-un). A doctor who specializes in pregnancy and birth.

ovum. A female cell or egg. Can also refer to the fertilized egg in the first two weeks of pregnancy.

P

pacifier. A nipple attached to a plastic ring sometimes used to comfort a baby.

parallel play. Describes the play of young children who play independently while with other children, rather than interacting with them.

paraprofessional. A person with education beyond high school that trains him or her for a certain career field.

parent cooperative. A child care facility in which part of the supervision is provided by the parents of enrolled children, who take turns donating their services.

parenting. The process of caring for children and helping them grow and learn.

paternity leave. Time off from a job allowing a new father to help care for the baby.

pediatrician (PEE-dee-uh-TRISH-un). A doctor who specializes in the care of babies and young children.

peers. People one's own age.

perception. Learning from the senses.

personality. The total of all the specific traits that are consistent in an individual's **behavior**.

placenta (pluh-SENT-uh). The tissue which connects the unborn baby to the mother's **uterus**. It provides nourishment to the developing baby.

placid. Describes a person who is easy-going and not easily upset.

plaque (PLACK). A sticky, colorless film on teeth caused by bacteria. Plaque promotes tooth decay.

play group. A child care arrangement in which a group of parents take turns caring for each other's children in their own homes.

poison control centers. Hospital units that are specially equipped to advise and treat poison victims.

positive reinforcement. Something (for example, praise or attention) that rewards a particular **behavior** and makes it more likely to be repeated.

positive self-concept. Seeing oneself as good, capable, and important.

postnatal. Refers to the period of time after a baby's birth.

potential. The highest level possible of physical, intellectual, emotional, and social development.

pregnancy test. A test (laboratory or at-home) to determine whether or not a woman is going to have a baby.

premature. Refers to babies born before their development is complete.

prenatal. Refers to the period after **conception**, but before birth.

preoperational period. Piaget's second stage of learning, between ages two and seven. Children think about everything in terms of their own activities and what they see and hear at the moment.

prepared childbirth. Also called "natural childbirth." A method of giving birth in which pain is reduced through the elimination of fear and the use of special conditioning exercises.

preschool. See **nursery school**.

preschoolers. Children age three, four, or five.

primary teeth. The first set of teeth one gets. Often called "baby teeth."

professional. Someone employed in a position which requires at least a degree from a four-year college or technical school in a particular field.

proportion. The size relationship of one thing to another, such as between different parts of the body.

Q R

recessive. Describes a **gene** which can only determine a particular trait (such as eye color) when paired with a similar gene. If paired with a stronger, or **dominant**, gene, the dominant gene will determine the trait, and the characteristic of the recessive gene will not be seen.

reference. Someone a prospective employer can contact to find out about the applicant's character and abilities.

reflexes. Instinctive, automatic responses, such as sneezing and swallowing.

rooming-in. A hospital arrangement where the baby stays in the mother's room after birth instead of in a hospital nursery.

rooting reflex. Automatic response of a newborn; when something touches the baby's lips or cheek, the baby turns toward the touch and begins to suck.

running record. Observation recording method involving recording for a certain period of time everything observed about a particular child, group, or teacher.

S

secondary teeth. The permanent teeth that replace **primary teeth**.

self-centered. Constantly thinking about one's own wants and needs rather than those of others.

self-concept. How a person feels about himself or herself.

self-discipline. The ability to control one's own **behavior**.

self-esteem. Positive sense of self-worth.

sensitive. Describes persons who are more aware of their surroundings and changes in them than most other people are.

sensorimotor period. Piaget's first stage of learning, from birth until about age two. Babies learn primarily through their actions and senses during this period.

separation anxiety. A child's fear or stress when away from a familiar environment or familiar people.

sequence. A step-by-step pattern.

sibling rivalry. Competition between children for their parents' love and attention.

single parents. Divorced, widowed, or unmarried people with children.

small motor skills. Physical skills which use the muscles of the wrists, fingers, and ankles.

social development. The progress a person makes from a baby's complete self-centeredness to the adult's ability to live and work with others.

socialization. The process of learning to get along with others.

speech therapist. A **professional** trained to diagnose and help correct speech problems.

sperm. A male cell capable of fertilizing a female egg or **ovum**.

sphincter muscles (SFINK-ter). The muscles which control elimination.

sprain. An injury caused by sudden, violent stretching of a joint or muscle.

startle reflex. Automatic response of newborns to a loud noise or a touch on their stomach. The infant's arms are thrown apart, fingers spread, legs extended, and the head is thrown back.

stepparent. The relationship of a person to his or her spouse's children by a former relationship.

strained foods. Solid foods that have been processed to make them smooth and somewhat runny.

stranger anxiety. Stage when a baby screams when a stranger approaches.

subjective. Using one's personal opinions and feelings, rather than facts, to judge or describe something.

symbolic thinking. Using words and numbers to represent ideas.

synthetic fibers. Fibers manufactured from chemicals rather than natural sources. Polyester, nylon, and acrylic are common synthetic fibers used in children's clothing.

T

temper tantrum. Child's violent release of anger or frustration by screaming, crying, kicking, pounding, and sometimes even holding his or her breath.

therapist. A professional trained in helping people handle problem situations. Some provide support for those with emotional problems; others specialize in helping people overcome physical limitations.

time out. A method of **discipline** in which a child who is misbehaving must spend time sitting away from the activities of the group.

toddlers. Refers to children from the time they take their first steps (about 12 months) until about age three.

training pants. Heavy, absorbent underpants used during bladder training.

transitions. In a child care setting, times between scheduled activities in which children put materials away, use the restroom, and get ready for the next time period.

trial-and-error learning. Learning in which a child tries several solutions before finding out what works.

U

ultrasound. Technique of using sound waves to make a video image of an unborn baby to check for health problems.

umbilical cord (uhm-BIL-ih-kuhl). Long tube which connects the **placenta** to the developing baby and through which nourishment and oxygen are carried to the baby.

uterus (YOOT-uh-russ). The womb. The organ in a woman in which a baby develops during pregnancy.

V

vaccine. A small amount of a disease germ introduced to the body (usually by injection) so the body can build a resistance to the disease.

variable expenses. Costs over which people have some control and which can cut back if necessary.

vocabulary. The number of words a person knows.

W X Y Z

weaning. Changing a baby from drinking from the bottle or breast to drinking from a cup.

Credits

Abbott Laboratories, 145

Richard Alcorn, Colgate-Palmolive, 356

Amoco Corporation, 305

ANCLA Production/John Wentland, 40

Apple, 481

Jim Ballard, 118

Lynn Bannon, St. Francis Medical Center, 86, 143 (left)

Roger Bean, 93 (bottom right), 266, 310 (right), 341, 342, 349 (left), 376, 393, 448, 456 (bottom right), 466, 488

Boy Scouts of America, 388

Bradley Childcare Center, Roger Bean, 160 (bottom right), 277, 283, 307, 335, 346, 430 (bottom), 437, 443, 444 (top), 499, 501, 505

Bradley University Childcare Center, 328, 360

Robert Brisbane, 329

Bristol-Myers Co., 47, 140 (right), 392

Burlington Coat Factory, Charles Hofer, 175

Barbara Caldwell, 278, 283, 322 (bottom)

California Birthplace, 136

Barbara Campbell, 27, 29 (top), 200

Campbell Soup Company, 159

Todd Carroll, 274 (top)

Todd Carroll, Friendship House, 103, 201 (top)

Carter's, 303

Century Manufacturing, 121 (bottom), 131

Pete Christie, 213

Coleco Industries, Inc., 294 (top right), 371

Corning Glass Works, 411

Crittenton Crisis Nursery, 463

Don Fahrenbrink, 424

Findout Products, Inc., 166, 180 (top)

Fisher Price, 229 (left), 292

James Gaffney, 101 (bottom), 447

Bob Gangloff, 127, 128, 129, 130, 132, 207

Gerber Products, Inc., 34, 108 (bottom), 247, 251 (top), 256 (left), 365

Good Beginnings, 49, 170, 188, 210, 216 (top) 228, 294 (bottom), 485, 510

Good Beginnings/YMCA, Charles Hofer, 450

The Gorilla Foundation, 195

Hasbro Inc., 245

Hewlett Packard, 70 (top)

Charles Hofer, 36, 81, 82, 91, 143 (lower right), 165, 167, 179, 190, 197, 214, 221 (left), 222, 229 (right), 230, 239 (top), 266 (top), 275, 281, 344, 400, 468, 487, 491

Impact Communications, 26, 37 (bottom), 42, 43, 48 (left), 51, 68, 90, 93 (bottom), 94, 95, 96, 97, 115, 139, 146, 221 (right), 233, 240, 250, 257, 311 (left), 313 (right), 321 (left), 334, 354 (right), 380 (left), 381 (right), 417 (top left), 423, 432, 435

Thomas Jefferson School, Roger Bean, 308, 366, 367, 369, 370, 420, 425, 455 (top), 455 (bottom), 456, 509

Johnson & Johnson, 156 (bottom right)

Vicky Kee, 174, 176, 177, 231, 252, 379 (right), 405, 469

Warner Lambert, 446

Bob McElwee, 29 (bottom), 269, 288 (left), 315 (left), 351 (bottom), 417 (right)

Manual High School, 28 (bottom), 39

March of Dimes, 19, 70 (bottom), 74 (top), 75, 79, 80, 85, 101, 300, 312, 440

Mead Johnson Nutritional Group, Evansville, 180 (bottom), 194, 310 (left)

Methodist Medical Center of Illinois, 135

Paul Miller, 293

P.C. Morse, 48 (right)

Index